D1364591

About the Author

Tom Hallman Jr. is considered one of the nation's premier narrative writers.

During his career, he has won every major feature-writing award, including a Pulitzer Prize. A common thread in all of Hallman's stories is the exploration of the character's heart and soul.

Hallman and his wife, Barbara, were born and raised in Portland, Oregon where they raised their two daughters, Rachael and Hanna, now grown women. Living with a storyteller showed the importance of being curious about all kinds of people. He graduated from Drake University in Des Moines, Iowa in 1977. He's worked at a car wash, a grocery store, a greyhound racetrack, and volunteered at a VA hospital. His first journalism job was in New York City as copy editor for Hearst Magazines Special Publications. He returned to Oregon as a reporter at *The Hermiston Herald*, before landing a job at the *Tri-City Herald* in Kennewick, Washington.

In 1980 he moved to *The Oregonian* where he covered crime for ten years. He is now a senior reporter specializing in storytelling. He is also a teacher, speaker and story consultant. He can be reached at www.tomhallman.com

Dispatches from 1320

The Collected Works of Tom Hallman Jr.

TOM HALLMAN JR.

Copyright © 2015 Tom Hallman Jr.
All rights reserved.

ISBN: 0692494936
ISBN 13: 9780692494936
Library of Congress Control Number: 2015911857
Hallman Publishing, Portland, OR

I swear to God, I think you are about the finest writer to ever stroke a keyboard. I'm frustrated that I haven't cultivated a keen eye, ear and heart for stories the way you have. I heard Chief Burke of the Umatilla Tribe say once: "We are not human beings here having spiritual experiences, but rather spiritual beings here having human experiences." Thanks for sharing your human experiences with me. -- *Karen Spears Zacharias, author of "Mother of Rain," soon to be a stage play.*

Tom Hallman is one of this country's finest wordsmiths. He's a reporter, but he's more than that. He tells great stories. He does it by conveying the emotions of his subject very well. – *Bill Cooper.*

Tom is, above all, a storyteller. He mines the extraordinary from the lives of seemingly ordinary. Ferreting out the indelible details of his subjects, Tom writes in a way that enables readers to recall the nuances of his stories years later. – *Carolyn Donohoe Marieb, essayist.*

I read the last portion of your story today and just sat in my office for a while and reflected on it. All of it reached me on a number of levels both personal and professional; some painful – some very satisfying. Thanks again for a great piece of work and give me pause to reflect on my life. – *A reader.*

Thank you very much for writing this great story. I will read it through again every now and then to encourage me. – *A reader.*

Reading Tom Hallman is a full contact sport emotionally. There's something about his writing that seems brisk and to the point technically, but as he draws you intimately into the living rooms, city streets, court houses and phone calls in his stories, Hallman adds layers of emotion and complexity to his narratives about people that make you feel what he felt. In the end, you're left with a raw glimpse into human nature and you're all the more better for it. His work is pure artisanship. -- *Emily Clingman, editor, The Park County Republican and Fairplay Flume*

Our editor passed your story around the newsroom, saying you are the one of the only reporters he consistently reads. -- *A reporter.*

As one writer/reporter to another, I simply wanted to thank you for showing the power of narrative. It's the type of writing I'm drawn to and your work inspires me. -- *Rosette Royale, writer.*

Written by Tom Hallman means the story will be compelling and full of "heart." -- *A reader.*

Well written, Tom Hallman. I know when you and I met at the Starbucks a few years ago about my sister's murder, the amount of caring and empathy you showed while just listening to my story, was comforting. -- *Karen Pilgram-Forkner*

You help us rise above ourselves. You give us examples of everyday people dealing with stress and life-and-death decisions, and their fortitude. You give us empathy because we know, but for the grace of God, that situation could be ours. As we hope and pray for them we hope we can handle whatever comes our way as well as they do. – *April McKechnie Ober*

You are an inspiration. I so enjoy and respect your stories about people and life. – *Martha Hendricks*

I sat here at my desk, with coffee, and quietly read your words Tom. I am again dumbstruck with the power of story and the unique ability that you have to connect with us, your lucky readers. Thank you for adding grace to our world. – *Carrie Ohlson Stevens*

I'm writing to tell you what a beautiful story you wrote on Abby's closet. This is one of the best stories I have ever read in the Oregonian, and this is the first "fan" letter I have ever written. -- *A reader.*

You always take me along on your journey and let me feel the air, taste the food and smell all the elements that make your job so interesting. You also let me feel their pain and share in their joys. *A reader.*

Thank you for sharing your gift with us and reminding us about how well a story can be told. – *A reader.*

I had a tear rolling down my check by the time I finished it. You have a real talent for this. – *A reader.*

This is a story marvelously told by Pulitzer Prize winner Tom Hallman. His style is as clear as glass. Throughout this narrative, he is the unseen observer, who has the grace, humility and good sense to let the story unfold on its own terms. – *Book reviewer.*

Thank you for that piece of journalism. I am so exhausted with the negative. This was about something very beautiful. I need to hear these kinds of stories. -- *Thomas Wells.*

I want to thank you for your story. I am sending it to my grandchildren. I was about to cancel my Oregonian subscription as the paper these days only brings news of the worst of everything. -- *Kate Smith*

I am an 18-year-old freshman at OSU. I live in a fraternity, and my normal routine is to eat a bowl of cereal each morning and read the sports. Today was different. Someone had the sports. I began to read the front page. I read your story. I had to leave the room. I was crying, but I took the paper with me. I finished the article, and realized I was still reading through tears. – *A reader.*

Thank you for your work. It has lifted the heart and soul. – *Mary Frances Doherty.*

I just wanted to drop you a line and thank you for writing such a great article. I just loved your writing style and wanted to take a second from the day to say you communicated the emotion/empathy. -- *A reader.*

Tom Hallman, Jr.'s narratives give a graceful voice to the universal struggles everyday people face. He isn't one of those celebrity journalists, looking at the world from afar. He writes from the news trenches and touches readers with beautifully written pieces daily. Tom Hallman, Jr. is required reading in the narrative writing courses here at Stonehill College—along with Truman Capote, Tom Wolfe, and Gay Talese. He is one of the best in the business. -- *Maureen Boyle, Journalism Program Director, Stonehill College*

Tom was one of the finest writers I ever worked with at Reader's Digest. – *Gary Sledge, former Assistant Managing Editor Reader's Digest*

Tom Hallman, Jr. is that rare and wonderful combination: a master storyteller and an elegant writer with a deeply perceptive heart. He has an uncanny ability to see the profound in the everyday and make you see it, too—in ways that will remind you of what's really important in life. I defy you to read his work and not be moved, enlightened, and inspired. -- *Bryan Smith, writer-at-large, Chicago Magazine*

Tom Hallman, Jr. is one of America's foremost feature writers, one who knows how to judge—and tell—riveting stories. Above all, he understands that the most moving and insightful tales reveal the hearts, minds, and actions of real people who face wrenching challenges and eventually find redemption. —*James Sinkinson, publisher, Infocom Group*

As an editor and a story scout for *Reader's Digest*, I've read the work of some very special writers. Tom Hallman heads the list. Through beautifully structured, easily accessible narratives, he draws readers into stories that touch the soul. -- *Brian Summers, Reader's Digest story scout*

The reporting is outstanding; the writing is extraordinary. This is journalism at its highest level. -- *Missouri Lifestyle Journalism Awards, University of Missouri*

My 16-year subscription to The Oregonian is partially influenced to the frequent writings of my favorite journalist Tom Hallman. In morning ritual, I eagerly scan the newspaper knowing that his stories are inspiring, soul stirring and sincere. His writings never disappoint. Many times after reading I set the book or newspaper aside and just quietly reflect on the story -- just allowing the words to fully sink in. -- *Krista Miller*

Tom Hallman writes with color and grace. His heart is apparent in every sentence. -- *Judges, Scripps Howard National Journalism Awards.*

This is the kind of reporting that really means something. -- *A reader*

Please, please, write more articles like this one. -- *A reader.*

We don't usually allow reporters around us but we made an exception for Tom Hallman Jr. and I'm glad we did. In our life everyone has an opinion about the club without ever meeting one of us, so they parrot another man's words to base their opinion about us. Not Tom! He wrote what he saw!! He has the ability to go to new and uncomfortable environment and not only fit in but put onto paper an unbiased account of what he witnessed. Thank you again Tom for your pride and integrity as a man. Because of those traits you helped us honor our brother -- *Jon Jon, Hells Angels, Sonoma County*

Your stories are by far the most worthwhile and meaningful of all areas of the paper. – *A reader.*

Tom does everything that students of storytelling are encouraged to do. He puts readers on the scenes of stories, magnificently so, with details that not only tell but also illuminate.

But what he does best is to place readers into the heart of the characters he writes about.

This is the rarest of gifts, for it requires the ability to listen, really listen, and the desire to understand another person's life and circumstances. Most of all it requires thought – in what way does this person or this story tell us something about all of us?

In the end, a Tom Hallman story does not call attention to the reporting, the writing or the structure but to the humanity, the subject's and our own. Because he cares, we care, and we look forward with great anticipation to the next dispatch.

He's so good that most writers I know – a group not exactly famous for being charitable toward another's work -- are too inspired by Tom's stories to be jealous. *--Ken Fuson, award-winning writer and author*

Hallman's writing is crisp and affecting. – *Publishers Weekly*

Tom Hallman Jr. belongs to a generation of writers who are pushing the literary envelope. His style is transparent and unclouded, projecting the reader directly into the minds and lives of his subjects. – *Jon Franklin, two-time Pulitzer Prize winner and author of Writing for Story*

Hallman is a marvelous journalist-storyteller. -- *Los Angeles Times Book Review*

Gripping…Compelling drama, driven by Hallman's factual narration of events. – *Rocky Mountain News*

I loved this story because of its humanity and relevancy. I very much enjoy the way you write, the way your stories flow and speak with a true voice. But the thing that I love most is their humanity. – *Molly Hottle, writer.*

Tom Hallman's work – captivating, urgent and reported and written with tremendous discipline – has inspired a generation of journalists. I will never forget the first time I read 'The Boy Behind the Mask' and came to the moment where the nurses write the sign that says 'Sam I Am'. That detail knocked me down, and I have never forgotten it. Journalism is better because of Hallman. *–Tom French, author and winner of the Pulitzer Prize.*

The role of a storyteller takes me into worlds where people who are not newsmakers play out the great themes of life in private. The best stories are about "something," not just a recounting of an event. A story reveals, gives meaning and – on some level – provides lessons about life. I am grateful for all the people who graciously allowed me into their lives.

Tom Hallman Jr.

Foreword

I chose the title for this book – Dispatches from 1320 – because the stories that appear in this collection were written in a newsroom that no longer exists: The Oregonian, 1320 S.W. Broadway.

Long ago, when I began exploring the art of storytelling, I learned it's more effective to write about a person than a place. A character draws a reader in, provides a point of view, and allows an emotional connection to a story.

But now I want to tell you a story about a place.

Like all my co-workers at The Oregonian, I did my part to make the transition to a new building and a new newsroom. I emptied my desk drawers, cleared everything from a file cabinet. Notebooks, files and cassette tapes of long-forgotten interviews were taken home, tossed in the trash or dumped into recycling containers.

We moved to a building within walking distance of our old building. It's a nice place. We have new furniture, state-of-the-art technology and stunning views of Mount Hood and the Willamette River.

But an era ended.

If you've worked in a newsroom, you know what I mean.

And if you haven't, well, you've missed something special.

I got my introduction to The Oregonian newsroom in 1975, when an editor gave a kid majoring in journalism a chance to be a summer copy boy. I served the reporters and editors. I handled the mail, ripped the wire and ran errands. I collected money from reporters and went to a deli to buy sandwiches, returning to the newsroom to deliver them desk-to-desk.

I changed typewriter ribbons and made the morning and afternoon runs, stopping at the police station and city hall pressrooms to collect reporters' typewritten pages that I'd carry back to the city desk. Like I said – errand boy. No matter, I could truthfully say I worked in the newsroom.

I returned to The Oregonian the next summer as an intern, and I was eventually hired as a reporter in late 1980, assigned a desk in the middle of a group of veteran reporters who decided to take a young man under their wings and show him the ropes. Some smoked cigarettes at their desks, enjoyed the occasional drink at lunch and trash-talked and swore as they pursued the stories that people would read the next morning. And I got to be part of it, watching and learning from men and women whose names I will never forget.

An editor, fed up with a reporter's messy desk, once tucked a turkey sandwich under a stack of papers and then walked around the newsroom taking bets on when the reporter wound discover the gift. A month later it was still there.

One reporter bought a universal television remote control, figured out the code for an editor's office television and used it to drive him nuts by sitting far away and ever so slowly turn up the set's volume. The editor, irritated, would adjust the volume and then return to his desk. An hour later, the reporter would slowly turn down the volume.

Another reporter signed an editor up for a subscription to a nudist magazine. He'd wait each month for the mail to arrive, stifling a laugh when the editor would stand up at his desk and yell, demanding to know where the magazine came from.

A reporter had a remote-control robot he used one afternoon to deliver his story to the city desk, taping the story to the robot's arm. The editor heard a whirring noise, looked up and snatched the story without uttering a word.

A high-ranking editor used a squirt gun on people passing by his desk.

A mild-mannered clerk, so shy that he could barely speak to a woman, once became frustrated over something that forever remained a mystery. He tossed an electric typewriter through an inner-office window, adjusted his shirt and sat back at his desk and got back to work.

Brilliance.

Creativity.

Jealousy.

Tension.

Craft.

Friendship.

You found all of it – and more – in the newsroom.

People were always talking, grumbling or arguing. The police radio always crackling, a telephone always ringing.

When visitors wandered in, they saw chaos and wondered how anything ever got done. You had to be a part of it – be one of us -- to understand and love the magic of the newsroom.

Within that grand room, everyone had a mission.

Someone was sorting through negatives looking for the perfect photo, or figuring out how to get a source to talk, or crafting a sensitive opening to a feature, or studying documents to hold a politician accountable, or editing a story to make it understandable, or designing a page or writing a headline.

A paper was born.

And then we did it again.

And again.

And again.

I spent more than 35 years in that newsroom, more time than in any home or apartment I've ever lived in.

Earlier, I wrote that the newsroom was a place.

I was wrong.

The Oregonian newsroom – first on the third floor and at the end on the fourth -- was a character, a living thing.

I see it now, late in my career, that the newsroom was a fine bottle of red wine, aged with the character, grace and heart – precious gifts from all who ever worked there.

1320

Rest in peace.

© The Oregonian. All rights reserved. Reprinted with permission.

The Graduate

He Wasted Too Many Years Dreaming And Wandering.

The house is just outside of Portland, the last one on the right side of the street, not too far from the freeway and just across from a self-service car wash. Patches of moss cover part of the roof, some of the siding is missing, and the grass hasn't been mowed in weeks. With each knock, the front-door glass rattles and threatens to fall out of the frame.

The man who answers the door has hands that are tough and calloused. The hands of a man who uses them to work. On this Sunday morning, he wears a suit he bought a day earlier at a used clothing store for $8. He borrowed a blue tie with red stripes from a friend. The white shirt and the black wingtips are his. He bought them at what he calls a real store, a good store. He pulls them from his closet only when he goes to church. Or for special occasions.

"This is where I study," says Juan Morales as he leads the way to the kitchen, which has cracked counter tops and a sagging floor. Next to the microwave is a stack of World Books published in the 1960s. He bought the set at a used bookstore. When he eats, Morales randomly selects a volume and reads. He does not care what he reads. Any subject will do.

"I wasted too many years," he says. "Too many years dreaming, wandering, not doing anything."

He shakes his head.

"Let me show you something," he says.

He walks into the living room and points to a dirty wall that needs paint. Earlier this morning, he pounded a nail into the wall.

"That," he says, "is where the diploma will hang."

He nods firmly.

"That wall," he says. "That nail." His mother makes first trip to U.S. He returns to the kitchen and sits at the table. He looks at his wristwatch. He does not have to be at Lewis & Clark College in Southwest Portland until 10 a.m. to meet his mother. She has made her first trip to the United States to witness his graduation. He thinks now of his mother and of the old man, the stranger. Today, he feels the old man's presence. Without the old man, he would be on the streets.

In 1984, Juan Morales, the youngest of eight children in a poor family, decided to leave his hometown of Torreon, a city in northern Mexico, to come to the United States. He had heard stories of people who had come north and found the good life.

"I was naive," he says with a chuckle. "I believed them and all their stories of the lush life. I sold some things to get the train fare to the El Paso border. I walked across the border by myself and then asked which train tracks led West. I jumped on a freight train to Los Angeles."

The train was later stopped and searched by officials, who sent Morales and others back to Mexico.

"I crossed and recrossed the border eight times," he says. "I didn't know what else to do. There was no life in Mexico."

Morales eventually ended up in Oregon, in Washington County, working the fields as an illegal migrant farm worker. He later drifted to Portland, living on the streets in Old Town. Each morning he'd scrounge up money and walk across the Burnside Bridge to a McDonald's restaurant on the east side of town.

"I'd wash my face, clean up and then have something to eat," he says. "Somehow I became friends with an Anglo, a man who was a regular there. He was in his 70s. I never knew his name, but we became friends."

In time, the two men ended up sitting together. The Latino with the poor English, the Anglo with too much time on his hands.

"He told me that time is wasted on the young," Morales says. "Most young people, he told me, wander without direction. I told him that was me. I told him my life was hard and that I was not sure if I could do anything remarkable with it. He talked with me about the importance of education. He said I should go to school."

The stranger suggested Morales enroll at Portland Community College to take a course in English as a Second Language. The man helped Morales enroll and find the money for tuition.

"Then he passed away," Morales says. "I did not know of his death until weeks later when I found out from others at McDonald's. I was angry. I felt he left me. I really needed his advice and guidance. Suddenly, as I was beginning to pursue something, he was not there."

The telephone rings, and Morales excuses himself to take the call. He returns to the room, smiling. His mother, he says, is excited. She will be brought to Lewis & Clark with a couple that Morales considers his adopted U.S. family. He met them when he was picking strawberries, and people from their church brought food to the workers in the field.

"My mother is proud of me," he says. "But I don't think she really understands what I went through."

After Morales' mentor died, he continued to go to school and held down several jobs to earn tuition. He worked at the McDonald's and as a busboy at a truck stop.

"I took whatever came around," he says. "I would work, save money and go to school. Then when I ran out of money, I would quit school and go back to work."

In 1993, he found work as a janitor at Lewis & Clark. He later took an opening in the library, working the graveyard shift. And he learned that employees were eligible to take courses at reduced rates.

"My English was better, but not good," he says. "I wandered around the campus, scared. I was just a poor man. Who was I fooling? But I found another mentor -- a history professor who remembered me from cleaning his office. I decided to take his class. I became enchanted and decided that I wanted to study history."

He took classes when he could. He worked full time on the graveyard shift in the library and held down other part-time jobs, scrimping and saving for food and books. At times he thought he could not make it, that he did not belong. But on Sunday, he would join them.

Juan Morales, 38, the youngest child of a poor family, would receive his bachelor of arts degree in history.

"I wanted my mother there to watch," he says. "In March, she went to the U.S. Embassy for a visa. My family and I all chipped in for an airline ticket for her. Tonight, I plan on taking her to dinner.

"The money?" he asks.

He smiles and rolls up his right shirt-sleeve. He points to a dark spot on his skin.

"I am very familiar with the plasma clinic," he says. "I got $25 yesterday. We will use the money for dinner."

He closes the door to his home in Fairview and walks to the car he bought for $100. To start it, he must connect two wires under the dashboard. He lets it idle for a while. Blue smoke pours out of the tailpipe as he heads to Lewis & Clark.

He is not sure what he will do now. He plans on getting a job this summer to pay debts and to save money. Graduate school is a possibility, but the tuition frightens him. He has considered teaching history, but he finds he is drawn to somehow working with high school students.

As he pulls into the campus, a Latino security guard spots Morales and gives him a thumbs up. He stops Morales, shakes his hand and then pounds on the roof of his car. The guard can't stop smiling. Morales parks his Datsun 210 next to a Volvo and joins the hundreds of young graduates making their way to the student center.

"I know every single office on this campus," he says. "I cleaned every one of them."

In the student center, he goes to the restroom to wash his hands. He looks at himself in the mirror, in his cap and gown.

"I cleaned this bathroom," he says. "Me, Juan Morales."

He adjusts his cap and joins the other graduates. He receives his material and learns that he will be student No. 247 out of 404 to receive a degree this Sunday. He clutches his number close to his chest and walks away, quickly swallowed up by a roiling sea of black.

THE CHAPERONES

From a kid's perspective, a chaperone is nothing but trouble.

Max Davidson, the senior class treasurer at Southwest Portland's Lincoln High School, didn't want to send the e-mail. Truth was, he didn't even want to tell his parents about the problem. But he had no choice. So with great reluctance, the 17-year-old hit "send." Within minutes, responses from his fellow students flooded his in-box: "No way." "Are you kidding?" "Absolutely not."

He expected as much. But now, months of planning would be wasted because of one terrible word that high-schoolers consider more horrific than "SAT," "homework" or "grades."

Chaperone.

If he didn't round up 30 parent chaperones, Lincoln's homecoming would be canceled. The event, scheduled days before Halloween, had been billed as a costume party, and nearly 1,000 tickets had been sold. Now, though, pulling it off hinged on Davidson.

He'd checked with Cameron Neil, a school vice principal, looking for a break. Neil was adamant: No chaperones, no dance. Neil was sympathetic, though; he doubted his own two high-schoolers would let him chaperone their dance.

High school students do everything in their power to make parents disappear. The boys and girls who once held on tightly to their parents' hands and jumped in the car to tag along on errands suddenly demand they be let out of the car three blocks from school. They juggle identities like undercover agents, simultaneously existing in two separate worlds.

From a kid's perspective, a chaperone is nothing but trouble. They see mom in her sensible skirt and shoes, telling everyone to have fun but

5

terrified she'll reveal secrets about life at home. Or dad dropping the names of musicians from the 1980s and maybe hollering at the most popular guy in school.

Davidson was well aware of that, but he sent a second request anyway. Like all area schools, Lincoln counts on parents to help. Having them run the concession stand at the basketball game is tolerable. What isn't OK is being on the dance floor, preparing to make a move -- and catching your mom's eye.

Throughout the city, high-level negotiations ensued. Some parents wrote Davidson to say they wanted to help, but their kids wouldn't hear of it. Davidson's parents, Anne and Martin, signed up. A little too quickly for Davidson's liking, but desperate times require extraordinary measures.

Other parents volunteered -- with as many stipulations as a real estate contract: They had to leave at 9 p.m. They could only take tickets at the front door. Under no circumstances could they work the dance floor.

The list grew. And then it hit 30.

C ameron Neil pulled open the door to the Melody Ballroom in Southeast Portland and stepped into the foyer. The metal door slammed shut, and the sound echoed through a two-story building that, in an hour, would be a playground.

He sighed, walked to a table and read a note left by a parent who'd been by to decorate the ballroom: "A walk through downstairs reveals many "nooks" with unlockable doors. Chaperones should circulate through those areas."

"Oh, boy," Neil muttered. He headed downstairs to examine those nooks. Proactive, he looked at them the way a teenager might: dark, cozy and isolated. And nothing but trouble. He walked upstairs, running his hand over his face and devising his plan. He'd be overseeing 30 chaperones and three teachers. He had to deploy this meager squad wisely.

The reinforcements arrived, and Neil asked a father to look for all the exits in the building to make sure no one sneaked into the event. He sent another father to double-check the nooks. Six parents settled in behind long tables to check identification cards against a master list. Other parents were sent to the coat room. The rest roamed the foyer, basement and second-floor ballroom.

Neil motioned to Beth Burczak.

"I need you to stand here," he told her, putting her in front of the basement steps. "No one goes down there without checking in first."

Burczak's 16-year-old daughter, Sarah, had agreed to let her chaperone. With conditions. Her mother couldn't talk to Sarah. She was permitted to talk to Sarah's friends, but only --and this was stressed many times --if the friend initiated contact. Hugging and waving were prohibited.

Her mother also had to dress appropriately. In Sarah's eyes, that meant her mother couldn't look like she was 20. Nor should she look like she was 60. She had to look like a mom. Not a nerd mom. Cool. But not too cool.

"I wouldn't have wanted my parents at a dance," said Burczak, who wore a long skirt, black tights and a sweater. "Being seen with your parents wasn't good. My sister and I rode home from an awards banquet with my parents, and they decided to pull into a McDonald's full of kids. My sister and I dove to the floor and hid."

"Are we ready to man our stations?" Neil called out as he hustled upstairs to check the coat room.

Parents traded horror stories about childhood. One father remembered being at a high school football game with a blind date who threw her arms around his neck at the exact moment his father appeared. Moms talked about sons hiding when they saw them approach. Dads talked about being able to hug their daughters only in certain situations. Before leaving home, their children issued the final rules: Don't hover, don't watch me dance, don't yell at my friends.

"We're a minute from showtime," Neil yelled. "There's no turning back."

He took a deep breath, threw open the doors and got out of the way.

Hundreds of teenagers – "You look great," "Is she here?," "Can you believe her?" -- rushed up the marble steps to the dance floor, where the lights had been dimmed. A DJ stood behind a control board, and music blasted from speakers.

Walt Peck moved aside, trying to casually catch a glimpse of his two sons in the pack.

"I have great kids," he said. "I'm the fog lines in their lives. As long as they're going in a good direction, I give them space."

He walked up the steps and headed toward a far corner of the dance floor. Neil had asked Peck to sit by an exit near the stage. "I brought my ear plugs," Peck said. "My wife handed them to me when I walked out the door."

Bruce Thompson roamed the crowded dance floor. His daughter, a 15-year-old freshman, allowed him to come as long as he stayed downstairs. But Neil assigned him to the dance floor. He spotted Justine, smiled and raised his hand. Justine shook her head and walked the other way.

"As long as he stays away from me, he'll be OK," she said. "Don't get me started on all the ways he could embarrass me: 'Who's that?' 'Who are you dancing with?'"

Chastened, Thompson stuck his hands in his pocket.

"She doesn't realize what a cool dad she has," he said before disappearing into the dark room.

From the walls, where parents linger, the view is familiar: The nervous boy preparing to talk to a girl, his buddies alternating razzing and cheering him on. A girl running to her friends to spend the rest of the night analyzing a boy's every gesture or comment.

And yet it's like a foreign language they spoke once, long ago. They remember "hello" and "goodbye" but little else. The music, fashions and culture they once were a part of have changed, and they're lost in the way that parents have felt when the next generation is ready to leave.

They see young men and women in front of them, but they remember the children.

And on a Saturday night, they continue to let go of the past and hope that the future is kind.

THE SALESMAN

All his life he's struggled to prove them wrong. He will not quit.

The alarm rings and he stirs. It's 5:45. He could linger under the covers, listening to the radio and a weatherman who predicts rain. People would understand. He knows that.

A surgeon's scar cuts a swath across his lower back. The medicines and painkillers littering his night stand offer help but no cure. The fingers on his right hand are so twisted that he can't tie his shoes.

Somedays, he feels like surrendering. But his dead mother's challenge reverberates in his soul. So, too, do the voices of those who believed him stupid or retarded, incapable of being more than a ward of the state. All his life he's struggled to prove them wrong. He will not quit.

And so Bill Porter rises.

He takes the first unsteady steps on a journey to Portland's streets, the battle-field where he fights alone for his independence and dignity. He's a door-to-door salesman. Sixty-three years old. And his enemies -- a crippled body that betrays him and a changing world that no longer needs him -- are gaining on him.

With trembling hands he assembles his weapons: black wingtips, dark slacks, blue shirt and matching blazer, brown tie, tan raincoat and pinched-front, brown fedora. Image, he believes, is everything.

He stops in the entryway, picks up his briefcase and steps out onto the stoop of his Northeast Portland home. A fall wind has kicked up. The weatherman was right. He pulls his raincoat tighter.

He tilts his hat just so.

———◆———

O n the 7:45 bus that stops across the street, he leaves his briefcase next to the driver and finds a seat in the middle of a pack of bored teenagers.

He leans forward, stares toward the driver, sits back, then repeats the process. His nervousness makes him laugh uncontrollably. The teenagers smirk. They don't realize Porter's afraid someone will steal his briefcase, with the glasses, brochures, order forms and clip-on tie that he needs to survive.

Porter senses the stares. He covers his mouth, stifles a laugh and regains his composure. He looks at a boy next to him. He smiles. The kid turns away and makes a face at a buddy.

Porter looks at the floor.

His face reveals nothing. In his heart, though, he knows he should have been like these kids, like everyone on this bus. He's not angry. But he knows. His mother explained how the delivery had been difficult, how the doctor had used an instrument that crushed a section of his brain and caused cerebral palsy, a disorder of the nervous system that affects his speech, hands and walk.

Porter came to Portland when he was 13 after his father, a salesman for a neon sign company, was transferred here. He attended a school for the disabled and then Lincoln High School, where he was placed in a class for slow kids.

But he wasn't slow.

His mind was trapped in a body that didn't work. Speaking was laborious, as if words had to be pulled from a tar pit. People were impatient and didn't listen. He felt different -- was different -- from the kids who rough-housed in the halls and planned dances he would never attend.

People like him were considered retarded then. What could his future be? Porter wanted to do something and asked the State Vocational Rehabilitation Division for help. They sent him to several social service agencies, but it did no good. He couldn't use a cash register, unload trucks or solicit funds on the telephone. "Unemployable" is what they called him. He should collect government disability checks for the rest of his life.

His mother was certain, though, that he could rise above his limitations. She helped start a workshop for people with cerebral palsy, and Porter sold redwood planters to raise money for it.

People listened.

With his mother's encouragement, he applied for a job with the Fuller Brush Co. only to be turned down. He couldn't carry a product briefcase or walk a route, they said.

Porter knew he wanted to be a salesman. He began reading help wanted ads in the newspaper. When he saw one for Watkins, a company that sold household products door-to-door, his mother set up a meeting with a representative. The man said no, but Porter wouldn't listen. He just wanted a chance. The man relented and offered Porter a section of the city that no salesman wanted.

It took Porter four false starts before he found the courage to ring the first doorbell. The man who answered told him to go away, a pattern repeated throughout the day.

That night Porter read through company literature and discovered the products were guaranteed. He would sell that pledge. He just needed people to listen.

If a customer turned him down, Porter kept coming back until they heard him. When apartment managers refused to admit him, Porter waited until someone else was buzzed inside and then walked in behind them.

And he sold.

He was rewarded with the Laurelhurst sales route in Northeast Portland. His parents made deliveries because he couldn't drive. He prospected the area for 13 years before concentrating solely on Portland's westside, a bigger market.

For several years he was Watkins' top retail salesman in all of Oregon, Idaho, Washington and California. Now he is the only one of the company's 44,000 salespeople who sells door-to-door.

He's headed back to his route today. The bus stops in the Transit Mall, and Porter shuffles off.

His body is not made for walking. Each step strains his joints. Migraines and other aches are constant visitors. His right arm is nearly useless. He can't fully control the limb, and it's pressed close to his body and thrust backward as if he's pushing off with a ski pole. His torso tilts at the waist; he seems to be heading into a strong, steady wind that keeps him off balance. At times, he looks like a toddler taking his first steps.

He walks 10 miles a day.

His first stop today, like every day, is a shoeshine stand where employees tie his laces. Twice a week he pays for a shine. At a nearby hotel one of the doormen buttons Porter's top shirt button and slips on his clip-on tie. He then walks to another bus that drops him off a mile from his territory -- a neighborhood near Wilson High School.

He's been up for nearly five hours.

He left home nearly three hours ago.

———————

The wind is cold and raindrops fall. Porter ignores the elements and the sluggishness in his thighs. He trudges up one hill and down another until he reaches the edge of the neigbhorhood.

He stops at the first house. This is the moment he's been preparing for since 5:45 a.m. He rings the bell.

A woman comes to the door.

"H e l l o."

"No, thank you, I'm just preparing to leave."

Porter nods.

"May I come back later?" he asks?

"No," says the woman.

She shuts the door.

Porter's eyes reveal nothing.

He moves to the next house.

The door opens.

Then closes.

He doesn't get a chance to speak. Porter's expression never changes. He stops at every home in his territory. People might not buy now. Next time. Maybe. No doesn't mean never. Some of his best customers are people who repeatedly turned him down before buying.

He stops again.

"No, I'm babysitting for friends, and I have three toddlers in here. I can't talk now."

The door shuts.

He makes his way down the street.

"I don't want to try it."

"Maybe next time."

"I'm sorry. I'm on the phone right now."

"No."

He makes his way up and down the hills. His briefcase is heavy. He stops and shifts it to his bad hand, forcing the handle between his fingers. He walks 15 feet and stops.

His hand hurts.

He catches his breath.

He walks on.

Ninety minutes later, Porter still has not made a sale. But there is always another home.

He walks on.

He knocks on a door. A woman wanders out from the back yard where she's gardening. She often buys, but not today, she says, as she walks away.

"Are you sure?" Porter asks.

She pauses.

"Well . . ."

That's all Porter needs. He walks as fast as he can, tailing her as she heads to the back yard. He sets his briefcase on a bench and opens it. He puts on his glasses, removes his brochures and begins his spiel, showing the woman pictures and describing each product.

Spices?

"No."

Vanilla?

"No."

Pasta toppings?

"No."

Jams?"

"No."

Potpourri?

"No. Maybe nothing today, Bill."

Porter's hearing is the one perfect thing his body does. Except when he gets a live one. Then the word "no" does not register.

Cinnamon?

"No."

Pepper?"

"No."

Laundry soap?

"Hmm."

Porter stops. He's a shark smelling blood. He quickly remembers her last order.

"Say, aren't you about out of soap? That's what you bought last time. You ought to be out right about now."

"You're right, Bill. I'll take one."

Because he has difficulties holding a pen, Porter asks his customers to complete their order forms. The woman writes him a check, which he deposits in his briefcase.

Then he is on his way.

No sale.

No sale.

No sale.

Finally, a woman and her daughter invite Porter inside. The woman and Porter talk about the neighborhood -- who's moved away and who's sick. After a few minutes of small talk, Porter takes off his hat and raincoat and sets them on a chair. Out come the glasses and the brochures.

"A good buy on detergent. No phosphates. Do you have a brand you already buy?"

"Yes, the biggest one Costco sells."

"Oh."

"We have a new kind of pepper."

"I don't do much with those kinds of things."

"Hot spices?"

"No."

"All natural, pure pasta toppings."

He glances at the customer. She's teetering and just needs a push.

"Sure would make a nice gift."

He studies her face, searching for clues as to what she needs to hear.

"Nothing synthetic."

"Really?"

Touchdown!

"How much is a set?" she asks.

"$22.99, and they go a long way."

"OK, I'll give it a try."

"I think you'll like those toppings. They have a good flavor."

As the woman fills out her order form, Porter suggests another item.

"How about some vanilla."

"How much?"

"$10.19."

She adds it to the form. Porter removes his glasses and places everything in his briefcase. He pulls on his coat, replaces his hat and follows the woman to the front door.

He turns to her.

His bent body makes it appear as if he were bowing.

He struggles to get out one final sentence.

"And...I... thank ... you."

———◆———

He arrives home, in a rainstorm, after 7 p.m. Today was not profitable. He tells himself not to worry. Four days left in the week.

At least he's off his feet and home. He and his parents moved here more than 30 years ago. They're both gone now. Not a day goes by that he doesn't silently thank them.

After his father died, his mother lived off a small pension with help from Porter's income. When she passed on eight years ago, she left only the house and a voice he still hears.

Inside, an era is preserved. The telephone is a heavy, rotary model. There is no VCR, no cable. His is the only house in the neighborhood with a television antenna on the roof.

He leads a solitary life. He's met a couple of women over the years, but nothing serious developed. Most of his human contact comes on the job. Alone, he does paperwork, reads and watches television, especially sporting events.

Now, he heats the oven and slips in a frozen dinner, a staple because they're easy to fix.

As his food warms, he opens his briefcase and stacks the order forms. In two weeks, he will use a manual typewriter to write detailed directions to each house so the women he hires to make deliveries won't get lost. He can use only one finger and one hand to type.

The job usually takes him 10 hours.

He's a weary man who knows his days -- no matter what his intentions -- are numbered.

He peddles his goods in downpours, snowstorms and sweltering heat. He does not know how much longer his body can take the pounding. In quieter moments, he wonders if the day is fast approaching when the world will no longer answer his knock at the door.

At many homes, the woman of the house is off working. And if someone is there, they buy in bulk at superstores. They'd rather save a dollar than deal with a stranger who talks about money-back guarantees.

He works on straight commission. He gets no paid holidays, vacations or raises. Yes, some months are lean.

In 1993, he needed back surgery to relieve pain caused from decades of walking. He was laid up for five months and couldn't work. He was forced to take a loan on his house to eat, consolidate past debt and pay three years of back property taxes.

When he returned to the street, business was slow. He fell further behind. Eventually, he sold his home, cleared the books and started over. The new owners, familiar with his situation, froze his rent and agreed to let him live there until he dies.

He doesn't feel sorry for himself.

The house is only a building. A place to live, nothing more.

His dinner is ready. He eats at the kitchen table and listens to the radio. The afternoon mail brought bills that he will deal with later this week. The checkbook is upstairs in the bedroom.

His checkbook.

He pays a gardener. He pays his medical insurance. He pays a woman to shop for him, clean his house, do his laundry and make his lunch when he knows his daily route will take him far from a fast food restaurant.

He types in the recipient's name and signs his name.

The signature is small and scrawled.

Unreadable.

But he knows.

Bill Porter.

Bill Porter, salesman.

From his easy chair he hears the wind lash his house and the rain pound the street outside his home. He must dress warmly tomorrow. He's sleepy. With great care he climbs the stairs to his bedroom.

In time, the lights go off.

Morning will be here soon.

The Flagger

These characters slip unannounced into your life

He showed up about two months ago, just appeared on the street one afternoon and eased his way into the city. No one knew his name or anything about him. But he stuck it out, day after day, shift after shift. Before too long, people got used to seeing his face.

That's the way it always is with these characters. They slip unannounced into your life and -- in a strange way -- you start counting on them to always be there. The barista at the coffee shop, that familiar face behind the checkout counter, the security guard at the front desk. Not one of them is doing anything special. They're just, well, they're just there.

Our lives intersect for only the briefest of moments. A few words, a nod, a wave. Yet in time they're subtly woven into the fabric of our daily routines. They offer that elusive sense of community. When they vanish -- and most of them do -- we miss them.

So, yes, Tom Potter and Rosie Sizer and Nate McMillan are big shots, important and newsmakers in every sense of the word.

How about Arvin Bradley?

Not familiar? He's the man who holds the stop sign each afternoon at the west end of the Hawthorne Bridge, directing traffic as it heads east.

Ah, that guy.

Bradley ambled his way onto a small corner of Portland's larger stage because of the massive construction project that has torn up long stretches of Southwest Naito Parkway. The northbound lanes are closed at the Hawthorne Bridge, and traffic is diverted onto the bridge's eastbound on-ramp. That causes congestion during the evening rush hour as pedestrians, bikes and cars headed out of downtown converge at one small choke point. The project required a flagger to control traffic, and KM Services -- a company that supplies flaggers across the state -- was told to get one.

But it would be a tough post. The flagger would have to work alone and deal with the public up close in ways not typical for the job. Men and women rotated through the post. One quit after a single shift. Another said the stress got to him and he felt like pulling drivers from their cars and beating them up. The company's dispatcher, Kim Lee, realized filling the spot could be difficult. So she asked Bradley, a laborer's union member and flagger since 1990, if he'd try it for just one shift.

"I told him it wouldn't be easy," she recalled. "There are no breaks or lunch at regular times. You have to stand there and concentrate because it's so crowded that it's easy to have an accident. It's one of those posts that burns people out. He came back after that first day and said he was fine. He's been there ever since, which is very unusual for a flagger."

He works a four-hour shift that begins at 3 p.m., Monday through Friday. By his estimate, Bradley figures at least 5,000 cars, trucks, buses, motorcycles, bikers and pedestrians pass by him each shift. And because he works rush hour, most of them travel the same route at the same time day after day. All that has combined to make the 53-year-old Bradley perhaps the metropolitan area's most recognized anonymous man.

That may not be any great distinction. And yet, something special is going on at the west end of the Hawthorne Bridge, something quaintly small town, something that affirms what we desperately want to believe: When given a chance to connect, no matter how briefly, most people bring out the best in one another.

For the commuters who pass by him day after day, Bradley has become "their guy," a character in their lives.

Drivers roll down their windows to say hello. They wave and smile at him when they drive by. Bus drivers pull over to the side of the road, swing open their doors and offer Bradley bottled water or candy bars. Bike riders and pedestrians who wait to cross the street ask how he's doing.

They know nothing of his life -- married to a retired elementary-school teacher, no children -- or the details of his job -- buses get priority and he has to act like a conductor making sure every lane of traffic moves smoothly.

What they sense is something more important: Bradley cares.

Sure it's a job, but the man is not just standing there in the hot sun and pounding rain pulling in $19.22 an hour and bored out of his mind. He tells drivers that he's sorry for delays and that he understands why they may be frustrated. He smiles and mouths "thank you" to every driver.

"I look at these people every day," he said, keeping an eye on traffic during a busy weekday afternoon. "I start every shift the same way, with a prayer where I ask that I have a good attitude and that no harm come to anyone."

Just a man with a stop sign at the end of a bridge.

Dianna's Choice

What does it mean to be mother?

After all this, she still flinches at each cough. One . . . two . . . three . . . He hacks and wheezes and gasps, like an old man in the grip of emphysema.

Five . . . six . . .

She shoves her cereal aside and stands guard outside his bedroom door.

Ten.

Silence.

She eases in, peers into his crib.

"Are you ready, honey? Are you ready to go on a long trip?"

Nothing.

"Oh, my son," she whispers. "I . . . "

She kisses her fingertips and slides them across his cheek. She lingers, eyes closed, memorizing the curve of his face. She lays hands on his chest and feels the life beating there.

Then she turns to confront the suitcases that taunt her from the living room. The choice, her husband said, was hers to make.

Never has she felt so alone. She gave up on God long ago. If only someone could tell her what to do.

No.

Yes.

No.

YES.

She packs his few, small things. A shirt. A sleeper. A pair of shoes whose soles will never be scuffed. Her husband appears, wordless, and takes over, leaving her to dress her boy one last time.

He whimpers when he hears her enter his room. Now it's just the two of them.

"Shh, it's OK. Mommy's here. Your mommy's here."

She rubs his back, but her touch carries no comfort. She struggles to wrestle pants and shirt over limbs that flop and sag. She hears her husband, outside now, loading the suitcases into the car. She has but moments left.

She scans the room.

His favorite animal?

Yes.

His blanket?

Without question.

A musical toy?

She kicks it away. "Rock a Bye Baby" fills the room, mocking her.

———◆———

"I used to think the worst thing that could happen to a parent would be to have their child die. Was I wrong. Wrong! When someone dies, it ends. But my boy . . . Well, my boy is just . . . He's just there.

"Most people don't know how I really feel. It's funny how good I got at hiding what's there. I guess I keep everything inside to make it easier on everyone else.

"I'm the one who wonders what's really going on in his brain. Is he scared? Does he miss me? Does he wonder where I am?

"This is right, I know this is right.

"But there are moments when I'll glance in the mirror, and I'll ask myself: What kind of mother does this to her son?"

———◆———

Pressed to name a hometown, Diana Sullivan picks Albany, an Interstate-5 industrial hamlet 60 miles south of Portland.

Truth is, she took root in people, not places. Her family followed the crop farm harvests across the Pacific Northwest, until Diana's senior year in high school, when her father found steady work in Albany.

Even now, at 26, she honors the small-town ways. Strangers get a howdy. Waitresses get respect. She knows how many children the grocery clerk has and likes it when a man holds the door.

The past rides in her blood. Musty scents remind her of clothes stolen in the dead of night from Goodwill boxes. When her parents pulled together the money for a winter coat, they let Diana pick the color; she knew she had better choose wisely because she would wear that coat for years.

During the worst times, relatives offered to take the kids to live with them. But her father, abandoned as a child, wouldn't hear of it. Family is everything, he preached, as important as life itself.

After high school, Diana toyed with notions of college. But she never considered herself book smart. And she wanted to experience some of the world.

She joined the U.S. Navy in 1988 and was shipped to San Diego, where she trained to be a firefighter. There she met Mike Sullivan, a slender Navy welder, 2 years older.

Mike knows a lot about things -- carburetors and buckshot and tools. But when it comes to feelings, he speaks as if he pays by the word.

They were married a little more than a year when Brandon was born. Books and classes taught Diana how to care for a baby, but nothing had prepared her for the enormity of the love. Brandon was just 5 months old when Diana was shipped out to sea for two weeks; she thought her heart would break.

And so it was that Diana Sullivan made a choice: She would find a way out of her standard six-month duty tour at sea. She would be home when Brandon dared his first steps and cooed his first words.

She scoured the Navy's rule book and found an exemption from sea duty: pregnancy. Mike said he wasn't ready for a second child yet. So Diana just decided: She stopped taking her birth-control pills.

———◆———

The pregnancy is unremarkable until one night in the seventh month. Her stomach hurts. Diana thinks it must be the hamburger she ate. She lies down, tries to relax. When she can't stand the pain any longer, she asks Mike to take her to the hospital.

The doctors find nothing. Her cervix isn't dilated. No contractions. Blood tests and amniocentesis are normal. The baby's heartbeat is strong and steady.

But this pain . . . she's never known anything like it. The soft touch of the hospital bedsheet on her stomach makes her writhe.

And suddenly the baby's heart is racing, 200 beats a minute. Contractions rip through Diana. The doctor says she has little time to decide: Bear the pain and risk of a vaginal delivery, or have an emergency Caesarean section.

Mike can't help.

She doesn't know what do.

The doctor is waiting.

It hurts too much.

End it, she begs.

After it is over, after the tiny creature is lifted from her womb, she lets Mike name his second son.

Christopher.

Christopher Sullivan.

He tells his wife the name sounds so innocent.

———•———

Christopher weighs barely 5 pounds. The top portion of his right lung is hyperinflated, trapping oxygen like a balloon; blood flowing through receives no oxygen. And he has bronchiopulmonary displasia, dysplasia is an asthmalike condition in the main branches of the windpipe.

These are minor problems, the doctors say, all to be expected. A ventilator will help him breathe. He will outgrow the displasia. And, when he is older and stronger, surgery can fix his lung.

Diana sits beside Christopher's plastic-walled crib in the pediatric intensive-care unit, watching him doze beneath the heat lamp. How does she mother this child?

She can't cradle him lest she disturb all the tubes and wires that attach him to the terrifying machines. She can only touch his fingers and wonder what he feels like, smells like.

For the first five days of his life, he lies motionless in the incubator. On the sixth day, he opens his eyes. They are brown.

It is another two months before Christopher meets the criteria for release from the hospital: Maintain a normal body temperature, feed by bottle and sleep in a proper crib.

When Diana gets him home, she does not want to be apart from him. She holds him constantly, showering him with kisses and gentle hugs. His stomach is so small that he must be fed every three hours. But he's a good suckler and easily drains his bottles. Mike takes the first night feeding and alternates with Diana until morning.

Friends drop by. They pack the boys in strollers and wander the mall. They stroll through the park. Brandon, 19 months, wants to hold his brother and give him his bottle. He shares his toys.

They are a family.

———◆———

The coughing begins on a Friday, on Christopher's ninth day home. Nothing alarming. Just little baby coughs that signal a baby cold. Maybe four an hour.

Just to be safe, Diana takes Christopher to the pediatrician, who sends her home with medicine.

On Saturday, he is still coughing, 10 times an hour now.

On Sunday, it's up to 20. He sounds like a barking seal.

The pediatrician's office is closed. Mike is at work. Diana bundles the boys into the car and drives to the emergency room. All kids have coughs, she tells herself.

By the time they reach the hospital, Christopher's cough is almost constant. He is whisked to a room jammed with doctors and nurses and machines. They cover the baby's face with a breathing mask, draw blood from his arm, scrape cultures from inside his mouth.

The tests show that Christopher has respiratory syncytial virus, which clogs the airways of the lungs, blocking his breath.

It is a common enough illness. Perhaps Brandon, who has a cold, spread it to a toy that spread it to Christopher. But given the baby's medical history, the doctor wants him in the hospital, on a ventilator, until the virus runs its course. About five days, he says.

Diana isn't sure. Maybe she should just take him home. She wants to talk to her husband.

No time, the doctor says. You must decide.

She signs the admission papers.

Two days later, Diana receives an urgent message at work: Call the hospital.

She dials the number.

Christopher had a series of bronchial spasms. They were so severe that his heart stopped.

Twice.

———— ◆ ————

"You know what haunts me? Maybe I shouldn't have taken him to the hospital. If I had taken him home, maybe this wouldn't have happened.
"So was this a consequence of my choice? There was no answer. No one to say if it was fate. Or if it was me."

———— ◆ ————

The young mother stumbles off the elevator in a stupor. She asks questions. The answers make no sense, incomprehensible terms rushing by.

" . . . Gastroesophageal reflux . . . "

" . . . Atypical hyaline membrane . . . "

" . . . Hyperbilirubinemia . . . "

She does not consider herself book smart. But certain words leap out, and they stick.

Mental retardation.

Cerebral palsy.

Blind.

Failure to thrive.

She stares at this . . . this . . . thing in front of her. A tube runs from his stomach. Machines click and rumble and whirl. He cannot breathe on his own. His arms move a bit. Twitches, really. Mostly, he just lies there.

He had a cough.

Just a cough.

"You may hold him," a nurse tells her.

His gaze up at her is blank, empty.

"He can't see?"

"You'll have to discuss this with the doctor."

This can't be her son.

No.

"All he had was a cough."

She gathers him up. He feels the same in her arms. He smells the same.

"He wasn't that sick."

"You'll have to talk with your doctor."

The nurses watch.

"He didn't even have a fever."

She asks for a bottle.

They hesitate.

She asks again.

She places the nipple in his mouth.

He will not suck.

The formula dribbles down his lips and chin.

Now come her tears.

"He's OK."

She tries again.

The nipple slips from the slack rosebud of his mouth.

She tries again.

Again.

Again.

"Mrs. Sullivan, he's not going to eat. You're going to wear him out."

She pulls away.

Again.

"He needs his rest."

Again.

"Mrs. Sullivan."

"Mrs. Sullivan, please."

———————•———————

"*W*hen *Christopher was born, I pumped my breasts so I'd produce milk until he came home. I wanted to breast-feed him. I figured he'd be home in a week. Well, you know what happened. He stayed in the hospital a long time, and I quit, and my milk dried up.*

"Now what I'm going to tell you makes no sense, but the day I saw him all hooked up to those machines, I went home and looked for that breast pump. I dug in the closet and looked in the drawers. I yelled at Mike to help me find it, but he couldn't, and he got frustrated and said I was crazy and to give up. I finally found it and started pumping. Of course, my breasts were dry.

"Like I said, this makes no sense.

"But I tried and tried.

"You see, I never got a chance to bond with my son. I never got to nurture him. Eleven days is all I had.

"Tell me, what you can do in 11 days?"

———————•———————

The doctors hedge. He is young, and, please understand, it is impossible to accurately predict the future with someone so small because, of course, there are many variables and . . .

She demands the truth.

The central portion of his brain has been severely damaged, if not destroyed. He will never sit up. He will never eat on his own. He will never walk. He will never talk. He will never use his limbs. He will never see.

Why?

They don't know.

The tiny lungs.

The hyperinflation.

The virus.

Fate.

Please understand, they say. His heart stopped for a total of 45 minutes during the seizures. His brain received no oxygen. If doctors had not performed heroics, if machines and drugs could not work have worked miracles, he would have died.

Christopher, they tell her, is lucky to be alive.

———————

A mother's first priority is her child. That is the only truth Diana knows. She will quit work to care for Christopher. That is what a good mother would do.

But people can't just quit the Navy. The doctors write letters describing her situation, but her commander denies her request for a release.

"I know it's hard to take care of two kids," he says. "I have two kids. My wife works. What we do is use day care."

Diana is in full uniform for the meeting and chooses her words carefully.

"Sir, your wife is not in the service. My job requires more time than a civilian job. My son has many problems. I cannot drop my son off at day care. I don't have that option."

Her commander reconsiders the file.

"The Navy has a program for outstanding children," he says finally. "Kids who are special and need help."

Diana controls her rage.

"Sir, I don't need your counseling."

"What do you need?"

"To be with my son."

———◆———

Diana blames herself. She should have been a better person. She should have accepted sea duty. She should have stayed on birth control.

She tries explaining it to Mike, how guilty she feels, and confused. But he won't talk to her. When tears threaten to betray him, he turns away.

Maybe he thinks that silence will protect her, that words will only reopen the wounds. She doesn't know how to tell him that she never healed.

The staggering medical bills add to their tension. Insurance covers 80 percent. But without her salary, they fall farther and farther behind, trying to make it on Mike's monthly take-home pay of $1,500.

Diana hates the solution: She will take the boys to Albany to live with her parents. Mike will move into base housing until he can get a discharge.

The U.S. Coast Guard flies Christopher to Portland, a courtesy to a military family. A special ambulance charges $1,500 to take him to Doernbecher Children's Hospital for lung surgery. It costs $15,000.

The day before the baby is released, the doctors suggest that Diana spend the night in his room. Christopher hardly sleeps. He cries. Diana asks if something is wrong.

"No," the nurse says. "This is how he is all the time."

Diana's parents share their modest Albany home with an aging parent and a son. To make room for Diana and Christopher, they give up their own bedroom, moving into a 15-foot trailer parked in the driveway.

Christopher's crib goes up near Diana's bed. She monitors his feeding tube and administers his medicine. He screams and chokes and vomits. He sleeps no more than an hour at a time, and then only when she rocks him.

She doesn't watch television. She doesn't read or go to the movies. Friends don't visit. The bedroom becomes her prison, the rocking chair her bed, Christopher her tiny cellmate.

Sometimes, when she is alone and too tired to stop herself, Diana takes stock of her life. If Christopher was deformed, if his face was hideous, she could detach, look at him as though he was a piece of broken machinery.

But his cheeks are plump and kissable. His eyes deep brown. His brown hair has grown in thick and silky. And when he sleeps, she can adjust him so he nuzzles her neck, the way Brandon used to. She likes to feel his soft breath on her cheek.

She knows he is little more than a doll with a beating heart.

To complain would be to betray him. What happened to him happened because of her. She chose to give him life. She is responsible.

Brandon wants her to hold him.

Not now. Christopher needs her.

Brandon cries.

She ignores him. Christopher is fussing.

Brandon wants her to play.

She can't. It's time for Christopher's medicine.

Brandon can wait. Mike can wait. She can wait.

Christopher needs her.

When he screams and screams, she tells herself it's not his fault. He is innocent. Be patient with him.

And so it goes for three months. Until one morning, when Christopher screams, Diana screams back.

"I can't handle this," she shrieks at her mother. "I'm taking Brandon. He's my baby. You want to take care of Christopher? You take him."

She runs to another room and locks herself in. She slumps to the floor, sobbing. She dreams of driving somewhere no one knows her. Her mother knocks, asking if she can help.

"Leave me alone," Diana screams.

She hears Christopher choking.

She doesn't care. Let him die.

She hears Brandon crying.

She doesn't care.

She hears her mother pleading.

"Don't give up. Christopher needs you."

My God. She doesn't want Christopher to need her.

"Diana, open the door."

She sobs.

"Diana."

"Go away."

She slumps in the room, her mind blank. She can't think. She hears voices -- her mother, her sister, her aunt. They cry and call to her, begging her to come out, to let them help.

Beaten, she opens the door. They hand her a Diet Coke, hug her and promise that everything will work out, that she isn't alone.

They lie. They will leave. They will go back to their lives.

Only Diana will be left.

—————•—————

"*L*oneliness is heavy."

—————•—————

The Navy arranges a temporary assignment for Mike in the Salem recruiting office. He moves in with Diana and her parents and commutes from Albany.

Being together feels awkward. Mike seems distant. Diana is self-conscious about the weight she has gained. She has little time to fuss with makeup. She longs for him to hold her, to tell her that everything will be fine.

Nothing. He goes to work. He comes home.

Two days before his return flight to San Diego, she confronts him.

What's bothering you?

Nothing.

Tell me.

He hems.

Mike?

It's just that he can't handle this. Life used to be so good.

No kidding.

And . . .

What?

He's not sure he wants to, well, stick around.

Diana thought she had spent her tears. She is wrong. Frantic, she wonders what she can change, what she can do to make him happy, to make him stay.

Then she knows.

Nothing. There is nothing she can or should do.

This time, the choice is his to make.

She rehearses her speech all day the next day. She steels herself not to cry. When Mike gets home from work, she asks him to sit down.

"If you leave, don't come back."

He blinks at her, stunned.

"No one will ever love you like I will. But the good comes with the bad. This is our life. You have one day to decide if you want to be a part of my life or not."

The next morning Mike tells her he loves her. But he is scared.

So, she says, am I.

When his discharge comes through, the couple rent an apartment on the north edge of Albany. Mike sells used cars for a while, but the lot goes under. He builds mobile homes and takes roofing jobs when he can, bringing home about $400 a week.

They no longer have Navy insurance coverage, and Christopher's Social Security benefits are minimal.

The baby's intravenous feeding bags cost $600 a month. And they still owe $10,000 for various surgeries.

Diana feels as though she has been sentenced to eternity with a colicky baby. Sometimes she drifts, thinking she could let him cry until he suffocates. Who would blame her? Who would ever know?

One morning, Diana settles Christopher on a blanket on the living room floor. She sits down to rest and watch a little television, perhaps nap a few minutes.

He begins to cry.

"Oh, Christopher," she snaps.

He stops.

She glances at him.

He is smiling.

"Christopher?"

He smiles.

She shakes his leg.

"Christopher?"

He grins.

———— • ————

She calls Mike, laughing the news. She calls her mother. Her younger sister. The pediatrician.

For the first time since Christopher fell sick, Diana remembers how good it feels to be a mother. Maybe God is telling her that if she just tries harder, He will cure her son.

"Christopher."

He smiles.

She can't remember such happiness.

She plays games with herself.

If she could choose to change just one thing for Christopher, what would it be?

To see?

To walk?

To talk?

She cannot choose.

She will accept any blessing.

The pediatrician examines Christopher, now 19 months old, and notes that he is moving his hands.

Diana is ecstatic.

But the doctor gives a warning: Mentally, your son has the capacity of a 2-month-old. The doctor repeats himself, making sure she understands.

He doesn't know everything, she tells herself. Give me time. She works with Christopher every day. She talks to him, sings to him, tickles him. She lives for his smile. She sees progress where others cannot.

Smile, Christopher.

For the first time, she has hope. He doesn't cry as often or need as much medicine. He can lie on the floor and play with a toy. Well, not play, really, but the toy doesn't irritate him.

She hangs a mobile over his crib and watches him wave his hands at it. Maybe he can see.

He has a future.

She has a future.

She ventures back into the world.

Her mother baby-sits so Diana can attend a birthday party for a girl born a month before Christopher. The girl is the center of attention. She babbles and tries to walk. And somewhere after the gifts, but before the cake, it hits Diana so hard that she fights to stop the tears.

That should be Christopher.

He should be learning to walk.

And what does she get?

A smile.

A lousy smile.

———◆———

"*Anger grows. Not so much anger that it happened, but anger about why. I wanted an answer. Even if I found out it was my fault, at least I would have an answer.*"

———◆———

On their fourth wedding anniversary, Mike takes Diana on a date. Her brother volunteers to watch the boys.

Over dinner, Mike presents a small box. He has been saving each week, he says, for a surprise. The diamond earrings are tiny, but they match her wedding ring. Mike nods at the pianist, who plays their wedding song, and Mike sweeps Diana into his arms.

She feels like Cinderella.

She feels life a wife.

She feels normal.

A waiter interrupts them. There is an emergency phone call from Diana's brother. Christopher won't stop crying.

Diana storms home, the evening ruined, and retreats back into her world, a world with room only for Christopher.

She leaves dinner to Mike and Brandon while she attends to Christopher's feeding tubes. She sleeps when Christopher sleeps so she can wake with him, at least five times each night.

Her only outside contact is with social workers, who come to the apartment to check on Christopher. Diana relishes their visits with a sort of madness, cleaning the house as if she were throwing a party.

During a routine checkup, Christopher's pediatrician asks Diana how she's doing.

"Fine," she mumbles.

He waits.

"How are you holding up?"

She shakes her head. She won't betray Christopher.

"Diana?"

It leaks out. Her fears. Her doubts. Her loneliness. The doctor just listens. For the first time since her son was born, someone just listens to Diana Sullivan.

And when she is finished, the doctor tells her this:

There is life, and there is quality of life.

Christopher has life.

You, he says, have a life.

He pens a number on a piece of paper.

This is the Providence Child Center in Portland, he says. A nursing home for children. There are only about 10 places like it in the United States. And it's not what you think. This is a good place.

She takes the paper.

She would never consider putting Christopher in an institution. But she tells Mike she must see it, so she can tell the doctor she followed through.

It's up to her, he says.

———————

She signs in at the visitors desk. The literature says that parents pay nothing to keep their children here. Medicaid contributes about $150 a day per for each child, about 70 percent of the true cost. Fund-raising covers the rest.

A woman escorts Diana down the hallway, through the double doors, to the children.

She gasps.

She is back in grade school, in the lunch room, where the special education kids had their own table. She hated being near them, watching them eat, watching some of them be fed. It nauseated her.

A cry snaps Diana back. She is surrounded by babies and toddlers and teen-agers, none with mental capacity beyond that of a 3-month-old. None can walk or talk or feed themselves. Five sit in wheelchairs, gaping at a Chevy Chase movie on TV. Diana knows this movie, saw it in her life before Christopher.

Numb, Diana moves out of the way of the volunteers and nurses, who dispense medicine and adjust feeding tubes and chatter in cheerful, one-way conversations.

No.

Not this.

Not for her boy.

But Diana finds herself staring.

Why? she asks.

Why are they like this?

These are not the products of drug addiction or abuse. These kids children were simply unlucky. In earlier times, their viruses and defects and accidents would have killed them. Now technology keeps them alive. And hopelessness brings them here.

She peeks into a large dorm room. Four children sleep here, photographs of their families tacked above their beds, sharing space with a Michael Jordan poster.

They will live like this until they are 18 and move to an adult nursing home. Or until they die, which happens to about six children a year. Each death opens a spot on the waiting list for one of the 58 beds.

A girl, perhaps 13, follows Diana's path down the hall with her eyes. Two years ago, on a Monday, the girl told her mother she felt sick. On the following Friday, she suffered 30 seizures an hour and lapsed into a coma. Doctors have not identified the virus that destroyed much of her brain.

Diana smiles at the girl, uncertain.

The girl's eyes follow her, silent, haunting Diana with their silent hint of humanity.

Diana has seen enough.

She wants to go home.

Yes, Christopher is sick.

Yes, Christopher can be hard to take.

But he is different.

Different from the girl who fell into the family swimming pool and now sits in an eternal trance.

Different from the boy who was trapped in a house fire and now is imprisoned in a bed.

No.

Christopher will not live in their world.

———◆———

Sometimes, Diana wonders if whether she is going insane. And if she is, who will care for Christopher?

She calls the center one day. In frustration, she adds his name to the waiting list. Not that she would ever let him go, of course. But the center becomes her safety valve. Knowing it is there makes her job bearable.

And then the center calls her.

An 8-year-old boy died in the night. There is an immediate opening for Christopher.

She has two days to decide.

The choice, Mike says, is hers to make.

———◆———

She is his mother and must do what is best for him. Being with her is best for him. But at the center he will be cared for, constantly. She will not be so tired and angry. When she visits, she will be happy.

If only someone could tell her what to do.

———◆———

The first few days that Christopher is gone, she sleeps in because she is so tired. Then it is because she can't face the day.

She made a mistake.

She will leave him in the center just a little longer. Long enough to get some rest. Then she will bring him home. She leaves his room untouched. To box up his things, to tear down his crib, would be wrong.

Her family doesn't ask about him.

Only Brandon wonders.

"Where's Christopher?"

"He's sick and in the hospital."

"When is he coming home?"

"I don't know."

"I've been sick."

"This is a different kind of sick. Christopher can't walk or talk or do a lot of things that a big boy like you can do."

"Oh."

One day, Brandon snuggles up and asks her to read to him. She thumbs through the pages but can't concentrate on the simple words. She hasn't read to Brandon in more than a year. She hasn't done a lot of things.

"Just be good, Brandon."

"I don't have time."

"Christopher needs me."

That night, she makes dinner for Mike. They make forced small talk, like as though they are on a first date. She has been with this man for more than four years. She hardly knows him.

"Later."

"Can't you understand?"

"Christopher needs me."

She can't do this. She must choose.

Christopher's life?

Or hers?

———◆———

A volunteer tucks the sleeping child in a baby seat near the nurse's station. His mother is coming.

They dress him in clothes from home. They spray a medicine mist near his face to help him breathe.

Diana hangs back when she arrives. She wears a tag that labels her a visitor. The volunteer motions her forward, but she does not move.

"Oh, Christopher," the volunteer croons. "Your mama's here. This is what you've been waiting for."

The volunteer slips away. Diana perches in front of her son.

"Christopher," says Diana.

She wishes she could be a better mother.

"Hey, buddy."

She wishes he had never gotten sick.

She touches his cheek.

He stirs.

She pulls him from the seat and cradles him in her arms. She holds her little boy and rocks him.

She says nothing.

She feels his soft breath on her check.
She listens to his heartbeat.
And she knows.
He has life.
She has a life.

———◆———

"Don't call me courageous. And don't tell me what you'd do, because you don't know.

"Every day I tell myself that he doesn't know any different. That he doesn't feel the same emotions we all do. That he's getting wonderful care. That he's happy.

"I do this so I can turn around and walk away."

———◆———

She stands by his bed.
Now it's just the two of them.
"My sweetie."
He smiles.
She adjusts his pillow.
"There you go, buddy."
She can't move.
"My precious son."
She reaches onto a shelf above his bed and pulls down his teddy bear. She tucks it under his arm and pulls his blanket over him.
"Christopher . . .
Her voice breaks.
"Christopher, I will always be your mother."
He smiles.
"Christopher, I will always love you."
She swipes a tear from her cheek.

"Christopher, mommy's going bye-bye.

———◆———

An epilogue:
Christopher Sullivan will turn 3 on Dec. 7. His condition remains the same and is not expected to improve. Nurses at Providence Child Center say he likes being cuddled.

Brandon Sullivan is 4 and attends preschool, where he is learning how to tie his shoes and is working on colors, shapes and numbers. He says he misses his baby brother.

Mike Sullivan was working in construction until the job ended two weeks ago.

Diana Sullivan works as a sales clerk in Albany. She would like to attend school to gain certification as a paramedic but can't afford to quit her job.

The Sullivans continue to live in Albany with Diana's parents until they can afford their own apartment. They still owe more than $5,000 in medical bills.

They visit Christopher several times a month.

BRIDGE DAY

For 70 years they met for lunch each month.

With hands that sometimes tremble and eyes that need help, they mark calendars to fulfill a promise made long ago. They agreed to the second Thursday of each month, and nothing -- not World War II, marriage or children -- got in the way.

Once there were 12 of them. Now, 70 years later, only five remain.

On this Thursday, 92-year-old Lois Tupling arrives first. She sees no familiar faces and waits on a settee near the Waverley Country Club dining room. Back in 1934, when her Pi Beta Phi sorority sisters were leaving Oregon State University, Lois proposed that the close friends meet monthly in Portland for lunch and bridge. They rotated duties as hostess, meeting in one another's apartments and, later, homes. When babies arrived, the group temporarily met at night and let the husbands watch the children. Once the kids enrolled in school, though, it was back to lunch. Although their families socialized occasionally, the real friendship lay with the women.

The women attended one another's weddings and other celebrations. Eventually, they stood together when fellow sorority sisters were buried and supported one another when their husbands -- the remaining five women are widows -- passed on. Only one woman in the group still lives at home. Only two still drive. The others are in retirement centers and travel by bus or taxicab. The group alternates the monthly lunches between Waverley and the Multnomah Athletic Club.

"We're very fond of each other," Lois explains. "When we look at each other, we don't see wrinkles. We see the girls we once were."

She keeps an eye on the front door, knowing her sisters are prompt. She beams when she sees the "girls" arrive: Shirley Ditewig, 88, Arline Maylie, 92, Gail Martindale, 92, and Luddy Schweiker, 90. After a round of hugs, Lois surprises them by singing a song from their past: "I'm glad that I'm a Phi Pi, not a K.A.T. or a K.K.G. or Tri Delt, Alpha Pi or Delta G. I'm glad I'm a Phi Pi and will be 'till I die."

Gail claps her hands. "Oh, Lois that's remarkable," she says. "I can't remember the words even though I was the song leader in the house."

A waitress leads them to a circular table. They order wine and, as they sip from their glasses, Lois passes around a group photo taken decades before. "I just can't believe how many people in this photograph aren't living," Luddy says. "Wasn't Betty the first to go?"

There's a long discussion, but, finally, they agree that, yes, Betty was the first. The photograph makes its way around the table. At each stop, a woman cradles the photo in her hands and stares into the young faces -- her face and the faces of the women sitting with her at this table -- and then gently touches the picture. No one speaks during this private moment in a public place.

"Loss," Arline finally says, "means pain."

They nod.

"When your spouse is your best friend," Lois says, "the world changes when he's gone."

Luddy pats Lois on the arm.

"I know," she says. "My husband and I did everything together. After all these years, I still miss that."

The table falls silent. Each woman is lost in her past. One mentions a friend who developed Alzheimer's. The woman picked up her bridge hand one afternoon and admitted to her friends that she didn't know what the cards were for or what to do with them. She never played again and now lives in a nursing home.

"That's what I think I'm getting," Gail says. "I'm worried that I just forget things."

"Oh, Gail," Lois says, "at our age we just have so much stored up in our minds that it's easy to get mixed up. None of our memories are that good."

"Lois, you're so kind."

At every lunch, someone notes just how remarkable it is that they've been meeting for seven decades. The monthly get-together may have begun as a lark, but over the years it developed into something important. The women grew up together, learning about one another's hopes and fears each month.

Some of the original 12 dropped out of college because of the Depression -- their families thought it made no sense to waste money educating a girl. Lois excelled in chemistry and wanted to go to medical school. But her father told her to concentrate on home economics because she was just going to get married when she graduated.

The world changed around them, sometimes dramatically: civil rights, women's rights, two more wars and a change in what society expected from a woman, a mother and a wife. Through it all, the one constant has been the second Thursday of the month.

A light lunch arrives: half a sandwich, a cup of soup and fruit. As they eat, the friends relive their past: the parties, the crushes on boys, the dances and the honor of a Pi Phi membership.

———◆———

Boys, they remember, were never allowed in the sorority house. But they could hug them and sneak a kiss on the front porch until Mother Drake appeared and said it was time to come inside. Alcohol was never served at a dance, only tea. And a good girl never smoked in public; she sneaked a drag behind a woodpile.

"We didn't know what we were doing," Luddy says.

"But wouldn't it be fun now?" Gail says with a smile.

The table laughs. A few cheeks redden, but maybe it's just the wine.

"But the world," Gail says, "just sees us as another table of white-haired ladies."

Lois sets down her glass.

"Would you girls like to play a little bridge?"

They push back from the table. Gail helps Luddy from her chair. Luddy grasps a cane in each hand and leaves the dining room. Arline uses just one cane but stops to rest. Lois, Gail and Shirley walk to the elevator and hold the door.

"Don't you run," Lois calls. "We'll just wait here for as long as it takes."

On the second floor, they slowly walk down a hallway and into an empty room where a deck of cards, a notebook and pencil sit at a table. They settle in their seats. Lois volunteers to sit out the first hand and the four remaining women pair up.

"Who would have thought this after all these years?" says Arline. "Just try and remember something from 70 years ago."

"That's asking a lot," Shirley says with a laugh.

"I don't want to think about this all ending," says Luddy.

No one speaks.

"It won't," Lois says firmly. "We'll just be playing up there in heaven."

Gail takes the deck of cards and tries to shuffle. The cards spill onto the table.

"My hands just won't do it anymore," she says quietly.

Lois takes the cards from her.

"Then I'll do it, dear."

The Elevator Girls

It's nearly impossible to understand how impressive an elevator once was.

In their day -- before cellphones and pagers and voice mail --- the only place to meet in downtown Portland was under the clock. And so their plan was to meet there one last time before they went upstairs to say their goodbyes.

The three women, all of them in their 80s, made their way through the nearly empty aisles in Meier & Frank. They moved slowly -- one was blind, the other used a cane, and the third pushed a walker -- until they were under the art-deco clock that hangs from the ceiling near the department store's first-floor escalator.

"Well, here we are,' said Violet Calhoun. "Here we are."

Libby Gordon, who can no longer see, had her hand on Violet's arm.

"Oh, those were the days," she said. "We were something then. Weren't we?'

"Ambassadors," said Margaret Smith. "That's what we were, ambassadors."

Violet patted Libby's hand.

"I think it's time," she said.

"Just wait a moment, Vi," Libby asked. "Can we wait just one more moment?"

And so they stood there -- three old women under the clock on a Saturday in May -- until Libby finally spoke.

"OK, Vi," Libby said softly. "I'm ready to go."

They made their way back through the aisles until they were at a bank of elevators. They pushed the button for No. 22 and waited and waited. Violet looked up. No. Twenty-two was stuck on the 10th floor.

"That," she sniffed, "never would have happened in our day."

———◆———

In this computer-driven fiber-optics age, it's nearly impossible to understand how impressive an elevator once was. It changed American business by allowing employees and customers easy access to floors higher than three. But in those early years, no one just walked in and pushed a button on an elevator.

They were mechanical contraptions, beasts sometimes, that had to be run by an operator who controlled the speed, aligned the car with the floor and opened and closed the doors. When elevators were installed in Portland's downtown Meier & Frank in the 1930s, the company needed operators.

Anyone who lived in Portland during the 1950s remembers the crew. They were called the elevator girls during an era when calling an adult woman a girl was considered appropriate.

The operators called out each floor -- the boys always snickered when they said "women's lingerie" -- and helped customers find their way around the store. On the first floor a stern supervisor attracted attention with a hand-held clicker and directed customers to the next available elevator.

Becoming an elevator girl was the first taste of a bigger world. To be hired, applicants had to have poise, good looks and height -- they had to be at least 5-foot-5.

A strict woman they all called Aunt Mary trained -- and sometimes terrified -- them. She taught them how to stand correctly and how to speak. She insisted they stay well informed about the store, and they studied the newspaper each day, reading ads so they could help the customers. She demanded an impeccable appearance -- a tailored uniform that discreetly showed a bit of leg. Painted nails. Hair done.

Each morning Aunt Mary inspected them. She noticed it all. A run in a stocking, a chipped nail, hair out of place. One flaw and Aunt Mary pulled the operator off her elevator and sent her upstairs to the beauty salon for a tune-up.

"She thought my voice was too harsh," Libby said. "I had to take voice lessons for two weeks. I had to say, "how now brown cow" over and over and over until Aunt Mary thought I was ready to run the car."

Each operator made about $50 a month.

"You had to learn how to land right on the floor," said Violet. "We had to throw the wheel in the right direction. I was petrified. I had never run any kind of machine before. They were tricky things. I remember once dropping from the eighth floor to the fifth and the superintendent coming down to chew me out."

For most of the operators, it was a first job. Some stayed for several years. Others moved on. They got married, sent their husbands off to World War II and then welcomed them home again. They had children.

In the 1950s, Meier & Frank installed escalators and eventually self-operated elevator cars and the elevator-girl era ended. But there was something about being an elevator girl that had created a bond among these women. For the past 52 years they have met on the third Saturday in May to have lunch.

On this Saturday -- May 20, 2000 -- the group decided to hold its last lunch. Once, 60 women came to these lunches. But death and disabling illness visited. The group shrank.

The girls grew old.

Most of them are widows with infirmities that make life difficult. It's hard to get around -- many of them can't drive any longer. And so the plan was to meet once more, and then say goodbye to one another. Most of them suspected they would not see one another again.

But the 16 remaining wanted one last meal together in the place where it all started -- in the restaurant on the 10th floor at Meier & Frank.

They wanted to do it the right way.

They wanted to ride the elevators.

The elevator door opened and the three old women walked into their past. There was Marie and Babe and Nancy. One woman had flown in from Arizona, another from Palm Springs in California.

A few days ago, Violet learned that a member had just died. She mentioned it to Rose Thomson.

"That's where we are all headed, Violet," said Rose. "But I've had a good life, a full life."

They showed pictures of kids and grandchildren. They looked in scrapbooks and traded tales.

Ruth Sconce said when she was first married her husband would come down to meet her. She would take him up in her elevator and stop the car between floors for a quick kiss.

"Now, if Aunt Mary had known," she said.

Rose said she may have been one of the last elevator girls to see Aunt Mary. "I heard she was in a nursing home," she said. "I went to visit her, and she was in a wheelchair. I think she was in her 90s. She didn't remember me or anything. She died not too long ago. She never married, you know."

"I think we were her family," said Georgia Shaw.

At promptly 11:30, the doors to the restaurant opened and the elevator girls made their way inside.

They helped each other.

Those who could see easily led the way.

Those who could walk unaided offered an arm.

They were together once more.

The Ghosts of Mister Coakley

For just a moment, he is alone. And then the ghosts appear.

Paul Coakley needs to be out in the hallway, but he is tethered to his desk by an unexpected midmorning telephone call that won't end.

"Yes, yes," he interrupts. "That's great, but . . ."

Coakley gives into it, slumping into his chair, waiting for an opening.

The seconds pass so slowly that he begins to fidget. He glances three times at the clock in his principal's office at Harriet Tubman Middle School.

His office is a cramped bunker, and his world is ground zero -- a school that draws students from some of the bleakest neighborhoods in North and Northeast Portland.

Too many of the sixth, seventh and eighth graders here are no strangers to bloody bodies and crack and 9mm handguns. Too many come from broken homes where food stamps, social workers and cop calls are a part of everyday life.

And though some have graduated to high school, college and jobs, too many have dropped out. Some reside in the state's prisons or rest in the city's cemeteries.

Coakley glances at the clock again. "Yes, yes," he says. "That's great. OK, we'll . . ."

The caller is off on another tangent. Coakley frowns, listens and waits.

"The books? Wonderful, just wonderful. Look, I'll set up a conference call with the teachers. It's been great talking with you, let's keep in . . ."

He rubs a hand across his face and stares at the clock -- 9:12 a.m.

Coakley stands, cradles the phone against his shoulder and uses both hands to stuff blank, white slips of paper deep into the pockets of his suit jacket.

"OK, goodbye," he finally says. "Goodbye."

He drops the phone into the cradle and rushes out of his office with a quick wave to his secretary, a woman so used to his hectic pace that she doesn't bother to look up from her stack of papers.

With two minutes to spare, Coakley steps into the hallway and strides toward the intersection every student must cross on the way to first-hour class.

He stops and leans against a wall.

For just a moment, the halls are quiet. For just a moment, he is alone.

And then the ghosts appear.

Mister Eperson.

Miss Malone.

Miss Smith.

Miss Peters.

Mister Herod.

He feels their presence, their steady hands on his shoulder, their words in his heart.

The morning bell shatters the silence. The charge of children spilling out of homerooms sweeps toward him.

Soon they will be here.

Once again, it is time for Paul Coakley to pay his debts.

Few people know his story.

Oh, his wife and two sons have heard most of it. But he is a private man, and so it dribbled out in bits and pieces -- when he heard someone complain, when family came to visit, when a song stirred his memory.

Mostly, though, Paul Coakley is a mystery to the administrators and teachers he works with. Certainly to his students.

He is built like a linebacker and his voice rumbles like a diesel engine. And in an era of casual Fridays and lax dress codes, he wears a suit and tie to work every day. Without fail. All because of Mister Eperson, but that's getting ahead of his story.

The tale began 41 years ago in a Detroit ghetto.

Ghetto.

That's a word used so frequently these days that it has lost its meaning.

Coakley's early years read like a cliche. The youngest of eight children. Dad was a barber who went door-to-door in search of customers. Mom scrubbed floors at the local hospital.

He and his brothers and sisters slept five to a bed, blanketing each other in winter when the heat was cut off.

One Christmas his only gift was a tiny spinning top. His father held him on his lap that morning and apologized: "Santa wished he could've done more. Santa wished he could've done more."

In the second grade, he changed schools six times because the family was repeatedly evicted for not paying rent.

He skipped school, smoked cigarettes, committed petty crimes. He seemed destined to follow the path of his brothers and sisters; only one graduated from high school.

His parents divorced, and he shuttled back and forth between their apartments. Life was so unstable that the child welfare department prepared to take him from his family and make him a ward of the state.

That's when a visiting uncle decided to intervene. He and his wife were unable to have children and agreed to raise the 9-year-old boy as their own.

And so a small suitcase was packed and money scraped up for a ticket. Paul rode the train with his aunt and uncle back to Gallatin, Tenn., a small town just north of Nashville.

It might as well have been Mars. Shortly after the train chugged out of Detroit, he looked out the window and saw a cow. Then green pastures and the vast open spaces.

His uncle lived in a proper house. With a garden. And Paul would have his own room and his own bed.

But if one life began -- and a good life it seemed to be -- an old one, lived in a certain innocence and trust, ended.

In Gallatin, he learned he was a nigger.

And his uncle, even though he was a teacher, was called boy by men half his age.

Back in Detroit things were tough; but toughness was an equal opportunity employer. Here in Gallatin, he found two separate and unequal worlds: white and colored.

Whites bought tickets to the movies out front; Negroes paid in a back alley and sat in the balcony. Whites worked at the counter in the town's fast-food restaurant; Negroes washed dishes in the back.

White kids went to one school; coloreds to another.

Paul and his classmates thumbed tattered, outdated books and sat at rickety desks handed down from the white school.

His teachers paid no mind.

Miss Malone taught them to ignore the slurs. Within the school's walls, she promised, you will learn that skin color has nothing to do with ability.

Miss Malone organized plays. She taught the kids how to speak and act, and that words have the power to move people, to make them angry or joyful or sad. She made them memorize poetry, and the language of the ages came alive for Paul.

Miss Smith took them on field trips to the big cities, where blacks were not just dishwashers or janitors or servants -- they were bus drivers and small business owners and salesmen.

Mister Eperson, the shop teacher, ditched his work clothes every Friday and wore a suit and tie. Four days a week he showed them how to use their hands. On the fifth day, he showed them a world where they could use their minds to make a living.

Mister Martin tolerated no nonsense. Students were in his class to learn, not play. They could not afford to be average. He once gave Paul two paddlings within one hour for fooling around.

When Paul stumbled over the years, his teachers steadied him.

Mister Herod.

When he had doubts, his teachers shooed them away.

Miss Robertson.

When he was lost, his teachers provided the map.

Miss Doyle.

When he thought he was doing well enough, Miss Peters ripped into him. He was the laziest student she had ever seen. If he worked harder, he could earn straight A's and go to college.

College.

No one in his family had ever considered it.

College.

His grades improved. He discovered he was a good reader. He liked history.

He applied to the junior college in town and was accepted.

One afternoon before classes started, he came home and found a cake outside the back door. Written in the frosting was a sentence: "Congratulations. Good luck in college."

The note with it was signed: "Love, Miss Peters."

Little wonder Paul Coakley wanted to be a teacher.

To pay his way through school, he bagged groceries at a local store. He was the first black person hired there. When he was promoted to checker, white customers refused to come through his stand because they didn't want him touching their food.

He would not back down. He would wait in his stand, smiling, looking those customers straight in the eye.

One day, when he was the only checker available, a white customer went through his line.

Then another.

And another.

Customers ended up liking him so much that he was named the store's head checker.

He graduated from the junior college and then from Middle Tennessee State University. He taught at a state vocational high school and caught the eye of Portland school administrators when he attended a seminar in Oregon.

He was recruited to teach at Tubman in 1980, the year the school opened. Two years later he was promoted to vice principal. In 1985, he was offered the top job.

But it was no prize.

If he took the post, he would be the fifth principal in five years at a school acknowledged by the Portland district to be in shambles.

He prayed, seeking God's guidance. Finding his answer in faith, he accepted the job.

Because so many teachers had quit, he was able to hire others who shared his commitment. Almost overnight, Tubman became Paul Coakley's school.

And then the ghosts returned.

Mister Eperson.

Miss Malone.

Miss Smith.

Miss Peters.

Mister Herod.

He hadn't talked with those old teachers in decades. Some were dead. Others had moved.

And yet they found him.

He was their legacy.

Now it was his turn.

He looks like a politician 10 points behind in the polls a week before the election.

Every morning he stands in the middle of the hallway, shaking hands, patting backs and calling students by name. He is a fisherman, casting out his line and reeling in those who require help, encouragment or a kick in the rear.

He has an innate sense of who needs him.

And why.

One girl seems lost in the crowd until Coakley spots her and pulls her over to him.

"I'm going to talk to your teacher about the writing contest. I want you involved."

The girl looks scared.

"No, Mr. Coakley. My handwriting is too bad. No."

He waves his hand.

He shakes his head.

He will not hear of it.

"No, no, no," he says. "We can clean that all that up. I read what you wrote and it comes from here."

He slams his fist into his chest.

"From the heart, girl. From the heart. Can't teach that. No you can't. You're good. Very good."

He speaks loudly, so every child within 30 feet can hear his praise.

The girl smiles.

"OK, Mr. Coakley. I'll try."

Then she is gone, back into the rushing river of students.

He checks his watch, then bellows, "One minute!"

He claps his hands.

"Let's go. Let's take care of business today. Let's move it. Time to learn."

The children nod. A few reach out to touch him, to shake his hand, just to have him smile at them.

He spots a boy he knows has been in trouble with the police -- gangs, stealing, hints of worse. He pulls him in, puts his arm around the boy and whispers to him.

"We OK on that situation? You taking care of business?"

The boy nods.

Coakley pats him on the back.

"You need to talk, you come see me."

He hugs him.

The boy nestles into Coakley's chest. There is no sign of embarassment or shame, even though hundreds of kids pass by.

"Now go take care of business."

Then the bell rings. Again, the halls are empty and quiet.

Coakley is about to return to his office when he hears someone whistling. He waits like a cat hiding for a mouse. Then he pounces.

"You're walking through my halls, toot-toot-tooting?" he yells. "My halls? This ain't no band. And you get to class on time. This is not acceptable. You're better than this."

He glares at the boy.

"What's your GPA?"

"I don't know."

"Tell me your grades."

"Let's see . . . C, C, A, B."

Coakley softens and lets a smile creep onto his face.

"That's good. Could be better."

He points toward the classroom.

"Now, get going now."

As the boy hustles away, Coakley's rumbling voice shoves him along.

"And hey! You want to toot, you go join a band."

He expects things of these kids. Work hard. Respect adults. Get to class on time.

Not all of them will be straight-A students. But everyone must strive to do their best, whatever that may be.

And don't use racism or being poor as a reason for not trying. Yes, those are difficult hurdles. But they can also be excuses that invite failure.

"Kids live up to or down to your expectations," he says during a rare moment of quiet in his office. "A lot of these kids may not have much going on for them outside these walls. But in here I want to expose them to success and show them it comes not from me, or their teacher, but from within themselves."

If a child needs extra help, Coakley gets it. If they need guidance outside of school, he looks for it. If a student is in trouble, he brings parents in to talk.

And while supportive, he is not soft. When a student disregards the rules, Coakley demands they be sent to see him. And his greeting, which comes out like a growl, is always the same.

"Sit down."

The youngster slides into a chair and stares at the clock on the wall and the photograph of the Rev. Martin Luther King Jr. on the shelf behind Coakley.

"You look at me," Coakley barks.

The boy complies.

"Why is your teacher upset?"

The boy shrugs.

"She don't send people out of her class," Coakley says. "When she does, I take it seriously. What's going on?"

"I was just fooling around."

Coakley eyes widen and he looks around the room, then leans forward and spits out the words.

"Fooling around? Fooling around. I'm expecting great things from you. I don't want you messin' up, I want you up working! Understand?"

"Yes."

The boy sits up straight, like a Marine facing his drill instructor.

Coakley leans back in his chair.

"Say, you got a new haircut, didn't you?"

The boy nods.

"I like it," Coakley says.

He sits forward again.

Now he is speaking man to man. Father to son. Big brother to little brother.

"I expect you to get your act together. Hear me? If I send you back to class and you come back, it's going to make me look bad. And I don't like to look bad. Do I make myself clear?"

"Yes."

"OK, you go back and take care of business."

Once a month, Coakley holds a schoolwide assembly to talk about goals and the future: Have you done everything to be a success? Do you believe in yourself?

Each morning he comes up with a word of the day -- maximum, teamwork, integrity, achieve, responsiblity -- and has his teachers pass it on to their students.

Throughout the day he stops students in the halls or drops into classes to ask about the word. The reward for remembering the word is one of those blank slips of paper he has stuffed in his jacket pockets. The reward for spelling a word is another slip.

Sometimes he walks into class with a quiz about a math problem or asks if anyone can spell a word such as "complicated" backward. A right answer gets a slip of paper.

At the end of the day, students write their names on the slips and give them to teachers. During each monthly assembly, Coakley draws names of three winners whom he treats to lunch off campus.

Students who raise their grade-point averages a full point automatically get lunch, as do all 4.0 students.

Sometimes it works. One boy raised his GPA from a .57 to a 3.0.

Other times there are failures. The gang bangers. The dropouts. The delinquents. The dead.

"We're going to lose some of them," he says. "And that makes me sad. But I'm never going to give up. Never."

Students believe him.

If it wasn't for Coakley, 14-year-old Johnell Cleveland would have dropped out. Now high school is a sure thing. And maybe college.

"My Dad lives in San Diego and I don't hear from him much," he says. "Mr. Coakley is like my father because he keeps me on the right track."

Jathiya Rushdan, 12, likes Coakley's spirit.

"He makes everything fun," she says. "He makes me laugh and I know he cares about all of us."

Artelia Spruill, a sixth-grade teacher, says Coakley is the male figure missing in so many students' lives.

"He is their father, their big brother, their mentor. Whatever a child needs, he becomes."

Coakley reveals a sad smile when he hears that.

"I know where they're coming from," he says softly. "I see myself in the faces of those children."

Rukaiyah Adams grew up . . .

Well, since she's paying for this long-distance telephone call, let her tell the story.

"I grew up in a poor family, the stereotypical inner-city family," says Adams, who attended Tubman from 1985 to 1987. "My mom raised us alone, and my older brother was in and out of prison. I didn't know where I was headed.

"I knew a lot of kids in gangs, I saw a lot of violence and I guess I was starting to drift into some serious trouble. And then one day, Mr. Coakley called my name."

Adams laughs at the memory.

"He was in the hallway, yelling at all of us to get to class. And he called my name."

She falls silent.

"My name."

She pauses, caught in the turbulence from a storm created when the past, the present and the future collide.

"It meant more than anything in the world."

She is back there now.

"He knew who I was. He called me over to him and said that he had read something I had written in class. He encouraged me to write an essay. I wasn't sure, but he offered to help me with whatever I needed. And then he told me to get to class.

"I couldn't stop thinking about it that day. He told me I was good. I had never known any college-educated black men. None had ever talked to me. But he did.

"And he told me I was good."

The middle school years whizzed by for Adams.

"He encouraged me with the sternness of the father I didn't have. He was one of the first people in my whole life who cared about me for no other reason than to care for me."

She hesitates, unsure whether her words convey what she deeply feels.

"Do you know what I'm saying?" The words hang in the air.

"Do you understand?"

She is quiet for a moment.

"He had nothing to gain," she finally says. "He just did it. That was the first time in my life someone did that for me.

"And it made a world of difference."

Sometime next week, the mail will bring a letter to Paul Coakley's desk. When he returns from the hallways and the classrooms and handing out small slips of paper, he will read it.

He will learn that Rukaiyah Adams, child of Portland, raised on a street once called "Crack Alley," is now the student body president at Carleton College in Northfield, Minn., and will graduate with honors.

And in June she will begin work at Chemical Bank in New York City, specializing in global banking and financing.

Mister Eperson.

Miss Malone.

Miss Smith.

Miss Peters.

Mister Herrod.

Mister Coakley.

THE DRESS

Without a girl, a dress is nothing but fabric.

It's just a dress. Only a few yards of limp fabric on a hanger. Take the finest, most expensive silk ever spun and there's still no life. And certainly no magic.

What a dress always needs is a girl.

A girl in a dress takes a father's breath away. He turns from the television when his daughter walks into the room and is struck by how quickly the years have slipped away, gone in a heartbeat when he wasn't paying attention to all the changes.

A girl in a dress stands before her mother and they realize -- despite all those arguments over messy rooms and dirty dishes -- that they share a bond that doesn't need to be expressed in words, only in a glance that says "We're alike."

A girl in a dress stands before a mirror and sees her past and her future, the girl she is and the woman she will become.

A dress without a girl is nothing.

That becomes clear Saturday morning when one sees the hundreds of dresses hanging from racks in a large room at the Oregon Convention Center in Northeast Portland. Every imaginable color and size are available.

They have about as much character as towels.

But that's about to change. If you listen carefully, from the other side of locked doors you can hear the sounds of girls.

There's probably no more pressure-filled time in a young girl's life than right now, when the prom season is unfolding.

During the day, a girl can blend in wearing any old thing. Prom is about glamour, the night when every girl is a princess.

But a prom dress can cost as much as $350. Some families drop a few bills for the memories. But for other families, $350 might as well be $5,000. In those families, a girl doesn't bother asking. She knows.

Four years ago, Abby Egland, who lives in West Linn, cleaned out her closet while getting ready to attend the University of Oregon and found the pink gown she had worn to her high school prom. She felt bad about just tossing it out.

"I have three older brothers," said Egland, now 22. "I didn't want to give it to the Goodwill because I didn't want some guy to buy it and wear it for Halloween."

Egland talked to her mother, Sally, to see whether there was a way to give the dress to another girl. Her mother had heard about groups in other cities that collected and distributed prom dresses to girls who couldn't afford them. She checked around Portland and found nothing.

So she and her daughter started Abby's Closet, asking friends to donate prom dresses.

"The first year we ended up with 500 gowns in my garage," Sally Egland said. "A hotel donated space to hold an event to give them away."

During the year, volunteers collect dresses that have been cleaned and are ready to wear again. They pay to keep them in a storage unit and have an annual giveaway event at the convention center over two days.

This year, volunteers sent packets of information to high schools within a 150-mile radius of Portland. To get a dress, all a girl had to do was show a high school identification card.

"The stories you hear from the girls are amazing," said Jen Ingber, a member of the group's board. "Last year, I helped a high school senior from Portland. She was a foster child and lived on her own. She worked during the day and went to night school. She had a full scholarship for college, but couldn't afford a prom dress. She came and I helped her find her dress. It was one of the most rewarding experiences of my life."

Sally Egland organizes a team of volunteers -- there's a "no guys zone" -- to help girls. The volunteers range in age from early 20s to 70. They have different body shapes, so girls feel at ease having someone help them. The dresses are organized by size and color, and 50 girls are let in at a time to "shop."

"We want them to have better service than at Nordstrom," Egland said. "We don't want them to feel this is a charity. The goal is to make them feel valued, beautiful and respected."

Girls began arriving at the convention center by 6 a.m. Saturday, waiting in line, being friendly with one another, but maintaining a certain level of privacy and dignity as they waited for the doors to open.

Some mothers said their daughters would be unable to attend prom if it wasn't for a free dress.

Ursula Shepherd, 17, is a foster child who lives with Starla Bradley in Aumsville. They drove to Portland with Tila Motzko, 17, and Motzko's mother, Erika.

"We might be able to afford a dress off the clearance rack at Ross," Bradley said. "Maybe."

Shepherd said going to prom is "a special moment for a girl."

"It's a chance to go out and be pretty," she said. "I'd like to find something that looks good with my skin tone, maybe something green."

By 9:30 a.m., about 30 minutes before the doors would be unlocked, the line was filled with girls of all races, backgrounds and sizes.

All of them beautiful.

Behind the closed doors, Sally Egland stood in front of more than 30 volunteers to give the final instructions.

"You'll see and hear some very emotional things here today," she warned. "We have tissues scattered around the room.

"I'm serious," she said. "You will get choked up. Be respectful of the girls. Respect confidentiality. You will hear things, hear stories about the girls. Be careful about repeating them."

And then, as is tradition, Abby Egland took the floor to announce how many dresses had been collected this year.

"Drum roll please," her mother called out.

The volunteers pounded their knees and table tops, gathering speed.

"The final dress count," Egland said, "is 3,592."

A door swung open.

THE PATIENCE OF JOB

Day work is what the women -- all of them black -- called it

In the early evening, while her grandchildren busied themselves in the kitchen, Annette Steele lifted the Bible from an end table and cradled it in her arms. For more than a half-century she's carved out a moment at day's end to read from the book her father handed her as she left the family's small Georgia farm.

Within this Northeast Portland house few remnants of that old life remain. A letter or two buried in a drawer, and on the shelves, hidden behind knickknacks, yellowed photographs. Her parents and her precious grandmother are gone. This Bible -- a heavy, black, leather-bound edition as substantial as a big-city phone book -- is the last living link to her past.

Her seven children, and certainly her grandchildren and great-grandchildren, don't share her intense faith, and to them her relationship with this Bible is a bit of a mystery. She carried the big book to the dining room, pushed aside a pile of folded clothes and created a clearing at the end of a long table. Then she eased herself onto an old wooden chair. A self-professed "little bitty woman," she's a wiry 5-foot-2 and weighs a slim 130 pounds.

Earlier in the day she'd been on her nearly 70-year-old knees, scrubbing yet another toilet. The years have left nicks and cuts on her fingers, and her hands are scarred from barehanded cleaning with lye.

After settling into the chair, she adjusted her glasses. When she was a girl, she jabbed herself in the right eye with a pair of scissors. In the poor, black area of rural Georgia that she called home, going to a doctor was a luxury. Her grandmother calmed her down, pulled the blade and hoped for the best. The eye never healed correctly, and Annette wondered if that's why learning to read was such a struggle.

She bowed her head, reached out as if preparing to shuffle a deck of cards and ran her fingers along the Bible's frayed edges. When she felt the spirit move her, she flipped open the book to embrace the evening's message: the 34th Psalm. She tilted her head and moved close to the page in the way a scientist peers into a microscope. A power appropriate to the pulpit infused her voice: "I will extol the Lord at all times . . ."

Something crashed in the kitchen. She stopped and heard her grandson curse. "What's that?" she demanded, swiveling toward the door. "What did I hear?"

"Ship," he said sheepishly. "I said 'ship.'"

"I thought I heard something else," she said. "I better not."

She bowed her head. "I will extol the Lord at all times," she said, her voice rising and falling with a haunting rhythm. Her 14-year-old granddaughter, captivated, paused on her way up the stairs. "His praise will always be on my lips. My soul . . ."

Her grandson meekly approached with the portable phone. She patted him on the shoulder and smiled, keeping the phone pressed to her thigh until he, too, smiled. She lifted the phone to her ear. One of her clients, a Portland couple headed to the desert for the winter season, wanted Annette to clean their house. "Oh, yes," she said. "That'll be just fine. I'll see you tomorrow."

Her granddaughter took the phone. "You don't have to do this," she said to her grandmother. "Why do you keep working?"

Annette stared at the ceiling and ran her hand over her graying hair. How to explain that this old lady was once 14, too, and that she also had dreams? How to explain that she didn't discover them in Portland, a city where she and her husband were, they thought, just stopping over before settling down someplace else? How to explain?

"Child," Annette Steele said softly, "I just do. I just do."

Her granddaughter shook her head, slipped headphones over her ears, turned up the volume on her compact-disc player and continued up the stairs.

———◆———

D ay work is what Annette and the women -- all of them black -- called it. They'd see one another waiting with quiet dignity for the early bus leading out of Northeast Portland. The women, members in a sorority where admittance was a knowing glance and a nod, spent their days cleaning white people's houses.

For the most part, they're gone. Dead. Crippled with old age. The era itself drew to a close when the women were given opportunities. Only one woman from that past still does day work. She is here, in this wooden chair, reading this Bible.

The Good Book has been the constant in her life. While her children slept, she taught herself to read, sounding out words in this Bible. Her life is in these pages. Some are torn. Others are stained with tears and blood. When she realized her life was falling apart, when she realized she was alone, she reached for this book.

Tonight, as she turned the pages, she remembered the pungent scent of the Four Roses Whiskey her husband couldn't do without. Even in the quiet of this house, she heard the echoes of his voice. Without thinking, she reached up and touched his gift to her -- a scar above her right ear.

She bowed her head.

"I will extol the Lord at all times . . ."

———◆———

A nnette called to her grandchildren and told them to straighten the living room and wash the dishes before leaving. Pride, she likes to say, comes from doing the little things, a lesson passed on by her grandmother.

Annette's father was in the Air Force, and her mother followed him from base to base. Her grandmother raised Annette on a farm she sharecropped with her 16 children. Nanna Curtis, who had only a first-grade education, couldn't read or write. She worked the fields alongside her sons after her husband killed a man in a fight and disappeared. She'd never ventured farther than a few miles from the farm, and when Annette introduced her to the man she wanted to marry, her grandmother warned that he was a "city slicker."

That night, her grandchildren gone, Annette climbed into bed and dreamed of the past. She felt her grandmother's spirit. The dead, she believed, knew what the living were doing. So she hoped she'd made her grandmother proud.

Annette had wanted to be a nurse, a goal that seemed possible when she was among the first black children to attend the white school. But as a 16-year-old, while taking the bus to school, she exchanged glances with an older man in uniform. They fell in love and married.

There's no future here, he told her, and Annette knew he spoke the truth. When her father left the service, he had wanted to open his own restaurant, but he ended up working for a white man. Her father cooked and hired the crew; the owner took the profits.

Annette's new husband hoped to settle in Milwaukee, where many Southern blacks were migrating. But first, he wanted to travel. So she dropped out of high school and left with him. Their wandering led them to Portland, and somehow they never left. The first of her seven children arrived, and he started drinking. He refused to attend church, too, and he resented it when Annette faithfully headed out the door every Sunday morning. There was, he warned, but one boss in her life, and it sure wasn't God.

He was particular to Four Roses, whiskey with a label that pictured a Southern belle wearing a corsage of four red roses. Annette wondered how something so pretty could create something so ugly.

Then came the Sunday she and her daughter remember so well. She was hanging curtains when she smelled the familiar scent of Four Roses. She turned and saw him standing behind her. He cursed and pulled the curtains out of her hands. He grabbed an end table and threw it out the front door before turning on her. He shoved her into the corner. I'm sick of you, he screamed. He smashed her head with a pot.

Annette lay crumpled on the floor, feeling the blood run down her face. She heard a noise in the archway and saw her oldest daughter.

It was over then, although years went by before he finally left for good. Years that brought more kids, more drinking and more rages. He tossed a Thanksgiving turkey out the front door and trashed the Christmas tree. He cut her clothes with scissors and pummeled her with his fists. The children called police, but Annette refused to press charges. She needed his paycheck.

He stopped coming home, vanishing for weeks or months at a time. At first he'd leave money. That ended, and there were rumors he had a girl-friend and another child.

She thought about packing up and moving back to the South, where she and the kids could live on the farm. But Annette knew her children's future would be bleak. Their best hope lay in Portland.

The farm and the past? Or Portland and the future?

She decided to pray.

———◆———

She locked her front door, grasped the railing, gingerly made her way down the step and started walking. She never learned to drive and has no use for a car. At the corner she waved to a friend at the bus stop and kept hiking, past the small homes in her Northeast Portland neighborhood and up the long hill to Portland's affluent Alameda Ridge.

Unless there's a downpour, Annette refuses to ride. Her friends call her stubborn. She says she's independent. In the early 1960s, when she decided to stay in Portland, the employment office told her she wasn't qualified for any job. Friends advised her to live on public assistance. But her grand-mother raised her to take care of herself. She refused any help.

Twenty minutes after leaving home she neared the crest of the Alameda Ridge. She turned to see she'd beaten the bus to the top and smiled. She hates to lose.

After her husband abandoned the family, Annette learned people could pick fruits and vegetables on small farms along Northeast Marine Drive. She and her children walked to the fields to put food on their table. Winter approached, and the harvest ended. Friends again advised her to get help.

That would be quitting, she remembers thinking, and she worried about the message it would send her children. She applied for jobs, but nobody wanted her. One night, all she had for her family to eat was a single can of pork and beans.

Then, at church a parishioner said a wealthy matron living in Portland's West Hills was looking for a cleaning woman. She specifically wanted a Southern black woman. Annette considered it, but cleaning houses seemed demeaning.

She flipped through the pages of her Bible and discovered she'd stopped on the Book of Job. The devil tried to turn Job, an innocent man, against God by causing him to lose his possessions through a series of calamities. His children were killed, and he was stricken with boils. But Job never turned on God. The heart of the story, at least the way Annette understood it, was that Job clung to one truth: In all my disappointing times, I will wait until a change comes.

On nearly every level, Annette's life seemed a disappointment. She wondered if staying in Portland had been a mistake. A mother is supposed to make a better life for her children. She'd failed. And yet . . . in all my disappointing times, I will wait until a change comes.

Annette approached the top of the ridge at a lively pace that defied her age. The bus roared past as she waited for the light to change. The sidewalk crested the ridge, and she passed into a world of huge stucco homes with immaculate lawns and sweeping views of the city.

She's been cleaning houses for more than 40 years. That first cleaning job led to another and then another. Before long, day work was her life. She walked to a Lake Oswego cleaning job because she had no bus fare. She never asked for a ride or complained.

She worked six days a week. On Saturdays she cleaned house for a woman who owned a day-care center. In exchange, the woman watched Annette's youngest children during the week while the others were in school.

Annette's family used U.S. Navy surplus flatware. She made her kids' clothes. From time to time, employers gave her hand-me-downs their own children had outgrown. Annette took them home and tried to make her children feel as though they were getting something new.

She discovered a rhythm as she cleaned that allowed her to drift away from the dirt and tedium. When she dreamed, it was no longer about herself, but of her children. She insisted they do all their homework before playing. Or, if they had no homework, she'd make them read to her from the Bible. She grilled them on their multiplication tables. If they made a mistake, they had to start over.

During a career day, her daughter's classmates snickered when she explained her mother cleaned houses. The girl came home distraught, but Annette told her to stop feeling sorry for herself. They had clean clothes and food on the table.

When a white elementary school teacher told another daughter to mind her place, Annette appeared in the principal's office. No one would ever talk to her children that way. She enrolled them in a different school even though the family had to move from the neighborhood and into a one-bedroom apartment. Four kids shared one bed. Annette and the others took the floor.

She insisted her children go to a westside high school, where she believed they'd be academically challenged. Her daughter arrived home in tears after overhearing a classmate tell a friend about this "fantastic colored woman" who cleaned her family's house. Annette's daughter had realized she was describing her mother.

The other children said they, too, were ashamed. They didn't want to be seen with their mother. She wore a scarf around her head. The toes of her old shoes curled. She looked poor.

They were poor, Annette said. She was, after all, a cleaning lady. Other students had doctors or lawyers for parents. They lived in sprawling homes. They learned how to ski. They drove new cars and had allowances. But those were their lives. Not hers.

She washed out toilets and mopped down floors. She did work that no one else wanted to do. But she wasn't ashamed. Her money was earned honestly, through hard work and pride. The families who hired her were good people.

Never again did her children complain.

They picked fruits and vegetables during the summers. When they were old enough, they got jobs in offices, at grocery stores, in day-care centers. Every few weeks the children turned their checks over to their mother. They'd sit at the dining-room table and pay the bills. When the accounts were all settled, Annette offered a prayer of thanks.

The evil the Bible warned against surrounded her family. Some of the neighborhood girls drifted into prostitution. Or they got pregnant and dropped out of school. Some boys dabbled in drugs, or took up with gangs. More than a few went to jail or ended up in an early grave. Every child who fell by the wayside gave Annette the chance to teach her children about the dangers of wasting a life.

The Alameda neighborhood was quiet as Annette walked along the sidewalk. She approached a stately home and made her way up the steps. She'd start today in the kitchen, mopping the floor. She used a key to open the front door.

"Annette's coming in," she called out. "Annette's coming in."

———————

Annette nurtures vegetables, the kind she learned about on her Georgia farm, in the small strips of soil on each side of her driveway.

On a warm autumn afternoon, she walked out her back door, plucked collard greens from her little garden and dropped them into a bowl.

Pots and pans banged back in the kitchen, where every burner on the stove glowed orange in preparation for Sunday supper. She expected nearly 30 children and spouses, grandchildren and great-grandchildren at her table. Missing would be only her youngest son, who lost direction in his life after high school and has been in and out of jail ever since. His mother believes she did her best. No longer does she cry.

In the kitchen she stood before the sink and looked through a cracked window held in place with pieces of duct tape. When the winter rains come, the roof will leak. Portions of the front steps are rotten. She worries they will give way and she will fall.

But those things do not matter. This is the home she bought when she managed to save $200 for a down payment. The women whose homes she cleaned asked their husbands -- men who knew their way around real estate, mortgages and banks -- to help. They cut through red tape and restrictions. They negotiated. And now Annette Steele has roots in a city that was never supposed to be home.

With her Social Security check and the money she gets for cleaning, she brings home just over $1,100 a month. She knows her children worry. She's never asked for help. Nevertheless, when they visit they write checks and leave money on the table before slipping out the door.

One by one the children arrive for supper.

The attorney, the two middle-school teachers and the state worker who looks after children. The grocery-store executive and the medical technician.

Her legacy.

They crowd into the kitchen as Annette slips into the dining room. At each place is a setting of gold flatware, gifts over the decades from the wealthy families whose homes she has cleaned.

"We're ready to eat," Annette calls. "Come sit down."

No one hears her. They are busy talking about their careers, the economy, problems at work and how their children are doing in school.

She walks to the living room and sits briefly on the sofa. With her right hand, she reaches out and touches the black Bible on the end table. She closes her eyes, thinking about what she will say before the meal is served.

"Let's go," she calls. "It is time to pray."

Everyone crowds together.

"Join hands," she says. "No talking. All eyes closed. All heads bowed."

She pauses and then leads the prayer.

"O Heavenly Father, we thank you again that we can again be together for the day," she says. "Thank you for the health and strength of the family and for continuing to lead us."

Two of her grandchildren look at each other and smirk. One touches his watch. This is going to be one of Grandma's long prayers.

"You brought us from a long way," she says. "A long way. Without you, we could not have made it. I could not have made it. Thank you. Thank you for giving me a mind."

She pauses.

"Lord," she says. "You told me to wait . . . to wait until my change comes."

She bows her head.

"I waited," she whispers.

"Amen."

THE GUIDE

No God would allow a child to live that life.

For most of his life, the man believed he could escape his past. After he buried his parents and their demons, he left the neighborhood and never looked back.

By the time he was 45, he was married, had two children and owned a company that occupied most of the 17th floor of a downtown Portland building. In the quiet moments, when he wasn't hammering out million-dollar deals, he was drawn to the windows, which offered a spectacular view of Portland's East Side.

He recalled the promise, something he had whispered to himself when he was a boy. A prayer of sorts on the nights he cried himself to sleep after the cops left and his parents stumbled off to bed.

He found himself thinking less about business deals and more about the children living where he once lived. On clear days, he could stand in front of the office windows and peer right into his old Northeast Portland neighborhood. Then he made his decision.

Now the man on the 17th floor touches the lives of 240 children every day. Next year, the number will grow to 256. In two years it will be 274.

His story is theirs . . . and theirs his.

———◆———

Well before lunch, Duncan Campbell pushes back from his desk. He tells his assistant he will be out of the office for a while.

Out on the street he looks like a 53-year-old tourist ready to explore the city. He wears khaki pants, a white short-sleeved shirt, a blue sweater vest and loafers. The only time he slips into a business suit anymore is when new clients pay him a visit at The Campbell Group.

He's a good-looking man in a rugged way, stocky and strong through the chest and shoulders, built like a middle linebacker. During his life, he's led with his face, and it shows. This is a man who's thrown a punch and taken a few.

Campbell does not need to make these frequent trips back to where his journey began. He has pleasant distractions -- a house on the Oregon coast and another near Bend -- and memberships in some of the city's most prestigious athletic and social clubs. He travels back to his old neighborhood because of the promise.

He crosses the Willamette River and with each passing block, Campbell sees the world once again through a boy's eyes. Soon he's a man traveling with memories and ghosts.

He drives through inner-Northeast Portland streets, through neighborhoods where many of the children watch, with sad eyes, a world filled with things they should not know about.

Campbell stops in front of a small, brown house. He kills the motor, leaving silence broken only by the ticking of a hot engine. The leather seat creaks when he leans forward to gaze out the passenger window.

"This," he says, pointing, "is where I grew up."

A few men wandering down the sidewalk gesture toward the $35,000 Chevrolet Suburban. They wonder why a middle-aged white guy is just sitting there, staring at a run-down house.

"I come here quite a lot," Campbell explains. "It keeps my life in perspective. Sometimes I bring my kids, but they get bored."

He smiles.

"They can't believe it was as bad as I say it was."

He pulls away from the curb and eases into traffic. Each block he passes holds a memory.

There, to his right, is where he walked, alone, when he was 3. He woke up late at night after hearing sirens. He ran from his bed to look for his parents, who, of course, were drinking. He headed to the tavern. On the way, a cop found him, wandering in his pajamas, a scared kid looking for his mom and dad.

They were the neighborhood lushes. When they had to root through drawers for quarters, they drank beer. When they had a few bucks, it was bourbon. When they got kicked out of Black's Tavern, they'd wobble across the street to the Alberta Tavern and drink the night away.

Some nights Duncan waited for them in the car. If they had an extra buck, they'd send him to the Silk Hat, a nearby Chinese restaurant. Most of the time, though, he sat in the car and listened to the radio. When he was older, he stayed home alone, where he sat, dreading the sound of the front door opening. Someone bumping into furniture, screaming matches, telephone lines being cut, the cops showing up at the front door.

The screaming matches ended for a time when his father went to prison for kiting bad checks.

"My parents were mean to each other," he says. "To be candid, they were pathetic."

Up one street, down another.

That building, straight ahead, that's where Campbell went to join the Cub Scouts. Rules required that his father attend. But the night of the ceremony he sat alone. When it was over, he ran toward the door, embarrassed. Then his father burst in, dead drunk, yelling at the top of his lungs.

"You have to understand that we started at the bottom and worked our way down," he says. "My parents lost their house, had to move to a duplex and then to an apartment. They ended up in a small room and had to sell their car for $35."

On Sundays, while his parents nursed hangovers, Campbell went to church, the one over there on the left. By the end of high school, though, he quit and considered himself an atheist.

"No God would let me go through that childhood," he explains. "The horrible scenes and fights. The bars and the poverty. No God would allow that to happen to any child."

He never invited friends to his house. The fathers of kids he knew became his role models. One was African American, a porter on the railroad. The other white, a truck driver. They set a place at the dinner table for him, let him spend the night. They showed him how to fish, how to fill out a scorecard at the baseball game. Their homes smelled not of stale smoke and booze, but of pot roasts and bread.

He was a smart kid, but a classroom troublemaker. He neglected homework and stayed up watching television movies, staring at the screen and doing jigsaw puzzles. In high school he was suspended twice for fighting.

But his parents didn't care. When he graduated from high school, they ignored the ceremony.

He worked three summer jobs to raise money to enroll at Portland State University. Then he transferred to Oregon State, graduated, hitchhiked around the country, worked in a steel mill and returned to Portland. He enrolled at the University of Oregon law school, but quit after the first year. He discovered, he said, that "being a lawyer was not about justice."

In Portland, he stumbled onto a job as a caseworker for delinquent boys. But he quit after two years, convinced there was a better way to help such children. He vowed to himself that if he ever had the money, he'd make it happen. He returned to law school and graduated.

His parents didn't attend that graduation either.

"They died when I was just starting out in my career," he says. "Within a year of each other from the hard life they led. I was never able to talk with them about growing up. The closest my father got to talking about it was when he told me that one day I'd understand how bad life was. He said then I'd learn why a man had to drink."

———◆———

Duncan Campbell turns his Suburban away from his past, toward downtown Portland and his other life.

After law school and a stint as a CPA with an accounting firm, he quit and took to the road to sell the idea of using timberland as an investment vehicle. The company he formed takes money from investors and finds timberland for them to buy. It then manages the land for the investors, harvesting and selling the timber, replanting trees and making sure operations comply with timber-management regulations.

Harvard University now has more than $200 million invested with the Campbell Group, and total investments top $1 billion. The company occupies most of the 17th floor of a building not far from the west end of the Hawthorne Bridge in downtown Portland.

Campbell lived two lives. Down the long hallways, his employees knew him as a successful businessman. When he looked out the windows, though, he was right back on the streets, a poor kid from Northeast Portland.

He offered to serve on various commissions and task forces dealing with juvenile issues. Society, he came to believe, was taking the wrong approach. Agencies spent resources on children long after the kids already were in trouble.

Campbell was fascinated by the children who lived in his old neighborhood. He hired researchers to study their resiliency. Why, he wanted to know, did some children -- children like him -- overcome hard times.

The researchers confirmed what Campbell knew in his gut: Resiliency develops in children through a caring relationship with an adult role model. If not with a parent, then an aunt, uncle or grandparent.

As Campbell looked at his own life he realized it was friends who showed him there was a better life. His fifth-grade teacher, a high-school football coach, his friends' fathers. He was convinced he had lived the life he had so he could understand and help children in a way that few others could. And that's when he remembered the promise he made to himself when he was a boy: Nobody should be alone like I am, he'd said then. When I grow up, I'll do everything I can to make sure this doesn't happen to somebody else.

In 1990, Campbell sold his company. The new owners asked him to stay and run the operation. He agreed, but he also decided it was time for him to do more with his life.

And he discovered once more he believed in God. But not with the unthinking faith of a boy who went to church only to get out of the house.

God, he decided, gave humans free will. The choices people made had led to the conditions in which people were forced to live. There were adequate resources to take care of one another if people chose to do so.

Three years later he hit on his plan.

Campbell was convinced high-risk children needed help before they were sucked into the juvenile justice system. He was thinking of children who might have a parent in prison, or on welfare, the kind of children who, if not helped when young, would one day end up in prison themselves or would cost society hundreds of thousands of dollars in welfare benefits, not to mention the human tragedy and loss of potential.

What they needed, he believed, was just one good adult friend.

For his program, he wanted to avoid volunteers, who quit when the novelty wears off. He planned to hire friends, to pay them salaries comparable to what first-year teachers earned. And while most social workers had caseloads of up to 100, Campbell vowed that each of his employees would oversee just eight children.

The friends would not be substitute parents. They wouldn't give the family money or help out family members when they dealt with state agencies. A friend's relationship would be strictly with the child, one-to-one, not with a family.

When Campbell told his own friends about his plan, they said he was wasting his money, that he was a businessman, not a social worker. But he would not be deterred.

He wrote down goals: Each child would get a library card, be taken downtown and shown a world he or she could be a part of. The friend would meet with the child several times a week. They'd go on field trips, do homework together, play in the park, ride bikes. But most important, the friend would be someone the child could count on for the next 12 years.

To find the children, Campbell turned to first-grade teachers who knew them and their families. He christened his program "Friends of the Children," put up $1.5 million of his own money and in May 1993 hired the first three Friends.

They went to the school Campbell attended long before -- King Elementary -- looking for 24 first-graders. They met with the teachers, made a pitch for the most at-risk kids in the school and asked for help.

Some of the teachers were so deeply moved by the idea that they broke into tears.

Before the school year ended, 16 boys and eight girls were assigned to the three Friends. Campbell set the $1.5 million up as an endowment and picked up the annual budget.

The 6-year-old program now has 30 Friends, and each year it grows by two Friends and 16 children.

Last year, the state office of Services to Children and Families decided to refer a handful of the children to the Friends program, says Betty Uchytil, assistant administrator for field operations.

"What makes them so good is that they have the ability to forge a one-on-one relationship with a child and make a difference in the lives of kids who have come from demolished backgrounds," she says. "One person, over time, can turn a life around. It is not something state agencies can do."

From the outset, Campbell wanted to make sure Friends of Children was not perceived as an African American program. By chance, the first child accepted into the program was a white girl. Now, 43 percent of the children are African American, 47 percent white, 5 percent Latino and 5 percent mixed race.

Through the program's development, Campbell has maintained a low profile. Few Oregonians know his personal story. And outside of a handful of social workers, few have heard of Friends, as the program is now generally called.

But as reports rippled across the United States, social service officials from other cities traveled to Portland to pick Campbell's brain. Three other cities now plan to replicate the program, and earlier this year, the nonprofit Public/Private Ventures, a Philadelphia think tank that studies youth issues, turned its sights on Friends.

"In my professional life, I've seen only a few programs that I think have a shot at really making a difference," Gary Walker, the think tank's president, says. "I don't casually toss words around like 'brilliant' and 'unique,' but what Campbell did is brilliant and unique. What he created in Portland could change the way this country tries to help its children."

While Campbell moves money around the Northwest's timber economy, Friends do the work he considers most important. On this day, Steve Wick is outside King Elementary School after the last bell, looking for one missing child. Other kids tell Wick they haven't seen the fifth-grader since last period.

"How's he been doing?' Wick asks an 11-year-old wearing short pants and a small green backpack.

"Bad."

Wick walks to his car, starts it and pulls onto the street. He wants to find an 11-year-old we'll call Phil, a bully and a loner with just one true friend: 31-year-old Steve Wick. At each intersection, Wick slows his car. Hookers and crack dealers assume he is buying. He waves them off.

Wick is paid to befriend and mentor eight fifth-grade boys. He has been with the same group since they were in first grade and will remain with them through high school. He's white; they're African American. He's country; they're city. And yet he knows a side of these boys that they hide from the rest of the world. Each boy has his pager number with instructions to contact him whenever they need to talk. They reveal secrets. They cry on his shoulder.

Wick, like all of the Friends, meets individually with his kids several times a week to play, to do homework, to go on field trips and to form bonds that will help guide the children through life. He pulls them back from the precipice that looms before all the kids in the program.

One child was left in a shopping cart at a grocery store. Another was born addicted to crack. His mother is a street addict and the boy lives with his grandmother, a reformed addict. A girl will be forced to spend this summer in a foster home because her mother is in jail. Another girl was abandoned by her mother. She lives with her father when he's out of jail. When he's locked up, she bounces to her grandmother.

Since Phil was born, his mother has moved 12 times. She's had six children with six different men. The kids wander the streets. The older boys have dropped out of school and are in gangs and selling drugs. Their mother is on welfare.

But the system offers no help unless kids are physically abused or subjected to horrible neglect, and then acts by removing the child from the home. So teachers recommended that Phil be placed in Friends.

"There are no miracles with these kids," says Wick as he drives down an alley toward Phil's apartment. "This is a long, slow road. But the beauty is that we have time. I can spend years with each child."

He stops the car and walks to the apartment. On the door he finds a note from Phil's mother. She's moved again, apparently to a motel along North Interstate Avenue.

Wick heads that way.

"Some days I go home, and I think I have not helped at all," he says. "Some days I feel great. This is a very emotional job."

He pulls into the motel's parking lot and knocks on a door. No answer. He peers in a window. The place is vacant.

Wick stands in the parking lot. "Where is that kid?' he mutters.

Wick checks six other places. He finds the boy at his cousin's. He learns Phil's mother has been kicked out of their apartment. She tells Wick that she's found a place she can afford, but it's infested with fleas. She wants to wait a couple of weeks to see if the fleas die before she moves in.

Wick can only nod. He must maintain a relationship with Phil's mother. Parents can pull their children out of Friends at any time, although only a handful have done so.

"I have to have tunnel vision," Wick says. "I see a lot of bad things in a lot of homes. Drug paraphernalia, partying all night, living off of chips and soda pop."

A Friend must report cases of sexual or physical abuse, but for other things they turn a blind eye.

Wicks was born and raised in Banks, a quiet town on the way to the Oregon coast. After graduating from college, he got into social work and was a counselor at the Boys and Girls Aid Society.

"I dealt with 100 kids a day," he says. "Always different faces. I felt I just couldn't make an impact. One day I heard about this program that a guy named Duncan Campbell was starting. It sounded amazing. I looked him up in the phone book and called him at his office. I told him that he had no idea who I was. I said I wanted to work for him."

As word about the program got out, job applications flooded in. The average age of a Friend is 26, but some are in their early 20s, others in their 50s. All have a bachelor's degree and experience working with children. They go through extensive criminal and background checks. Half are men, 50 percent are African American, 30 percent white, 10 percent Latino and 10 percent mixed race.

Some, such as Wick, grew up in traditional homes. Others, such as Rodney Clemente, a 30-year-old African American man, have experiences similar to the kids'.

A single mother raised Clemente in a San Francisco housing project. "In my environment it was normal to see someone doing drugs or to see some kid killed," he says. "When I was a senior in high school my friend got shot and killed by a drug dealer. From there, it snowballed. At one point I was going to a funeral twice a month."

What prevented Clemente from getting in trouble was a cop who coached a neighborhood football team.

"I met him when I was young, about 6," Clemente said. "He was in my life for the next 20 years. He was a positive person for me, a male who was not stealing and fighting and selling dope. He showed me there was a better way to live."

Clemente played football on a Portland State University scholarship. After graduating he wanted to become a probation officer to help kids in the system. When he heard about Friends he saw a chance to do something before they got into trouble.

"These kids are so similar to me," he says. "The more I talk with them, the more I realize how scared they are. Only two of them have a father in the home. One kid was born addicted to drugs. He is good in school, but he talks slow because of what the drugs did to him. The other kids tease him, and I sit and talk with him and tell him that he is not dumb. I have an 8-year-old boy who is in a house full of women. His mom is an addict and is always telling him to be tough, to not cry. With me, he can cry."

As his program has grown, Campbell has solicited donations from acquaintances, other individuals and foundations. He wants steady growth, but only when he has money to make a long-term commitment to a child. And he wants to make it clear to the Friends that this is a career. He offers 401(k) benefits, insurance and a modest monthly expense account.

The program has a headquarters, where Campbell keeps an office, for a four-person administrative staff. Campbell also bought a house in Northeast Portland where the Friends can take their children. Many of the kids' parents don't want the Friends coming to their homes because of what they might see or hear. At the house are computers for the children to use. In the kitchen, Friends teach them how to cook. Some need help with simple hygiene, or something as routine as how to set the alarm clock to get up in time for school.

Although the program has its roots in King Elementary School, Friends follow their children if they transfer. They now track children in 67 metropolitan area elementary schools.

Northwest Regional Educational Laboratory in Portland, a nonprofit organization financed by the U.S. Department of Education, has launched a 10-year study of the program. In addition to monthly reports from Friends, the laboratory receives assessments filled out by teachers, school principals, parents and the children themselves. Interim reports show that none of the children has had contact with the criminal justice system. Nearly all of them avoid drugs and alcohol.

Schools report remarkable turnarounds. "In one case, I don't know how this boy would have made it," says Joseph Malone, principal of King Elementary. "He would have been expelled if not for the attention and guidance of his Friend."

Other schools offer similar reports. A boy whose father was in prison was literally the worst kid in school. Now he's one of the best. A bitter and withdrawn girl is now active in dance. A former problem child was recently given a character award.

Wick knocks on the door nearly 20 times before someone answers. He has come for Phil on a Tuesday morning. He steps into the house and sees Phil's mother passed out on the living room floor. Two men Wick has never seen before are sleeping on the floor, too. The boy who opens the door yells to the basement, where Phil sleeps with three other boys on mattresses laid out on the concrete.

Phil emerges and leaves the house with Wick. His mother never stirs.

At the Friends' house Wick makes Phil breakfast, and they sit at the kitchen table. While Phil eats his oatmeal, he and Wick talk about what they will do that day. Phil wants to go swimming. Wick asks Phil how things are going, what he thinks about all this moving.

"It's OK," Phil says.

He sips his hot chocolate.

"Not really," he says. "I miss my friends, but I meet new ones. I know kids in gangs, but I'm not scared."

Have you seen guns?

"Yes."

People beat up?

"Yes."

People selling drugs?

"Yes."

Phil pushes his cereal away and warms to a story.

"Dealers don't scare me," he says. "Some are my cousins and uncles. I'm not scared of anything. One time me and my cousin were riding our bikes, and this dude pulled a gun and told my cousin to give him his necklace. Then he shot the gun in the air and pointed it at my head. I rode my bike away fast."

Not scared at all?

"Nope."

A little?

"Yes."

He looks at Wick.

"When are we going swimming?'

Soon.

Phil smiles.

He slowly reaches across the table until his hand touches Wick's. Without a word, Wick takes the boy's small hand in his.

Down the hall, Duncan Campbell's executives are gathered in a conference room. His presence is required. He pushes away from his desk, crosses the office, but stops. He walks to the windows.

"I bring the kids up here," he says. "I see myself in those small faces. You know, a lot of those kids have never been out of their neighborhood. They've never been in an office building."

He smiles.

"So I bring them in here," he says, "and I have them stand in front of the window. I want them to see the bridges and the river. I want them to see the world out there."

Phones ring. Employees hustle down the halls.

But the man on the 17th floor is motionless, staring out the windows, silently looking at the view.

PORTLAND: 3 A.M

At 3 a.m., the city is a poem.

What you search for at 3 a.m. in the city is an oasis of light, some sign of life on the banks during the journey along a river of darkness.

A handful of cars on the road. A man walking, a sack in his arms. A janitor pushing a mop back and forth, headphones on, head down, lost in thought. A patrol car on a side street, lights flashing, the cop's right hand resting gently on the butt of a gun as he leans down to peer in the driver's window.

At 3 a.m., Portland is a poem.

It's Tom Waits' lyrics. A Raymond Carver two-pager. An Edward Hopper. The power comes not from what's in front of you but from what you can't see.

At 3 a.m., you feel your way, letting the current push you into the still waters. Finally, out on Northeast 122nd Avenue, lights are on at Shari's. When someone walks in, people look. Not subtly, either. Maybe it's a throwback to something deep inside all of us, this survival instinct that comes out late at night.

Fellow traveler?

Nut?

Once they pass judgment, they talk.

That's the way it is at this hour. Kind of like when a snowstorm blankets the city. Strangers open up. Darkness brings forth this need to connect. What you get then is this partial friendship, this funny bond that bumps right up against the gray edge of loneliness.

A story, at 3 a.m., is only partially told.

So you get a 21-year-old at the counter who's finished a chicken-strip dinner. He lives nearby and likes coming here. Doesn't sleep at night. So he lingers, no rush -- no reason -- to go back home. He once did night work as a janitor, he explains. He discovered he's more comfortable in the shadows.

And now?

He shrugs.

He smiles.

He carries his leftovers out the door and slips away in the dark.

What's left is a work crew sharing a table, wide awake, loud and raring to go. Nearby, two assistants at a pizza parlor, worn out, try to stay awake. At a table by the window, three people laugh and trade inside jokes about "The Rocky Horror Picture Show."

Hovering over all of them is waitress Shelly Williams. She's 37 and calls people "honey" in a natural way that doesn't seem phony.

She used to be a bartender, she says, and calls herself a night owl. People, she believes, are born more suited for the day or night. She found her place long ago. She dropped in here awhile back for pie and coffee -- in the middle of the night, of course -- and noticed they were short of waitresses. She flagged down the manager.

The interview was short. Williams said she'd work the graveyard shift. Now, a few days later, she's pulling the 10:30 p.m. to 6 a.m. shift.

And in a few minutes -- when the other waitress, Stacy Christenson, checks out -- she'll be on her own for the first time. The people won't be a problem. It's the register she worries about.

To stay alert, she's had three cups of coffee.

Business, she knows, is slow. Receipts show that last week, though people were in the restaurant, no one paid between 3 and 4 a.m. It picked up a bit the next hour -- $6.27.

But things may change. Night people, she knows, are good tippers.

Williams steps outside for air while the other waitress checks out.

"There's something so quiet and beautiful about 122nd right now," she says when she returns. "Morning changes everything."

Christenson walks through the restaurant, calling out to the customers.

"Everyone be nice to Shelly," she says. "She's new."

And then Williams is on her own.

———◆———

When it comes to loosening the tongue, silence and boredom are as effective as scotch and soda. So the two men behind the counter trace the arc of their lives and explain how they ended up working the graveyard shift at an auto parts store.

Only two businesses remain open at 3 a.m. along this long and lonely stretch of Southeast 122nd Avenue -- a porn emporium and Thrifty Auto Supply. One parking lot is full. The other empty. It doesn't take a genius to guess which draws the crowd.

Thrifty is the only 24-hour auto parts store on the West Coast, according to manager Robert Foster, who, at this moment, is home and probably fast asleep. In 1984, the chain decided to keep one of its six local stores open all night, figuring it would draw the night-owl business and get a jump on daily paperwork needed to stock the other stores. The shifts have always been hard to fill.

From the store's open doors, it's possible to see Diego Juarez and Andy Cocom behind the counter, tapping pencils and making small talk while waiting for customers. Windshield wipers are a popular item, but they've also sold water pumps and transmission seals to customers who need it now and drive from as far as Salem.

The boss doesn't provide stools or chairs, telling the pair that sitting will make them lazy. The in-house radio station can't be changed. It plays nothing but oldies.

So Juarez and Cocom stand and wait.

This Friday night has been slow -- just eight customers since midnight. Maybe it will pick up. Cops, the two men say, have been known to pull over motorists for not having a brake light and waiving the ticket if the driver heads straight to the store for a replacement bulb.

But now the shift is passing slowly, giving the 19-year-olds time to think.

They're not sure how they ended up here. They're not sure where they're headed. This is their first job out of high school. Sure, they have big dreams.

But they whisper them quietly, shyly, almost as if to themselves while looking down at the counter.

They both attended Reynolds High School, knew of each other but weren't friends. What they had in common was a lack of interest in school. They skipped classes, didn't care. The one constant, the thing that pulled them back, was auto shop. They found purpose in the garage where they could tinker with cars.

They graduated but didn't know what to do next. So they drifted here. Cocom came on first. In six months, he went through five partners. Then one night a familiar face walked in. Juarez had been hired and assigned the graveyard shift. The partnership has worked, and the two are now friends.

Two customers appear out of nowhere. They're edgy, with ratty clothes and darting eyes. The aisles are chained off to prevent shoplifting, so the customers wander as far as they can, talking to each other. Five long minutes later, one motions to Cocom, who walks to the cash register to ring up a sale.

"Acetone at 3 a.m.," Cocom says when he returns to the counter. "Got to wonder what that's all about."

Juarez shrugs.

"One night some guy kept getting too close to me," Cocom says. "He freaked me out. Made me nervous."

They haven't been robbed, but they're cautious. They've seen it all: drunks, meth heads, car buffs, strangers who drift in because they're lonely and want someone to talk to. The two men oblige.

"A bum used to come in here all the time," Cocom says. "We let him warm up. We'd give him empty boxes. He'd take them and go make up his bed."

He stares out the door.

"Haven't seen him for a while," he says. "I always wonder what happened to him."

The store falls silent, just two counter guys passing the time.

"Think we'll be here a year from now?" Cocom asks.

Juarez ponders the question. "Maybe," he replies. "Probably."

"That's what I figure," Cocom says.

Letting Go

She is my little shadow who wants to tag along wherever I go.

The clock radio goes off, but no alarm is necessary. I've been awake more than an hour.

Lying in bed, I realize this is it. In less than three hours, I will tell my little girl goodbye.

Rachael is starting kindergarten, and her baby sister and her mother and I are taking her to her first day of school.

During my life, I've said plenty of goodbyes. Schools, college and jobs around the country have taken me from home, but I was always the excited child ready and eager to fly away from a parent.

Today will be different: I will be the parent. I will be a father saying goodbye to his 5-year-old daughter.

In the morning's early light, I ponder what role I should fill. What wisdom can I pass on to her? What should I tell her that she will remember?

But my mind is blank.

I shower, dress and eat and then come back upstairs. I stand over Rachael's bed to watch her sleep.

Tucked in next to her is a stuffed doll that was once her favorite possession. These days, it spends most of its time in the corner. But last night I put the doll in bed with her -- not for Rachael's sake, but for mine. For just a little while longer, I could remember her as the baby she will always be to me.

As I stand there in her room, listening to the rest of the house wake up, I realize I'm thinking in cliches. Time flies. I remember when.

But looking at my sleeping daughter, I do remember. The day she was born and how I cut the umbilical cord and then gave her the first bath. That first visit to Santa Claus and how she cried and wanted me to hold her. The first time she called me "Da Da."

For now, I can do little wrong in Rachael's eyes. I am Daddy, strong and all-knowing.

She is my little shadow who wants to tag along wherever I go. She holds my hand in public. She gives me kisses.

Today, that will begin to change.

Although she will spend just a few hours a day at a school less than a mile from home, I know she is embarking on a journey that will pull us apart.

Now she wants me to walk her to school. In coming years, she will die of embarrassment if I get within five blocks of her school. I mean, someone might actually see that Rachael has a dad.

A part of me wants to shut her bedroom door and lock it, do anything in my power to stop time, to keep Rachael inside this room where I can alway watch and protect her.

"Rachael," I call out as I stroke her hair. "Time to get up. Time for school."

As she stirs and nods, I walk downstairs to make her breakfast. I wonder again what I should say when I leave her at school. But I am still not feeling wise or witty enough.

I don't have much time to think about this failing. Before long, the house is alive. Hanna, her sister, is drinking her bottle. Barbara, her mother, is combing Rachael's hair. And for once, Rachael is not arguing about it.

Soon it's time to leave.

Rachael and I walk the blocks hand in hand, just ahead of her mother and sister. She skips and jumps until we get near the school. Then she slows when she spots the big kids hanging around the door.

I file the necessary forms at the office, and then we walk down the hallway to her classroom. Other children and parents are gathered by the door, and we all file inside when her teacher arrives.

After a few minutes the parents begin saying their goodbyes and leaving their children, who then sit cross-legged in the middle of the classroom floor.

In a moment it will be my turn. As I wait, I realize I am doing what my parents and their parents and all before them did.

I am letting a child go. And that's the way it should be.

It is then that I know what to say:

"Rachael, I love you."

She kisses me.

Her hand slips from mine.

THE PIONEER

When he was a child, he dreamed of being a journalist. It was a ridiculous goal.

The door leading to his fourth-floor office in The Oregonian's executive suites does not have a nameplate. Nothing indicates that this is where William A. Hilliard ended up.

Once, everything in the newsroom revolved around this man. Promotions went through him. His memos to the paper's city desk meant action. Since last year, however, when he announced he would retire as editor this spring, Hilliard has taken a less active newsroom role.

A new editor directs and controls the paper. Soon, Hilliard's name will vanish from the paper's masthead on the editorial page and his 42-year career will end.

He will be remembered not so much for his skills as a reporter or editor, but for a more personal legacy. This is a man who, at age 11, was denied a paper route at The Oregonian because managers said whites did not want blacks delivering their paper. Now, at age 66, he sits in the editor's office at that same paper.

When he was a child, Hilliard dreamed of being a journalist. It was a ridiculous goal because in the 1930s Negroes were maids or waiters or redcaps. They cleaned toilets, cleared tables and carried luggage.

That didn't deter Hilliard. When he was 10, he started a neighborhood paper in Southeast Portland. The Coppy Cat Gazette had 75 customers who paid 2 cents for the two-page weekly that reported on such matters as which girl was kissing what boy and how the family down the street mowed its lawn last Saturday.

In college, a University of Oregon professor told Hilliard that Negroes couldn't be journalists on mainstream papers. Hilliard transferred to Pacific University and earned a journalism degree. He could not find a job at The Oregonian or the Oregon Journal when he graduated, and he ended up working at the train station as a redcap, carrying suitcases for tips.

He returned to The Oregonian once more, when a family friend heard that the paper was looking for a copy boy to run errands. Hilliard got the job.

He was 25. His boss was a high school student.

Later, as he moved through the reporting and editing ranks, Hilliard was always the first black in any particular post. For a younger generation used to seeing blacks in leadership roles in the 1990s, it might be easy to underestimate the significance of Hilliard's journey.

When Hilliard was hired, white reporters and editors wondered if he would bring what was called the "Williams Avenue look" to the paper. Would he talk funny? Listen to odd music? Wear strange clothes?

During his career, Hilliard was the scout, leading the way for all who would follow. Minority reporters and editors now are scattered throughout the paper. Hilliard considers that his most important accomplishment.

On this April day, Hilliard's office is in disarray. He is cleaning out his desk, sorting what he will take with him when he leaves in a few weeks. He motions a visitor to sit -- on the blue leather sofa that has been in his office since he became the editor -- and he pulls up a chair.

He is a gentle man who speaks softly. Yet he radiates a steady pride and strength. He smiles often, and it's easy to imagine what he looked like as a kid. He quickly shares facts and dates but guards his emotional core. Reaching it requires a special tenacity.

When he's asked what working at the paper has meant to him, Hilliard is caught off-guard. There is a long pause. His office grows so quiet that it's possible to eavesdrop on people talking in a hallway 30 feet away.

Finally, he speaks.

"When I was in grade school, everyone had to get up the first day and say what their parents did," he says.

He shifts in his chair. It appears the conversation may end.

But he continues.

"I lived on the edge of a pretty nice neighborhood, and most of the kids had dads with good jobs," he says. "When it was my turn, I'd stand up and in front of all those kids and I'd have to say that my mother was a domestic and that my stepfather shined shoes at the bus depot."

He looks around his office, the editor's office.

"This paper gave me the opportunity to feel worthwhile, to have self-esteem, to feel I was somebody," he says. "I knew that when my kids had to stand up in class, they could say I worked at The Oregonian. They could say their father worked at The Oregonian."

Hilliard's parents divorced when he was a baby, and for the first eight years of his life, he and his two sisters lived with his grandparents in Arkansas. His mother, who worked as a maid, moved west with a family and sent for her children when Hilliard was 8. By then she had remarried and the family rented a house in inner Southeast Portland.

"My stepfather was not a father figure," Hilliard said. "He was my mother's husband, that's all. He drank and he'd disappear for days at a time, or come home drunk. He had no interest in our lives."

Although other black families lived in the neighborhood, most of Hilliard's friends were white. When he ventured out of the neighborhood, however, he heard racial slurs and taunts.

Blacks were allowed to eat in only a handful of Portland restaurants, and Hilliard remembers going downtown with his family and being stopped at businesses by signs that read: "Whites Only."

Hilliard found guidance from a neighbor. His name was Stephen Wright. He was a black businessman who owned the Melody Hotel, the only hotel in Portland that welcomed blacks.

"I cut Mr. Wright's grass and he took a liking to me," Hilliard said. "It dawned on me that there were no blacks that I could see as role models.

But here was Mr. Wright, a black man who was not a waiter or a Pullman porter."

When Hilliard was 13, his mother and stepfather moved to Northeast Portland. Hilliard didn't want to go. Wright's family took him in.

"My mother may have been hurt from time to time, but I think she saw it as a good influence," Hilliard said. "Mr. Wright took me on business trips. He taught me how to drive. At his hotel I met black entertainers and businessmen. Mr. Wright told me, showed me, that there were blacks doing things with their lives. He told me to do what I wanted to do. Get good grades in school, go to college and don't pay attention to what anyone else says."

Hilliard attended Benson High School and worked on the school paper but, because he was black, was not named editor. After graduation, he was drafted by the U.S. Navy and served for a little more than a year. While in the service, Wright sent him small, comic book-sized copies of The Oregonian that the paper produced for servicemen.

Hilliard returned to Portland and studied journalism at Vanport College, which was organized to accommodate the returning servicemen. Two years later, he transferred to the University of Oregon, where a professor told him that he was wasting his time. Hilliard transferred to Pacific University, graduated, but could not find a job. He worked as a redcap at Union Station and started the Portland Challenger, a weekly paper that covered Portland's black community.

A few months later The Oregonian hired him as a copy boy and then made him a part-time clerk in the sports department.

"I was working in sports, as a redcap and running the Challenger, which was losing money," Hilliard said. "I was way behind in my bills, so I took out a loan to pay off the printer and shut the paper down."

While in the sports department, Hilliard met another clerk, a high school student named Jack Rosenthal.

"Hilliard and I sat next to each other," said Rosenthal, now editor of The New York Times Magazine. "Until then, I had known one black, a kid at my high school. Hilliard was my first experience with integration. I remember thinking that I had never known a Negro up close before. I realized they were just folks. It sounds stupid now, but it was a segregated world then."

Rosenthal left the sports department to attend Harvard University.

"My family had no money and I could not afford to fly," he said. "I was going to sit up for three nights on the train to Boston. As my parents and I entered the train station, a redcap came rushing over and grabbed my luggage. I hung onto it, because we didn't have any money to give for a tip. But he was insistent and took my luggage.

"Suddenly, I looked up, and under the cap was Bill Hilliard," Rosenthal said. "He was grinning. We tried to offer him money, money we didn't really have, but he would not take it. He said this was his contribution to see me off to college.

"I remember feeling such a complicated set of emotions. I was thrilled that my friend Bill Hilliard would do this for me, and yet I was embarrassed for him that he was a redcap. Here I was going to Harvard and he was hauling my luggage."

Hilliard continued to work as a redcap until L.H. Gregory, the sports editor, showed up at the train station on his way out of town on a story.

"I was in my uniform and I said, 'Hello, Mr. Gregory.' He looked down at me and said, 'Bill? Bill Hilliard? What the hell are you doing here.' I told him I was working an extra job to make money. He just looked at me, and it was kind of awkward so I quit (as a redcap)."

Eventually, Hilliard was hired as a full-time sports reporter. White reporters, even part-time reporters, were sent out of the office to cover stories, but not Hilliard. His first outside assignment was to cover the Harlem Globetrotters, the black basketball team, which was putting on an exhibition at Lincoln High School. Hilliard got his byline, but other reporters told him the paper had never before covered the Globetrotters.

Friends in the department told Hilliard to contact the newspaper union, the Guild, to complain about the disparity in assignments. A few days later the sports editor warned Hilliard to get the union off his back or he'd run him out of the paper.

"The Guild came to me, and I said I had no problems," Hilliard said. "They said they knew I was. I told them I was happy and they were not going to get any information from me."

Hilliard asked J. Richard Nokes, the city editor, if any openings were available in the newsroom. None were, but Nokes, aware of Hilliard's problems in the sports department, brought Hilliard over to the city desk as a religion and general assignment reporter as soon as possible.

John E. Guernsey, a longtime reporter who retired in the 1980s, remembers when Hilliard joined the news staff.

"It was tough," he said. "There were comments, issues he had to deal with. Not everyone was supportive. But an assistant city editor took Bill under his wing, and it was understood that if anyone gave Bill crap, they'd answer to him. That stopped most of it, or at least drove it underground."

In 1959, the Guild authorized a strike against The Oregonian and the evening paper, the Oregon Journal.

"Most of us had no beef against The Oregonian," Hilliard said. "But we felt compelled to support the craft unions. I hated them. They were a bunch of bigots who put up with me only because I worked in the newsroom. I felt guilty walking out, because the paper had been good to me."

Hilliard stayed out for five months and worked for a time as a longshoreman. Other striking reporters told Hilliard that he should return to the paper because he had more at stake than they did. They had other opportunites that Hilliard did not. Hilliard returned to the paper.

Now, new pressures arose. The black-power movement was sweeping the nation, and Hilliard faced scrutiny from inside and outside the newsroom, Guernsey recalled.

"The whole country was at unrest over civil rights and Martin Luther King," he said. "There was a lot of struggle and strife, and as the only black on the paper, Bill got caught in it.

"Parts of the black community considered Bill an Uncle Tom because he ran in the white community," Guernsey said. "That was tough. A bunch of us played golf every Monday, and I got to know Bill very, very well on the course. We'd talk and some of the things he heard pained him.

"Some days he would do all the talking; others he wouldn't say a word, but we could tell he was angry," Guernsey said. "I don't think I would have handled it as well. If I had to name on one hand the super humans that I've met in life, people that have the components that I consider important, Bill would be on that hand."

Hilliard has heard criticism from the black community throughout his career. The complaint is that he's not involved enough in black issues and that he has not been a leader within the community.

It's one issue that makes Hilliard angry.

"I have no desire to be a black leader in this community," he said. "I prefer that anything I do be seen through The Oregonian and what it does. A lot of the criticism of me does not reflect whatever influence I may have had on this newspaper, or what this paper has done.

"This paper was the second paper on the West Coast to cover the national meetings of the Urban League and the NAACP (National Association for the Advancement of Colored People)," he said. "We did that before The Seattle Times and the San Francisco Chronicle."

Hilliard said racial prejudice has been so damaging to blacks that some "tend to be resentful of blacks who have done well, like there is some sort of black society.

"If you're not part making a lot of noise, then you're not recognized as being black," he said. "My noise has to be heard by the whole city, not the so-called black community."

In 1965, Hilliard was offered the chance to leave reporting and become an assistant city editor. He took the position because he saw it as an opportunity to have more of a say about what was in the paper. In 1971, he was named city editor and 11 years later, the executive editor. Four years later he was named editor, with control over both news and editorial departments.

Publisher Fred A. Stickel said he made the historical choice for "a number of reasons."

"Bill was a man who had faced tremendous odds in accomplishing what he did," Stickel said. "I saw a strength and tremendous dedication to his job and The Oregonian. There was never any doubt about his loyalty to the paper or to me."

Hilliard recalled being "stunned."

"There were people who were getting very political about the position," Hilliard said. "I never thought I would be editor of this paper."

But the appointment, which should have been Hilliard's moment of glory, turned sour one month later, when Stickel told Hilliard that within months he planned to merge the staffs of The Oregonian and the Oregon Journal and close the Journal.

Stickel said that no staff members would lose their jobs and that Hilliard had to absorb managers from the Journal and place them in key posts at The Oregonian. The ultimate effect was to prevent Hilliard from assembling his own management team.

The merger set the stage for one of the most controversial, turbulent and troubling times in Hilliard's career.

When it was over Stickel, would once more make history, this time by choosing a person from outside the organization -- something that had never been done -- to be the next editor of the paper.

Hilliard believes that one of his qualities as an editor was his ability to pick people for the right job. Yet none of his proteges were chosen to succeed him.

"Bill picked a lot of good people, but they didn't succeed him because of tension in the newsroom," Stickel said. "I went outside the paper because I felt it was time for The Oregonian to change, substantively. If I stayed with an inside succession, nothing would change. I had no complaint with the product, but the whole culture of the newsroom had to be changed, and I had to find the strongest editor I could find to lead that change."

Some people say that because of the merger, no one will know what kind of editor Hilliard would have been. They say he was dealt a hand of cards and told to play them.

Others say that Hilliard's personality worked against him. He operated behind the scenes and was not seen as a take-charge leader with a plan for the paper. What power he had began to slip away as others saw an opportunity to fill the void. The result was that the paper drifted while the newsroom split into camps as people jockeyed for power.

Hilliard said the merger forced him to stop implementing many of the changes he had planned for the paper.

"It was a pretty rough time," he said. "Without the merger, things would have been a lot different here. But that isn't the way it went. It went the other way."

During Hilliard's tenure, he carried out the publisher's goal to start suburban zoned coverage. The paper also hired columnists and featured more in-depth and investigative reporting. Circulation grew. Minority employment at the paper has increased 168 percent, from 45 minority employees to 121.

Did any of this matter to readers?

Few people will go on the record when they talk about The Oregonian under Hilliard.

One who will is John Armstrong, who worked at the paper in the 1950s as a reporter and later as an editor. Armstrong left during the strike and was later the news director at KOIN (6) and a journalism professor at the University of Portland.

"Number 1, the days of the all-powerful editor are over," he said. "Anyone who has been an editor of a paper in the last 20 years has had a hell of a hard job. That said, The Oregonian is one that shows flashes of greatness, but is not a great paper."

Another observer, however, had this to say:

"There's nothing glamorous about setting up bureaus in the suburbs to lock up the market, which the paper has done," he said. "You don't get Pulitzers for that, but that's a successful newspaper.

"Bill has left The Oregonian in an incredibly strong position," he said. "There are much more celebrated papers in bad shape. The Oregonian is in great shape. There are different ways to look at success."

In 1993, Hilliard was named president of the American Society of Newspaper Editors.

Again, he was the first black to hold that post.

As his successor -- Sandra M. Rowe -- took the reins of The Oregonian, Hilliard turned his attention to the editors organization. During the last year, he has been little more than a figurehead at The Oregonian.

To much of the staff, he remains an enigma.

At his request no fanfare will mark his leaving The Oregonian. No good-byes to the staff, no public acknowledgment of what he has accomplished.

And so, his moment of glory came not in Portland, not at the paper where he battled discrimination to rise to the top, but nearly 2,000 miles away at the ASNE annual meeting in Washington, D.C.

"The Oregonian did not fire a white male reporter to make room for me," Hilliard told the editors in his farewell address. "And I was not promoted at the expense of more competent or deserving colleagues. Nobody lost because I succeeded. On the contrary, I want to believe that, over the years, scores of young people of color have looked at me and said, 'It can happen.'"

At a luncheon banquet, Hilliard met with President Clinton, the guest speaker, and then made the formal introduction to the assembled editors.

"Ladies and gentlemen, the president of the United States, accompanied by Bill Hilliard."

The president of the United States. And Bill Hilliard.

When Hilliard relinquished his national post, the incoming president, Gregory E. Favre, said Hilliard "has been a leader who has served with grace and passion, with energy and vision. He has served with a sense of sharing and a sense of caring.

"And because of Bill and many others in this room and newspapers across the nation, we no longer are stumbling around in the total darkness of exclusion.

"Throughout his career, Bill has helped plant the seeds that have blossomed in our newsrooms, seeds of all colors, both genders, all ages, all desires, a broad range of human experiences. Seeds of diversity."

Favre then handed Hilliard a package. Inside was a silver gavel. The editors applauded and gave Hilliard a standing ovation.

Hilliard fought back tears.

The last vestiges of power have been removed from Hilliard's office. Work crews have put drywall over a door to an adjoining office. Painters have touched up the walls. His blue leather sofa now sits in the lobby outside the executive suites.

No one knows how the space will be used. Maybe it will be turned into a conference room.

In less than three hours, Hilliard will leave The Oregonian and his story will end.

He is not sad.

Thoughtful.

Reflective.

But not sad.

He regrets that Stephen Wright didn't live long enough to see him here. The man saw something in a little boy, nurtured a dream and helped it come true.

Hilliard shakes his head.

He says he's an emotional man. He just doesn't like to show his feelings, and he doesn't want to break down.

Beyond his office, out in the newsroom, reporters and editors are producing a paper.

"They are a part of me," he says. "I'll see their names in the paper, and I'll never leave The Oregonian."

He turns back to his desk.

He has papers to sort, boxes to pack. And time is passing too swiftly.

THE BARBER

The cards tell the real story.

In the quiet moments -- when he'd cleaned his clippers, snapped off the lights and locked his door for the night -- Bob Schlick headed to his Beaverton home and mulled over a question: Do people like me?

He had a steady customer base at his shop on the mezzanine level of the PacWest Center in downtown Portland. A man doesn't survive for 44 years as a barber without talent. He'd stayed relevant, changing from crewcuts to flowing locks to something in between.

But Schlock, 64, a quiet and proper gentleman, couldn't help but compare himself to other cutters he'd known through the decades. The ones who were so easygoing, so quick with a joke and able to carry on conversations with their customers.

Barbering is an intimate act. A man puts hands on you and gets to know you from your reflection, glancing into your eyes in the mirror to make a connection. Did customers, Schlick wondered, come to him only because he was convenient and competent? Or did they like him? A wise man, Schlick knew it was a foolish question.

And so he shared his concerns only with Lynn, his wife of 34 years.

On Oct. 27, Schlick's life would be forever altered. He'd lose a piece of himself.

But he'd also get the answer to his nagging question.

———◆———

Schlick was heading into the city on Southwest Scholls Ferry Road near the Portland Golf Club about 6:40 a.m., when he realized that a sport utility vehicle had veered into his lane. Knowing he was in danger, Schlick laid down his motorcycle -- going into a controlled slide along the pavement -- to avoid getting hit head-on. When he stopped, he looked down. His left leg was tucked under him -- attached to his body only by strands of muscle.

"I picked it up and laid it where it was supposed to be," he said. "The pain was excruciating. When the EMT arrived on the scene, he almost lost it. I don't think he'd ever seen anything like this."

A team of doctors met Schlick in an OHSU Hospital operating room. One showed Schlick an X-ray and explained that everything had been shredded away. They could try to save the leg, but it would be risky. Even if they managed to reattach it, Schlick would face nearly two more years of surgeries.

"I told them to take it," Schlick said. "I needed to cut my losses."

While he was in the operating room, his wife went to his shop -- Pac West Hair Design -- to post a note on the door about the accident. On the way out, she grabbed his appointment book.

Back at the hospital, she waited for news from the operating room and began calling customers. Four people had come to the shop but found the doors locked. She called 30 others who had appointments that week and then began notifying still others listed in the book.

When Schlick came out of surgery, he contemplated his future. Doctors said he'd need more operations. Sometime next year, when the wound finally healed, he'd be fitted with a prosthesis.

Unable to stand, he couldn't cut hair for months.

In just weeks -- on Monday, Dec. 1 -- Schlick would turn 65. Maybe it was time to call it a career. In a fickle world, why would his customers wait?

The first card arrived the next day.

It was from one of his clients, an attorney in a firm in the building, who wrote that there were no words to express how concerned he was for the man who cut his hair.

Schlick's wife put the card on the window sill.

During the next few weeks, nurses brought in stacks of cards. Hundreds. All from customers. Word, it seemed, had spread that Bob Schlick was in trouble.

Whatever you need. Come back. I need a haircut.

Flowers and telephone calls.

Each day, Schlick learned something more about his customers and their hearts.

"Thank you for being a ray of sunshine."

"Your smile and wave makes our day bright. Don't lose that gift."

"We realize the little, but significant impact others have on our lives."

In one way or another, the cards all said the same thing: When you come back, we'll be there.

Schlick had never cried over the loss of his leg.

But the cards?

He couldn't stop the tears.

———————

On Wednesday, Schlick went home. He must stay in bed for two weeks. A Washington County grand jury will review the accident. Medical bills are piling up, and insurance companies are getting involved.

He plans to be back at work in late January. He's looking for a stool that will allow him to sit and cut hair.

He has to get back.

His customers are waiting.

Life's been so hectic the past few weeks, his wife has been unable to stock the pantry, let alone plan a Thanksgiving meal.

So today, she'll root around the cupboards and throw something together.

It will be just the two of them.

The cards tell another story.

THE LAST BUFFALO SOLDIER

God, he hated the name and all it represented. Who hung it on him?

In the early morning, as his head throbbed with the familiar pain brought on by too much whiskey, Vinegar Red tried to figure out what had gone wrong last night.

Like most recent evenings, it had ended in a fight. Not with a stranger this time, but with his wife.

"What's bothering you?" she had asked.

"Nothin'," replied Vinegar Red.

But she knew. Oh, how that woman knew. For some time she had been picking away at him, trying to get him to talk, to open up and spill the secrets that caused such hurt.

"Nothin'" was all Vinegar Red would say.

Most of the time she catered to him. Last night, however, she pleaded, then yelled. And Vinegar Red, fueled by liquor and frustration, matched her word for word until, finally exhausted, they both shut up.

His wife wanted him to put down roots and make a home. Impossible. For Vinegar Red knew if he stopped moving, his past would find him. His past would haunt him.

Like this name "Vinegar Red."

God, he hated it and all it represented. Who hung it on him? Jabo Martin? Oklahoma Slim? The Black Diamond? Didn't matter. All these years it had stuck. Just like that other name.

"Nigger."

Vinegar Red never talked about his past. He just wanted to forget. But he'd see something or hear something or maybe a memory would just

111

bubble up and then the past would be right there saying, "How's it going, Vinegar Red?"

And he would move on.

Texas, Arizona, California, North Dakota, Georgia, Arkansas, Louisiana, Tennessee . . . hell, where hadn't he been?

Now, as he sobered up, he knew it was time to leave this place, Albuquerque, N.M.

Florida.

Just popped into his mind.

Weren't no cowboys in Florida.

No one knew Vinegar Red.

Florida.

Worth considering.

About then his wife woke up.

"Jeff," she called out. "What's wrong?"

"Nothin'," said Vinegar Red.

———◆———

That night he went looking for a place to drink, which always helped him forget. Only in the mornings did he remember and wonder how it, how he, had come to this.

"Give out, son," his father had always preached, "but don't give up."

He thought a lot about his father these days, a life in Manor, Texas, a small town near Austin, where he was known as Jeff Parks, not Vinegar Red.

He ordered a straight shot and let the fire fill his belly while his mind drifted back to another time and place.

What was he, he thought, all of about 5 when he first realized what the color of his skin meant? Yeah, about 5. He and Daddy had gone into town and had walked by a group of white men when one called Daddy "nigger."

Jeff didn't know the word. But when he looked into his father's eyes, he saw pain and humiliation. And if he was just like Daddy, what was he?

After that, whatever innocence he'd held about life in Manor in the 1920s vanished. His parents showed him the parts of town where he wasn't welcome. They pointed out the signs, "Whites only" and "Colored," and taught him to use the side door in restaurants and sit quietly in the back. They were lessons taught not in anger but in resignation and recognition of life as it was.

His father held out hope for a better life. Not for himself, but for his son.

"Give out, son," he'd say, "but don't give up."

Now, as he sat in the bar, Vinegar Red wondered if he had given up and what his father would say if he could see him sitting there intent only on getting drunk.

His father was a rancher, and Jeff took after him, rising early for chores before walking to the colored school where he first heard the legend of the Buffalo Soldiers.

Brave and tough, these colored men had continued to serve in the U.S. Army after the Civil War. They fought the Comanches and rescued homesteaders under attack during the settlement of Texas. The Indians, who had never seen such men, called them the Buffalo Soldiers because their kinky hair looked like the dense hair on buffalo hides.

When he heard the stories, Jeff decided he wanted to be like them, a cowboy, a Buffalo Soldier.

He was good with animals and considered that his ticket out of Manor. He didn't plan to spend his life saying, "Yes, sir, that's right, sir," to men he knew were no better than he. No way was he going to use a side door.

When he was 16, Jeff headed for a New Mexico ranch that was hiring. He learned to operate trucks, tractors and other heavy machinery. On the weekends, he entered Negro rodeos held near the ranch.

He liked the fairness of the rodeo. The best man won. That didn't happen outside the ring. This small New Mexico town was no different than Manor. He was a colored, in some people's eyes no better than an animal. So he quit the ranch and followed his love, the rodeo.

Oklahoma, Alabama, Mississippi, Colorado.

Small events called jackpot rodeos, these gatherings of Negro cowboys were held all over through the spring and summer. Each entrant had to toss $20 into the pot, winner take all. When Jeff ran out of rodeo winnings, he'd stop somewhere, work a while and then move on. When the rodeos ended in the winter, he'd find a job running heavy equipment until the spring, when he was off again.

He was a star, and the kids from the colored sections of town would come watch him ride bulls and bucking broncs, wrestle steers and rope calves.

Once in a while, his travels would take him near places where a whites-only rodeo was being held. He'd stand outside the ring and watch, knowing he could beat them if he only had a chance.

In one small town he tried entering a rodeo. He walked up to the organizers and said he wanted to ride. They stared at him as if he were crazy. Then they laughed and told the nigger to get lost.

He didn't want trouble. He did what they said. He moved on.

He couldn't always walk away. A Negro traveling alone was an easy target. He was beaten up, cut with a knife and threatened with a gun. There wasn't much to do about it. Who could he go to for protection? The police? He had no rights. He was a colored man living in a white world.

The anger smoldered inside until finally it caught fire. Over time, he began hitting back. He began using his own knife.

He took out his frustrations on the rodeo. He rode harder than anyone. He accepted any challenge. He was very good but not very friendly.

One day at a rodeo, he heard someone call out "Vinegar Red."

He looked around. They were calling to him. He ignored them. He cornered a few of them.

What's with this name? he asked.

Well, they said, your skin is lighter than ours, almost a hint of red in it. And you're so mean and sour-looking. Like vineger.

Yeah, so what? he said.

Well, that's your name now, they said.

Vinegar Red.

———◆———

He hated the name. It seared like a brand, reminding him of all that was wrong with his life.

He became a loner. Life revolved around the rodeo, an occasional job and the road. As a kid, he had allowed himself to dream that he could be anything. Now, he knew different. He knew what his future held.

As long as he kept moving, it didn't hurt. Only when he stopped did he feel pain.

No one knew what he thought or felt. He liked it that way. He never showed any emotion. Other riders came and went, weary of the road. Vinegar Red rode on.

He became one of the best. But the praise always came as one of the best Negro cowboys; Vinegar Red wasn't allowed to ride against the whites.

Occasionally, he'd get a call from a white promoter offering him a chance to ride an exhibition at an all-white rodeo. He was a good draw. A Negro cowpoke was something to gawk at.

If he stayed on a bull that hadn't been ridden before, he'd get as much as $500; if he fell off, nothing. He always accepted. To ride was to show what he could do.

He'd enter the arena and someone would realize that the Negro was going to ride. The catcalls would start, quiet at first, then louder.

"Get that nigger out of here."

Someone threw a bottle.

Vinegar Red kept walking.

"We didn't come to see a nigger."

The promoter was out back, maybe wondering if it was worth it. Things were getting out of hand.

Vinegar Red concentrated.

"I hope the nigger gets hurt."

He eased himself down onto the bull's back.

And then Vinegar Red rode.

That bull shook and bucked, and Vinegar Red had to use every trick his daddy had showed him breaking horses on the ranch.

Move with the animal. Become one. Don't fight it. No time to think. All instinct. Up there on that bull, there was no doubt he was good.

Then it was over.

He'd push himself off the still heaving beast, fall to the ground, stand up and brush the dirt from his pants. A smattering of applause, a few boos. Vinegar Red didn't give a damn. Just get the money and move on.

For years it went on. The Negro circuit, a job for the winter, a rare exhibition, and the road. Finally, in the 1950s, the white rodeos began allowing Negroes to enter.

Vinegar Red was in his 30s, and his body was beat up and worn out. But he couldn't wait to prove himself. At the Albuquerque State Fair, he finished first in some events, rankling some whites who believed no Negro could be top cowboy.

He began traveling the white circuit. He knew his days in the saddle were ending, and he had to show what he could do. But nothing got easier. In some places, the judges scored him just low enough so the white would win. Other times, the promoter wouldn't pay his winnings or his fair share.

He didn't complain. Time was running out. He moved on, hoping for better luck in the next town, the next event.

In restaurants, he was forced to sit in the colored section. When hotels wouldn't rent him a room he'd go to the colored part of town and hope somebody would let him bed down. If not, he'd sleep in his car.

He married a woman who followed him for a while, then asked him to quit. He rode a few more events, stopped and got a job running bulldozers and dump trucks.

He tried to settle down, but without the rodeo the anger had no place to go. Restless and frustrated, he told his wife he wanted to move.

So began an odyssey that took them from state to state to state. Vinegar Red always found something wrong. The town was too big or too small. He couldn't make enough money, or it cost too much to live.

His wife never understood. Vinegar Red did. The problem was with him. He couldn't come to terms with the frustrations, the taunts and the lost opportunities.

He told himself to forget it but found the past wasn't dead. He couldn't forget. The past, he found, was alive.

So he ran from it.

One night, he was in an Albuquerque bar when a man challenged him to a fight. Words were exchanged, then a few shoves. The man pulled a gun. Vinegar Red saw the barrel just inches from his face. The bar fell silent. The patrons backed away.

Vinegar Red stared at the man. He laughed. Then spoke.

"Shoot me."

For an instant, the man hesitated.

In that instant, Vinegar Red reached out and up, grabbed the man's wrists and wrestled the gun away.

But instead of throwing it to the floor, he held it. His palm wrapped around the butt, his fingers found the trigger. At that moment his rage boiled over and he swung the gun toward the man.

He pulled the trigger.

Click.

Click.

Click.

Click.

———•———

He took the gun's misfiring as a sign to move on. He thought of Florida, and he and his wife ended up in a Tampa motel room.

Although Vinegar Red got a steady job working heavy equipment, the frustrations, the fights and the drinking never stopped. One day, he left his wife and went looking for a place where he could be happy.

Arkansas. Alabama. Missouri. North Dakota.

He did odd jobs, gambled and drank away what he earned, then moved on. He landed in Salinas, Calif., and heard about a bull that hadn't been ridden. He rode it but was hooked by the bull's horn and thrown against the chute. He broke his shoulder and fractured his skull.

He knew his days as a cowboy were over and returned to his wife. She wasn't going to put up with this any longer, she said. He wanted to change but couldn't. They fought one night and Vinegar Red left for good.

He started driving, not caring where he went, just so long as it was away. He ended up in Atlanta, found a bar and got drunk. Hours later he stumbled out to his car.

Where to go?

He opened his glove box and found a United States map. He turned on the overhead light and stared at the country. He wanted to find someplace far from his past.

He picked Portland, Maine.

He put the map away, drove to a service station and asked for directions.

"Portland," he slurred. "Want to go to Portland."

They showed him the way to the freeway. He drove in a drunken stupor, stopping only when he needed gas, directions to Portland, or a drink.

He sobered up somewhere in Utah and realized he was headed west, to Portland, Oregon.

Well, he thought, never been there. Why not keep going?

He arrived in the city on a rainy night and wondered if he had made a mistake. The town looked as miserable as he felt. He took stock of himself. He had the clothes on his back, a car and a hell of a hangover.

He pulled out his wallet.

He took out all the money he had. One by one he counted the bills.

$8.

———◆———

Vinegar Red ceased to exist. He never returned to his wife. He introduced himself as Jeff Parks and said nothing about his past.

Portland's blacks had no use for him. It was the 1960s, black power and Afro haircuts. And here was this guy with a Southern accent and a cowboy hat. He was known as "the black cowboy," a name meant to ridicule.

He went looking for work, but the union always said he was just one spot away from being sent out on a job, always, he noticed, just behind a white man.

When black activists threatened to sue, the union relented and found spots for blacks, including Parks.

Some people in the black community thought he was strange. A few of them owned cowboy boots, but only Parks had the boots, the hat, the belt buckles and the walk that looked as if he had just climbed off a horse.

Some thought him a joke. He'd be drinking, hear the heckling and turn to see men pointing at him while women laughed.

"Niggers can't be cowboys."

He'd ignore them.

"Nigger, get out of that suit. You some kind of hillbilly?"

Then one of the men would push it, walk over and tease him up close. Parks wouldn't say a word. Just start punching.

Children brought out his gentle side. He bought a horse that he rode weekends. Right down the center of the street and through the parks.

Portland kids had never seen a black cowboy. They'd spot him and chase him until he stopped. Some had never been close to a horse. He'd let them touch the animal, lift them up and let them sit in the saddle.

"Mister, are you a real cowboy?" they'd ask.

"Once was."

That's all. Then he'd jump on his horse and be gone.

Adults didn't know what to make of him. He'd ride his horse into a tavern, order a drink then ride away. He carried two guns in holsters. Some said they were toys. Others said they were real. No one wanted to find out.

Distant was the best way to describe Parks. He'd make conversation, but he'd never open up and talk about life before Portland. To many, he was just the funny-looking cowboy dude.

It went on this way for years.

In time, Parks retired, found he was bored and got a job at the Royal Esquire Club, a black social club on Northeast Alberta Street near 17th Avenue.

One day he learned the club hadn't paid its loans and the bank was ready to foreclose. He considered buying the place but wondered at his sanity. After all, he was near 70 and the business was in sad shape.

The building itself needed work and was in the middle of a high-crime area. Drug dealers, gang members and prostitutes controlled the streets. After dark, good people were afraid to leave their homes.

Parks wrestled with his options.

Don't get involved.

Do it.

In the end, he listened to his heart. He put down roots.

<hr />

Banks don't consider drifters good risks. But a club member who worked for the bank persuaded loan officers to give Parks a break.

He remodeled the building himself. He improved the bar and made a restaurant and social area where families and young people could come.

When he was done, he had business cards made up.

"The Texas Restaurant and Lounge," they read. "Jeff Parks. Owner."

He could hardly believe it.

"Owner."

By day, business was good. At night, however, there were shootings and fights. Drugs and sex were sold and traded. Parks called police. It didn't help. Officers made arrests, but the criminals came back.

Parks worried about the older people who lived in the neighborhood, the men and women his age. He worried about the families and the children. All of them, he thought, held hostage.

One night, Parks knew what he had to do.

He put on his cowboy hat. He put on his leather vest. He slipped on his cowboy boots. He buckled his big belt. Then he walked out of his bar and stood on the sidewalk.

Vinegar Red, the last Buffalo Soldier, was ready to ride again.

He crossed Alberta Street, this funny-looking cowboy dude, and stopped in front of a group of drug dealers.

"Leave," he said.

"What?" they said.

"Leave," said Vinegar Red.

They looked at this guy, old enough to be their grandfather.

They laughed.

"Leave the area," said Vinegar Red.

He turned and walked away.

Every night he was out there. So were the dealers.

Showdown.

The dealers wanted him to go away. He was bad for business, made their customers nervous.

Vinegar Red was crossing the street one night when he heard a motor roar and tires squeal. He looked up to see a car heading toward him. It swerved at the last moment.

He never broke stride. He thought of bulls he had tamed over the years and how a bull is tougher than any man alive.

The prostitutes and their pimps cursed and threatened him.

He ignored them. He remembered how he had once heard far worse in small towns across the South.

People threw bottles at him.

He never ducked. No bottle ever stopped him in the past. It wouldn't happen now.

Someone shot at him.

But Vinegar Red was out there the next night.

Night after night, week after week, it went on. Aren't you afraid? people asked.

He smiled. He shook his head.

"I fear no man," he said.

One night, Vinegar Red stood on the sidewalk and looked up and down the street. They had moved on.

From where he stood, he could hear sounds floating out of his tavern. His business.

Music. Laughter. Happy sounds.

The old cowboy took one last look at the street, then turned and walked inside.

THE WOODSMAN

Almost everybody he knew in his youth is dead. What remains are the words.

He sits in a small room in the back of this cabin he built by hand nearly 45 years ago and waits. He's a widower whose only companion is Dolly, the dog he rescued after somebody dumped her out of a car near his place.

Each day Herbert Miller's world shrinks. He can't drive because his eyes are bad, and he needs a magnifying glass to read even large-print publications. He doesn't miss the television he gave away when he could no longer see the images on the screen. Almost everybody he knew in his youth is dead.

What remains are the words that take him back to the mines and the logging camps, the woods and the rivers. The words, he's discovered, are more precious than the gold he once searched for in Alaska, California and Mexico. They are elusive, these words, but he is patient. A man lives to be 100 -- he's a century old today -- and he discovers a truth about time that has nothing to do with clocks and calendars.

But no words will come today. He's learned to let them appear when they're ready. When they do, he captures them with pencil and tablet. Hunting and pecking with one finger frustrated him, and he gave his typewriter away years ago.

The words don't come as easily as they once did. His time, he knows, is drawing to an end. Before he passes on, he'd like to write a final story. To leave pieces of his grand adventure behind.

He eases himself out of the love seat and moves to the kitchen. The man who used to roam the Coast Range hunting bobcats and trapping animals for their fur is afraid of falling. He walks cautiously, with two canes.

Back in the old days, he was a legend. His appendix broke while trapping and the pain was so terrible that he couldn't walk. He crawled under a log and spent the night in the woods. The next day he made his way to town, where he spent 18 days in the hospital. Three weeks later he was back out in the firs and cedars.

He steps into his front yard and lifts his face to the sun. A burgundy and white flannel shirt covers a thin frame. A belt cinched tight holds up his brown pants, its leather tip dangling. A brown, baseball-style cap is pulled down low, hiding his eyes. He stands about 5 feet 7, but is hunched over. He starts each day guided by thoughts he's used through the years: "Don't overeat, speak no mean words and don't kick no one's dog."

"That last one could cover a lot of territory," he says.

"Think about it."

As a young man, Hub Miller scratched out a living for his wife and their two children by dabbling in more than 40 jobs. Among them: window washer, gravedigger, deputy marshal, gunsmith and truck driver. In the dusk of his life, though, he's a writer, looking for words.

He took a writing class at the community college on a whim when he was in his early 70s. The words, he discovered, not only gave him a way to make sense of the past, but also became the way for him to leave a legacy, a memorial to the time that he was here. He had a column in the local newspaper and became a bit of an institution. The Tillamook Senior Center will throw a party in his honor today from 1 to 3 p.m.

He also wrote poems and stories, some published in the Mother Earth News and the American Rifleman, as well as in national publications specializing in hunting and trapping. He self-published a collection of his work, and a few weeks ago the commissioners named him Tillamook County's poet laureate.

"You're not going to get blue skies and daisies with me," he says. "None of that. What you get with me is reality."

"Widows and Widowers" begins with this stanza:

Some several weeks ago,
To a meeting I did go

And looked around to see what I could see.
T'was a dozen friendly widows
Sitting in a row,
And three or four old codgers just like me.

He smiles when he hears the verse.

"Love, the nice stuff?" he asks. "That's not what I write about.

"I think about stories all the time, ordinary happenings."

He steadies himself, holding his canes. "Even though I'm crippled up now," he says, "stories make my spirit buoyant."

Miller steps off the city's dial-a-ride bus, focusing on the placement of each foot. The Tillamook Senior Center's president, who's been watching for him, descends concrete steps and offers her arm. But he shakes his head. Five minutes after starting this little journey, he sits in a chair next to a wall heater and lays his canes on the table. He made them himself out of driftwood he spotted on the beach. "Never had store bought," he says. "These are good enough."

He's been a widower for nearly 20 years. Even though his son and daughter don't live in the area, they call often and come to visit when they can. Miller waves off talk about his family life. "We won't go into that," he says. "That's personal history. But what I tell you is accurate and true. I've been on everything from a covered wagon to an airplane."

His parents lived on a homestead near Roseburg. His grandparents brought him to Bay City in 1907, where his grandfather, a doctor, built Tillamook Bay Hospital. His parents joined them in 1909. His mother was the community's first telephone operator and ran the operation out of her house. Miller liked to hang out in the general store listening to trappers and hunters talk about life in the woods. His writing imparts not just the facts of a bygone era, but also the texture of life in what was still a frontier community.

"Second Look" deals with Miller's work on a road crew in the 1930s. No heavy machinery, just men and horses living in a camp far from civilization. The men passed around a newspaper called Heart and Hand, a collection of ads from men and woman who wanted to get married. A one-eyed laborer named Red decided to contact Molly, described in her ad as tall, good looking and an excellent cook.

He wrote to her, and they exchanged letters for a few weeks. Then he sent her money for train fare to the village, two miles from our camp.

Molly takes the train to the camp and is met by Red, Miller and a friend named Jack. On the way there, Miller picks a handful of roses.

The train stopped, only one passenger stepped off. She walked towards us, a tall, thin woman as red-haired and freckled as Red himself, and almost unbelievably, it was apparent that she, too, had an artificial eye.

Jack walked away. Red and Molly looked at each other for a long moment that I thought would never end. Then she looked down, just stood there, thin shoulders slumped forward. Suddenly I felt a strong surge of pity for this ill-favored woman in this uncertain predicament, and angry at Red for prolonging it.

What in the hell is he going to do, standing there like a dolt?" Then, he took her hand and held it. I gave her the roses. Red said "Molly, I thought that you might not come."

She blushed, as only the fair-skinned can.

Winter had passed, and it was spring. Suddenly I thought, she's not really homely, in fact, she is almost beautiful. An illusion? Perhaps.

And then what happened?

"Let me think a second here," Miller says. "I'm kind of getting it now. They were later married. Yes, they settled down together. It took a little urging, but it got me going. I remember meeting that train."

He closes his eyes.

"Hub, would you like some hot chocolate?" the club president asks.

"That would be nice."

He takes a sip and sets the mug on the desk. He reaches over and turns up the dial on the wall heater. He closes his eyes and clasps his hands in his lap as if praying. He's here, but not here, a man from another time.

He returns home carrying what remains of his lunch at the senior center. He pets Dolly and lingers outside, enjoying the warmth. "I'll live one day at a time out here until I die," he says. "At this age, I don't make plans."

He extends his hand.

"Strong grip, eh?" he says with a laugh. "I still use a chainsaw to cut my firewood."

He still makes his own breakfast and lunch, too. And he takes care of his dinner with the food he brings home from the senior center.

He steadies himself between his canes.

"Every boy has a dream of who he will be," Hub Miller says. "When I was a young man, my ambition was to be on a fur-trading boat in the north county, and by God, I made it. And then I had this notion for stories."

He looks at his little cabin in the woods, at the wild salmonberries he will pick for his breakfast.

"I want people to remember me," he says. "Some will and some won't. I know that. Once you pass away, you're forgotten. But maybe someone will read my stories. I know they'll never be classics.

"But they matter," he says. "They matter."

Fire Death

There's a stillness on this side of the yellow tape

There was this brief moment Sunday morning when all was right in their world. A before, an after. A time when they were able to stand on the other side of the yellow line.

And then came this early-morning phone call that shattered the silence in their home. The boy's grandfather was on the line, in a panic, asking Thomas Faull about a deadly house fire and desperately wanting to know if the boy was at home. Of course, he wasn't.

Faull remembers hanging up and awakening his wife, Shirlien. They threw on clothes, anything they could find lying around their Fairview home, and ran to get Hannah, their 2-year-old, from her bed. Faull drove like a madman all the way to Milwaukie. As he turned onto the 3500 block of Southeast Concord Road off McLoughlin Boulevard, he saw firetrucks, police and crowds.

He parked his car and ran toward the mobile home park where his stepson, Shanan Vockrodt, had spent Saturday night with his wife's aunt, Deloris Priest, a 73-year-old childless woman who lived alone. She considered Shanan, who just turned 11, her surrogate son, and he frequently spent the night with her. They both considered it a treat. As Faull ran down the street, his wife hurrying to catch up, he saw smoke coming from Priest's home. When he reached the edge of the trailer park's driveway, a cop stopped him.

You can't come in here.

Our son's in there.

He remembers the police officer lifting the tape, the plastic barrier officials use to surround areas where bad things happen. And just like that, with one simple little step, Faull and his wife moved into the world that exists on the other side of the yellow line.

The boy and his great-aunt were dead, victims of smoke inhalation. Their bodies remained in the home while investigators tromped in and out. Capt. Jamie Karn of the Clackamas County Fire Department said no one knew how or where the fire started. His department got the call at 5:28 a.m. There was no smoke detector in the home. When firefighters got inside, they found Priest in the front and Shanan in the back.

"He was in the bathroom," Faull says. "The water was running in the bathroom. He must have been so scared."

There's a certain stillness on this side of the yellow tape. Investigators and firefighters huddle, talk quietly and haul equipment in and out of the house. They tell the medical examiner who is waiting to take the bodies to the morgue that it will be a while.

"I'm holding my own," Faull says. "I have to be strong for my wife. I've got to be there for her. That was her firstborn."

The randomness of being here haunts Faull. Right now, about 11 in the morning, he should be picking up Shanan to go to church. And then for a swim. That was the plan.

"See, he comes here a lot on the weekends to spend time with Aunt D," Faull says. "And then when school's out, he always spends the first week of summer with her. He's been doing that since he's been a baby. He came out on Friday night. This was going to be a good week for him."

Family friends gather around, talking about Shanan in the present tense.

"He's going to be in the fifth grade."

"He loves to draw."

"He loves animals."

Faull says Shanan had autism but was highly functioning and attended the Multi-Sensory Learning Academy, a charter school in Gresham. He just happens to have the boy's yearbook in the car. He points to Shanan's photograph.

"He is, I mean was," Faull says, "an easygoing boy."

Life doesn't stop behind the line.

Someone gently asks Faull about funeral arrangements. He starts to say something, but hems and haws. The pastor from their church, the one the family knew so well, just moved out of state. Faull isn't sure how he's even going to pay for the funeral. He was just laid off from his job as shop manager for a painting contractor. His wife, who is pregnant, works reduced hours as a cashier at Wal-Mart.

"To be honest," he says. "We live paycheck to paycheck. We're not wealthy people. We just found out last Monday that we're going to have another girl."

"The baby's due in October," he says with a smile. "Shanan would have liked another sister."

Faull paces, nodding when a friend pats him on the shoulder. He walks over to cradle his daughter, still in her pajamas, and sets her stuffed animal on the hood of a car.

"I know how life is," he says. "They're going to have to bring his body out, and I want to be here for him. I asked if I could go in and see him, just to hold him, just to pick him up one more time. They wouldn't let me. They said he wasn't viewable."

A group of well-dressed men and women skirt the outside of the yellow line. A trailer park resident, an elderly man, died of cancer and a memorial is about to start in the park's recreation center.

One life lived to the full, the other cut too short.

Bookends on a Sunday.

Shirlien Faull has been trying to stay warm in the car. She comes outside to see how things are going in the mobile home, the one with an American flag on the front.

"My son is everything to me," his mother says. "Every breath I've taken in the last 11 years has been for him. If I could just go in there and hold him, I almost feel like I could make it better."

Heather Hummell, her best friend and Shanan's godmother, stands beside her.

"I know he's trying to be there for me," Faull says of her husband. "He's OK for now. But he's not really OK."

She starts to cry.

"It really hurts," she says as she rubs her stomach and feels the life within her stir.

"Do you need a tissue?" her friend asks.

"I have pockets full of tissues."

She turns from the home.

"I can't do this anymore," she says. "I don't want to be here anymore."

There's a commotion down the way. Two men pushing a gurney with a little lump under a white blanket.

"He's coming out," says Faull.

"Yes, he is," whispers his wife.

HELLS ANGELS LEGEND

They don't welcome outsiders.

The first pack arrived early in the morning, the unmuffled roar from the engines echoing off buildings and setting off car alarms as they raced their choppers from the freeway off-ramp to the Sonoma County Hells Angels clubhouse. At their destination, they squealed to a stop, tires smoking, and carefully backed the bikes to the curb.

Ray-Ray, the chapter president, heard the commotion. He ignored a closed-circuit television monitor mounted on the clubhouse ceiling just above the bar. Members always keep watch over the street, alert to anyone who doesn't belong. But on this day, Ray-Ray knew that only a fool would wander down this street without an invitation.

A few citizens -- middle-class men and women, kids on bikes and families jammed into sedans -- had tried getting a better view of the clubhouse, a nondescript tan building in the middle of the block. But they'd been turned away by two beefy Hells Angels in sunglasses, who told anyone ignorant enough to cross an imaginary line that the event was a private affair. They didn't have to repeat themselves. The spectators obediently moved across the street and waited in a light rain for the spectacle to unfold.

More than 800 Angels from around the world had descended on Santa Rosa for Norm Greene's April 18 funeral. The former chapter president was the only Hells Angel ever to spend 50 years in the club.

Greene was one of the founders of a group whose roots reach back to the years when World War II veterans were starting motorcycle clubs. In 1954 one took the name of the Hells Angels B-17 bomber group. By any measure, the Angels grew into the world's most famous, feared and respected outlaw motorcycle club. All of the rituals associated with outlaw motorcycle clubs come from the Angels: colors, which are the patches worn on leather jackets and vests; the patches that read "1 percent"; and the requirement that members ride only Harley-Davidsons. From the moment motorcycle clubs came into existence, the police labeled them "bikers" and targeted them as troublemakers and criminals. In the 1960s, the American Motorcyclist Association tried to distance itself from such groups, saying they represented only 1 percent of the motorcycle-riding public. Many clubs seized on the 1 percent label as something of a badge of honor and a way to mock the establishment.

And while some Hells Angels have run afoul of the law and served prison time, much of the public sees members as modern-day cowboys who live in a brotherhood bound by loyalty and respect. The club occupies a special place in American culture. Weekend bikers who dress in leathers and put patches on their vests want to be seen as "1 percenters" even though they may be riding only to the local coffee shop.

An autobiography by Sonny Barger, the spiritual leader of the Angels, was a worldwide best-seller and is the basis for an upcoming movie on his life and the club. The Angels have incorporated and own a copyright on both their name and their familiar winged death's head insignia. Individual chapters have Internet sites and sell support items such as stickers, mugs and shirts.

Even so, the world of the Hells Angels remains cloaked in secrecy. Members don't use last names, even with one another. Just a first name. More often than not, a nickname. They greet each other with a hug, two pats on the back and sometimes a kiss on the cheek. They don't welcome outsiders.

When news of the funeral got out, the clubhouse phone started ringing. Reporters wanted details. A Hells Angel funeral always attracts attention. Members, usually just from a chapter or two, appear en masse, leading a motorcycle procession to the graveyard. But because of Greene's stature, his funeral would be unlike any that had preceded it.

Ray-Ray, an intense man with dark brown eyes, listened to the reporters' requests. He swore, two curt words, and slammed down the phone.

"We don't look for publicity," he said.

He moved out from behind the bar and made his way through the clubhouse to greet his Angel brothers and swap stories about Greene, who died April 9 of heart failure at age 75.

"He carried himself like Clint Eastwood in a movie," Ray-Ray said as he stood in a doorway, surveying the street as it filled with bikes and bikers. "He had a presence, intimidating. He walked tall and proud. He was as active in our chapter as the younger members. At the last party, he was there until 2 in the morning."

Greene, according to his daughter, forged documents and joined the Army when he was 15. After WWII, he drifted to California and lost track of his two Illinois sisters. He joined the San Francisco chapter of the Hells Angels, literally fighting his way into the club, in 1954. At the time, there was just one other chapter, in San Bernardino. Now, there are chapters all over the world. And all of them sent representatives to Santa Rosa for a funeral that would be full of what the Hells Angels value above all else: respect.

"We bury our own," said Smilin' Rick, president of the Washington State Nomads, another Hells Angels chapter. "We don't know the person doing the burying, and we don't want a stranger throwing dirt on a Hells Angel. Every Hells Angel at the cemetery shares in the burial."

He looked out the doorway. A Santa Rosa cop -- a young woman in a patrol car -- made her way down the street. She stared straight ahead, not acknowledging the Angels.

"About an hour to go," Ray-Ray said. "At high noon, we move out."

While waiting for the order, the Angels mingled in the clubhouse. When it got too full, they spilled out onto a side patio and then the street. While some drank beer or hard liquor, many drank bottled water. Few smoked cigarettes. The ground rules in the clubhouse are simple. They're not posted, but clearly understood by everyone. If it's not yours, don't touch it. If it doesn't concern you, stay out of it.

No one postures or tries to act tough. Everyone is tough. So everyone is exceedingly polite, saying "excuse me" and backing away to let someone else pass through the door first. At the same time, an electric undercurrent flows. If trouble breaks out, the Angels also live by another motto, "Taking care of business," which they do swiftly and surely. No one gets a second chance.

"I'd go anywhere to honor Norm," said Hammer Joe, a Hells Angel from Switzerland who said he dropped everything and flew to California when he heard about the funeral. "Norm was a hero."

Greene had two grandchildren and two great-grandchildren. Even to the end, he was cantankerous. When he was dying in a hospital, a nurse tried to lift the sheet off of him. He yanked it out of her hand and told her he didn't know her well enough to let her see him that way.

"He was a man's man," said John-John, the Sonoma chapter vice president. "He was intimidating to people who didn't know him, and he wasn't close to most people. He was bulletproof. And I mean that literally."

Ray-Ray laughed.

"He was cocky and cool, big and bad," he said. "Cowboy boots, Levi shirt and a knife on his side. He was a complete man, the good and the bad. He didn't hit anyone unless it was justified. The man meant something. He was a legend in our club."

The president shook his head, thinking back to the last time he'd seen Greene.

"He didn't want to talk," he said. "He didn't want to lie in a bed. He wanted to let go."

Members from Maryland and Illinois and Germany examined a memorial platform built by the Sonoma chapter in the heart of the clubhouse. Made out of hardwood, the memorial features a photograph of Greene and a plaque honoring him for his years of service to the club. His motorcycle, a gift from the club on the 40th anniversary of his membership, would be on permanent display. Ray-Ray planned to ride it one final time, at the head of the procession, to honor his friend, leader and mentor.

"He will be missed," Ray-Ray said, "but he will not be forgotten. When some people die, they can't get more than 20 people at their funeral. One week notice, and look how many people are here for Norm. He's gone, but his legend will live on forever."

Ray-Ray stepped into the street and walked to the end of the block. He climbed on Greene's motorcycle and kicked the starter. A prospective member stopped traffic on a main street and the club president led the procession four miles from the clubhouse to the funeral home. When they ran out of room in the funeral-home lot, the Angels parked their bikes on the street, sometimes blocks away, and walked. Nearby neighbors pulled up chairs in driveways to watch and take photographs.

Red and white flowers -- the colors of the Hells Angels insignia -- filled the front of the chapel. Guests studied photographs of Greene over the years and signed first names in a guest book. His daughter and his sisters sat in the front row.

"We hadn't seen our brother in more than 50 years," said Marlene Werner, from Joliet, Ill. "We thought he had died. About two years ago we searched the Internet and found him. We sent him a letter and came out to see him. We didn't know anything about the Hells Angels. It's been so wonderful today to see how many people's lives he touched. So many people have praised him."

Greene's daughter, Christine Carevich, said her father "dedicated his life to the club.

"He lived and breathed the Hells Angels," she said. "He had a soft spot in his heart for family, but he had a set of values that he believed in, and he lived up to them."

The casket was open and Greene would be buried in his colors. The Angels stopped, either one at a time or in small groups, to say a few words to Greene, wiping tears from their eyes, unashamed to show how they felt. Rusty, a Hells Angel from the Sonoma chapter, led off the service.

"Brother Stormin' Norman Greene, we will miss you," he said, "but the stories about you will be passed on by Hells Angels forever."

He said he'd first met Greene when he was just a kid and saw "patrons diving out the windows of a bar. I walked in and there were only two people in the room," Rusty said. "The bartender and a guy sitting at a table with his hands hidden. That was Norm. I remember thinking that maybe he had a .45 under his shirt."

The mourners laughed.

"Just kidding," Rusty said. "The point is, Norm was around way back then, one of the men that started the Hells Angels legacy. The old-school legendary Hells Angels who set the standards that we strive to live up to every day. The standards that define a Hells Angel today, tomorrow and forever."

He paused to gather his thoughts.

"Hells Angels are not the Boy Scouts," he said to more laughter. "And I doubt Norm ever compared felony convictions to merit badges," he said.

"He never whined about how unfair life is. If he screwed up and got caught cracking safes, or accidentally put a bullet through a guy's head in a crowded bar, he paid the price like a man does.

"If Norm was convicted of a crime, he would try to make the most out of doing time, further his education while learning a new trade and come out a wiser man," Rusty said. "With 54 felony convictions, he had the time to take a lot of classes." The crowd roared.

Rusty said Greene had a "memory for detail that a lot of ex-members found to be their undoing and the reason they are ex-members.

"If a brother was honest with him but in a pinch, he'd give the shirt off his back without thinking twice," Rusty said. "But Norm never could or would tolerate a liar or anything trying to rip off a brother."

Several women then spoke about how Greene took them under his wing.

"He helped me get through college," one woman said. "He helped me with my three daughters and give them a better life. He taught my daughters how to be strong women."

A Hells Angel walked to the lectern to tell about the time he and Greene were in what he called a "hot chase."

"A car had run over our brother, and we chased it and caught up to it," he recalled. "We got the guy out of the car and were working him over when the cops showed up. There were some billy clubs, and then a cop pulled out a gun. Norm put his hand on the gun and told the cop, 'I wouldn't do that.' I kid you not. That was Norm."

The funeral director, a man in a suit and tie, stepped forward and gingerly asked if anyone else wanted to say anything. When no one did, he announced that the hearse was leaving for the cemetery. The Angels left the funeral home and fired up their bikes.

The streets were lined with spectators, many of them waving when the Angels roared out of the funeral home. Ray-Ray and the Sonoma chapter members led the way, surrounding the hearse. Other bikers raced ahead to intersections, blocking traffic so that the procession, which stretched out over two miles, could stay together. Police watched from a side street. A highway patrolman staked out a freeway overpass. A biker blocked traffic on the freeway, but the patrolman didn't intervene. The procession drove down the freeway for three miles, then looped back and headed to the cemetery.

Hells Angels wearing white gloves lifted Greene's casket from the hearse and carried it to the plot. They set it on a silver stand. Members came out of the crowd to touch the casket and put stickers identifying chapters from around the world on the front of the casket.

The casket was lowered into the grave. A Willie Nelson song -- "Angel Flying Too Close to the Ground" -- played on a portable stereo. Then the Angels dropped the white gloves onto the casket and threw flowers into the hole. Ray-Ray drank from a bottle of red wine and passed it to another member, who took a swig and then poured the wine into the grave. The cemetery crew lowered a cement slab onto the casket and then Greene's brothers began burying their own, shoveling dirt and handing the shovel from brother to brother.

When the plot was nearly full, a Hells Angel called out to Greene's sisters, sitting nearby.

"This is what it's all about," he said. "Honor. Devotion. Respect."

He bowed his head.

"That's Norm Greene," he said. "Hells Angel forever."

THE WRITER

He will look into their eyes and see the soul of a child.

He sits outside the brick institution Tuesday morning, waiting for an official to lead him inside.

In the eyes of the law and society, the children behind these walls are nothing but trouble. He'd have but one precious hour with them, an hour, the way Ernest Gaines saw it, to alter the course of a life. He has no grand illusions. At 70, he's a realist, but still a man with hope. Gaines will look into their eyes and, behind the swagger, bluster and posturing, see the soul of a child.

He climbs out of the car, cracking his arthritic knees, and grabs a cane to steady himself. He makes his way into the Donald E. Long Home, Multnomah County's juvenile detention hall, and stands before a thick-glass window where a guard asks if he is carrying any weapons. "No," Gaines says, with a low chuckle. "I'm a writer."

Gaines, who has won several major awards, traveled to Portland from his Louisiana home this week as the grand finale to Multnomah County's "Everybody Reads" project. The goal was to have as many people as possible read and discuss Gaines' book "A Lesson Before Dying" during the past two months. Gaines plans to talk about his life and his book during a presentation to paying customers tonight at the Arlene Schnitzer Concert Hall.

But on Tuesday he came at no charge to the Donald E. Long Home, where those inside had read the book, which deals with the relationship between a black schoolteacher and a young black man sentenced to die for a murder during the 1940s in rural Louisiana. The young man, Jefferson, did not pull the trigger. He happened to be in the wrong place at the wrong time with the wrong people. The backdrop is plantation life in an era where seg-regation flourished. During his trial, Jefferson's attorney calls him a "hog" as a way of imploring the jury to look at the uneducated young man and show mercy on him because he is little more than an animal. Even so, he's con-victed. Grant, the plantation schoolteacher, is persuaded to teach Jefferson so he can walk to the electric chair as a man not as a hog.

As he waits for security clearance, Gaines stands quietly, thinking about what he'll tell the children about himself. Character, not penal codes or jails, is what he wants them to discover. The character of Jefferson and Grant. His character. The character that might lie buried and untouched in each of them. All in a little more than an hour.

Gaines is a celebrity. Four of his books have been made into movies. He has received a MacArthur Fellowship, known as the "genius grant," for a lifetime of achievement as a writer. He has met Oprah, movie stars and presidents. And yet, as he waits for the security door to buzz open, he knows that had things been different in his life he might have ended up just like the children now gathering to hear him. Over the years, he's spoken at similar institutions in other parts of the country. So many young people in those jails and prisons identify with Jefferson. They lack education and role models. Many feel they were born to die, that they will never live to see 30.

The guards lead Gaines to a chair on the basketball court, near the foul line. He sits quietly and watches as the nearly 75 inmates file into the gym and sit on floor mats. Black, white, Latino and Asian. Fewer than a dozen girls. He watches them carefully, not smiling, not nodding. Just staring. In the children, he sees his own story.

He was raised on a plantation in Louisiana, the oldest of 12 kids. During the war years, his stepfather and mother moved to California to find work and opportunities for their children, who because of the color of their skin had limited futures. In the new city, Gaines, out of loneliness, went to a library and devoured the books. Over time it dawned on him that he wasn't finding books written by blacks, or any books about blacks. At 16, he decided to be a writer. It was a long, arduous journey.

When asked, he explains that the genesis for the book came when he was going to college in San Francisco, right across the bay from San Quentin prison. "I wondered what a person thought about when they know they are going to die on a certain day," he says. "What goes through their mind? The best way to get rid of the nightmare was to write about it. I set it in the 1980s, but then brought it back to the 1940s, to a plantation. I went to a school like that. It took me seven years to write the book."

He moves close to the microphone and begins reading a chapter. After two pages, he stops.

"When I am reading, you will not laugh or talk among yourselves," he says.

He looks over his audience.

"OK?"

He continues. The words wash over the young men and women. Some lie on their sides. Others smile at friends across the court. A few study their hands and yawn. And yet here and here, some listen intently to this man, his words and this story. The phrases -- "Dignity and heart" -- and individual sentences -- You have the potential. . . . Show the difference between what you are and what they think you are. . . . We are all pieces of driftwood until we decide to become something better" -- strike home.

He answers questions, telling those who dream of being writers that they have to read and read and read. And then sit at a desk and write. He stops in midsentence and points to the second row.

"You two want to be cool," he says. "Don't be laughing when I'm talking."

He taps the microphone.

"They need to understand what I'm talking about."

Writing is difficult. Whenever he wanted to quit, he thought of his brothers and sisters, and his aunt.

"I started working in the fields when I was 8," he says. "I always wanted to learn. I wanted to set an example for my family. I could not afford to fail. I was the first male in the history of my family to go beyond high school."

There are a few more questions and then the hour is over. Time for lunch. The young men and women stand and stretch. They talk or laugh, and prepare to file out of the gym. In the last row, though, a young man ignores those around him. Taller than the others, he peers over the crowd, staring at Gaines. He waits until he catches the writer's eye. And then slightly, ever so slightly, he nods.

JOHNNY'S TOWN

With Johnny, everything's the best. Except his own life.

I think about him when I walk past the old Portland police station, down-town at Second and Oak. Once that bunkerlike building was the beating heart of the city, a hive of cops and gamblers, head cases and hookers. No security. No visitors' badges. The gritty character of the town flowed in and out of the station's double set of big wooden doors. If you stood around long enough, as I did as a young police reporter, you'd eventually see the whole face of Old Portland. And, of course, you'd see Johnny Howard.

In a way, I realize now, they were one and the same.

He looked like James Dean in those days. Lean, clean-shaven with angular features, and a head of dark, wavy hair that women loved to touch. A real ladies' man. Other cops remember him showing up at parties with a blonde on one arm and a brunette on the other.

And a talker. Intense, gesturing, promoting. Always promoting. A beauty contest, a uranium mine, a movie. Even though he received more letters of commendation from citizens than anyone else in the bureau's history, he seemed to have a hand in everything but police work.

I never met another cop like him. He walked a downtown beat, and he knew everybody. He bubbled with so much enthusiasm that even a crisp blue uniform and the black. 38 Special riding on his hip couldn't take the boy out of the man. So they always called him Johnny, never John or Howard or even Officer Howard.

He met every celebrity who passed through the city: Bob Hope, Red Skelton, The Beatles, Archie Moore, Elvis Presley, Richard Nixon, Ann

Landers and hundreds of bit players. He once set himself and Andre the Giant up for a double date with two Portland women.

In his heart, he was a born promoter. He found a drug addict named Chester with a hand mummified by repeated injections of Seconal. Johnny took him on a tour of schools to tell kids to stay off drugs. The partnership ended when Chester's hand finally fell off.

But that was a long time ago. Johnny held court in a different city and a different time, one that I find myself missing as I grow older.

Now Portland has a new police station, high-rise, designed by a famous architect. The old bunker at Second and Oak is mostly abandoned, broken windows covered with rotting sheets of plywood.

I hadn't seen him in years. And then last January someone phoned me and said he was dying. For reasons I couldn't quite fathom, I found myself haunted by Johnny Howard.

I checked with the Police Bureau, but no one there knew anything. And only a handful of people even remembered Johnny. A few calls revealed that, like most things surrounding Johnny's life, this rumor contained an element of truth, but was heavy on drama.

Still, the call brought back memories . . . of Johnny and quite a bit more. And so I headed up the steep drive to the hospital on Pill Hill. I found him in Ward 8CVA.

He'd been running errands with a friend who apparently swerved to miss another car on a narrow road up in Portland's West Hills. His friend's car ran off the road, plunged 35 feet down a bank and slammed into a tree. It was a nasty accident -- his friend was in bad shape and would later die. Johnny had broken two vertebrae, had a deep cut in his leg and was stuck in the gully for more than two hours.

No one looks good in a hospital gown. But even allowing for that, the Johnny I saw in that room wasn't the man who once nearly won a national jitterbug contest. This Johnny's hands shook when he tried to adjust his pillow, and he struggled to catch his breath.

When a nurse came to care for him, though, he somehow found the strength to describe the accident the Johnny Howard way.

"Black," he said, raising his hands to the ceiling as if preaching. "Oh, look at these hands. Black from climbing up that embankment inch by inch. That dirt will never come out. Let me tell you, swear to God" -- Johnny swears everything to God -- "I thought we were goners. I had to kick out a window and slide out of that car. I hurt my back something fierce. Listen to this, swear to God I'm telling you the truth, when that ol' car went down . . ."

The nurse waved her hand, telling Johnny she had to get back to work.

"We'll talk later," he called, reluctant to end the tale. "Let me tell you . . ." He trailed off as she left the room. Johnny says "Let me tell you" a lot, too.

With the nurse gone, Johnny looked out the window and stared at the evening sky. He didn't seem to recognize anything. The world he'd known, I found myself thinking, was gone. The prince of the city was an old man.

On the other hand, I wasn't a fresh-faced police reporter anymore either.

I asked Johnny how he was doing.

"Everything I touched in my life turned to water," he said. "I've done so damn much that you'd think I'd have one success story. I'm not a boozer. My weakness is trying to be a success."

I'd known that for years. What I didn't know was just how deep that weakness reached, and how it eventually had slipped over the line into obsession.

"I'm a little tired now," Johnny said as he pulled the sheets up to his chin. "On your way out, would you mind closing the door?"

After that, Johnny became a part of my life again. He'd spent eight days in the hospital and then another three weeks in a nursing home. When I hooked up with him, he looked a little better.

He lives alone in a little Northwest Portland walk-up. No wife. No kids. Nobody to take care of him.

We met at the Dockside, an old Portland tavern surrounded by train tracks and warehouses under the western approaches to the Fremont Bridge. It's not far from Johnny's apartment. He knows the owner, Terry Peterson, and all the regulars. He was sitting in a window booth. Past him, an old pay phone hung on the wall and a keno game played out on a television hung from a ceiling mount.

This was the second time I'd seen him in 20 years. I slid into the seat opposite him, and he gestured grandly to the owner. "This is my best friend, Tom," he said loudly.

Peterson looked as though he'd heard that line before.

Johnny turned back to me. "You gotta eat somethin'," he said. "I been comin' here for years, and Terry makes the best food in town."

With Johnny, everything's the best.

Except his own life. . . .

He was born Johnny Holzman in Kingsville, Texas. His parents died when he was about 6, and his early childhood remains a mystery. He isn't even sure what killed his folks.

The thought of that childhood can still strip away the happy-go-lucky veneer Johnny wears everywhere. In the gray industrial light that streamed through the Dockside's window, his shoulders sagged. Outside, a train rumbled by.

He reached around in the tight confines of the booth and pulled out his wallet, black, beat-up and stuffed with the debris of an old man's life. But, unlike most men his age, he still carried a faded, photo booth-sized picture of his mother. He pulled it out.

"What I remember is being taken into the room to see her and about 10 minutes later someone coming out and saying she was someplace else," he recalled. His eyes wandered around the room, avoiding mine.

"A while later my father got sick," Johnny continued. "He passed on, and I was alone."

Johnny, it occurred to me then, has been trying to get reconnected ever since.

After his father died, an older sister, married and living in San Diego, sent for Johnny. She and her husband adopted him and changed his last name to Howard.

World War II broke out, and Johnny dropped out of high school. He lied about his age and tried to join the Marines. The recruiter knew he was just a kid, told him he'd be killed and turned him down. So he joined the Navy, serving on an aircraft-carrier supply ship. There Johnny discovered that he craved an audience's applause.

Tenderly, he slipped his mother's picture back into his wallet.

"I was quite a dancer, and the captain assigned me to be in a big Christmas show for the troops," he said. "Bigger than all bird, I was introduced to a nurse, and we worked out a routine. We tore the house down. Damnedest thing you ever seen.

"When I got out of the Navy, I entered a national jitterbug contest. I told my partner that I was going to do something so damn sensational that they'd never forget it. I told her I'd throw her over my head, and that she'd drop her handkerchief, and I'd do a deep knee-bend and pick the handkerchief up with my hand. Well, the bandleader damn near fainted when I did it."

He turned to the waitress, who was standing next to the booth, listening.

"Yes," he said. "I did it."

He sipped his coffee.

"But then I fell off the stage, broke my ankle and couldn't get up. We came in fourth."

Fourth.

Third.

Almost.

Nearly.

You want to trade bad-luck stories? Johnny has you beat.

"I wanted to find the next Miss America," Johnny said. "I figured I'd manage her, and that's how I'd get to Hollywood. I was looking all over the city. Then one day I pulled into a filling station in Dunthorpe, and there she was -- Miss Dorothy Johnson -- as beautiful as could be.

"Her father owned the station, and I told him what I wanted to do. He was all for it. She did some modeling around here, won Miss Oregon, and then it was off to Miss America.

"She was the runner-up," he said. "You know what killed her? One simple question. They asked what kind of man she'd want to marry, and she said, 'A wealthy one.' I damn near fell out of my chair. She wasn't lying, but that wasn't the right thing to say. If she'd just said, 'Any man that treats me and my children nice is all that matters,' we'd have won."

According to the clippings, Dorothy Mae Johnson actually said her ideal man was "a tall, dark one with a good job." But after the pageant, she dated Conrad Hilton. So maybe Johnny had the sequence of events a little confused.

He sat his coffee cup down and stared out the window.

"We'd have won," he whispered.

———————◆———————

After our meeting at the Dockside, Johnny kept dropping in and out of my life. His back flared up, and he had to go back to the hospital. Then he went into long stretches of rehab. At times he seemed to vanish. Then my phone would ring, and Johnny would launch another tale.

Following Johnny's tales on the phone is impossible. You have to see the hand gestures and the glances to see where the story is headed. So I asked him to meet me for a cup of coffee in downtown Portland.

We set off down Broadway -- the heart of Johnny's old stamping grounds. He wore a yellow shirt and a pair of frayed gray slacks. I asked Johnny, once one of Portland's best-dressed men, if he still owned any suits.

"No reason to own one," he said. "That was another time. Hell, my time isn't drawing to a close; it's stopped."

Every step brought back a memory.

"God be my witness," Johnny said, "those were exciting days. This was my place. Amato's Supper Club was right down there. After I'd work my shift, I'd go over and work as a maitre d'. I saw Sammy Davis Jr. there."

Sammy Davis! In Portland. A glimpse of the city I'd seen from the outside as a wide-eyed 11-year-old riding through downtown on a bicycle. By then, in the mid-'60s, it was winding its way down to extinction. The suburbs were fundamentally changing the character of downtown, a place where all types came together in a social mix that, to me, seemed exotic and oh-so-desirably grown-up. A Dashiell Hammett city with supper clubs, after-hours joints and bars filled with off-duty cops, boxers, gamblers, businessmen and . . . Johnny Howard.

It was the world that, as a kid, I'd romanticized in my own vision of adult life. It guided my own path toward newsrooms filled with clacking Underwood typewriters, clouds of cigarette smoke and bourbon bottles tucked in bottom drawers. I saw myself working with characters right out of "The Front Page" and writing about characters off Johnny's beat. It was inconceivable that jails would be called "justice centers," that ranch houses would fill Washington County or that newsrooms would be smoke-free.

Johnny paused on the sidewalk for a moment, catching his breath.

"Take it easy, will you," he said. "Kind of different than the old days when I'd bound right up Broadway."

We paused, and he turned philosophical. "Lot of dear friends are gone," he said. "Kind of sad."

He continued down memory lane. "I wonder if I did enough? Did I enjoy life enough? I think I came close, but there are times when I think of myself as a loser."

"What do you mean, a loser?"

He waved his hand in dismissal, and we wandered down Broadway in silence until we reached a Starbucks. I motioned toward it, and Johnny nodded. We walked in.

"Never had one of these fancy coffees," Johnny said to the barista. "What should I get?"

"Do you like sweet drinks?"

"No."

"You like milk?"

"Yes."

"Then get a cappuccino."

We sat at a table. Johnny opened the lid and stared into the cup.

"Kinda soapy looking," he said. "I could put my pajamas in there."

He sipped it and made the face of a kid forced to eat his vegetables.

"That's bitter as heck," he said. "You pay for this?"

He pushed his cappuccino aside and stared out the window. Then he excused himself and wandered out into the city that had grown so unfamiliar to him. As I looked after him, it suddenly looked different to me, too.

The bus mall and the Starbucks had crept up on me, gradually pushing aside the city's old character.

———◆———

A couple of weeks later, he called and asked me to meet him in front of The Oregonian. I walked outside, heard a horn and saw him sitting in his car, a burgundy 1975 Cadillac Fleetwood. Duct tape covered the passenger-door handle, and a pine tree-shaped air freshener hung from the ashtray.

Johnny, still stiff from his accident, swung out of the driver's seat, braced himself against a door and slowly stood. He held onto the roof and worked his way back to the trunk. He pulled out two old Samsonite briefcases and handed them to me.

"Take a look at these," he said.

He lowered himself back into the driver's seat and pulled away.

I carried the briefcases up to the fourth-floor newsroom. At my desk, I popped them open.

The first thing I saw was the nameplate off a trophy: "Meg Patterson: Most Beautiful Girl, 1960 Merrykhana Parade."

I hadn't thought of the Merrykhana Parade in more than 30 years. When I was a kid, that was the city's best parade, even better than the Rose Parade. There was something wild, almost sexual, about the Merrykhana.

The queen, called Miss Raindrop, wore a bathing suit. So did many of the other women in the parade, which was really just an excuse for ordinary folks to get in their cars and trucks, to drive through downtown and to toss water balloons at the spectators. The parade ended sometime in the 1970s, a victim, most likely, of political correctness and fears of lawsuits.

Below the Merrykhana memorabilia were three binders crammed with black-and-white photos, many of them connected with another of Johnny's goals: He wanted to be a Hollywood talent scout.

So half the photos were of Johnny with beauty queens. Or of beauty queens by themselves, in various poses. One in a helmet, high heels and short shorts, carrying a football. Another in high heels on a ladder. All Johnny's discoveries.

For a while, Johnny was involved in something called the Miss City of Roses, an event he held at the Oriental Theater. All that women needed to enter was to look good in a bathing suit. Johnny paid for trophies that were almost as tall as the girls. He'd emcee the show, do a jitterbug for the crowd and then bring on the contestants.

His goal was to find a girl good enough to make it in Hollywood. None did, although more than a few ended up on the pages of The Oregonian in poses that would raise a hue and cry these days.

There was lots more. I recognized a photograph of the boxer, Archie Moore; the wrestler, Andre the Giant; and the bodybuilder, Arnold Schwarzenegger. A photograph with then-Mayor Neil Goldschmidt, his arm draped around Johnny's shoulder. A signed letter from Ann Landers, who had visited Portland. "It appears the whole town," she had written, "is made up of your closest friends."

In a thin folder was a seven-page detailed story about the two days Johnny spent being Bob Hope's bodyguard when the comedian visited Portland.

An envelope bulged with letters of praise from citizens. Letters from a succession of Portland mayors, praising Johnny to various police chiefs.

In the second briefcase, I stumbled across the obsession that has held Johnny for a half-century.

Atop the litter of paper was a movie script: "DeAutremonts: Wanted Dead or Alive." It was a professional job, 139 pages written by somebody named Greg Walker, all laid out in standard script format. Beneath it was a bound 23-page budget for the movie, detailing every expense down to the catering costs. Then there was a hard-bound book, "All for Nothing," by Larry Sturholm and John Howard. The flap carried a blurb by Tom McCall:

"Larry Sturholm has interwoven historical events of the Roaring '20s with the vast amount of research material provided by John Howard into an exciting, spellbinding reconstruction of one of the most amazing sagas of American history."

I started to read.

———◆———

Johnny Howard's obsession, aptly enough, revolves around a footnote to Oregon history, three brothers left behind as time marched into a new era. Just like Johnny.

In 1923, Ray and Roy DeAutremont, identical twins, and their younger brother, Hugh, waylaid the Gold Special, a train that made a regular run carrying bullion from Portland to San Francisco. They heard the train might be carrying as much as $500,000 in gold.

The brothers, armed with a case of dynamite, scouted the line and decided to strike near the crest of the Siskiyou summit, where the engineer stopped to check the train's brakes before making the long descent into California. The DeAutremonts figured they could jump the slow-moving train as it headed into the summit tunnel. They'd force the engineer to stop at gunpoint, and then they'd blast open the mail car in the tunnel, which they figured would muffle the sound.

On Oct. 9, 1923, they dressed as loggers, covered their faces in grease-paint and soaked their shoes in creosote to throw off tracking dogs. They jumped the train, all right, but then everything went wrong.

They blew open the mail car with a blast so powerful it was heard at a train maintenance camp miles away. The explosion ignited the mail car and killed a clerk inside. The flames were so intense the brothers couldn't even look for the gold. As they fled, they panicked and killed three crewmen.

The fiasco was one of America's last great train robberies, and the four-year hunt for the brothers extended across the planet. One was caught in the Philippines while serving in the U.S. Army. The two remaining brothers were caught in Ohio.

After reading the book, I called Johnny, and we met at the Overlook Restaurant in North Portland. He settled into his favorite window booth. A waitress stopped by the table.

"Honey, can I get a cup of coffee?" he said. "And give me a smile, will you?"

He poured in cream and stirred.

Johnny heard about the DeAutremonts right after World War II. He got out of the Navy and did some gold prospecting in Southern Oregon. He found nothing -- Johnny's schemes never seem to work out -- and he ended up in Medford, working the orchards. An old pear picker pointed up to the hills and said that there'd been a train robbery up at the summit tunnel.

"I got so fascinated that on my day off I hiked all the way up there," he said. "I hiked 23 miles. Can you believe that? That there was the start of this whole damn thing. I've been thinking about that robbery most of my life."

Two of brothers died -- one shortly after being paroled from the Oregon State Penitentiary, the other in an Oregon nursing home after going insane and having a frontal lobotomy. The third dropped out of sight.

Even in a restaurant, Johnny seems to hold court. In a matter of minutes, a couple from the next table were listening in. Johnny turned his chair, telling them about a crime that took place nearly 80 years earlier.

Before long, the conversation turned -- as it always does with Johnny these days -- to The Movie. "My whole life," he said, "is that movie."

He believes his movie on the robbery is his last chance to leave a mark in this world. In his quiet moments -- and there aren't all that many with Johnny -- he'll say that all his life he's been driven to be someone, to show the world that he mattered, that he could be a success.

And he always came up short.

Remember that uranium mine? It's a classic Johnny Howard story, a yarn with enough color and one-of-a-kind character to satisfy Mark Twain. Let Ralph O'Hara, a retired Portland police officer who serves as the bureau's unofficial historian, tell you about it:

"Johnny and a bail bondsman ended up getting a stake in a uranium mine near Bakersfield, California," O'Hara said. "Johnny promoted the hell out of it. Judges and district attorneys were putting in dough. I bet 50 percent of the cops in the city, including yours truly, bought shares. We thought we were going to be millionaires.

"Finally someone was smart enough to say that we ought to look at this mine. About 12 of us drove down there with picks and shovels. Most of us couldn't walk 100 yards without huffing and puffing, and this damn mine was up one hell of a hill. We'd poke around and end up back to the motel having a few drinks.

"Then we got hold of a couple cases of dynamite. We had a hell of a time blowing holes in the ground -- we're lucky no one got killed. Finally we brought in an expert. He took one look at the samples Johnny'd been passing around and said they had come from a mine in Utah.

"Well, Johnny fell apart right then and there. The damn mine had been salted. Turned out he got the sample from his brother-in-law's friend, who passed the thing off as legitimate. None of us blamed Johnny."

"Yeah," Johnny said, back at the Overlook. He sighed. "Everyone was going to get rich. I had 37,000 shares of stock. Can you imagine 37,000 shares? I'd have been the richest guy living. I'd finance my own damn movie."

He thanked the waitress as she cleared the table.

"I've talked to every rich guy you ever thought of," he said. "You know Phil Knight, that Nike guy? He was sitting in the doctor's office, bigger than all bird, and I recognized him. Now that man has money. Whoee! He was reading a magazine, but I interrupted to tell him about my movie. He said to send him a script. So I did. And what did I hear? Nothing."

He pounded the table for emphasis.

"I wonder if Paul Allen might be interested?" he muttered. "Got to figure out how to talk with him."

He paid his bill, leaving a $2 tip for a $6 meal, and sauntered out to his car. He got in and started it, and I climbed into the passenger seat. How many years, I wondered, had Johnny been working on this project? I asked him how old he is. He was coy.

"I don't have a girlfriend right now," he explained. "I don't want any woman I might run into thinking she's getting involved with some old man. Just say early 70s. But make sure you tell 'em I still got it."

He pulled away from the curb.

"You know, I was married once," he said. "My wife wasn't a dog person so I kept my apartment for my dogs. Don't believe me, do you? Swear to God. We stayed together six years, and when we got divorced, I moved back to the apartment. Those dogs treated me better than that woman."

His left foot rested lightly on the brake while his right tapped the accelerator. He drove for two miles with his right blinker flashing, oblivious to the cars that passed him, drivers shaking their heads. He approached a pair of freeway entrances and stopped in the middle of the street. He hesitated and then gunned the motor, pulling in front of an oncoming semi with a blaring horn. Once on the freeway, he realized he was headed the wrong way.

"The story of my life," Johnny Howard said with a sigh. "Two roads, and I always seem to take the wrong one."

———◆———

He eventually figured out where he was going and pulled to the right lane and puttered along the freeway, this time with the left blinker flashing.

"So, where was I?' he asked. "OK, well one night back in the late 50s . . .."

He'd just gotten off duty and was sitting in his car in front of the Police Bureau when a young woman knocked on his window. She recognized Johnny from her neighborhood and wondered if he'd give her a ride home. When they got to her place, she invited him up for a Coke.

"A Coke, I'm telling you," Johnny said. "That's all it was. A Coke."

"She was a nice girl."

While she was in the kitchen, Johnny wandered around the apartment. He noticed a large painting on the wall, bent down to see who did it and was stunned to see the name: Ray DeAutremont. He figured he'd found the last of the three brothers.

"Fate had hold of me," he said. He turned to look out the car window. "Wonder why that fool keeps honking?"

He got off the freeway and headed toward Portland.

"I asked her if she knew this guy," Johnny said. "She said her father was a minister and had befriended Ray after he'd been in a little trouble. She didn't say nothin' about no trains. I said if she gave me Ray's address, I'd be the happiest man alive. He lived in Eugene, and I pulled up at the littlest house you've ever seen.

"I thought he'd be a monster," Johnny said. "He was a little guy who'd spent 34 years in prison. He invited me in. He kept the fire in a wood stove so high that I was soaked to my shorts. I sat there for five hours. I never was so hot in my life. I thought I'd been sent to hell. But bigger than all bird, I finally got to see Ray face to face."

Seven years passed before DeAutremont agreed to tell his story. Johnny recorded the interviews and dug up everything else he could on the DeAutremonts and the robbery. Then he hooked up with Larry Sturholm to write the book that Tom McCall eventually introduced.

The cop and the killer became friends. Fellow officers criticized Johnny's relationship with Ray DeAutremont, but Johnny always said the man he'd befriended wasn't the man who'd done the crime. When DeAutremont died in the early '80s, Johnny paid for his casket and burial suit. Then Johnny launched his campaign to turn the book into a movie.

"I've made so many trips to Hollywood trying to talk my way into studios," he said. "I've had two scripts written, one by a stuntman. I bet I spent $75,000 of my own money on this thing."

The closest he ever got to making a deal was when he ran into an executive producer who traveled to Oregon to make a movie. Johnny, who had retired from the Police Bureau, was hired as a contact man -- helping the crew secure locations and get permits.

"The second thing he told me after I met him was that he had a movie," recalled Terry Morse, who lives in Los Angeles. "I gave his script to some people, but it never went anywhere. I hear from him every few months, wondering if I can help him. But I'm almost retired, and I don't have the contacts anymore. But he's never given up, and I admire that. With the right ingredients it could be a good little movie."

———◆———

Once off the freeway, Johnny drove toward his apartment. He was still several blocks away when he pulled to the curb and turned off the motor. His back was killing him, he said, and he was tired.

"I've got diabetes, and eight years ago I had a heart attack," he said. "I guess I know where I'm headed. On my grave I'm going to have a tombstone that says: 'He tried. He died.'"

He chuckled.

"Ever hear that one before?" he asked. "Boy, I got some one-liners."

He shook his head.

"If I had one dream in life, it would be to make that movie," he said. "And who pushed me to make it? No one but me. If a man has nothing to hope for, or dream of, he has nothing to live for. But of all the damn things to dream of, I would have to pick making a movie."

He climbed out of the car and walked to his trunk, popped it and rummaged through a box and found the movie budget that I had returned to him. He got back in the car.

"Let's see," he said as he thumbed through the pages. "Way I figure it, I need $14 million."

He said nothing. But the silence spoke the truth. The number might as well have been $14 billion -- the movie would never be made. Johnny's time was over. And, I realized, a big part of mine was, too, with more slipping away all the time.

Johnny sat for a moment, then dropped the budget on the car seat. He started the car, gripped the steering wheel with both hands and pulled out into the traffic.

"I have a hell of a memory," he finally said. "Did I tell you about the time I was on duty, and someone dynamited a restaurant? Bigger than all bird, it blew me right out of that car."

The Caddy picked up speed, the blinker flashing, while Johnny Howard rode toward what used to be his town.

CHEMO FARIES

Where it began is impossible to trace. That makes it all the more beautiful.

The women who find themselves in this room deep inside a Northeast Portland hospital cling to anything offering a bit of hope. Doctors, drugs and treatments play a role.

But so, too, does a simple story.

When a woman arrives at Transitions, a Providence Portland Medical Center program where women deal with cancer's aftermath, she often feels alone. As a way to reassure her, someone in Transitions often tells the story of the "chemo fairy" as a gentle reminder that many women have also made this journey and she is part of a sisterhood.

The word "fairy" implies a bit of fiction, and it's true that over time the particulars surrounding the story grew foggy. But that never mattered because the meaning was always clear.

Last summer, Renee Koch, Transitions coordinator, had finished telling the story when a woman who had recently volunteered to work in Transitions walked up to Koch to say she had overheard the tale.

And then she identified herself to Koch as the chemo fairy.

"At that point," Koch recalled, "chills ran up my spine."

———◆———

"This journey can be so tough. But you are tougher! You have the strength within to make it through this."

Just before her 60th birthday, Kathy McKenzie learned she had an aggressive breast cancer that required eight chemo sessions. She was the first in her circle to receive such news, and her friends weren't sure what to say or do. McKenzie felt isolated and consumed with grim thoughts. When McKenzie, who lives in Welches, arrived for her first treatment at Providence, a receptionist handed her flowers and a card. Inside the card, in tidy writing, were words of encouragement -- but no signature.

She assumed it was from a friend needing emotional distance to speak of this disease and of McKenzie's will to live. When she returned home she called her friends to see who'd been so kind. None claimed the card.

Eight days later, it became clear she was in a brutal fight to survive. Chemicals attacked her body. She fainted and felt as if she were burning from the inside out. When she returned for the second session, she was exhausted and scared. Once again, she was handed a card: *"Sending prayers and positive thoughts to you as you begin this healing journey. Be strong."*

She began crying.

At each appointment she received a card with a message: *"Stay faithful."* *"Thinking of you today." "You are not alone in this."*

She studied the handwriting with the intensity of a detective looking for clues.

"The underpinnings of my life were taken away," she said. "All I could think about was death. These cards told me I was strong, and I started to believe it. In the midst of treatment, when I felt so isolated, someone put an arm around me and told me I could do it. I sensed the cards came from a woman who had done it, too."

On the last visit, McKenzie received a final card: *"Congratulations. You did it."*

She was upset there was no signature so she could thank this stranger.

Where it began is impossible to trace. That makes it all the more beautiful. It just was, is and will be. But once upon a time a woman somewhere did something kind to a stranger, who later did the same to another stranger. On and on, until one day a domino fell in Welches, a small community along U.S. 26 on the way to Mount Hood.

McKenzie's husband, Wally, is a dentist in town, and she worked for him as a hygienist. One of their patients, a woman named Maggie Yamnitsky, heard about McKenzie's diagnosis through the small-town grapevine: Her sister attends the same church as the McKenzies, and members had been talking about the terrible news.

"I knew who Kathy was," Yamnitsky said. "But we weren't friends and didn't know each other."

Years earlier, when Yamnitsky was diagnosed and treated for breast cancer in Portland in her 40s, she'd been the recipient of anonymous cards left in the treatment center.

"I was scared, but at each appointment, I'd find a card waiting for me," she said. "I wasn't alone. Those cards got me through hard times."

When Yamnitsky arrived for her last appointment, there was no card. Disappointed, she went inside for treatment. When she emerged, she was greeted with a card and flowers.

"It was a woman my husband knew through work," Yamnitsky said. "She'd been through cancer, and someone had left cards for her. She wasn't my friend. If you'd said her name, I wouldn't have been able to place her face. But what she did for me was impossible to describe. There was no way I could ever say thank you."

But, of course, there was.

It takes a team to pull off something like this because hospitals and doctors are prohibited from releasing patient information. Yamnitsky's sister contacted Wally McKenzie and told him what was going on. He sent her emails telling her what day and time he'd be taking his wife to Providence for her treatment.

"I was sworn to secrecy," said Wally McKenzie. "I saw how intimate and important this was for my wife."

At the time, Yamnitsky was living in Gresham. She'd take a card to the receptionist -- she was in on it, too – and leave. When McKenzie's treatment ended, Yamnitsky had to find a way to reveal herself, and decided it would be at a party at her sister's house. Her sister's husband contacted Wally McKenzie and they created a plan to have the couple drop by, saying some people they knew would be there. Kathy McKenzie, still feeling the effects of the chemo, didn't feel like going. Her husband told her they'd stay just a few minutes.

"I walked in and I was given a plate of cookies," she said. "On top was a card. I recognized the handwriting."

Hugs all around.

"Everyone cried," she said. "Even the men."

———————

Not too long ago Kathy McKenzie heard through a friend about a woman who had been diagnosed with breast cancer. McKenzie had never met the woman and knew nothing about her. McKenzie's friend said the woman had moved to the area from the South, didn't know many people and had no family in the area. There's nothing, her friend said, anyone can do for her.

McKenzie knew otherwise.

And so it goes.

Model of a Man

He respects the boys by calling them gentlemen.

"**P**ay attention!"

The big, bald-headed man barks out the command, pauses to make sure the whispering in the back row stops and then resumes pacing back and forth in front of the classroom, a lion on the prowl, lost in thought, while the 17 boys fall silent.

Their heads move slightly, back and forth as if watching a tennis match, while keeping an eye on Roy Pittman. He'd been so easygoing moments earlier, welcoming them to a classroom at Tubman Middle School in North Portland with a handshake and a broad smile. "Gentleman," he'd called them, and -- with a wave of his hand -- told them to take a seat.

Now, he paces, ignoring the sound of a school having fun, trying to figure out how to teach life's lessons one hour at a time.

Lunch is over, and the boys fidget. They know some of their buddies are on their way to the gym at this very moment to play basketball. All that stands between them and a jump shot is Pittman: a solid 5-foot-5 and 210 pounds. His demeanor makes it clear he won't be calling recess.

"Pay attention," he says.

He has but an hour with them each Wednesday, and he acts as though he doesn't plan to waste a second. He looks into 17 faces and sees himself. He remembers when he was 12, a floundering kid helped along life's path by an older man who cared. And so each Wednesday, the 61-year-old comes to the North Portland school to repay a debt.

He stops pacing and stands before them, waiting for Debra Meskimen, who runs the school's volunteer mentor program, to leave the room and close the door behind her. This is a time for men.

Most of these boys are being raised by grandparents or mothers. Every boy in the class knows someone who has been -- or is now -- behind bars. Some have family members or friends who've been caught up in violence. When someone once suggested a field trip, a few boys asked for a tour of the state prison.

Pittman says these boys need a place where they can talk to a man. None of the students is forced to meet with him, but teachers refer boys who could benefit from guidance. Nobody tracks the results formally, but teachers say they notice a difference.

The street stays outside this room -- no fancy handshakes, no slang, no hats. The boys learn that they're not to interrupt, that they must look people in the eye and that they must address adult males as "Mister." They shake hands like businessmen.

Pittman talks about grades and homework. He wants them to be part of the community and to demonstrate their commitment by doing little things, such as picking up litter they find in the hallways and looking out for one another.

The door closes.

Pittman stops pacing and smiles.

He takes a seat and holds a piece of paper in his hand. He reads the boys a poem called "I Need to Belong." It was written by one of his former wrestlers, a young man who, it seemed, had everything life had to offer. And then he drifted into drugs and gangs, finally taking his own life.

"What's that mean to you?" he asks the class. "What does it mean to belong?"

Several boys shrug.

"We all want to belong," he says. "But we have to find good things to belong to, good people to associate ourselves with."

Pittman, a community legend who runs the wrestling program at Peninsula Park, tolerates no excuses. In wrestling, a competitor leaves it all on the mat and, win or lose, walks away with head held high. That's the message he wants these boys to learn. Success, he likes to preach, is doing the best you can with what you have at hand.

Slowly, he pulls answers from the boys. He talks; they listen. They talk; he listens. They discuss social skills, how to act in public. Pittman doesn't lecture, but engages the boys in conversations. How does a man treat a woman? What is peer pressure?

Pittman stands and paces again.

"Do you know we have more African American males in prison than we do in college?" he asks.

The students sit silently.

"Some of you think this is a joke," he says. "This is no joke."

He points to a boy in the back. "You need to pay attention, brother."

He paces again.

"I want you all to give me a definition of a black man," he says. "When I say black man what comes to mind?"

The hands go up.

"Good for nothing."

"A man who thinks the streets are a good place."

"Doesn't support his family."

Pittman's round face is expressionless.

"Now," he says. "Give me the definition of a white man."

He points to first one boy, then another.

"Educated."

"Nice cars."

"Studies and goes to college."

Pittman sits on a chair.

"A man is a man is a man," he says gently. "It is not about color. There's no difference. The only difference is how you think about it. You're going to be black men someday. How are you going to live your lives?"

He tells the boys to give him honest answers and asks how many of them give 100 percent in class?

Not one hand goes up.

"Why not?" he asks.

One boy mumbles.

"That's how you answer?" he asks. "With a 'huh'? You can do better than that. Try again."

He listens, nods and smiles.

"Much better," he says. "By not getting an education, you're sentencing yourself to a lifetime of misery. I want you to survive. We all give in to the pleasure of the moment, and that does us no good."

The students talk about how studying and doing well in school is not always seen as cool. A "square," they say, is someone who goes to school and turns in all the homework. One boy wonders why he needs to learn math if he plans on being a basketball player.

"Life is about distractions," Pittman says. "You're going to be distracted. I'm going to be distracted. You must stay focused; I must stay focused. What you need to do is to separate yourself from people who distract you. If you compare yourself to others, you will always find someone who is better than you, and someone you are better than. The only person to compare yourself to is you."

A bell rings. The hour is up.

"Report cards come out soon," Pittman says. "Men, when you get yours see how you can improve, how you can do better."

He moves to the door.

He shakes each hand.

"Thanks for coming," he tells each boy. "See you next week."

The Guy, the Girl and the Car

The car was a beauty. So, too, the girl.

Before the girl, there was the car. And now, after more than 50 years of twists and turns, the girl and the car remain at the heart of a love story. Some things, it seems, are meant to endure.

If you've lived in Portland a long time, there's a good chance you've seen the car, most likely cruising in Portland's West Hills where John and Arlys Chesnutt live. He's 77, and she's ready to turn 75. They have three sons and nine grandchildren.

But when the couple stand next to the car, his hand gently resting on her shoulder and her arms wrapped tightly around his waist, you see them as they once were, fresh-faced kids peering at the road ahead, into the future.

What a ride they've had.

It began in 1958 when John, then living in Seattle, had a friend visit from Montana. He was glad to see his buddy but more taken with the man's car: a 1957 Chrysler 300C.

This was an era when cars had personality, style and chrome that could blind you if it caught the sun just right. It was a time when driving meant freedom, when no one cared about emissions or miles per gallon.

And the copper-colored Chrysler was a sight to behold. Only 1,767 were produced that year -- a two-door with fins, push-button instruments and leather seats. Inside the behemoth -- just more than 18 feet long and nearly 4,300 pounds -- rumbled a 375-horsepower high-performance racing motor.

"I wanted the car," John says. "I told my friend that if he ever wanted to sell it, to call me. In June 1958, he said the car was mine. Dealers, he told me, didn't want it. He said he couldn't interest anyone in Montana. So if I wanted it, it was mine.

"New, it was $5,400," he says. "I bought it for $3,000."

Today, John figures he could get $60,000 for the car, a collectible, or maybe more than $100,000 if it was restored.

Even in its early days, the car was distinctive. When John worked as an accountant, his boss asked him not to take the car to visit clients. "He told me that people would think we were overcharging them," John says.

The girl, too, was a beauty.

John met her shortly before buying the car. He came down with a terrible sore throat. At the doctor's office, a nurse named Arlys Gibson told him he needed a penicillin shot.

John rolled up his shirtsleeve. Not in the arm, Arlys told him. Down there. He dropped his drawers, and she jabbed him.

The sore throat subsided, but John's interest in Arlys didn't. He couldn't stop thinking about her. He called the doctor's office. She was out, and the staff wouldn't say where she was or give her phone number. John, though, remembered her last name and scoured the phone book. He started dialing and finally hit paydirt.

Arlys was in California, her mother told John. But she'd be home soon. John called again, and this time Arlys answered. She said it was her birthday and invited him over.

Arlys had been raised on a farm in South Dakota and didn't live in a home with electricity or running water until she was 13. Her mother had learned to drive in a Model A but had sold the car when the family moved to Seattle. In Portland, the family got around on the bus.

Then here comes John in the Chrysler.

"He showed up in this car," Arlys says. "It was a huge deal in the neighborhood. Everyone came out to look at this car of his."

They went out for a drive that night. Soon after, in September 1958, they went on their first official date. John wanted to make it special. He picked her up in the car, and they set off to Sunset Park near Mount Rainer.

At a viewpoint, he pulled over. The couple got out to look at the scenery. He asked if he could take her picture.

She posed -- a bit coyly -- on the front bumper of the car. The car is stunning, but so, too, is the woman he was falling in love with. In the photo, she's spunky and cute, with bright red lipstick and a smile that says she, too, is smitten.

That Christmas, he gave her an engagement ring. They married on July 25, 1959. With that, the car became hers, too.

On their honeymoon, they drove to California on U.S. 101. At one point, while passing, they hit 115 mph. But Arlys felt safe with her husband behind the wheel. The car -- what they took to calling the beautiful brute -- was sturdy and hugged the road.

Over the years, they packed the car with life: playpens and diaper pails, backpacks for Boy Scout camps, gear for hiking mountains and swimming in rivers.

They took the car to South Dakota to see where Arlys was born and to Seattle to see her mother. They got a ticket once, on the way to church. They brought each of their babies home from the hospital in it. Later, the boys slept in the big back seat. During a road trip, one threw up in the car.

Arlys drove the car in snowstorms, the powerful motor always bringing her and the boys home safe.

In that car, they went to funerals.

Over the years, the car needed two replacement engines. John needed a new heart valve.

Now the interior is scuffed, and the leather seats have more than a few tears. But when John slides into the driver's seat and starts the engine, it sounds pure and strong and ready to travel the highway. As it rumbles, John looks at his wife.

"We fell in love in this car," he says.

He guns the motor.

A Life Lost ... and Found

He played the tape back to himself -- listening to his voice was better than silence.

A bed, a dresser and an overhead light. The bedroom was as barren as a $30-a-night motel room.

The only personal touch was a photograph taken during a rafting trip on the Clackamas River. The picture showed him grasping an oar and standing between three men and two women. He was smiling. He kept the picture because it was his last link to a lost life.

Other artifacts -- service papers from the Navy, pictures from around the world, yearbooks filled with the best wishes of old friends -- lay buried at the bottom of a closet.

The man who lived here kept a small tape recorder beside his bed, and on it he recorded his thoughts and feelings. He played the tape back to himself -- listening to his voice was better than silence.

Gary Wall reported for work at noon, but he set his clock radio for 7 a.m. so that he could spend the morning trying to remember who he was. In the morning, his mind was empty, like a computer that needed rebooting.

He turned off the radio and lay quietly in bed. On his headboard shelf was a black, pocket-sized datebook. He reached for it to see what he had written the night before.

The page was blank.

He turned it to start a new day.

February 14, 1997.

Valentine's Day

He prayed, asking for strength and courage, then closed his eyes, trying to remember if he'd dreamed during the night. Nothing. There had been no dreams in six years, not since the day he died.

From his bed, Gary saw a small yellow Post-it Note stuck to the inside of his paneled bedroom door. He had written to himself: "Turn off the kitchen light." He got out of bed and walked into the hallway, where he found a second note: "Turn off the coffee maker." As he made his way through his Northeast Portland apartment, he followed a trail of more than 60 such notes: "Turn on the dishwasher." "Get gas." "Clean the refrigerator."

At breakfast Gary swallowed a ginkgo biloba tablet -- he'd been hoping the Chinese herb would help him remember. He gave it 30 minutes to enter his bloodstream, then tested its effectiveness by reading Bible passages and seeing if he could repeat them out loud. Some days he saw improvement. But then he'd wonder how a 39-year-old man could forget to turn off the kitchen light.

Like all mornings, this Friday passed slowly. He read his Bible and listened to a soft-rock radio station. He walked through his apartment reading notes and following instructions. He activated his answering machine out of habit. He received only one call a day. Every night at 6:35 his mother checked on him, and he was always there.

He locked his apartment and walked past his car. Although he'd learned how to drive again, Gary rode the train to work. While other passengers read the newspaper or thumbed through a paperback, he studied his datebook.

Gary was worried about the napkins the supplier was supposed to store in a cupboard in the Blue Cross lunchroom. They had started turning up under the sink, and he kept forgetting where they were stored. He stuck a yellow note to the sink, but the night crew kept taking it off. He complained to the supplier, who got mad and told him to just remember. But the problem had been keeping him up nights and making him doubt the effectiveness of the ginkgo. Today he wrote in his datebook: "Napkins under the sink."

Gary got off the bus downtown, walked into his building and took the elevator to the seventh floor. He punched in and changed into his overalls.

After he'd been rehired, he often stopped on the floor where he had worked as a claims analyst, back when he wore a coat and tie to work. He had been in rehabilitation for nearly two years; so when he reappeared, there were handshakes and slaps on the back. Over time, though, things changed. His old colleagues transferred or moved on. New employees saw only a stranger in a janitor's suit. Gary stopped going to his old floor.

He used to say hello to employees he met on his rounds, but that ended when he heard two women talking about him. One said it looked as if Gary had a light on, but that no one was home. He'd been a friendly extrovert. But in his new life strangers made him nervous. He feared they assumed he was stupid or retarded. And so, over time, Gary Wall became a loner.

He was the quiet guy picking up cigarette butts in front of the Regence BlueCross BlueShield of Oregon building. He stood about 5-foot-7 and had a slight build and a smile that women once had called sweet. When someone stared at him, though, he averted his eyes and looked like an abused dog who cowers before a raised hand. He was an invisible man, moving silently among them, listening to their conversations and their laughter as he wiped down tables and straightened chairs.

On the way home that Friday almost two years ago he wrote himself a note: "I did the best job I knew. To live is good in itself."

He wanted to put the note on the inside of his bedroom door so that it would be the first thing he'd see each morning. He opened his front door and was putting away his coat when the answering machine's red light caught his eye.

He pushed the button.

"Hi, Gary . . .

It was a woman.

"Your assignment at Blue Cross has ended," she said. "Do not report to work on Monday."

———◆———

Monday drifted into Tuesday and into Wednesday. A week went by. Gary ended up at his mother's house, where he sat on the sofa and ruminated like a man in the throes of a failed love affair. What had gone wrong? What could he have done differently? The napkins, he told his mother. It must have been the napkins.

On a day in early March, while his mother was off on an errand, he opened a scrapbook she kept. It was his story. On the first page was a press release from the Gresham Police Department.

On June 16, 1991, Gresham police officers responded to a serious motor-vehicle accident at S.E. 202nd Ave. and S.E. Stark St. about 12:30 p.m.

He turned the pages. He thought it strange how he could forget to turn off the kitchen light and yet remember details about the day the man he was died.

Sunday.

Home from church.

Mom called.

Come over for lunch. Sun roof open.

Listening to music.

Mr. Wall was transported by Life Flight Air Ambulance to Oregon Health Sciences University Hospital, where he remains in critical condition.

The other car smashed into the left side of his car. The impact crushed the left side of his car. His head slammed into the doorjamb. Rescuers had to cut him out of the car. On the flight to the hospital his heart stopped twice. His jaw was broken. His arm was slashed. And his brain had been smashed against the inside of his skull. He lay in a coma for seven days. His eyes opened after a week, but he didn't speak for two months. His first word was "Mom."

He had to remember how to swallow. How to control his bowels and bladder. For two months he wore a diaper. He fell out of chairs and had to learn to walk. A therapist set a fork, pen and scissors in front of him and asked him to pick up the fork. He had no idea what a fork looked like. Or a toothbrush. Or a shoe.

Therapists taught him how to tie his shoes. They trained him to stay on the sidewalk instead of blundering into traffic. This is a quarter, they told him. This is a $1 bill. Here's how you make change. Nearly two years after the wreck he was declared rehabilitated. His brother helped him invest $180,000 in settlement money in mutual funds to pay for living expenses and future medical bills. He received $700 a month in disability income from Social Security.

He didn't look different, but he was. If he was making lunch and he answered the telephone, he'd forget to finish the lunch. Doctors called it short-term memory loss. He wasn't stupid -- the knowledge was in his brain, but he couldn't retrieve it. He'd remember junior high school but forget if he'd paid his bills. He could deal with the memory loss only by writing yellow notes and keeping detailed datebooks and a computer diary. Blue Cross rehired him and found a job he could handle -- a janitor in the lunchroom where he used to eat when he was a claims analyst.

What frightened him, though, was that he had lost the essence of himself. His sense of humor was gone. Subtleties in conversation and gestures were lost on him. He realized that he was missing the things that had made him Gary Wall. One by one his friends stopped calling. The man they had known no longer existed.

After losing his Blue Cross job, the life he'd so carefully reconstructed splintered. Gary felt as if he were being held inches below the surface of a river, so close to safety, but drowning still the same.

As the weeks passed, he could not help reflecting on where he should have been in life. After graduating from Gresham High School, he'd joined the Navy and became a hospital corpsman. He had traveled the world. When he left the service, he returned to Portland to work in a hospital, and later, in a laboratory where he was the assistant section head. He took the claims-analyst job to broaden his knowledge of medicine.

With the future apparently hopeless and the past too painful to recall, Gary turned his thoughts inward in the same way a prisoner in solitary confinement keeps company only with his heartbeat. He started hearing irritating noises from his neighbor's apartment. He called 9-1-1 to say the tenant was grinding glass. But police arrived and found nothing. When he heard the sound again, he called his mother, Doris Shaw. She came over, talked with the neighbor and apologized for the intrusion. Gary was convinced he was losing his mind. He called to tell her that two men on the bus had stared at him. He thought they were going to attack him. His mother asked him what they said or did. Nothing, he told her. But he knew. He knew. Black was now white. Up was now down.

Even the Post-it Notes seemed to fail him. He'd call his brother for advice and write down the information. But he'd have to call the next day and ask the same questions again. He called his mother as often as seven times a day. And the noises didn't stop. His brother spent the night in his apartment but heard nothing.

His family grew concerned, and in early summer 1997 his mother contacted Dr. Danielle L. Erb, a Portland doctor who specialized in helping brain-damaged patients rebuild their lives. She had been Garry's doctor since 1996.

Gary's file revealed that during his weeklong coma, he did not open his eyes even when doctors inflicted pain to get a response. A series of X-rays determined there was bleeding in his brain from above his eyes to behind his ears. The damage was to the frontal lobe, the last portion of the brain to develop and the part that makes adults emotionally and intellectually different from children. The lobe makes it possible to remember past events and to use them for determining present and future behavior. That lobe is where adults wrestle with choices. That's where hindsight takes place. That's where human beings organize and carry out multiple tasks, an ability Erb calls "executive function." A child can handle one assignment at a time, while an adult can juggle numerous projects, shifting from one to the other with ease. Gary could not rely on his memory to put events into context. Nor could he use executive function.

In many ways, he was a child. A child afraid of two strangers on a bus.

———◆———

G ary Wall stood with his mother in the basement lobby of the Legacy Good Samaritan Hospital & Medical Center's neurological science center, waiting to see Dr. Erb. Other brain-injured patients surrounded them. The high-ceilinged room was dead quiet. A man waited with his wife and two young children. Another man sat in a wheelchair. A woman stared at the floor while her husband, seated next to her, read a magazine. None exchanged glances with any of the others. They all sat in their own worlds.

Gary grew agitated. When he started rehashing his job at Blue Cross and the noises in his apartment, his mother shook her head in frustration. She was grateful when a nurse appeared. The woman led them down a long hallway and into a small room. Gary sat on a molded plastic chair and shrank into a corner, next to his mother. He fidgeted and stared at the ground, silent.

They both looked up when Erb opened the door. She was 5-foot-8 and slender, with curly, dark brunette hair that fell to her shoulders. She was in her late 30s and known in the field as talented, no-nonsense and all business. She sat down on a wheeled stool and scooted close, knee to knee with Wall, a manila folder stuffed with his medical records unopened on her lap. She brushed back her hair and smiled the kind of smile a woman saves for a friend.

"Gary, how are you doing?" she asked.

Gary opened his datebook. He fumbled through the pages.

"I'm doing fine," he said. "And . . ."

He fell quiet, and Erb waited for him to fill the gap.

"You know I liked my job at Blue Cross," Gary said. "I think that . . ."

Erb raised her hand.

"Gary, what are you doing these days?"

He looked at his datebook.

"I went to church."

"What else?"

Gary shrugged his shoulders.

"I keep myself busy."

He looked in his datebook.

"I went to church twice last week."

"Gary, I'm concerned how you're filling your day. What are you doing?"

For the next several minutes Gary rambled about reading the Bible and creating computer files and writing letters he planned to send to Blue Cross administrators. The words themselves made sense, but Gary jumped from subject to subject, getting lost on tangents. Erb opened his medical records and scanned them, listening to Wall but not paying attention.

"Because of your disability, you want to make sure you understand things," Erb said. "You want things logical. Gary, science is logical. People are not. What happens are variables. Every human reacts differently to the same situation. You believe something should be Z. And when it isn't, you interpret it as something wrong. And then things snowball for you."

Gary brought up the missing napkins. He told her how he tried to find them. His voice rose. He scooted the chair forward, closer to Erb. He looked up from the floor, and he waved his arms as he spoke. He told Erb that losing the napkins could have been the real reason Blue Cross let him go.

"You're talking about specific examples," she said, "and I am talking about generalities."

Gary deflated. His eyes dropped back to the floor. He slouched in his chair. When he did speak, his voice was so soft that Erb had to lean in to hear.

"Dr. Erb," he asked, "do I have a mental illness?"

Erb reached forward. She touched Wall's knee.

"Gary, you are not mentally ill," she said. "You have a traumatic brain injury."

Gary looked up at her. He tilted his head to the side. His eyes opened wide.

"Honest?"

"Yes."

"I've always thought I was mentally ill."

"No, you're not."

Erb shut Wall's folder.

"Gary, look at me," she said. "This is important. You are not sick in the brain. You are not a schizophrenic or psychotic. You are not retarded. You have a brain injury. But you can have a life. A different life than most of us, but still a life. It will be up to you to determine what kind of life you find."

———————

In the weeks that followed his visit with Dr. Erb, Gary Wall quit hearing noises. Strangers on a bus no longer bothered him.

Erb had given him hope.

The worried phone calls to his mother ended. Their relationship subtly shifted away from caretaker-patient and back toward mother-son.

She had him over for dinner one night, and, when the plates were cleared, told him a story from her life when she was married and living in California with her first husband.

She told her son that she decided she had to divorce her husband because he was abusive. She was 29 and had four children and no way to support them. The only job she'd held was as a teen-ager working as a waitress at a drive-in. She went to a state welfare office and told a caseworker that she needed money, but she also needed to learn a skill. Teach me, she said.

The agency placed her in a program that provided welfare benefits, but also put her to work as a hospital clerk. Eventually the hospital hired her. Eleven years later she was an assistant supervisor in charge of 40 employees.

"I know all about starting over," she told her son. "Don't let yourself be pushed down, Gary. Try. You will fail. But try again. You will make it. You are my son, and I believe in you."

Gary had been dry-eyed since the accident. But tears welled in his eyes. He told his mother he was proud of her, too.

"You've been a good mother," he said.

The next day he sat at a desk in his apartment and wrote himself a yellow note: "Increase effectiveness by strength and realization of who I am and what I can do." He stuck the note to his bedroom door so that it would be the first thing he would see each morning.

He knew he needed a plan and a structure to follow. He needed a job. Social Security limited how much he could earn, but he needed to work not only for the money, but also to find his place in the world.

He contacted Ben Koerper, a counselor with Oregon's Vocational Rehabilitation Division. Wall had met Koerper after he'd finished his rehabilitation and was working in a head-injury program with Goodwill Industries. Gary had such a hard time solving even simple problems that program administrators labeled him unemployable. But then Blue Cross rehired Gary as a janitor.

Koerper was unsure of exactly what Gary could do. Head injuries are difficult to evaluate because no one knows what's missing. It's as if a telephone book has pages ripped out, but no one realizes what's gone until it's time to make a call.

Koerper enrolled Gary in a group of disabled job-seekers. Some had back injuries. Others had lost limbs. A few had debilitating diseases. The group, which was led by counselors, met to find ways they could work again.

On the first day, the meeting room felt like a singles bar where people feel as if everyone is checking them out when they walk into the place. Gary avoided looking anyone in the eye and found a seat in the middle of a long conference table. He sat quietly as the table filled up around him. Other participants found common ground by making small talk about sports or the weather. Gary wished the class would begin so that he wouldn't feel so self-conscious. He opened his datebook and read two notes he had written to himself that morning.

"Change."

"Talk."

He took a deep breath and turned to an older man to his left.

"Hi," he said. "I'm Gary."

They shook hands.

"So what do you think of this class?' the man said.

Gary didn't know what to say.

The man looked at him, waiting.

"Well?" he said.

Gary blushed and stared at his datebook. The man shook his head, turned to a woman on his left and started talking with her. When the man wasn't looking, Gary wrote himself a third note: "Always have something to say."

The counselors walked into the room and announced the group would meet twice a week from 8:30 to 11 a.m.

Gary raised his hand.

"Do you have any paper?'

A counselor slid four sheets across the table.

"We assume that when you come here you are ready to work."

Gary raised his hand again.

"What time are we supposed to be here?

"8:30."

He wrote it in his datebook and underlined it twice.

After talking about how to look for a job, the counselors took several students, including Wall, to an outer office. They used a computer to search a database of available jobs. Gary punched in his qualifications. Three jobs popped up on the screen: Glass-former. Engine-installer. Doughnut-maker.

He sat for a second, staring at the screen. Without writing anything down, he rose from his chair and walked back to the conference room. He stared out the window and watched the traffic along Southeast 122nd Avenue.

When the class was over, Gary walked out to his car. Inside he saw a sticker in the center of the steering wheel: "Get gas." He sat in the driver's seat and watched his classmates walk to their cars. Several continued the friendly conversations they'd begun inside. He started his car and prepared to go back to his apartment. He pulled the sticker from the wheel, crumpled it in his fist and threw it out the window. For six years, Gary Wall had remained hidden from the world. But his sessions at the Vocational Rehabilitation Division made him realize that he wanted a life.

He pulled Post-it Notes off his apartment walls to see if he could function without them. He started with little things, like turning off the kitchen light, and found he could remember. As the months passed, the number of notes scattered through his apartment dropped from 60 to 40.

He pried himself out of his apartment and began three-times-a-week workouts at an athletic club.

Other clients found work and moved on. But he stayed. Koerper sent Gary to CCI Enterprises Inc., a private nonprofit agency that offers intensive help to disabled people.

Gary connected with a counselor named Lori Jean Conover. She spent several weeks getting a sense of Gary's abilities. While he prepared a resume, Conover scoured the metropolitan area for jobs. She found two, and asked Gary to bring his resume and meet her at an Elmer's restaurant near his apartment.

They found a booth and sat across from each other. When the waitress left the coffee, she told Gary that she found his brown jacket attractive. He looked up, stammered something and blushed.

Conover dropped a stack of papers on the table, and Gary looked like a man who had done something stupid and was going to hear about it from his wife. He said nothing while Conover kept up a steady stream of conversation about jobs, interviews and what she had planned for him. She studied Gary's resume and said she'd refine it for him and return it when he came to her office for a practice interview.

"At what point in an interview do I mention my disability?" Gary asked.

"If you have a disability that doesn't interfere with your ability to do the job, you don't have to tell," Conover said. "People who are disabled often appreciate a job in a way that others do not. Employers are aware of that and sometimes take being a little slow as a tradeoff."

Conover told Gary that she had two stock-clerk jobs at Safeway and Target. She had picked up an application from Safeway but wanted him to get one from Target. Gary started to write the information down but dropped his datebook. He ducked under the table to find it.

"What am I supposed to do?" he asked when he emerged.

"Get an application from Target."

He wrote that down.

"Target would be a good place to work," he said. "I want a 401(k) plan."

"Gary, I have to be honest with you," she said. "Most part-timers don't get that kind of benefit."

"Oh," Gary said.

He slumped into the booth.

"But Gary, either one of these would be great jobs for you," Conover said. "Don't give up."

"I have to get an application where?"

"At Target."

"When?"

"Monday."

He wrote it in his datebook.

"And what time are we meeting next week?"

"At 10 in the morning."

He flipped through his pages.

"What week?"

"Next week."

"What time?"

"At 10."

He closed his datebook. Their business done, they sat quietly, drinking their coffee. Gary wanted to say something to her, but the words wouldn't come.

"Well," he finally said. "I guess I better get busy." He took his bill and shook hands with Conover. After paying the cashier, he walked outside and stood on the sidewalk.

The car?

Where had he parked his car?

He scanned the parking lot.

He was lost. Nothing looked familiar.

He moved away from the front door so Conover wouldn't see him. And for the next 10 minutes, Gary Wall wandered the parking lot, looking for his car.

———◆———

Of all the things Gary Wall had lost with his old life, he missed his friends the most. He told himself that he needed people in his new world. At the brain-injury support-group meetings, he forced himself to talk with his neighbors.

He was drawn to Jim Hardman, and, eventually, the two sat next to each other at every meeting. Hardman was eight years older than Gary. He had injured his brain in a 1972 car accident, and his memory loss was worse than Gary's. He also suffered seizures that made it impossible for him to drive. He had two daughters and had been married at the time of the wreck. His wife later divorced him. He could not work and lived in a small house by himself.

One night, Hardman told Gary that he liked him but didn't know what he could offer as a friend. His memory, he said, was so poor that he often forgot what he and Gary talked about.

Gary persisted. He found things that he and Hardman could do together. They went to dinner or to Gary's apartment to watch a video. Their conversations were stilted. Sometimes it seemed as if they were amateur radio operators talking on different frequencies. But Gary didn't mind. Hearing a voice other than his own made his apartment feel full of life.

Gary was at his athletic club one morning when a woman walked up to him and said hello.

He was stunned.

No one ever talked to him at the club.

She introduced herself as Diane Foster and said she recognized him from church. Gary didn't know what to say. He forced himself to calm down, to pretend he was talking with Hardman. He and Foster talked for about 15 minutes before she left for work.

As she walked away, something stirred deep inside Gary. As a young man, there had been plenty of women. Before the accident, he had broken up with a serious girlfriend. He'd heard she was now married and had a daughter.

But Gary hadn't spent any time with a woman who attracted him since his accident.

He was self-conscious, afraid women would think him odd. Even simple flirting was difficult. Unstructured social settings, with their lack of rules, confused him. He couldn't banter or understand the nuances that define a relationship between a man and a woman.

This Diane Foster awakened something in Gary Wall, something he thought was dead.

He learned Foster was in a Bible-study group at church. He joined. At his first meeting, he made his way to the table where Foster sat. They said hello again. Each week a church leader would give the group an assignment to read, write about and then discuss.

Gary could never finish his work. During the meetings he had a hard time answering questions. He rarely said anything and had difficulty concentrating on the discussion as it bounced from one person to another.

One night, several members turned on Gary, complaining that he was never prepared and hardly seemed interested in what they were doing.

He later remembered how ashamed he had felt. How he had considered saying nothing, just quitting the group and going home.

But Foster was there. He decided she was worth the risk.

"I'm sorry,' he said. "I have a brain injury."

And then they were apologizing to him.

After the meeting, Diane sought out Gary. She told him that 10 years earlier she had been in a car accident. Her brain bounced off the inside of her skull, tearing tissue. For two weeks after the wreck, she felt simple-minded. She called a brain-injury support group.

She asked Gary about his accident, his past and how he functioned. He told her, the first time he had been so open with a woman other than his mother. Diane told him he was doing fine and to not worry about the study group.

They started talking on the telephone. Eventually, Gary gathered his courage and asked if Foster would like to meet him for lunch at a restaurant after church.

She said yes.

He didn't dare call it a date. The word itself scared him. He woke up early and searched his closet looking for the perfect outfit: A shirt that looked stylish, pants that made him look trim. He spent extra time in the bathroom. He ran through imaginary conversations in his mind, thinking of things he could say, telling himself to not be nervous. At lunch, Gary was cautious.

"I hope you don't mind me asking this?" he'd say before asking a question.

When lunch was over, they agreed to split the bill. Gary was flustered. Did that mean this was a date or not? Should he shake her hand or hug her? He could not read her. Nothing made sense.

He shook her hand.

When he got home he stewed for an hour and then called her. If he had done, or said, anything wrong, he apologized.

"It's the brain injury," he said.

"Gary, don't worry," she said. "You were fine."

———◆———

Gary visited a Target and a Safeway near his apartment. Safeway looked easier. To him, stock clerks appeared to concentrate on specific aisles and spent most of their time loading shelves, as he used to do at Blue Cross. He knew he could do that job. At Target, the clerks seemed to move throughout the store and frequently had to help customers.

He decided on Safeway. And then he reconsidered. For the first time in years, he thought about his future. He wanted more out of life. He talked with Diane Foster and said he wanted to break out of his isolation. He wanted to be in the world. He called Lori Jean to tell her that he was going to apply at Target.

Conover called the store manager to tell her about CCI Enterprises Inc. and Gary. The manager agreed to interview Gary but made no promises. Conover told Gary she'd happily go along.

Gary thought about it. Having Conover along would relax him. He needed her. But he knew she would not be around forever. He needed to do this by himself. He called to tell Conover he would go to Target alone.

"Why?" she asked.

"Because I want to be needed."

"Of course you'd be needed," Conover said.

"I don't want sympathy," Gary added. "Everyone feels sorry for someone like me. I don't want a job because they feel sorry. I want the job because they think I can help the company."

Conover asked him if he was sure of what he was doing. He would have one chance at this job.

"Yes," he said. "I don't want to be a sympathy hire."

"It's your decision, Gary."

She met Gary at the CCI office, where she briefed him on Target's history and its philosophy toward customers. She worked with him on his interviewing and then set up a practice interview. Conover and Mary Oliver, another counselor, told Gary to wait in an outer office while they settled in a conference room to play the part of Target managers. They sat at a long table and called Gary into the room. He stood with his hands in his pockets.

"Hello, Gary," Conover said. "This is my associate, Mary."

They shook hands.

"Please," Conover said, "have a seat."

He pulled a chair out.

"Gary, could you tell us about your background," Conover said, "and how it relates to this position?"

"I did stock and cleaning," he said. "And . . ."

His voice trailed off. He sat silently for several seconds, lost. Then he blurted out the only thing he could think of: "I wonder if you have a job description?" he asked.

"No," Oliver said.

Gary sat back. He took a deep breath.

"I worked at Blue Cross for three years," he said. "And I cleaned the cafeteria and was in charge of restocking items."

Conover looked at a piece of paper in front of her.

"What is important to you in a job?" Conover asked.

Gary thought for a moment.

"I was way too isolated in my last job," he said. "This sounds strange, but I would like a job where I could say hi to people."

He watched Conover take notes.

"Gary," Oliver asked, "how would you deal with an unhappy customer?"

Gary didn't know what to say. The night before he had read a magazine article on the 10 most-asked interview questions. This wasn't on it. He shifted in the chair. He looked to Conover, who suddenly became interested in a paper in front of her. Random thoughts reeled in his mind. "I've got to think," he said. "OK, that deals with miscommunication. I understand conflict resolution. As a matter of fact, I took a test at church. I typed it up last night. It was a full-page document on conflict resolution and . . ."

He was losing it and knew it. He slapped his hands on his legs.

"Wait, wait," he said.

He took a deep breath.

"Let me start over. OK, an unhappy customer, right?"

Oliver nodded.

"I . . . I . . ."

Gary shrugged his shoulders. He didn't know what to say. He was fooling himself. He heard Conover cough and looked at her. He stared into her eyes, and it seemed as if she nodded. Then again. Two small nods.

Gary turned to Oliver.

"An unhappy customer?"

"Yes," she said.

"I'd talk with them and see why they were unhappy," Gary said.

He took another deep breath.

"And then, then I'd go to the managers to see if they could figure out a way to make the customer happy."

Conover broke out in a smile. She gave Gary a thumbs-up sign.

He smiled, too.

———————◆———————

In December 1997, Gary Wall walked into the Target store on Northeast 122nd Avenue and Glisan Street for his interview with the store manager. The night before he had prayed, asking God for one favor.

He spent about an hour with the manager. Later that day, when Conover called him, he told her that he thought the interview had gone well. The questions and his answers were a blur. He remembered only that the manager said she'd make a decision in a few days. Gary was at home when he got the call: Report to work on Monday.

There were so many things to remember: Time cards, paychecks, his uniform and name tag. He sat and watched a videotape that outlined the store's policies and procedures. There was a set way to do everything. His boss, John Payne, took Gary to the automotive department and showed him how to move products from the back to the front so that the shelves looked neat.

And so his new life began.

He'd show up for work, and other employees would ask him how he was doing. He got to know the woman behind the desk. In the changing room, he heard his co-workers talking about what they were doing with their lives. And he decided he wanted to be like them.

He called Andy Thomas, a man he had known before the accident. Thomas had been the one friend who had maintained contact with Gary after the wreck. They went out to dinner and soon began getting together once a week for coffee.

He talked frequently with Diane Foster, whom he considered not a girl-friend, but a friend, a woman who had shown him that he had attractive qualities. She invited him to a Fourth of July party. Thomas had him join a weekly group that played cards. When someone at work asked what he had done that weekend, Gary had something to say.

He enjoyed work. But it was hard to deal with customers. He'd be restocking motor oil when someone would walk up and ask where the sheets or televisions were. He had no idea. He used the intercom to call for customer service. He sensed his co-workers were annoyed with him, and that bothered him.

He found a piece of paper and walked the entire store to make a detailed map. Each night he studied it. He would ask himself questions. Where were the cameras? Towels? Toothpaste? In time he quit asking for help.

One weekend, Andy Thomas told him about a Christian dance for single men and women. They went. He saw her standing across the dance floor. She was smaller than he was, about 5-foot-4, with light brown hair that touched her shoulders. He decided he had nothing to lose and walked up to her.

"Would you like to dance?" he asked.

"Yes," she said.

Her name was Susan Lassman. They danced once and went their separate ways. But Gary went to more dances, and he usually ended up dancing a few times with her. During the breaks, they found a table to talk. Lassman, a divorced woman 11 years older than Gary, was taken with this man's gentleness. Others wanted to move so fast. Or they assumed Lassman wanted more than she did. Gary was content to talk and listen. He told her about his accident. She said she knew nothing about brain injuries. He told her about his struggles, the Blue Cross job and his new place at Target.

Lassman told Gary that he was different than any man she had known. The others, she said, all brought pasts with them: an ex-wife, a failed relationship, bad memories. Gary, she said, had no past. Yes, he admitted, he was starting over.

He could tell that she liked him, liked him in a way that no woman had since the wreck. When Gary was with her, he felt intelligent and well-read. He found it easier to express himself.

She called him one day to meet her at Clackamas Town Center. They window-shopped and talked. While they were walking, Gary reached out to take her hand in his. He fumbled briefly, embarrassed. How did a man hold a woman's hand? He waited for her to pull away. And then he felt her slowly squeeze his fingers.

Eventually, Gary invited her to his apartment to watch videos. And at dances they no longer sat out the slow numbers. Gary didn't have to come up with words to describe his emotions.

At work, Payne gave Gary more assignments, sending him out to all areas of the store. He learned how to use a word processor and a hand-held inventory computer. He was put in charge of specific floor displays.

As the weeks passed, he discovered he didn't know enough about the items Target sold. So he rummaged around the warehouse and found product information publications sent by manufacturers. During his lunch break he read them. He took them home at night. When Payne mentioned that some companies sent instructional CD-ROMs to the store, Gary asked if he could take them home to study on his home computer. Then, if someone asked about a ceiling fan, Gary would know how it worked and which fan was the better buy. When customers asked him something, he stopped what he was doing and gave them his full attention. To them it seemed as if he was being extra polite. He was, but he also had to concentrate so he wouldn't get confused. Customers liked his attention and help. They wrote letters to management. He got a raise.

In August 1998 his family threw Gary a 40th birthday party at his mother's. The most important people in his life surrounded him: His mother, friends, people from church and, of course, Susan Lassman. They barbecued steaks and played Pin-the-Tail-on-the-Donkey, which made everyone laugh.

A few weeks later, Gary received an evaluation from Target. He was rated as excellent and got a second raise.

That was about the time that Lassman called to tell him that she had a boyfriend. She said she wanted to remain friends. Sure, Gary said, sure.

He sat alone in his apartment and wondered what he had done wrong. If there was something he could have changed. He realized there was nothing. He had sought a life and found one. He had rediscovered that a life is filled with hope and disappointment, of dreams and realities, of joy and pain.

That was life. Now he had to go live it.

———◆———

On Oct. 31, Gary Wall prepared to go to a Christian Harvest Festival Dance. The event was a costume party, and he had given some thought about what to wear. He finally decided to poke a little fun at himself. He would be, he decided, a brain-injured doctor. He would wear a blue dress shirt, sports coat and, around his neck, a stethoscope.

After showering he walked into his bedroom to dress. The room was cluttered. There were pictures on the wall. Artifacts that had been buried in a closet were now on display. Athletic trophies he won when he was a kid and a photograph of his late father stood on a shelf. A stack of books perched on the nightstand. On his dresser were more pictures and bottles of cologne. He splashed some on. He wanted to smell nice. He never knew whom he might run into at one of these dances.

He glanced at the clock. Time to go. He wandered through his apartment turning off lights. He stopped at his door to read the only yellow note that remained.

"Believe," it said. "Don't doubt."

THE COP

Cops try to forget. But often they can't.

It began as a request from a 9-1-1 dispatcher that was about as low-key as it gets. A welfare check means a cop swings by a scene to make sure everyone's OK. Last year police answered more than 18,000 such calls in Portland.

Most were forgettable. Except for one.

Like all people, cops discuss politics, sports and current events when they gather. Eventually, though, their conversations turn to the job and the mysterious world-within-a-world where they work. Stories full of humor, drama and even absurdity spill out.

But given time, the mood changes and they talk about their ghosts. "You start this job and everything's exciting," said Matt Nilsen, a 41-year-old assigned to the East Precinct. During a typical year, Nilsen, whose father was a cop, handles about 400 calls. During his 18-year career that adds up to roughly 7,200 calls.

"Nothing fazes you at first," he said, sitting up against a table where officers fill out reports at the end of the shift. "In time, something changes. You learn you have to compartmentalize."

Cops try to forget. But often they can't.

"Sometimes when I'm on patrol I'll think about that boy," Nilsen said. "Maybe I see a kid on the street. Or I'm at coffee with some officers and they'll ask me if I ever knew what happened to him."

The strange thing about trying to forget is what you remember.

"His name," Nilsen said. "I'll never forget this name."

———◆———

Last Halloween, about 90 minutes into his shift, Nilsen took a break from patrol and met two other officers at a coffeehouse. While inside, their portable radios crackled with a call. It was about 8:30 a.m. The dispatcher requested a welfare check at a Southeast Portland home.

When Nilsen got there he learned a woman had called 9-1-1 to say she'd received a voice mail from her friend's father. The dad lived in Vermont and for the past two days couldn't reach his 40-year-old daughter, so he called her friend to see what was going on.

The friend went to check on Micaela Quinn and found the front door to her home unlocked. When she stepped inside she spotted Quinn lying on the living room floor.

Soon additional officers, detectives and medical authorities arrived. They determined Quinn, who they later learned battled a series of ongoing medical issues, had died of natural causes.

Left behind was her 2-year-old son.

"The little kid had been in the home for two days," Nilsen said. "He was all alone with his mother's body."

For a moment, Nilsen fell silent.

"You know what I remember?" he asked.

"I walked in that home and the first thing I saw was that boy's blond hair," he said. "I have three kids, including a 2-year-old girl. His hair curled just like my daughter's, you know, right before they get a haircut."

The boy was dehydrated and hungry, sickly and lethargic, and a police supervisor requested an ambulance take him to the hospital. Another call was made to the Oregon Department of Human Services, which would take the boy into protective custody until family could be contacted.

Paramedics loaded the boy into the ambulance. In his patrol car Nilsen followed to Doernbecher Children's Hospital. On the way he thought less like a cop and more like a father.

"Two days in a home with his dead mother," he said. "What did he think about? Imagine how scared he was. What was it like at night? Did he cry for her? Did he try to wake her up?"

Even more haunting was the boy's future.

"What will he remember?" Nilsen asked. "I hope he forgets."

After an exam, nurses gave the boy a bath, tucked him into a bed and gave him some grape juice. The staff assured Nilsen that the boy would be OK. Technically, the call had ended and hospital officials said Nilsen was free to go.

Instead he pulled a chair up alongside the boy's bed and sat down. He knew this child would be one of his ghosts.

"I just rubbed his head," Nilsen said. "I held his hand and prayed that he'd be taken care of and find peace."

When his shift ended that October afternoon Nilsen returned to the precinct and filled out reports before walking upstairs to his locker, where he changed into his civilian cloths. When he got home his wife asked how his day had been. He wasn't sure how to answer. Like most cops, he tries to wipe his feet clean to avoid tracking the dirt of what he does into the home.

Fine, he said, just fine.

The next morning, when he was in the kitchen, Nilsen said another prayer for the boy. When his wife walked in she told her husband that he didn't seem himself.

"I broke down right there," he said. "I began crying."

———◆———

The boy now lives with his grandfather on the East Coast. He's doing well. But his grandfather said he wonders about the lasting impact of those two days spent alone in that home.

So, too, does the cop.

But the calls keep coming.

When a gunman opened fire in Clackamas Town Center in December, Nilsen raced there to help customers escape. As dramatic as that scene turned out to be, the routine call with the boy is the one Nilsen knows he'll carry with him long after his career ends.

Last Wednesday he was starting his early-morning shift. He gathered his gear and was ready to head into the precinct garage when he stopped to offer a final thought about that October morning.

In the years to come, the details will fade away: the time the welfare check call came in, the home's address and perhaps even the names of the other officers who responded. What will stick with Nilsen is a simple image: a little boy, same age as his daughter, with curly blond hair and an uncertain future.

He moved to a thick metal door that leads to the precinct's garage. He opened it and then paused.

"I'll never know," he said. "But I'll never forget him."

The door slammed shut and he was gone.

DANIEL AND THE DOOR

That's my door.

With some stories it's difficult to see where a story starts and ends. In this case, pick a day in the fall of 2006, call it the beginning and let the story unfold.

"What I remember about that day is that it was cool," said Tom Patzkoski, warehouse manager for the ReBuilding Center, a North Portland outpost that resells building material.

He'd been sent to collect doors from the Estate Hotel, then a run-down Old Town property featuring small, bare rooms with concrete walls and floors. Even so, the place was a beginning for tenants collecting pieces of their shattered lives.

Central City Concern, the Estate's owner, contacted the ReBuilding Center, which daily collects roughly 6 tons of building material from the metropolitan area. Workers sort, price and sell it, recycling what would otherwise end up in the dump. By the end of that October day, 200 wooden hotel doors were stacked on the sales floor.

A few sold from time to time, but a year later more than 150 remained when leaders decided to panel a ReBuilding Center wall. In keeping with the spirit of the place, crews were told to wander the floor and randomly pick any 14 doors to serve as paneling. The Estate's distinctive doors caught someone's eye.

By the summer of 2007, the doors were hung on a back office wall.

In one sense, that's the ending of the story.

But it was also just the beginning.

Shortly after the doors were in place, a Central City Concern employee named Daniel Winters showed up with some volunteers he was supervising.

Besides giving people a place to live, Central City starts them anew with education, counseling and drug- and alcohol-treatment programs. Part of the transition to a new life is a mission to give back to the community through the center's Community Volunteer Corps. Teams of clients -- people in center programs -- are sent into the community to work with 12 area nonprofits, the ReBuilding Center being one of them.

Winters, who escaped the streets with the help of Central City, was leading a group planning to pull nails from incoming wood and help sort truckloads of donated items dropped off all day at the ReBuilding Center.

Before getting started, Patzkoski gave the group a tour. When they passed through a back room, Winters stopped and stared at a wall of doors.

He pointed to one.

That's my door.

Light blue, a vintage five-panel door with plastic numbers, 402, and a decal of an American flag off to the side. Winters told the warehouse manager that he'd lived behind that door at the Estate for 11 months. In that apartment, he said, he began a new life.

In the weeks following the tour, ReBuilding Center officials made some checks, looked at records and made a few calls.

Word came back that it was true.

"It's incredible when you think about it," said Shane Endicott, the center's executive director and co-founder.

About that time, people at the center began calling door 402 "Daniel's door."

Now, on every tour, whether it's with schoolkids, volunteers or construction crews, employees make a point of stopping and talking about the day a man walked in, pointed at a door on the wall and said it once was his.

———◆———

Though the door is now part of the center's lore, no one knows Daniel Winters' back story and why that door carries such meaning in his life.

Winters, 42, doesn't look like the kind of guy who appreciates nosy questions.

He stands 6 feet 1 with nearly 230 pounds of hard muscle. Much of his body is covered with tattoos -- too many to count, he says -- that are a graphic history of a life he once led. Back then, he was a tough guy, a hustler, a man who knew all too well the cramped back seat of a patrol car, the sound of a courtroom gavel and a jail cell's fetid air.

"I was born in a small town to an illiterate and drunk mother and father," he said bluntly. "I was passed back and forth between broken families. All were addicts. I spent most of my childhood in Spokane and dropped out of school in the 11th grade."

He drifted to Seattle and started using drugs.

"I was trapped in addiction for 24 years," he said. "I was sent by court order to treatment centers. I was in jail. All of it stemmed from addiction. I tried to run. I was in Minneapolis and San Francisco for a while."

He arrived in Portland in 2003 on a bus. In time, the way it always happened, he was picked up by the cops and sent to the Hooper Detoxification and Stabilization Center, which is run by Central City Concern just across the east end of the Burnside Bridge.

"I was taken there in handcuffs," he said. "When you're an addict, you're engulfed in crime. It's about low self-esteem. I was born into this disease. Those were the cards I'd been dealt."

After a short stint in the center, he was released. Soon, though, he was back to his old ways. Then one day he hit bottom.

"Desperation is what it's all about," he said. "I had nothing. No place to live, no job, no money. I was sick and tired. I was going to die a dope fiend."

Winters called himself a "garbage can junkie."

"I used anything that was around," he said. "I was a chronic alcoholic, smoked and shot cocaine, and used heroin and meth."

He's not sure what happened to him, or even why, but he decided to try one last time.

In late 2003, he had a friend with a car drop him at the Hooper center, where he voluntarily checked in for treatment. Nine days later he was released.

By chance, he ran into a Central City worker who offered to help him. Eventually, he met with a counselor and enrolled in an intensive drug-treatment program. But the beginning was when he was given a place to live, an apartment to call home: Room 402 at the Estate Hotel.

"I unlocked the door and it was gritty," he said. "It looked like a jail cell. But I had a bed."

He sat on that bed the first night and took stock of his life.

"I looked at the key in my hand," he said. "Room 402 was mine."

Winters spent 11 months there, laying the foundation to stay clean. He took classes at Central City's employment access center, learned how to use a computer and how to become a leader, which was why the director of Central City Concern eventually selected him to be the lead Community Volunteers Corps liaison.

"I love helping people in the same situation I was in," Winters said. "You have to figure out how to live life."

He's married now and earns a paycheck running the volunteer group.

"Addicts, and I was one of them, take from the community," he said. "We're a burden on taxpayers. Volunteering is a way to give back. This helps them build up skills. They learn how to pack a lunch, show up on time and dress right. The goal is to be self-sufficient."

Every other month, a group graduates in a Central City ceremony.

And then a new group begins.

In time, the volunteers end up at the ReBuilding Center to work. But first they get a tour. And Winters always takes a moment to go look at his door.

"I want to remember where I came from," he said, "and where I'm going."

THE ATTORNEY

The people's champion rang true with him.

Part 1

Friday drew to a close, and Darian Stanford realized time had run out. If he picked up the telephone on his desk and punched in the number he'd memorized months before, he couldn't turn back.

Through his open office door on the 21st floor of a downtown high-rise, he heard phones ring and the low hum of secretaries, legal assistants and lawyers ready to start their weekends. He set aside the antitrust lawsuit he'd been working on for Stoel Rives, Portland's largest law firm, and pulled out a yellow legal pad. One last time, he listed the pros and cons.

The cons -- why he shouldn't leave the firm that had recruited him out of Stanford law school -- filled most of the page.

He'd been at Stoel more than five years, and his salary had climbed to $130,000. In a couple of years, if he made partner, he expected his salary to double and keep climbing. He'd been raised by parents of modest means in a small Oklahoma town, but he'd studied hard and had gone to the best schools. At 32, he was married, had a 2-year-old daughter and lived in an old North Portland house that needed a new kitchen. He and his wife, Deana Julka, had toyed with buying a vacation home on the coast, and he wanted to replace his beat-up 1995 Toyota Corolla. He still owed more than $100,000 in school loans.

On the left side of the page was a single pro: a chance to step into the arena where law meets outlaw.

Stanford had spent more than a year putting out feelers, checking Multnomah County's Web page every few weeks and eventually walking across the street to meet District Attorney Mike Schrunk. The DA was stunned that Stanford, about to enter the prime of his career, was considering leaving Stoel and joining the prosecutor's staff. Schrunk warned Stanford to weigh his decision carefully. Stanford earned more than anyone in the DA's office, including Schrunk, the district attorney since 1981.

When Schrunk offered a job, Stanford got cold feet, knowing that if he went ahead there'd be no telling Stoel's senior partners that he'd made a terrible mistake. But he kept in touch. In the fall of 2004, Schrunk called again, and Stanford knew it was his last chance. He'd asked Schrunk whether he could get credit for time at Stoel. Schrunk said he'd start at the bottom, making about $50,000 a year -- an $80,000 pay cut.

Stanford gave himself a deadline -- decide, one way or the other, by the end of 2004 and get on with life.

He called his father, a man who'd worked a series of jobs, always living with financial uncertainty. The only time Stanford had seen his father cry was when he lost his job and had to work as a janitor at the family's church. His father's advice was blunt: A man supports his family. If you don't like your job, tough. Only an idiot leaves $80,000 on the table.

His wife, a University of Portland professor, said she'd support him whatever he decided. With tight budgeting and her income, the couple could probably adjust. Her friends called her crazy, saying they'd never let their husbands do something so foolish. His wife acknowledged that if she were Darian, she'd stay at Stoel.

His head agreed. But his heart spoke to him about larger issues, of wanting to give something to society and the city where he'd raise his daughter. As a boy, the values preached at home and church were about good and evil, right and wrong. Law and justice meant more than working for corporate clients with deep pockets. Part of the attraction to the DA's office was romantic -- he saw himself as a crusading attorney making arguments before spellbound juries. As naive as he knew it sounded, acting as the people's champion rang true with him.

At 4:49 p.m. on Friday, Dec. 10, 2004, he picked up the phone and called Mike Schrunk.

———◆———

Darian Stanford scanned the police reports. He fidgeted in his seat, the way he did when his 6-foot-1 frame was stuck behind a desk. From time to time, as was his habit when thinking, he ran his hand through the dark brown hair he carefully spiked with gel each morning. He fingered his new tie and fought the urge to loosen it. The dress code for Stoel Rives attorneys, unless they were meeting with clients, was casual. The DA's office required a suit.

In less than an hour, he would be in court for the first trial he'd ever argued on his own. He thought back to law school and tried to remember the rules of evidence. He glanced at his watch and sighed. He had participated in mock trials in school but had never faced a real jury. He closed the folder, leaned back in his chair and gazed at the ceiling.

The case had been dropped on his desk days after his orientation. He'd been assigned to Misdemeanor Row, where most DAs, including Schrunk, started their careers.

Each year, police forwarded more than 21,000 misdemeanor cases to the DA's office. Some were dismissed, others plea-bargained away. Even so, many went to trial, and the paperwork for them found its way to the Row, where Stanford was one of 14 assistant DAs. As the rookie, Stanford was easing into the rotation with one case. But within days, he'd be preparing four to six cases a week.

Stanford glanced around his office, windowless and one-third the size of the one he'd left behind. The room contained a small desk, a file cabinet and a metal chair. He hadn't thought to bring photos of his family, anything to personalize the room. The voice mail still carried a greeting from the woman who'd just moved out. Stanford had written his name on a yellow sticky note and slapped it on the outside of the door frame.

Sounds of the Row invaded the office, and he caught snatches of conversations, DAs calling to one another about files. Cops wandered the narrow hall, looking for the DAs handling their cases. His co-workers, all with trials that morning, did little more than nod when they walked past Stanford's door.

He opened the folder and reread the police report. Cops had arrested a man after discovering him on a fenced Southeast Portland recreational-vehicle lot. Stanford pulled notes he'd made Saturday when he drove out to look at the scene -- the crime scene. He liked the way that sounded.

He pushed back from his desk, bumping the wall behind him, and quietly rehearsed the opening statement he'd crafted Sunday afternoon. For the first time that morning, he smiled. The case hinged on circumstantial evidence, but Stanford thought he'd found a clever way to make the jury understand it. He'd tell a story about his 2-year-old daughter, Madison, drawing on the wall. Even if her parents hadn't seen her do it, and even if she denied it, the fact was that the green marks were just two feet off the floor.

He was about to run through it again when the phone rang. The property owner, the receptionist said, was in the outer office. Stanford took a deep breath, stood and straightened his new suit jacket, one of the two he'd just bought, denting the family budget.

In the lobby, the receptionist pointed out Morgan Philipp, the general manager of Curtis Trailers, who was reading a 4-month-old copy of U.S. News & World Report. The men shook hands. Stanford led Philipp out of the DA's office to a bench in the hallway to talk. "This is my first week on the job," Stanford said, running his hand through his hair. "Bear with me while I figure this out."

Philipp slumped a bit, leaned against the wall and turned away. Then, resigned, he sat up and leaned forward to tell his story.

He'd suffered a rash of burglaries, he said, items disappearing from RVs on the lot. Customers were angry about the damage, and Philipp had to pay for repairs. Then a neighbor spotted a man on the lot and called police. The suspect told cops he'd been trapped there and had to cut a hole in the fence to get out.

"Who believes that?" Philipp said, his voice echoing in the hallway. "No one. Now I have to take time off work to come down for this trial."

Stanford, who'd been taking notes, set his pen on the bench.

"This is my first trial," he said.

Philipp frowned.

"But I'll do the best I can for you," Stanford added. "Do you understand that in court I'm not supposed to ask you leading questions?"

Phillip nodded. "I've seen 'Law and Order.'"

Stanford laughed.

"I'm supposed to have you tell me what you know," he said. "Me asking if you inspect the fences on a regular basis is an appropriate line of questioning for me. But we can't talk about theft because he was only charged with trespassing."

Stanford slapped the folder shut. "In terms of what happens now, your guess is as good as mine," he said. The men stood. Stanford walked back to the DA's sixth-floor offices.

"I'm counting on you," Philipp called after him.

The words rang in Stanford's head as he made his way down the hall. He nodded to the receptionist and walked to his office. Over the years, he'd learned at orientation, even smart rookies who understood legal concepts had washed out. They missed the larger point, one that he was beginning to grasp:

The law in this office meant people -- victims, witnesses, defendants, judges, cops, defense attorneys and jurors. It had nothing to do with abstract rules applied to the business transactions that occupied his time before.

His fancy resume -- Baylor University, Notre Dame and Stanford Law School -- meant nothing. If he couldn't read people, he'd fail.

For Darian Stanford, the lure of the DA's office was the chance to work felonies -- murders, rapes and robberies, the kind of crimes that make news and scare people. But before he could be promoted to that unit, he'd have to prove himself on the Row.

As he walked back to his office, he began to think of the courtroom as a stage. The jurors were the audience, and he had a little experience with audiences. In college, he'd minored in theater and discovered that he liked applause. During the summers, he'd worked as a ranger at Yellowstone National Park, giving 30-minute talks each night to the 2,000 tourists who packed an amphitheater. He loved their rapt attention.

Going over his opening argument in his head, he spotted three cops standing outside his office. "New guy?" one of them asked, pointing to the sticky note.

"Ah, yeah," Stanford said.

"Welcome to the Row."

"Thanks," Stanford said, "come on in."

The cops glanced at one another. They knew the size of Misdemeanor Row offices.

"We'll wait out here," said Melissa Gray. She leaned on the door jamb. "So what's up today?"

Stanford opened his folder.

"I figure the defense attorney's going to make a big deal out of the fact that the guy who called 9-1-1 didn't see the suspect's face," he said.

"No pleas here?" Gray asked.

"No."

Gray frowned.

The disapproval flustered Stanford. "This is my first jury trial," Stanford said. "I've been on the job less than a week."

The cops exchanged looks again. Gray squeezed her way into the room and sat in a chair next to Stanford. "You're going to offer them a plea, right?" she asked

"What I've been told," Stanford said, "is that if they try to deal on the day of the trial, they've got to plead guilty to everything, all charges. No deals. Otherwise, all the defense attorneys would roll the dice. We'd make an offer in advance, and they'd wait to see if the officers showed up at trial. If no one shows, the case is dismissed. If the officers show, they'd take the offer."

He closed his folder.

"Why plead?" he asked Gray.

"It's a bone to throw," she said. "No trial, saves time and money for the system. Then I can go home and finish the work I have to do on my day off."

She stood and looked at Stanford.

"Look, I just moved, and I've got a ton of work to do," she said. "Tomorrow, I've got to be at work at 6 a.m. That's why a plea's good."

Stanford glanced at his watch. He had to be in court in 15 minutes, and he had no options. He led the officers out of the Row and found Philipp in the lobby. All of them made their way to the courtroom, and Stanford went inside. He emerged minutes later to say the case might be delayed because the docket was booked. Stanford and his entourage made their way to another court to see whether another judge could hear the matter. No go.

Philipp said it was the second time the case had been delayed, making him miss work.

"I need to get dates from you -- bad dates -- when you can't come to court," Stanford said. Everyone crowded around a cop's pocket calendar.

"No, not then. My birthday's that week."

"A friend's getting married."

"Going on vacation."

After five minutes, they still hadn't settled on a date, and the group broke up. Stanford stood alone in the hallway, his folder in one hand, the chart he planned to show the jury in the other. His shoulders sagged.

He walked back to the district attorney's lobby and nearly collided with Mike Schrunk.

"So how did your first trial go?" Schrunk asked. He smiled when Stanford explained the delay and the difficulty in setting a new date. "You're seeing the frustration that comes with the system," he said, sounding fatherly.

"I even went out to the property over the weekend," Stanford told Schrunk. "I can't believe it."

Schrunk laughed, knowing Stanford's enthusiasm would soon wilt under the pressure of five or six cases a week. "I used to do the same thing," he said. "I'd drive out to those damn scenes and make my wife nuts. I'd even take her out to places on a Sunday night. She thought I was crazy."

Schrunk headed down the hall. "You'll stop all that fairly quickly," he said over his shoulder. "You will."

———————

S tanford arrived for work one morning to find Misdemeanor Row buzz-
ing. The new guy was getting what everyone said was a once-in-a-lifetime
challenge. Stanford sat at his desk and opened the file. A woman had been
charged with third-degree theft -- shoplifting -- after taking three roasted
chickens and baby formula from a grocery store.

Deputy District Attorney Darian Stanford would have to prosecute her
in two days. When arrested, the woman was four months' pregnant. Stanford
looked at his calendar. Now she was nearly seven months' pregnant.

"You've got to be kidding," he muttered. "I left Stoel for this?"

Part 2

Darian Stanford held the case file in his hand and frowned. If ever a criminal
charge called for a plea bargain, this was it.

Multnomah County district attorney's office prosecutors offered a
deal, but Monica Espinoza insisted she was innocent. As was her right,
she demanded a trial. Stanford, the newest lawyer working small cases on
Misdemeanor Row, was supposed to prove that Espinoza, who he figured
would be nearly seven months' pregnant on her trial date, had stolen three
roasted chickens and some baby formula from a North Portland store.

He leaned forward in his tiny office, put the folder on the metal desk
and opened it. He ran his fingers through his spiky dark-brown hair, a habit
when thinking.

Before taking the DA's job, Stanford had read books by renowned
defense attorneys F. Lee Bailey, Alan Dershowitz and Gerry Spence, men
who made their reputations in front of jurors weighing life-and-death
matters. He hadn't left Portland's largest law firm to prosecute pregnant
women for shoplifting.

His phone rang. The receptionist said Israel Silva, the store's security
guard, was in the lobby, and Stanford quickly finished reading the report.
Espinoza had been seen putting chickens in plastic bags and dropping them,
along with the baby formula, into another woman's cart. The pair left the
store, and Silva stopped them. The other woman had a receipt for her goods.

Espinoza did not. She told Silva she thought her friend had also paid for her groceries, worth $42.30.

Stanford closed the file with a sigh.

When he was a small-town high school junior in Oklahoma, he took a date to a murder trial. A man had killed his wife with a ball-peen hammer, and Stanford felt the courtroom electricity when the prosecutor held up a bloody shirt and introduced it into evidence. At that moment, Stanford knew he wanted to be a part of the drama of big criminal trials.

Stanford slipped on his suit jacket, met Silva and led him back to his small office. Stanford, taking notes on a yellow legal pad, had the guard run through the case. Baby formula, Stanford learned, was one of the store's most frequently shoplifted items.

"It's important what she said to you, that she thought her friend paid," he said. "The sympathy factor is huge here. If I'm the defense attorney, I'm going to ask you if it is possible she forgot to pay."

"She stole," Silva said. "No way she forgets."

Stanford jotted more notes.

"In terms of facts, they support us," Stanford said. "She went to the store, came out and paid nothing. Come on, she didn't forget. No doubt about it, she stole."

He stood.

"Let's go do this," he told Silva.

———————◆———————

Stanford led Silva to a courtroom. Witnesses, police officers and lawyers huddled on benches along the walls outside. Marble floors and high ceilings amplified whispered conversations. Silva found a seat. The cop who'd taken Monica Espinoza into custody stood, waiting to testify if Stanford needed him.

Stanford pulled open the massive door to the courtroom and stepped inside. Other lawyers stood in front of the judge, discussing another case. He found a seat and watched.

Stanford heard the door open. He turned and saw a man motioning to join him in the hall. "My client isn't here," said Harry Carson, Espinoza's court-appointed defense attorney. "I called her at home, but there was no answer. I have no idea where she is. For all I know, she's at the hospital, in labor, ready to give birth. I'll keep looking for her."

Stanford returned to the court to wait for Nicole Jergovic, an experienced Misdemeanor Row DA, to finish a restitution hearing in front of Judge Ellen Rosenblum. When the details were worked out, Rosenblum disappeared into her chambers. Jergovic gathered her files, ready to leave. Stanford pulled her aside and explained the situation.

"This is crazy," he said. "Do I have the police go arrest her? That doesn't seem right."

Jergovic set her files on the prosecutor's table. She faced Stanford and said, "You're not cynical enough yet."

"What?" Stanford stammered.

"I said you're not cynical enough."

Stanford lowered himself into a chair. Jergovic, smiling, sat next to him.

"Maybe there's a legitimate reason," he said. "Maybe I should let her have the baby. I don't want to put stress on her and an unborn baby because of chicken and baby food. What's the point of that? For $42 and change?"

Jergovic slowly shook her head. "The taxpayers are paying for all this," she said. "The courtroom, your time, the time for the officer out there in the hall. Because he's here, that means he's either not on the street or he's being paid overtime. If there was a problem with her being here, she could've called last night. If she doesn't show because she didn't feel like it, you've got to ask for a bench warrant."

The door swung open. Carson walked in with Espinoza, who had two children with her.

"They're cute kids," Stanford whispered to Jergovic, who sighed.

Espinoza's eyes met his. She smiled. Unnerved, he looked at the floor.

"She looks like she's ready to give birth," Jergovic said. "Good luck when she takes the stand. Talk about sympathy."

Carson walked over to Stanford. "She wants to get it over with," he said. "She's ready for trial."

Carson returned to the hallway to talk strategy with his client. Stanford stood so quickly that he dropped a piece of paper. Jergovic picked it up and followed the rookie to the prosecutor's table. Stanford glanced around the courtroom. In high school, he'd participated in a mock trial of students who'd had minor scrapes with the law. He volunteered to be a defense attorney. A judge brought in to oversee the cases pulled Stanford aside after the session and praised him as "silver-tongued," a phrase Stanford had to look up in the dictionary.

Jergovic led him to the lectern where he'd question witnesses, and had him stand in front of the jurors' chairs. "You're going to be nervous," she said. "There's no jury box here, not even a bar, that separates you from the jury. You want to stand close enough so they can hear, but with some timid jurors, you can be too close."

They walked back to the prosecutor's table and talked about the rule every new DA needs to know: Stanford's first obligation was to show that the crime occurred in Multnomah County. Some new DAs got nervous and forgot to establish the location. Without that, the case could be dismissed.

Stanford took notes.

"She's not evil," Jergovic reminded him. "If you go after her, you'll look bad. Whatever you do, don't make her cry on the stand. That will backfire on you."

"Oh, God," Stanford said. "When my wife was eight months' pregnant, I just said 'hi' to her, and she started crying."

Jergovic stood. "Good luck," she said, raising her eyebrows. She walked away, and Judge Rosenblum entered the courtroom and took her desk. "Let's call the case," she said. "Go on the record."

"My name is Darian Stanford, and I represent the state," Stanford said. "Your honor, if I do something wrong, forgive me. I've never tried a trial in my life."

"I'll keep that in mind," she said. "I hope it's a good experience for all. Take a deep breath and relax."

The two attorneys questioned 15 potential jurors and selected six. "This is not a murder case," Stanford told them in his opening statement. "No one was hurt. There were no drugs. No weapons. No one drove drunk. This is a case where the state alleges theft of chicken and baby formula. Chicken and baby formula, that's what the state alleges.

"The defendant is not Darth Vader or Saddam Hussein," he said. "She's an extremely pleasant woman who happens to be seven months' pregnant."

Behind him, Espinoza sniffled.

"I can't imagine a more sympathetic set of circumstances," he continued. "The question you have to ask is: Did she do it?"

He ran through the case, sat down and listened to Carson's statement. The defense attorney said Espinoza had no criminal record, was innocent and wanted to clear her name.

Stanford, planning his line of questioning, saw Espinoza motioning to him. Slowly, not sure what to do, he leaned across the aisle.

"You're just doing your job," she said with a smile. "Thanks for not calling me Saddam."

During the lunch break, Silva, the security guard, pulled the DA aside to tell him he'd just remembered seeing Espinoza rip the sensor tag off the baby formula and throw it on the floor. He hadn't mentioned that in his report, and the rules require that both sides be privy to all the facts. Stanford sought out Carson.

When the trial resumed, Stanford stood. "The state," he said, "calls Israel Silva."

The judge smiled. "We don't have anyone to get witnesses here," she said.

Stanford apologized and walked to the hall to fetch Silva.

After Stanford questioned the security guard, Carson hammered Silva for not including the sensor in his report. Carson then called Espinoza to the stand. She cried during her testimony, talking about her high-risk pregnancy and an abusive ex-husband.

Stanford rose dramatically, slowly making his way to the lectern. He faced Espinoza, a dark-haired woman who smiled at him as if greeting an old friend.

"I recognize you're seven months' pregnant," he said. "If you crave french fries, that's what my wife craved. I've been told that I'm generally a nice guy. The baby's important, and this is obviously stressful. This is not a murder case, but this is serious."

Espinoza denied taking the items, sticking to her story about her friend paying for them. Stanford tried another tack, asking whether anyone had ever paid for her groceries. But Carson raised an objection, and the judge sustained it.

"I have no other questions for you," Stanford said. "I wish you the best."

Stanford started his closing argument. "We're here because a seven-month pregnant woman, a woman who's very pleasant and has been through a difficult life, stole chicken and baby formula. I can't imagine drawing a more sympathetic set of circumstances. But sympathy and prejudice cannot play a role in your job. If it does, our entire justice system is broken down. Justice must be blind."

In rebuttal, Carson said Espinoza wasn't trying to steal and blasted Silva. If the security guard had forgotten about the sensor until just before trial, how credible was the rest of his report? The business about the sensor, he said, created a reasonable doubt.

When the jury left the room, Espinoza reached over and touched Stanford's arm. "Thank you," she said. "Well," he said, "I'm sorry for the circumstances."

"Thank you," she said. "You did a very good job."

———◆———

As he waited for the verdict, Darian Stanford found himself thinking about Monica Espinoza. He wanted to win, but if he did, he'd feel sorry for her. Then the jury returned. Stanford fidgeted, looking at the jurors, trying to read the decision in their eyes.

The judge asked whether they'd reached a verdict. The jury foreman stood and told her that they'd found the defendant not guilty. The judge polled each juror, and each agreed.

Stanford put his hands flat on the table. He opened his mouth and leaned back in his chair. He felt someone tugging his left arm.

"I gotta give you a hug," Espinoza said.

He stood, and she wrapped her arms around him. Slowly, he put his arms around her.

"Can I have one of your cards?" she asked.

"I don't have one," he said. "I've only been on the job a week."

"Thank you," Espinoza told him.

"Ah, I guess you're welcome," he told her.

The courtroom emptied, but Stanford remained seated, his notes scattered in front of him.

"This was your first trial?" Rosenblum asked.

Stanford nodded.

"First, let me compliment you," she said. "You have a great demeanor; take advantage of that. Jurors will like you and trust you. You had a tough case. Look who you were prosecuting. You had a good theory, but the problem was sympathy."

Stanford sat forward and jotted her recommendations on his legal pad.

"You asked a witness to 'tell you,' " she said. "Have them tell the jury. You didn't object to leading questions, when he was spoon-feeding his client. During his closing, he got away with testifying. You should have objected. That was damaging."

The french-fry comment, she said, might have come across as uncaring. "You seemed uncomfortable when you cross-examined the witness," she said. "You were a bit sarcastic. Stay away from anything that makes light of the situation.

"The bottom line was, you didn't have much to work with. The report problem. That hammered you and made his testimony fall apart."

Rosenblum leaned back. She told Stanford that she was once a prosecutor. He told her he'd spent more than five years at Stoel Rives, practicing civil law.

"To me, the idea 'the pursuit of justice' is not a cliche," he said.

Rosenblum smiled.

"I wish you the best," she said. "Look at it this way, you'll never forget this day. In all my years on the bench, I have never seen a DA and a defendant hug."

"Six to zero! I can't believe it," he said, wanting to believe some jurors bought his arguments but caved under pressure to reach a unanimous verdict. "I'd have thought it'd be 5-to-1 or 4-to-2."

"It has to be unanimous," the judge reminded him.

"Oh, right," Stanford said. "Criminal has to be unanimous. I can go home feeling better. I think I had some of them."

Rosenblum laughed.

"Sorry to have to inform you," she said, "but I don't think you had any of them."

Stanford hung his head

"Beyond a reasonable doubt is a high burden," he said.

Rosenblum peered down at him.

"Do you want to go back to civil law?"

———◆———

Darian Stanford drove home in his 1995 Toyota with a dented front end, mulling over the judge's question. He felt like a loser, something he'd never felt at Stoel. His ego was wounded. At the DA's office, prosecutors younger than he was, some just out of law school, told him what to do. That never happened at Stoel, where he handed out assignments.

Deep down, he wondered whether he'd been right to leave. So he'd paused at Judge Rosenblum's question. But he'd answered firmly: No, he didn't want to go back.

When he walked in the door, his wife greeted him with news that would tighten the family's finances even more than they'd imagined when he'd taken a steep pay cut to join the DA's office:

She was pregnant.

Part 3

Darian Stanford stopped midstride in the Multnomah County Courthouse hall and stared through a window at a high-rise office building across the street. Stoel Rives, where Stanford had worked for more than five years, occupied several floors of the building, and seeing it brought back thoughts of his old life.

Since he'd resigned from Stoel, he had sensed private-practice attorneys treating him differently. The unspoken assumption was that the smartest lawyers end up in private firms, not making $49,500 at the Multnomah County district attorney's office. Stoel Rives was an elite firm that recruited the best graduates from prestigious law schools, and it carried a cachet that Stanford missed.

In his old life, he ate at the best restaurants, took European vacations and served on civic boards. As a rookie assistant DA assigned to Misdemeanor Row, Stanford made $80,000 less a year, worked out of a cramped office, handled the most minor of crimes and grabbed lunch from street vendors.

The complexities of the criminal justice system still confused him. He was discovering a world tinted by shades of gray rather than the black and white he'd expected.

He'd lost one case because the defendant, a drunken driver, was so funny on the stand that he'd charmed the jury. Even Stanford had laughed. He'd dropped theft and forgery charges against a woman because the felony unit needed her testimony in a murder case. If he'd won a conviction, defense attorneys in the murder case could have cast doubt on her credibility. He'd won a prostitution case because the defense attorney spent 45 minutes boring the jury while rambling about government conspiracies.

A judge tossed another case because police used excessive force while arresting a driver for failing to turn on his headlights. A judge had scolded Stanford because he'd pointed his finger at the judge four times while making a point. Jurors asked to be excused from trials because they didn't like judging people or didn't want to miss work.

His footsteps echoed in the empty hallway. No trials were scheduled on Friday. Nearly all of the courthouse activity was confined to a single floor, where Stanford and other Row attorneys met with defense attorneys to plea-bargain. Stanford carried a black metal container with files slapping against the inside, misdemeanor cases from the endless tide that flowed to him and the 13 other assistant DAs on the Row.

He rounded a corner and heard the murmur of the defendants and attorneys who huddled in corners and on hallway benches, getting ready to deal. He entered a jury room, greeted co-workers and sat at a long table.

Each day, delays and frustrations chipped away at Stanford's idealism. After he'd invested time and effort in one case, the victim refused to continue. He told Stanford he was fed up with coming to court, missing work, discovering that the docket was jammed and learning that the case had been postponed again. Stanford sympathized with him and others who found themselves immersed in a system that was slow, balky and, at times, on the verge of breaking down.

Dana Forman, a public defender, entered the jury room and slid into the chair across from Stanford. She opened her file and called out a name. Stanford pulled out the appropriate folder. He scanned the report and then sat poker-faced, waiting for Forman to make the first move.

"We'll trade a driving-while-suspended for assault," she said.

Stanford, impassive, read the file a second time. "Not a good trade."

Forman grimaced and walked away. A minute later, she poked her head back in the door. "My guy's still hemming and hawing in the hall."

Stanford smiled. "Let him hem. I'll still be here."

Every few minutes, the door opened and public defenders sat at the table, negotiating with Stanford or other DAs. Forman and Stanford worked out a deal, and Stanford worked his way through the files, reducing some charges, holding firm on others and occasionally granting an extension before trial.

As he opened each folder, he forced himself to remember the victim. As a father, it outraged Stanford when someone put children at risk. Out of principle, he'd never cut a deal for a drunken driver stopped with a child in the car.

A few weeks before, a public defender wanted to plead down a case in which a man had punched a panhandler and been found with a small amount of cocaine in his pockets. The victim, who needed 10 stitches, was afraid to file a complaint. With drug possession the only charge, guide-lines recommended 18 months' probation. But Stanford hated bullies and insisted on 50 days in jail.

The door opened, and Kenna Fisher plopped down across from Stanford. "Don't give me any trouble," she said with a smile.

Stanford returned a tired smile of his own. "Let me see," he said, "what trouble I can give you."

When all the deals were made, Stanford walked to the courtroom. He sighed as he sat at the prosecutor's table and scanned the faces of defendants who'd come to enter negotiated pleas. He fiddled with a pen until the judge arrived. The defendants, one by one, shuffled up to the defense table as the clerk called their cases.

"Darian Stanford for the state of Oregon," he said as he introduced each case.

No one paid much attention. They were simply words he repeated without much thought or feeling.

"Darian Stanford for the state of Oregon."

Two deputies escorted a burly man into the courtroom and helped him into a chair at the end of a long wooden table, where they remained standing on either side of him, waiting for the judge to start the hearing. A dozen nursing students taking a course on the mentally ill and soci-ety had come to watch. So had Stanford, who was curious about how involuntary-commitment proceedings worked.

The man at the table was 35, three years older than Stanford, who sat in the front row. The man had drifted from Iowa to Oregon, and he'd lost contact with his family. He'd been in Portland for nearly 15 years, often liv-ing on the streets.

Stanford, who'd never given the homeless much thought, leaned for-ward, studied the man's matted hair and watched as he brought his hand to his mouth and back to his lap every 10 seconds.

Psychiatrists had diagnosed him with paranoid schizophrenia. Social workers found him an apartment and provided him with medication, but he quit taking his pills, pulled a knife on neighbors and threatened to set fire to the building. Judge Lewis Lawrence had to decide what to do with him.

"How are you feeling today?" Lawrence asked the man.

"Pretty good."

"I'm here to determine if you suffer from a mental disorder and if I should order you back to the hospital. There are no beds available in Multnomah County. You'd have to go to Corvallis."

"I don't have a mental illness."

A psychiatrist asked the man questions to give the judge a sense of his mental state.

"Why were you in the hospital?"

"No idea."

"Do you hear voices?"

"No."

"Do you carry knives around?"

"No."

"Were the police at your apartment."

"Yes."

"Why?"

"No reason."

The judge opened a folder.

"What's your plan today if I release you?" Lawrence asked.

The man pondered the question.

"Go to the coffee shop."

The man's court-appointed attorney argued that he did not need to be committed because he'd shown the ability to live on the street for nearly 10 years.

"The court finds clear evidence he's suffering from a disorder and is unable to provide for himself," Lawrence said. "It's ordered that he be committed to the mental health division."

The deputies helped the man stand.

"Hang in there," the judge said.

After the courtroom emptied, Stanford remained seated, quiet, his hands on his legs as he stared at the floor. Left alone, the man could have stabbed someone or set fire to an apartment building, killing someone. He couldn't be set free, but would he spend the rest of his life moving in and out of mental hospitals?

Stanford stood and sighed.

At one time, Stanford thought, parents had loved the homeless man the way he loved his own daughter. And then fate had dealt a terrible blow, just as it had to Stanford's family a month earlier.

His wife had gone to the doctor for a routine pregnancy exam. A series of tests revealed severe birth defects. Stanford's wife called him in tears. Shortly after that, she miscarried.

Days later, Stanford, still reeling, had to oversee a probation-violation hearing involving a man who had fathered six children with six women.

He took his time heading back to the sixth floor, lost in thought. Once there, he made his way down the hall. He glanced out the window at his old building across the street but didn't stop. He walked to his office on the Row and found eight case files waiting for him.

———◆———

In the late spring of 2005, Darian Stanford learned he'd soon be transferred off Misdemeanor Row. As part of the standard rookie rotation, he'd move to the intake unit at the Justice Center, two blocks from the courthouse. There, he'd evaluate police reports and decide whether there was enough evidence to issue a misdemeanor charge. If there was, he'd send the matter to the Row for trial.

His boss, Fred Lenzer, the senior deputy in charge of the misdemeanor unit, told Stanford that the assistant DA's superiors had critiqued him in court and studied his paperwork. They'd continue their evaluations during the next year. Lenzer said Stanford had the makings of a good DA who eventually could land a promotion to the felony unit, where he'd prosecute murders, rapes and robberies.

Although the evaluation pleased Stanford, he realized how much more he needed to learn about the system and his place in it.

Darian Stanford flipped on his office computer one morning and read that his bosses wanted him to attend a two-day conference on driving while under the influence of intoxicants, one of the crimes that misdemeanor DAs often deal with.

He took Friday off, left his North Portland home in the morning and drove his old car to a Washington County hotel. He signed in and poured himself a cup of coffee.

More than 1,000 police officers, sheriff's deputies, social workers and prosecutors from throughout Oregon filled the room. Stanford didn't recognize anyone and wasn't sure where to sit.

Then he saw a familiar face -- Darke Hull, a Portland police officer whom he'd met in the cramped hallways on Misdemeanor Row. Hull asked Stanford to sit at his table with other officers and prosecutors from other agencies. They welcomed him with handshakes and introductions. The lights dimmed, and an honor guard presented the colors. Everyone stood, silent. And then 1,000 voices sang "God Bless America."

Stanford was the boy from Oklahoma, born and raised in a small town where flags fly on the Fourth of July, Veterans Day and Memorial Day. A child from a town where a man takes off his hat and places his hand over his heart when he hears the national anthem.

Stanford felt tears welling in his eyes. He was part of a team, someone who in court introduced himself as "Darian Stanford for the state of Oregon."

He put his hand over his heart and joined the chorus.

A Bygone Belonging

Only a few small pharmacies remain, their days most likely numbered.

As they rush past the building, hustling through the intersection on their way to something or someplace important, they hardly notice it. Few drivers realize that once upon a time the small business at the corner of Southeast Belmont Street and 60th Avenue was the place to go in the neighborhood, a place of quiet magic that served up a tonic for the soul.

If day-to-day existence is a swift-flowing river, Seaton Pharmacy has been the peaceful eddy. But now, after 70 years, the pharmacy is closing, victim of a way of life that crept up on Americans when nobody was looking.

What Seaton's provided was that elusive sense of belonging, that small-town feeling that sociologists like to call "community" or "being connected." The customers who came to Seaton's during the decades, though, never needed $2 words to explain what they felt in their bones.

It was two mothers commiserating while waiting to pick up a prescription for their kids' ear infections and then making a date to have lunch at the fountain later in the week. It was a couple of businessmen hashing out politics over a cup of coffee. Not a latte or one of those three-hyphen uptown drinks. Just a cup of coffee in a mug. It was a seventh-grade boy, fortified by a thick after-school chocolate milkshake, finding the courage to give a girl her first kiss while his buddies over by the magazine rack spied on him.

The curved soda fountain -- lined with 16 green-backed chairs that swivel on chrome pedestals -- hugged one wall. The menu hadn't changed in decades: hamburger, grilled tuna and cheese, fried eggs, milkshakes and malts made in sturdy Hamilton Beach blenders and plopped down on the

Formica counter in metal containers covered with frost. At Seaton's, you poured your own.

At the far end of the drugstore was a window that served as a Post Office. The neighbors could pay their utility bills there.

And tucked away in a corner was the actual pharmacy.

Small drugstores like Seaton's used to dot Portland's neighborhoods. They were another era's coffeehouses, the place where people from all walks of life met. They often had a grill and a fountain, and the aisles were packed with everything from perfume to greeting cards.

The pharmacist knew his customers. He watched the kids grow, handed out small pieces of candy and didn't complain when bored kids read Mad Magazine while their mothers waited to have orders filled.

As big drugstore chains moved into the city, they siphoned business away from the little guys. Now only a few small pharmacies remain, their days most likely numbered.

Yosh Inahara, the owner of Seaton's, started working for Layke Seaton, the founder, when he graduated with a degree in pharmacy in 1950. He bought the business in 1972. His son, Alan, started out as a stock boy, moved up through the ranks and has been the store's pharmacist for the past 25 years.

The margins from the drug companies and copayments from medical insurance plans are small, and pharmacies depend on volume to turn a profit. Alan Inahara says that on a typical day he might fill 80 prescriptions while one of the chain drugstores might fill 1,000.

When Alan Inahara's father finally decided to retire, the family quietly put the store on the market but found no takers. Seaton's had become a relic.

And so at the end of April, the Inaharas decided to close the doors. They sent letters to their charge customers and posted letters throughout the pharmacy.

"What are we going to do?" Inahara says. "It's a sign of the times. I remember when I wrote prescriptions on a manual typewriter, then an electric and then on a computer. Everything changes."

On Friday afternoon, the Inahara family held a final open house. Today is the last day of business. Four days from now, Alan Inahara will go to work at one of the chains that, in a roundabout way, put him out of business.

Traffic at Seaton's picked up in the past few weeks as customers stopped in to buy discounted Halloween decorations, Christmas wrapping and obscure items such as "Packers Pine Tar Soap." They made time to eat a final lunch at the fountain, to drink a real Green River and to say goodbye to friends, people they came to know only because they happened to share an adjacent stool.

At noon during the last couple of weeks, the counter continued to fill with what some of the regulars affectionately call the "Old Geezers Club," made up of men and women who have been lunching at Seaton Pharmacy for decades.

"Pretty near every day," says 64-year-old Fred Siebow, who has a sandwich named after him. "Fred's Special" -- fried egg, fried ham and cheese.

Jim Smith, 70, stumbled on Seaton's years ago when he was driving down Southeast 60th. He pulled in on a whim, ate lunch and has been coming back ever since.

"I have no idea where I'm going to go," he says. "I don't know where any of us are going. You can get a hamburger anyplace, but you can't duplicate this place and these people."

The pharmacy received a measure of fame in 1989 when it was featured in the movie "Drugstore Cowboy," a film about addicts who burglarized drugstores.

"There is a transom above the front door, and in the movie they walked by at night and crawled in," Inahara recalls. "Then one of them pulled out a drawer of drugs and ran out of the store. They shot the scene all night, and we threw a milkshake party for the crew."

Each weekday afternoon, for decades, the pharmacy has filled with students from Mount Tabor Middle School, just down the hill. They piled into the drugstore, buying licorice and finding spots at the fountain. The boys sat on one end, the girls on the other, but in time they gathered around one or two stools and talked. They borrowed money from one another, gossiped and complained about homework.

"Even though a lot of old people are here, this is a kid's place," explained Greg Stamm, a seventh-grader who held a bottle of root beer after school earlier this week. "It's a hangout. I don't know where we're going to go on Monday. Going to the grocery store isn't the same thing."

The Mount Tabor Middle School regulars, who think their generation discovered Seaton's and made it their own, planned to meet at the fountain Friday one last time. They intended to keep the Green Rivers and milkshakes flowing until their allowances run out.

"Hanna and Britta and Bobbi and Danny, everyone will be here," Greg said. "When you're in Seaton's, you don't have to worry about your parents doing something to embarrass you. If they pick us up, they wait in the parking lot or just honk out in front. We don't really want them in here. We were all in here one day, and the principal came in. It was freaky seeing her in our place."

When Greg and his crowd left, just two customers remained. Adrian Chandler, 55, heard the news about Seaton's and drove in from Woodburn with her 33-year-old son, Bryan Chandler. She wanted to make a final visit. Her grandmother first took her to Seaton's when she was 3, and she made countless trips with her mother, and then, through the years, with her son, to the little pharmacy.

After taking pictures in front of the building, they settled in and sat silently at the fountain, soaking in what soon would be gone forever.

Coaches Never Quit

He wanted to be known as a winner.

Had life worked out the way he'd so carefully planned it, an entourage would be hanging on his every word. He'd be written up in Sports Illustrated and featured on ESPN. Instead, there is only an empty parking lot. Steve Humann still looks big-city, though, a man ready to take on the world. He wears gleaming gold-rimmed glasses, dark-green slacks and a crisp white shirt under a sweater. His black dress shoes are unscuffed.

He moved here from upstate New York in 1980, a young man dragging his wife and three daughters to this speck on the map to head the men's basketball program at Southern Oregon University. It was supposed to be a temporary stop. In the coaching world, Humann, who had been an assistant at Cornell University, was a budding star. He was intense, a screamer who reminded people of a young Bobby Knight. He considered it a compliment. Knight, the Indiana University basketball coach, might be a walking volcano, but he was a winner. And in a world in which a man is judged on wins and loses, Humann wanted to be known as a winner.

The man whose voice once grew hoarse each weekend is silent tonight. The words, thoughts and feelings? They're in there. Just trapped in his body. When he speaks, it is slowly. He must concentrate, willing his tongue and lips to work together so he can be understood. The man who fiercely took pride in doing things his way now depends on others who lift him out of bed, clean his body, dress him and gently place his glasses on his face. His body flops as his motorized wheelchair gains traction. He moves through the parking lot by controlling a joystick with a trembling left arm. Alone, he moves up a ramp in darkness and bursts into the light that bathes the Ashland High School gym.

The young man with dreams is long gone. In his place is a 58-year-old grandfather who never imagined he'd end up in a small arena coaching a high school girls varsity game on a Friday night in the far reaches of Oregon.

In the middle of his third season at Southern Oregon, Humann underwent what was supposed to be routine surgery. He'd had a series of fainting spells but believed the problem was related to high blood pressure. As a precaution, the team's trainer suggested a brain scan. The scan revealed what Humann understood to be a life-threatening growth the size of an acorn. The growth, it turned out, wasn't life threatening, and everything that could go wrong in an operation went wrong. When he emerged from a monthlong coma, he could move only his eyes. He couldn't even speak. There were a lawsuit and eventual settlement.

After a year of intense therapy, his wife was warned that he'd never recover enough to lead a meaningful life. She refused suggestions to institutionalize him. Humann began nearly eight years of rehabilitation, always clinging to the hope that he'd walk. In the end, though, the best he could do was speak and partially move his left arm. The family had to move out of the house while it was remodeled.

On this Friday night, he used that left arm to move his chair out of the gym, into a quiet hallway and into his past.

"Everyone was watching me," he said. "My daughters, my wife, everyone. What was I going to tell my girls if I quit? What would I say? I wanted to stay strong for them. It was so hard. . . . You have to excuse me for getting emotional. I worked hard. The one thing that kept me going was my family. I didn't want to let them down. Coaches never quit. They might be frustrated, but they have no use for quitters.

"I never felt sorry for myself," he said. "I don't say that to glorify myself. It's not easy being in this chair. It's difficult when I poop in my pants and

225

have to sit in it until someone helps me. But I never ask why this happened to me. I'm not that kind of person. I grew up in a strong Catholic family, and I feel the Lord is watching over me."

He found support at church, but life seemed to have no purpose. He read books or watched television, but he had nothing to look forward to, no reason to start each day. He'd never be like other fathers. Never again be able to hug his daughters, play with them or be involved with their lives in ways that had once been so simple.

One day, he decided he'd go watch his daughter Katie, then 8, play on a recreational basketball team. Over the years, a group of friends and members from his church had volunteered to care for Humann, relieving some of the burden that fell to his wife. In the morning, friends arrive at his house at 6 to get him out of bed, showered and dressed. It takes 90 minutes. Throughout the day, he depends on others. At night, friends lift him into bed and cover him with blankets. Getting to Katie's game was a struggle.

"When I showed up in that gym, I was just a fool in a wheelchair," Humann said. "But I was out of the house."

The familiar sound of the ball and the clang against the rim stirred good memories. When the coach moved away the next season, and it appeared the team would have to disband, Humann volunteered to take over. It was a move no one would ever have expected. When it came to basketball, young children tested his patience. At one Southern Oregon University basketball clinic for boys, Humann grew so frustrated that he turned over the kids to his interns and retreated to his office.

"I had to learn to be extremely patient," he said. "I was in a wheelchair, and that was strange to them, and I was hard to understand. It got down to the basics: This is a basketball and that is the basket. I had to explain what the lines on the court meant. I started thinking less like a coach and more like a father. When I was at SOU, I'd see red on the basketball court, but when I got home with my girls, I saw pink. When I worked with the little ones, the world became pink."

There was no team for his daughter and her friends when they grew older. Humann started one. He persuaded a school principal to let his team use the gym on Thursday nights. He began coaching the girls, coming up with real plays and evaluating players. "He taught us how to shoot by flipping his wrist and then bringing someone in to demonstrate," Katie recalled. Humann rediscovered the intensity he thought he'd lost. He entered his team in a tournament, coached them as if it were the NCAA championship, and the girls -- his girls -- took home the trophy.

He preached fundamentals, working on the fine points of the game, and over the years, the girls he coached went on to play in high school and college. The coach who had once been given up for dead found a new life.

———◆———

One by one, the players and the team's two assistants walk into the band room where Humann holds his pregame meeting. Humann is the first disabled person most of the girls have known. His assistants demonstrate his plays and do the things he can't, but everything flows from his mind.

When he learned there was an opening for head coach of the Ashland High girls varsity team this school year, he called the athletic director and applied. He wanted to do it to thank the community that had once been nothing more than a stopover, but had become his home for the past 20 years. Any dreams of glory and prestige, of being called a brilliant young coach, were long gone. He wanted to do it for the girls.

"The first time I saw him, he scared me," admitted Marla Morin, 18, who started to play for him as a fifth-grader. "I couldn't understand him. I felt sorry for him. But he's never felt sorry for himself. He's never mentioned his disability. I'm graduating this year, and I realize that he's taught me that no matter what happens in my life, I should never give up."

Humann's coaching tips and speeches resonate with double meanings that apply to what happens off the court.

"I want you to focus," he says during the team meeting before the Grants Pass game. "You have to focus on what is at hand. No matter what happens, keep going. Adapt. You've prepared, and now you have to pay attention and execute. I've been lecturing you on this for how long? You know all this."

He struggles to move his head, swiveling so he can look into the eyes of each of his players. He smiles. "You're fine young women."

Humann looks down at his cheat sheet, a piece of paper that lists his players and plays he worked out during practice. Because speaking is difficult, Humann uses simple words -- colors or numbers -- to call out plays. He adjusts his chair and addresses his team.

"I don't like to lose," he says. "I never liked it, and we're coming out strong tonight. I don't care if it's Duke out there on that floor tonight. We're playing our game. Do what you do in practice. If you're a shooter, shoot. If you're a rebounder, rebound. If you do it all, do it all. Keep in mind what we have to do in this game. How do you win? You get on the board and you score big time. I can talk all I want. You have to do it."

The girls give a cheer and walk up a ramp and onto the court. In the stands, Randy Carlson cheers for his 15-year-old daughter, Alysse. Carlson is one of the volunteers who comes to Humann's house to help him.

"These girls have a bond with him that I can't explain," he said. "They would go to the ends of the world for him. It's been such a lesson for them to be around someone who's handicapped."

To make himself heard over the crowd during the game, Humann uses a wireless headset that connects to a small amplifier. "All right," he tells his players in a voice that only they can really understand. "Get out and go. Get out and go."

From the stands, he appears impassive. But he takes in every play, every shot, rebound and pass. When the referee calls a foul on one of his players, Humann begins shouting: "Terrible call! Terrible call!" He fumbles for the wheelchair's joystick and motors out onto the floor to confront the referee.

"That's a technical, Steve," the referee says. "Fine," Humann replies. "It's still a terrible call."

At halftime, Ashland is comfortably ahead 33-19, but Humann, who leads the girls back into the music room, isn't happy. "Shut that door," he demands of an assistant. "We need to regain our intensity. We are letting it slip away. We're going to crush these people. Let them know we are here."

He turns to face one player.

"You play hard," he says, glowering. "You play hard." His face softens and he moves his chair closer to the girl, who also performs with the choir and who gave a speech in the gym earlier in the week. "What you did this week was tremendous. You sang in that gym. You gave a speech in that gym. Now go out there and let them know you can play basketball in that gym.

"We want this," he admonishes his team. "We want it."

The Ashland team wins, 74-33, solidifying its No. 2 ranking in the Southern Oregon Conference. He congratulates his players and nods to their parents and supporters. In time, the players are gone, the gym nearly empty. Humann uses the joystick to move to the middle of the court. He lingers, alone with his thoughts. A man on Friday night in small-town gym. A coach.

AND THEN THERE'S HAROLD

The school is a place rooted in reality, not dreams.

Well before sunrise, Harold Roberts rolls out of his bed in the basement. Only after dressing does he dare dart across an icy concrete floor and trudge upstairs to make breakfast. Never cereal or toast or eggs. Always juice and a bowl of chicken noodle soup.

He first realized he was different three years ago, in the fifth grade, when he discovered that he liked school. That's when his classmates began teasing him. His parents tell him to ignore the taunts. He tries, yet he finds mornings, when he is alone with his soup and thoughts, to be the most peaceful time of the day.

He is soon joined by his mother, Veronica Roberts. The bus stop is only four blocks away, but she drives him to school. "African-American boys are an endangered species," she explains. She and her husband, Christopher, have jobs on opposite shifts -- he as a public safety officer at a community college, she as manager of information at an office -- so one of them will always be home with Harold and his younger brother and sister.

His parents approach life simply: Work hard and live within the law. Believe in God. Don't just meet standards, exceed them.

They understand, even expect, mistakes from their children. But not excuses. When they were unemployed awhile back, they told the kids that every life is filled with obstacles and that not having a job was one. There would be others. So they got by on unemployment, tightened the family budget and looked for work.

Veronica Roberts hands Harold the keys, and he slips away to warm up the car, a 1985 station wagon with ripped seats, a cracked windshield and more than 130,000 miles on the odometer.

They ride in silence the first few blocks. His parents know that Harold is slipping away from them. They are his launching pad into the world. They pray they have adequately prepared him for his trip.

Words between mother and son come when they both glance down a side street. They remember last year when Harold stumbled into a fight while walking home from school. He was behind a group of kids he did not know when one of the kids gestured at a passing car. The driver pulled a U-turn, jumped the curb and sped along the sidewalk, forcing everyone to scatter.

So now Harold doesn't catch the bus or walk home from school or wander alone through his Portland neighborhood, which borders Northeast Killingsworth Street about 11 blocks east of Martin Luther King Boulevard.

With each passing block, Harold fidgets in the front seat. He stares out the window. He clears his throat. When his mother turns into the driveway at Whitaker Middle School, the catcalls ricochet through his mind: "Smart boy, white boy." To calm himself he reaches in his backpack and searches for his calendar. He flips to a page where he has written himself instructions for this day.

"Really study for the test and ask more questions."

"Overdo yourself. Make positive changes."

"Have desires."

He is 13, a tall kid, about 5 feet 8, with the taut, slender body of a long-distance runner. Wire-rimmed glasses frame his face. His most distinctive feature is a deep, hearty laugh that hints at the man he will become.

He waves to his mother and heads alone toward his other world. No one raises a hand in greeting. No one asks about his weekend. He passes through the sea of students without a word.

When he opens the door, noise assaults him.

There are nearly 900 students here in the district's largest middle school. About 60 percent are minority. For the most part, it is a poor school.

Hats and caps and anything that could be considered gang attire are prohibited on school grounds. Officials, knowing that weapons can be hidden in pockets, require that coats remain in lockers. Sometimes it doesn't matter. When two students argued about a pencil a few months ago, one tried stabbing the other with a pair of scissors. During the past several years, two former students were gunned down and murdered by rival gang members. A third was shot and wounded while riding his bike.

Whitaker Middle School is a place rooted in reality, not dreams.

And then there's Harold.

———◆———

As he heads to locker No. 567, Harold feels out of place. In the hallways, boys talk only of basketball.

Harold: "I don't like basketball. I played one year in grade school because my mom said I should try it. We won all our games but one. I still don't see the purpose of the game."

Profanity and slang hang in the air like smoke in a bar.

Harold: "I don't live in an environment where that's spoken. And I don't say ` 'bouts' and `ain't'. My mom calls that `Yo, baby language.'"

He devours books, especially history. He likes the challenge of homework, especially social studies. He learned the piano by ear and plays at church. He would practice more often, but the $99 keyboard his parents gave him broke.

The first taunt comes near his locker.

". . . boy."

He can't make it out.

He swivels.

A blur of faces. And beyond, Edna Mae Pittman, waving to him.

Only then does he smile.

Most students avoid Pittman. She is 55 and her title is student services specialist, but she is more of a motivator and a woman who specializes in talking about real life. "I want these kids to understand that the world is bigger than this school, this city and this state." Although she is African-American, some black students call her racist because she doesn't cut them any slack during difficult times.

"Suck up."

Harold does not turn around.

Pittman calls to him.

"You come see me later."

He nods.

Pittman listens to the slang and watches him move on.

"Lord, have mercy."

Her speech still carries the lilt of her native Mer Rouge, La. Her father, a welder's helper on the railroad, never attended school. Her mother, who cleaned other people's clothes, made it to the eighth grade. Pittman, a single mother who raised six children, decided to go to college at age 38 and earned a master's degree at 44.

She stops her history lesson when a student slides into her office to hand her the daily report card she has requested from his teachers. The boy has not been paying attention in class.

"We don't want that, do we?" Pittman asks.

"No."

"You be better tomorrow."

She sends him away with a smile.

"Lord, have mercy," she mutters.

She studies the report card.

"That boy only wants to do work he thinks is fun. I called his mother -- I call parents, you know; yes, I do -- and told her that he will do all the work or he will sit in my office. And I know that boy doesn't want to be in here listening to me."

She admits to being pushy: "You know that saying -- You can lead a horse to water, but you can't make them drink'? Well, I make some of these students drink."

She laughs at being called a racist: "I know many of these kids are poor. Growing up I had it hard, so hard. My mother said people can take everything away from you but knowledge. Yes, there is racism. But I will not tolerate that as an excuse. We cannot continue to blame the white man for our situation. Yes, maybe we'd be further along if we had received a decent education earlier. Yes, there are going to be hard times. But I don't care about yesterday and I don't care about slavery and I don't care about what happened 100 years ago. I care about today and tomorrow."

Whitaker has more programs than most schools to help students. Pittman tries to steer students to tutoring sessions. Some days she is so discouraged that she wants to quit.

"I used to think I was going to save every child," she says. "Then a child in a gang was shot. Oh Lord, have mercy. I realized what I was up against. I could not save everyone. I asked the Lord to let me do what I could. I asked that in my attempt to save all, I might save some."

Last year, Pittman was registering students whose last names started with P, Q, R and S. "We were in the cafeteria. The place was chaos. Parents talking, kids yelling. I looked up, and this young man with glasses was standing there. There was something about his manner, his tone of voice. He radiated something. I knew, I somehow knew, that this was a child I could focus on."

She shakes her head at the memory.

"Lord, have mercy."

And so Edna Mae Pittman took Harold Roberts under her wing.

———◆———

Every student in the class must stand and read a sentence or two about what they did over the weekend. Most students mumble, barely more than a phrase or two.

Harold rises.

One sentence.

Two sentences.

He hears snickers.

Three sentences.

Four sentences.

Laughter.

He pushes on.

Ten sentences.

Motivational signs hang from the classroom walls: "I will listen and follow directions." "I will respect others." "I will work hard." "Enter the room quietly." "Be seated when you come into class." They seem as effective as speed-limit signs on Interstate 5 between Portland and Salem.

In Harold's Spanish class, the teacher is trying to get 32 students to understand the difference between the words "paper," "chair" and "desk."

A girl prances, yelping and waving her hands, as if on a game show. Four girls comb their hair. One complains that she doesn't want to be in class. Two girls argue. "Shut up," one yells. A group of boys laughs. Soon, seven conversations are taking place. Across the blackboard someone scrawls, "This class sucks."

The teacher asks the class if he is holding a piece of paper.

"Si," Harold answers. His book is open. He tries taking notes.

The teacher cannot hear him.

A girl starts to dance.

"Si," Harold tries again.

A boy punches another in the arm.

"Si."

Harold closes his notebook. He stares out the window.

Between classes, Harold sees Pittman and tells her about the Spanish class. "Keep on," she tells him.

She watches him walk away.

"How can a child learn? Lord, have mercy."

After first meeting Harold, Pittman took time to speak to him whenever she could. An operation on her left foot forces her to walk slowly, and eventually Harold offered to carry her books. Then he would linger in the doorway. Before long, he dropped by her office at lunch when other boys were practicing jump shots in the gym or after school while waiting for a ride home.

They talked about her past and his future.

From what she observed and learned from his teachers, Pittman knew that Harold was one of the smartest kids to pass through Whitaker. His parents had taught him that when a person masters one skill, he should find another to tackle. Pittman alerted him to a tutorial program run by the

Urban League, and his mother agreed to drive him there every night for two hours of study.

In his classes, in the hallways, he ignored the laughter and the snipes.

"He kept himself above all the madness that surrounds him," Pittman says.

And then his cousin was murdered.

Harold: "He was 20. He was a real friendly guy. He had a nice smile. I remember that smile. He was at his father's house, and a friend called and asked him to come over. It was raining, and his dad said no. He thought his dad was controlling his life, and he said he was going anyway. He was in the basement playing cards. His friend went upstairs through an outside door, and some guys came by and shot two times through the basement window. I heard there was blood everywhere. I think they were coming after his friend.

"My cousin lived a today life. He didn't think about the future. He finished high school and had a daughter, but he wasn't married. He had some kind of job in a nursing home. When he died it made me think about the choices a person makes and the people you hang out with."

He threw himself into school. Pittman arranged to have Harold and other top students testify before government agencies and neighborhood associations about school projects. Not so they could lobby or brag, but so they could practice public speaking.

She arranged for the students to take over a pizza parlor one evening as a fund-raiser. "The employees were there to watch them, but those kids did it all: Took the orders, made the pizza, served the customers, handled the cash register. A lot of the kids wanted to do the fun jobs. Harold? He stayed in back and washed dishes. I had to make him come out and do something else. He said someone had to do the dirty work.

"Oh Lord, have mercy.

"When the night was over, I sat those kids down and told them that their goal should not be to work in a pizza parlor, but dream of one day owning a parlor."

Harold makes the honor roll. His work is so good, so advanced, that teachers say he's the kind of student that comes along once or twice in a career. They marvel: "On par with any top student in any middle school in this city."

He dreams of becoming a lawyer but wonders if he has what it takes.

Pittman says he does.

My little lawyer, she calls him.

———◆———

Ignore them, his mother says. You will be a lawyer. One day you will defend the very ones who now mock you.

Harold decides to run for student-body president. He writes a two-page speech and practices it at home. His platform is to start a program in which students can tutor each other. And he wants to start an academic bowl to make scholastics as important as sports.

He wears a suit to the student assembly. He hears the kids laugh when he stands. He hears them say he looks like he's going to church. He reads his speech. But it is too long. He runs over his time limit and is cut short. He sits and listens to the other candidates. They are funny. The kids laugh. It is a different kind of laughter.

Harold comes in a distant third.

Pittman is in the principal's office when a call comes in from a Portland group called the Coalition of Black Men. It is looking for a male student who could be named student of the month. The principal asks Pittman if she knows of anyone.

"Harold Roberts," she says without hesitation.

The principal doesn't know Harold very well.

"Are you sure?" he asks.

"There's no one else," Pittman says.

The school must have a picture and a biographical sketch on Harold to the coalition by the next day to make the application deadline. Pittman tells Harold. She calls his parents. She works on his resume. She gets the packet to the coalition.

The days pass.

A week goes by.

Nothing happens.

Everyone forgets.

And then one day, Harold and his classmates are on a field trip in downtown Portland, studying various churches. They are boarding a Tri-Met bus when a classmate notices a poster in the bus.

Student of the month.

Whitaker Middle School.

Harold Roberts.

———◆———

He is invited to a Black Achiever's Annual Banquet where he must give a short speech. He arrives to find that he is the youngest person at the dinner. He is scheduled to follow Charles Jordan, a former city commissioner who is regarded as a gifted speaker.

Harold is not nervous. Government agencies, neighborhood assocations. This is no different, he tells himself. During his 10-minute speech he explains where he lives, what he studies and what he wants to do with his life.

This is how he ends his speech: "I'd like to thank Edna Mae Pittman. She was the one who helped me get to where I am. Without her, I would not have had the opportunities I had. She always pushed me along."

There is a round of applause.

When the banquet ends, a man named Tom Fuller introduces himself. He works for a Portland consulting firm and does recruiting for Yale University. Impressive speech, he says, and invites Harold to a meeting at Grant High School where an admissions officer will be talking with a select group of students.

Harold is the only African-American at the meeting. And all the other students are high school seniors. Harold stands and asks several questions about the law program.

Fuller has been talking with Harold's teachers and checking his school record. Now he asks the admissions officer what she thinks of Harold. She can't believe that he is in the eighth grade. She writes his name on her list. A few weeks later, Fuller sends Harold a letter telling him that they will be watching him through high school.

"This kid could go to any college he wants," Fuller says. "I've been interviewing kids since the early 1970s, and he's at the top of the list. He's gifted. No two ways about it."

Harold can't apply to college for four years. Fuller said that's only a technicality.

"And let me make this clear: Yale has a $4.8 billion endowment and admits blind to need. When he's accepted, we commit to his financial needs. The family pays nothing. Harold is the kind of person that makes a class at Yale what it is."

Fuller is white, a country boy.

"I grew up on a farm outside of McMinnville. Neither of my parents graduated from college. I was recruited to go to Yale. I got a scholarship, and it changed my life. I guess I'm trying to repay that debt."

He speaks quietly.

"I can relate to Harold."

He laughs.

"Except I wasn't as smart."

———◆———

They still make fun of him because he tucks in his shirt.

They still don't understand this thing of his with Pittman.

But . . .

There are students who want to sit next to him in class. They ask for his help. He doesn't just give them the answer, they say, he explains how he did it. They thank him.

"Don't make too much of all this," 14-year-old Jewlien Battles says. "A basketball player is looked up to more here. Way more. That's just the way it is. And as far as popular kids go, he isn't near the top."

For a moment he says nothing.

"But you know, in his own kind of way, Harold is cool."

1-2-3-Blush

They don't know. They can't know. They shouldn't know.

Life gets confusing when a boy turns 12. Perhaps not all of life, but certainly the part involving girls. When he's younger, girls are no big deal. Then he hits seventh grade and . . . BAM!

They change. Or he does.

At 12, a boy can find that just thinking about girls makes his hands sweat.

A grown man forgets what it's like to be a seventh-grader.

And so you spend a little time with Scott Dougherty.

He talks. You listen. You talk. He listens.

The years slip away.

You remember Melanie and Laddie and Becky. And even though you are 41 years old and married and the father of two daughters, the past returns so surely that your palms grow damp.

The process by which boys become men and girls transform into women is as subtle as the fade of daylight to dusk. It is possible to sense, but not see. Unless you wander into the Scottish Rite Center on the southwest edge of downtown Portland and stumble over your past.

There, on the second floor, you find Friday Evening Dancing Class, known to generations of Portland seventh-graders as, simply, dancing school. Since the school's founding in 1922, invitations have been issued to every westside middle school.

Classes run 10 weeks. By the end of that time, most kids truly can manage a fair fox trot.

But, truth is, dancing school is not really about dancing.

It is about boys and girls discovering the mystery of difference.
It is about children standing at the threshold of change.
It is about being 12.

The guide leading the children through this passage of life is Richard Walker, dance instructor. He is past 70, looks 60 and moves with the grace and confidence of a wide receiver in his prime.

Walker is Central Casting's perfect small-town postmaster. Serious, but not a fogy. Humorous, but not a comic. Mannered, but no fussbudget. His most distinguishing feature is a deep baritone, an instrument as rich and thick as maple syrup on a cold morning.

He uses it now to welcome a visitor to his home and introduce his wife, Dorothy. They have been married 47 years. For 35 of them, she has played his Ginger Rogers as he waltzes through the metropolitan area, teaching formal dance at social clubs and fraternal organizations.

Walker is only the third teacher in the long history of dancing school.

The first was Victor Christensen, a dandy with a Packard convertible and an uncanny talent for wooing women. When he died in 1937, at age 40, his cousin, Richard Billings, carried on.

Billings conducted himself like an English butler. He wore a tuxedo and made his students wear white gloves. Further sophistication was provided by a pianist, an older woman who never smiled.

Walker stepped in some 15 years ago, when Billings retired. He changed a few things -- boys no longer wear gloves, and the pianist gave way to a record player. But the basic tenets of dancing school, like good manners, have endured.

On this Friday afternoon, Walker ventures into his basement to find music for that evening's class. He rummages through a record collection that numbers more than 3,000.

"I use contemporary things," he says proudly. "Even Michael Jackson records."

Walker, who insists there is science in learning to dance, warms to the subject.

"First, you have to have a good beat," he says. "I try and find things that don't have lyrics because lyrics distract the kids. And, well, actually some of those lyrics are a little bit naughty."

He shakes his head.

"That Macarena, boy, you don't want them to listen to that."

Satisfied with his choices, he glides back upstairs as he explains why some records made the cut.

"New York, New York" -- "Kids like that for some strange reason."

"Hanging Out" -- "That's Henry Mancini. There's some whistling in it that the kids seem to like."

"Walk Between the Raindrops" -- "A modern swing beat."

He sets the records by a 41-year-old player, a "Califone Promenade," that accompanies him to dancing school. He escorts his wife to the sofa before he commences his demonstration.

"The first dance the children learn is the rhythm dance," he says.

His feet slide back and forth.

"Actually it's the samba, but I don't dare say that," he says. "It sounds too adult. What seventh-grader says he's going to do the samba?"

He sits down.

"Now we don't do the rumba or the tango," he says. "It's just too adult-ish. To do it right, you have to get close to each other. And I have the children dance quite far apart."

His wife nods her approval.

"Now on the fox trot they have to be a little closer together," he says. "The boy's right hand is on the girl's left shoulder blade. But clothes are not touching. We don't want seventh-graders close dancing. You know what kind of . . ."

His wife interrupts.

"Honey, tell about the problem with the cha-cha."

Walker hears music in his head and springs from his seat.

"This is the right way to do the cha-cha," he says. "You see that 1-2-3 rhythm? Smooth. It's supposed to be smooth. Well, when the kids do it they think it's fun to stamp their feet."

His wife looks pained.

"That's not dancing," she says.

Walker, still dancing, smiles.

"No, honey," he says. "That's adolescence."

———

The transformation begins about 5:30 p.m. when Scott Dougherty sheds baggy pants, his University of North Carolina basketball jersey and tennis shoes and heads to the shower.

He emerges wearing a blue blazer, gray slacks, a white shirt, a tie and black dress shoes. His mother selected the shoes. He didn't care what she bought as long as it wasn't anything fancy, which he describes as shoes with "dots on them."

His mother looks up from the stove and says her son looks wonderful. His father nods. His 17-year-old brother smirks. Dougherty returns to the bathroom to examine himself.

"I feel more mature," he says.

He squares his shoulders.

"Like 18."

He does not wear cologne.

"I don't have any," he says. "My brother does, but I don't think he'd like it if I wore it."

He stares into the mirror.

"My hair won't stay down."

He adds water to a comb.

He examines his hands and rubs them on his pants.

"They sweat. My friend's sister, who's older, went to dancing school, and she told me and my friend that she remembers having a guy's sweaty hand on her waist. So I'm always wiping them off."

He carpools to dancing school with best friend, Tommy Petroff, and Abbey Bowman, a girl he has known since fourth grade.

"You know, Abbey sure looks different in a dress," Scott says. "I've never seen her look like that."

He peers around the corner to make sure his brother isn't eavesdropping.

"You know, Tommy and I don't goof off as much around her when she's dressed up like that."

He checks his hair once more, then walks to the kitchen to wait for his ride.

The kid in him polishes off a handful of Oreo cookies, a glass of milk and a ribbon of spicy beef jerky.

The man in him pats his coat pocket to make sure he has his Certs.

———◆———

The boys trade punches and see who can jump the highest, shirttails askew. Shove a 12-year-old boy in a sport coat and slacks and he still acts like a boy.

The girls are something else.

Slip a 12-year-old girl into a fine dress and hose and a pump with a low heel and she is a creature who bears no resemblance to that skinny irritant who sits two seats away in social studies.

The girls exit from cars with grace and beauty, testing a power they don't yet comprehend. Only when they hurry to the ballroom do they give themselves away, running like little girls on the playground.

The boys scramble to the south side of the old-fashioned ballroom, beneath wall sconces and ceiling fans, while the girls hunker down on the north. They glance slyly across the room at each other, taking great care to look as if they are doing nothing of the sort. An anxious electricity ripples through the air.

Max Podemski appears shellshocked. He does not hear the question. Asked again, he repeats it.

"What's most embarrassing?"

He rubs his head.

"Dancing with a girl you don't like or one you really hate."

He looks across the room and grins.

"Or dancing with one you like."

Across the room, the girls register a change in the boys.

"They are so polite," Ally Estey says. "But their hands shake when they hold mine."

Abbey Bowman fiddles with her white gloves.

"Boys are nervous," she says. "They don't look at you. And their hands sweat."

———◆———

O ut in the empty foyer, at the foot of the steps, Roger Madden patiently sits through another class, attired in a proper business suit and tie.

Madden's family has run dancing school since 1940, when his mother took it over for a friend. In 1976, his wife took over for his mother. One day, Madden's daughter will be in charge.

Dancing school tuition is $65. That covers the invitations, the hall rental, insurance, Walker's tutelage and, on occasion, a minimal profit.

"I'm not into this for the money," says Madden, who has several business ventures. "If a child wants to dance, but the family can't afford it, I cover it. Every child should be able to come here."

Madden is 71. There are other places he could be on a Friday night. But he chooses to be here, to listen to the music float to him from the ballroom, to wait in the foyer and greet the children.

"Keeps me young to be around these kids," he says. "It's funny, though. When I told one boy that I knew his father he told me that was his grandfather."

He shakes his head.

"Where does time go?"

———◆———

G hosts are everywhere. In the ballroom, past, present and future collide and create something so timeless and life affirming that it overwhelms.

The dancers, though, are mercifully unaware.

"My mom made me come."

"I like to dance."

"My brother went so I'm going."

"My friends are here."

They don't know. They can't know. They shouldn't know.

They are children.

They are 12.

———◆———

Time to touch.

Walker bounds across the room to the boys and leads them, single file, to the girls, who also are standing in line. They pair up one by one, like gears meshing. A boy offers his arm, a girl slips her hand through the crook. It is strictly random. A girl who is 5-foot-7 links with a boy 4-foot-5.

Smiles are few and strained. Some girls talk with their partner. Others ignore the boy to chat with a nearby girlfriend. A few couples stare straight ahead, as if trapped in a bad marriage. Beads of sweat glisten on a few foreheads, twinkling in the dim light.

Walker leads the dancers around the ballroom, breaking them off in groups until three circles are formed, one inside of each other. Walker takes the middle.

"Boys, turn to your right. If you've met the young lady before, say hi. If not, introduce yourself."

The dancers stand two feet apart.

"Dance positions," Walker calls.

The dancers hold up one arm, as if dancing with an imaginary partner.

"Back to neutral."

"Boys check your shoes. Make sure they're where they should be."

"Dance position."

Walker wanders through the circles.

"That's great."

"Now the formal touch. Dance positions."

Each boy places one hand on the girl's waist, the other supporting her opposite hand.

"Back to neutral."

Hands drop.

"Touch."

"Neutral."

"Very good. Boys, check your right shoe. Now we're going to do the rhythm dance with music. You remember the steps from last week. This song has a good beat."

"Love Talks" blares from the speakers.

Some dancers are out of control. Many stare at their feet or off into the distance. When the music stops, Walker tells the boys to move to the next girl. And remember to introduce yourselves.

Max Podemski sighs.

Abbey Bowman looks up at a boy.

Scott Dougherty wipes his hands on his pants.

The music starts.

One boy can't see fit to make contact; through an entire song, he maintains a six-inch gap between his hand and her waist. Elsewhere, kids relax. They exchange glances. A smile. A gesture. A faint wistfulness when they next change partners.

Walker calls out the next dance, the "Lady Under." Back and forth, back and forth, and then the girl turns and spins under the boy's outstretched arm. Walker and his wife demonstrate.

"Boys, you do the side basic. And boys, please don't grab on to her fingers when she goes under."

"Shug-a-dee-bop" fills the room.

Walker beams.

"This is quite a modern record. The beat is a little faster."

He counts out the rhythm.

"One-two, one-two, one-two. Ready. Lady under."

Some girls get stuck in their partners' baseball-bat grip. A tall girl ducks to clear a short boy's arm. A boy steps on a girl's much-larger foot.

With great fanfare, Walker announces they will try the calypso. He shows them the steps. Instead of gliding, the kids stamp their feet.

"Adults don't make noise," he warns. "Four-year-olds do. If you are next to someone making noise, you know how old they are. Let's try again."

The stomping shakes the room.

"Hmm," he mutters. "I guess we'll have to forget the calypso."

They zip through the fox trot before the hour ends.

"Boys, before we go, I have a question. How many of you helped some lady with their chair at the dinner table?"

About half the hands go up.

"That's much better than last week. Let's see if we can be perfect next week."

Class is dismissed with a parting ritual. Each dance couple must greet one of several patrons -- parents who act as hosts to give the dancers the chance to practice saying thank you. The boy's task is to introduce himself and his partner.

A boy approaches.

"My name is . . .

He freezes. He plays with his tie.

"Thank you," he blurts before fleeing, leaving his partner stranded.

Another couple steps up.

"Um, good morning, I mean, good evening. Let me introduce Jenny."

Formalities complete, they spill out of the ballroom, down the steps and outside, where they wait for their rides.

A boy takes tentative hold of a girl's hand for a moment, before he yanks off his tie and uses it as a whip to chase his buddies.

Another girl whispers to her friends that, during "Walk Between the Raindrops" a boy said he liked her. When her father arrives, she runs to him, offers a hug and slips her hand in his as they walk to the car.

———◆———

They hover at a magical moment in life. A time of knowing it all and of knowing nothing. A time of big talk, and a thick-tongued stammer. A time before bills and jobs, before heartaches and reality.

In the coming years, it is unlikely they will ever formal dance.

Decades later, you barely remember the box step. But you hold the door for your wife, teach your children please and thank you, and are somehow mindful of the value of good manners.

And what you carry with you still is the seventh grade.

You remember the soft scent of a girl, her hand in yours and how, for the first time, your heart fluttered.

MOUNT HOOD'S DEADLY DECEIT

I'm a father who wonders whether he understood what happened.

In the decade since the mountain's betrayal, I have traveled back many times. Never once have I thought of anything but the children.

Now the anniversary approaches, and the mountain calls again. I share the front seat with memories that have not faded, with names as familiar as the faces of my own children: Patrick McGinness, Richard Haeder, Brinton Clark, Giles Thompson . . .

They were among the 13 -- three adults and 10 students from Oregon Episcopal School, an elite private school in Southwest Portland -- who failed to return from a one-day spring hike to the top of Mount Hood.

They set out in the wee hours of Monday, May 12, 1986.

By nightfall they were several hours overdue.

By the second day, two from the party stumbled down in a desperate gamble to get help. The other 11 were trapped above, huddled in a snow cave. Searchers cursed the blizzard winds that kept them grounded.

By the third day, spotters found three dead on the slope. One wore no parka, another no gloves. Two had peeled off their boots. The madness of hypothermia -- the severe loss of body heat -- made them think they were hot. Parents prayed aloud to the dark face of the mountain, where eight still were lost in the snow cave.

At the end of the fourth day, a searcher's probe found the cave. The eight climbers huddled inside were so cold that intravenous lines could not pierce their frozen skin. By midnight, only two survived.

Mount Hood stands a majestic 11,235 feet. It is Oregon's tallest peak, its post card and landmark and playground. After Japan's Mount Fuji, Hood is the most-climbed mountain in the world.

The climb to its summit is so pedestrian that 10,000 trekkers make it each year. So routine that OES made it a rite of passage for sophomores. So casual that one of the kids on this trip lugged along a six-pack of pop.

The days after the OES disaster -- the second-worst climbing accident in U.S. history -- were filled with funerals and memorials. Then came weeks of investigations and, later still, legal inquiries.

All but one of the families settled with the school's insurance company; only one, the Haeders, sued, winning $500,000 from jurors who found the school had negligently caused the death of their son, Richie. A report outlined mistakes made on the mountain and recommended changes in the school's Basecamp program.

Climbers continue to trek up Hood each spring, but few take it for granted now. They wear proper gear and carry cell phones. They watch the weather. They honor the mountain's dark power.

Later that summer, I encountered the parents of one of the lost climbers. Their presence embarrassed me. I felt awkward as I cradled my baby daughter, a cooing, living reminder. I made small talk and tried to ease away. But the father clutched my shoulder.

"Cherish her," he said quietly.

I thought it was over then -- until this anniversary, when I again travel this highway, a journalist in search of a sequel. Now that I'm at the base of the mountain, I'm a father who wonders whether he understood what happened on that mountain, to those who survived, to those who died, to those left behind.

—◆—

Firefighter Rick Harder hunkers on a bench outside the station house in Southeast Portland. Harder, also a master sergeant in the U.S. Air Force Reserve's Portland-based Aerospace Rescue and Recovery Squadron, was summoned to the mountain 10 years ago.

He doesn't want to remember. He leans away from the questions as if they were a swarm of hornets. At times his emotions threaten to breach some internal dam he has constructed.

"We thought we'd find them that first day," he says softly. "We gave it our best shot."

His descriptions come shrouded in the safety of cliches -- packed like sardines, stacked like cords of wood. But that's what rescuers found in that cave.

Those on the bottom had to be cut from their clothes, which had frozen into the snow. A girl's core body temperature was 39 degrees. A boy's teeth were clenched so tightly that medics couldn't maneuver breathing tubes into his mouth. They were raced by helicopter to Portland hospitals, where the formal declarations of death began.

By midnight only two -- Giles Thompson and Brinton Clark -- were left.

"I see death all the time on my job," Harder says. "But these were kids and . . .

"I've got kids of my own."

He mutters.

"You know, we searched that area four or five times," he says. "Everyone in the world tried as hard as they could. But they were buried under snow as hard as this."

He stamps his foot on the driveway.

"Buried alive."

He slumps in the seat.

"To die on the side of a mountain."

He bows his head.

———◆———

Brinton Clark has kept her silence these 10 years. The last time anyone heard from Giles Thompson, he was in college in Colorado.

Ralph Summers and Molly Schula-- the two who stumbled off the mountain the second day in search of help -- let it be known they don't want to talk. Summers, who was hired by the school to help guide the trek, no longer leads climbs. Schula, an older student who had the strength to make it down the mountain with him, later married one of the attorneys who represented OES in the lawsuit.

Eighteen people began the climb. Five turned back before they even eclipsed the Palmer chairlift. Among them were Sharon Spray and her daughter, Hilary. Spray, who now lives in Laguna Beach, Calif., is stunned by the telephone call.

"Mount Hood," she says. "Oh, my God. I moved away from that mountain. I couldn't bear to look at it any more."

She cries.

"I'm sorry. For years I had nightmares. Those kids calling for help and I couldn't do anything. I knew every one of them. One was my daughter's best friend."

From the moment they set out, Spray sensed it was a mistake. Most of the kids had been in a school play and had attended a cast party Saturday night. On a short night's sleep, they set out about 2 a.m. Monday, the standard time to depart. The ritual of Hood is to reach the summit in time for sunrise, then cruise back down in time for dinner.

But newfallen snow had sculpted deep drifts. The climbers were weary; an adult and several students were so slow they fell behind schedule within the first hour.

Spray had climbed Mount Hood before. She complained loudly that this march was ridiculous.

"You don't climb like that," she says. "We were all carrying 50-pound packs. And it was cold, the kind of cold where you feel it in the marrow of your bones. Your stomach is cold."

For some reason, the Rev. Thomas Goman, a teacher at OES and the climb's leader, didn't listen. They pushed on.

"Then a storm hit, and there was a whiteout," Spray recalls. "We had no sense of direction or balance. I said this was stupid, we needed to turn around."

When her daughter, a diabetic, grew nauseated, Spray told Goman they were turning back.

"My lasting image is those kids walking past us, disappearing into the falling snow," she says. "They were exhausted. None of them said a word.

"We never said goodbye."

They buried her daughter's friend, Erin O'Leary. At the funeral, the girl's grandmother asked Spray why she didn't grab Erin and make her come down the mountain, too.

"That will haunt me until the day I die," she says.

Eventually, the questions drove Spray into therapy.

"What if I hadn't been there? Why did Hilary get sick? What if Hilary had refused to turn back? I finally learned that for some questions there are no answers. I just, I just . . ."

The telephone falls silent.

Then comes a resigned, exhausted whisper.

"We came back. We just came back."

She clears her throat.

"Hilary and I turned back. And two people came out of the snow cave. And that's the way it was."

———◆———

The telephone rings.

"Yes, this is Brinton."

She listens to the question.

"Yes. Next week."

———◆———

The cold is a gentle killer.

When they found Patrick McGinness, he didn't have a mark on his body. He was 15 and sang in the school choir. He was different from other OES kids because he didn't come from money. His family lived in Northeast Portland, and he attended school on a full scholarship.

"At the hospital, they pulled down the sheet, and I looked at him," his father, Frank McGinness, says. "He looked like he needed to be kicked out of bed and told to get ready for school."

McGinness, sipping tea in a Northwest Portland coffee shop, apologizes because his thoughts tumble at random. In the month before the climb, he and his wife separated, and she moved to Philadelphia. Patrick and his younger brother were to join her when school ended.

"In early April I had a wife, two kids and a business," he says. "By late August, I was divorced and had filed for bankruptcy. I had no job, no money. One son was dead, the other was 3,000 miles away.

"I was drinking pretty heavily to kill the pain," he says. "I was doing a little consulting work to make ends meet, but not much more than drinking."

In the brutal days after the climb, McGinness was more approachable than most.

"You know, it was such a public thing" he says. "Not knowing for days, the media. Always the media."

Patrick was buried in Philadelphia, near his mother. The funeral was front-page news. Seven TV crews, two from New York, showed up at the church. When McGinness returned home, he says, he went through the floor.

"I had nothing to distract me from the grief," he says. "I cried, but I was in denial. One night I heard some music that Patrick liked and I realized never again would I hear him sing. I pulled the blinds and started drinking at night to go to sleep."

He failed to tend to his wood-finishing business; orders dropped off, and he was forced to let employees go.

"I crapped out," he says.

And so it went until 1990, when he met the woman who would become his wife.

"She stopped my freefall," he says. "I won't say I got better right away; it took time. But with her I felt safe."

What would Patrick think?

McGinness smiles. His eyes glisten.

"I'd like to think he's seen it all," he says. "He'd be proud because I've taken care of myself. I have flaws, but I deal with them. I'd like to think my son would be proud that his father had the courage to change."

———◆———

The woman at the front desk would be about his daughter's age. Another one of those reminders. He strides into the reception area, dispenses a handshake and leads the way to his office.

"The Oregonian made this dreadfully difficult 10 years ago," Don McClave says. "Pursuing information about the insurance settlement; harassing families about the investigation. Ghoulish behavior."

He shifts in his chair. He moves as if his shirt is too tight or the chair too small. He braids his hands behind his head, tucks them between his knees. Anger and disgust seep out of him. He hasn't been asked about the climb for eight years. But if there is to be a story, he wants his say.

He waits for the questions.

He gives terse answers.

Yes.

No.

He bristles against a long silence.

Then he fills the gap.

"Losing a child is the worst thing that can happen to a parent," he says. "All of us were beset by the media, by movie companies, by television producers, by insensitive and self-serving groups trying to capitalize on the incident."

He is proud that none of the families sold its story.

"We didn't hurt each other," he says.

He and his wife didn't know most of the other families. The climb was for sophomores. His daughter, Susan, was a senior. She had made the climb as a sophomore and went along to help.

Her father softens.

"It never goes away," he says. "You learn to live with it with the help of the church, professional help, friends. But we deal with it every day of our lives. We always will."

We face each other across a gulf miles wide, each in our roles. Me the inquisitor. He the guardian of the past.

He snaps to attention.

"My son is grown and married," he announces. "My wife and I are here. Other than that, I'm not going to talk about our lives. Anyone interested in reliving the accident can read the papers from 10 years ago. It was awful then. It is awful now."

———————

She is wary.

"I had lots of requests for interviews," Brinton Clark says. "I never gave one. I never wanted to be a public person."

She talks now, she says, because it seems right. But she is as evasive as a boxer. She ducks and bobs. A certain intensity radiates from her. Talking with her is like playing chess with a grandmaster. You think four moves ahead and find she is there, waiting.

When she was pulled from the cave, she was in critical condition. She spent six weeks in the hospital and nearly nine months undergoing rehabilitation to repair nerve damage in her arms and legs. She sustained no permanent damage. Doctors said she survived because she was dressed more warmly than the others and because Giles Thompson lay on top of her, his life stoking hers. At the time, doctors said she might never remember what happened.

"I remember a lot of things," she says. "I don't want to talk about them. They should stay private, with me."

She admits to mood swings and depression the first year. She does not know why she lived.

"I don't want to guess," she says. "I don't want to rehash it 10 years later."

She leans forward.

"Look, I was only 15," she says. "I needed to work on getting better. It's not productive to look back. I don't do a lot of second-guessing. I survived, and many wonderful things happened to me."

She graduated from Stanford University with a degree in human biology and joined the Peace Corps; she taught health education in a West African village. She plans to get a master's degree in public health and then a medical degree.

And she has been kissed by death. She has stared over the abyss. You can see it in her eyes.

She knows.

But she will not discuss it.

"It is an element of who I am," she says. "But only an element. It does not define who I am."

She knows.

We stare at each other.

She does not fill the silent gap.

"I lived," she says. "Why is not a question that has plagued me."

———◆———

She answers the telephone, but hands it to her husband, who does all the talking.

"She's crying," Richard Haeder says. "This is still too hard for Judy. The real tragedy of this is that it never ends."

From the beginning, the Haeders were different. On the mountain they wore city clothes. She carried a handbag. The rage they felt about their son's death was apparent even then and finally boiled over when they broke with the other parents and sued OES. They won a wrongful-death suit, but no comfort. They fled Portland and settled in Rapid City, S.D., near his parents and brothers.

He practices law, much of it pro bono. Only a few people there know about their past.

When the Haeders filed suit, some people thought them vindictive, unable to let go.

"The suit was not easy," he says. "It kept open an already raw wound. But the school would not take any responsibility for their actions. Their blunders put young lives on the chopping blocks for no more than pride in a program."

Long before it was fashionable for fathers, Haeder put his family ahead of his career.

And he feels cheated.

"I could have made more money, but I never missed it," he says. "Everything was for the family, not living through Richie and my two girls, but looking forward to being with them as we grew older . . .

"You cannot raise a person and lose them without heartache and regret. You see their potential. Not that they were going to be kings and presidents. But they had a future."

Richie's baby sisters are now older than he will ever be. They don't want to talk about their brother.

When the Haeders were flying out of Portland for the last time, the pilot announced he had a treat for the passengers. He instructed them to look out their windows for a breathtaking view of Mount Hood.

G iles Thompson is friendly on the telephone, but firm. No interview. We talk awhile. I ask again. He waits and waits. He goes to ask his wife and returns with directions to his home near Seattle.

I ask one more question: Do you remember?

"Yes."

I n the need to blame, a school is too vague to satisfy. A villain requires a face. This time it belonged to Father Thomas Goman.

He taught physics, ethics and math at OES and led the yearly climbs up Mount Hood for the school's Basecamp program.

An investigation noted that his decision not to turn around early in the climb was inconsistent with his long record of safe climbs. This, his last, was his 11th. His reasoning, the report noted, will never be known.

His widow, an artist, lives a quiet life in North Portland.

"Big anniversaries are important," Mar Goman says. "A decade is a way of measuring changes in a life."

Others can speak to the climb itself, the decisions made, the mistakes. But I turn to the priest's widow for questions about God and where He was that week. We sit near a window. From time to time, she says nothing, but stares out at a rainstorm. Her eyes twitch, and most of the time she looks away.

"God could have changed the weather," she says. "But that is not how God works. Tom would say that we only see a small piece of the picture. That what looks unjust to us is part of a larger puzzle. God doesn't make things well in life."

She remains a religious person. God did not let her down.

"What happened ripped my life open," she says. "I had to redefine myself as an unmarried person in a married culture. As painful as it was, there was new growth for me. My spiritual depth is there in hard times as well as in joyous times."

Yes, she says, her husband was at fault. But so were the school, the administrators and all those who oversaw the program. Tom was dead and unable to explain his actions.

"He was an easy scapegoat," she says. "People who knew him have memories of him. Those who don't know him can make up their own minds. He is out of this world. What is said does not affect him."

She does not think that she must defend her husband. But she says it is better that he died on the mountain.

"It would have destroyed his life if he had lived and those kids had died," she says. "He could not have lived with himself. They trusted him to bring them down safely. And he didn't do that."

She grapples with her own questions, not theological, but practical. Months after the climb, she visited a local sporting goods store and stared at the climbing gear. Goman didn't own any Gore-Tex, any special underwear. His gloves were U.S. Army surplus. What if he had spent $500 for better equipment?

"Would it have made a difference?" she asks.

She looks out the window. She answers her own question.

"Maybe."

"How I wish."

"How I wish."

She sighs.

"As a Christian I believe in the resurrection," she says. "I waited and waited for a vision of Tom. I dream about him from time to time. He still plays a powerful role in my life.

"He was the first person who loved me unconditionally," she says. "I never felt I fell short in his eyes. I miss his sense of humor."

She stares at her hands.

"I miss the smell of him."

———◆———

He moves so gracefully. It is hard to believe he wears prosthetics, that both his legs were amputated after they pulled him from the cave. Each year since the climb, OES has a memorial to mark the event. Giles Thompson does not attend.

"I learned not to count the years," he says. "For a long time, I wanted it to go away. I wanted to be like everyone else. And I wasn't going to be."

He cannot straighten his fingers. Thick, wide scars from skin grafts map his forearms.

"I will die this way because of something that happened 10 years ago," he says. "Something horrible."

There are no tears. No long pauses. He remembers everything. His wife, Marie, has heard the story, but he speaks with such passion that she stares at him, captivated.

"We should have turned around," he says simply. "We were only at the halfway point at the time we should have been at the top. And we kept going. Father Tom was focusing on one of the teachers, who was having a difficult time. He kept telling her that this was good for her, that she should push on."

The climb began to unravel when Patrick McGinness, suffering from hypothermia, fell over and knocked others off their feet. "He got up and pushed himself to continue," Thompson says.

They were all so tired. On a steep incline, they took one step up only to slide down two.

"Then all hell broke loose," Thompson says. "The weather got even worse. We turned around, but Patrick was in bad shape."

The group stopped to try to warm McGinness. They zipped him in a sleeping bag with another student and fed him hot water flavored with lemon. About an hour later, when they should have been approaching Timberline Lodge, they remained nearly 9,000 feet up the mountain. They continued their trudge.

"Ralph Summers was holding onto Patrick, who was like a sack of potatoes," Thompson says. "They were falling. Down a ravine, wandering off course. We'd lose sight of them. It was snowing like hell. I was carrying Ralph's pack and mine. The wind was blowing so hard that the snow was horizontal."

Goman was at the rear, tending to signs of hypothermia in the teacher, 40-year-old Marion Horwell. He and Summers devised a plan: Follow a 160-degree compass reading, which would veer them away from treacherous Zig Zag Canyon, where climbers often end up in whiteouts. The adults were busy helping the sick, so they passed the compass to a student.

Thompson, in his bright yellow gear, stepped out in front a few paces to serve as a compass beacon for Susan McClave, the next student in line. Step, read and follow. Step, read and follow. In that way, they would curve the group into the Palmer chairlift and follow it to the lodge.

"But we didn't start reading the compass at the right place," Thompson says. "We cut too early, missed the chair and started back up the mountain.

Then I fell in a hole. We were lost and thought we'd fall into a crevasse. But there were no crevasses. Turns out we were just on the side of a hill."

By now it was nearing dusk. They should have been sipping hot chocolate at the lodge and congratulating themselves.

Instead they were high above, trapped in the whiteout. No one could see. Summers took over the lead.

He instructed those with enough strength to dig a snow cave where they could ride out the storm. McGinness was tucked back into a sleeping bag; the others huddled under a tarp.

"I have no idea how the cave was dug," Thompson says. "It just was. It was so small."

The stowed their gear under a tarp. Summers led the climbers -- all weary, some sick -- into the cave two at a time.

"I went in first," Thompson says. "Brinton was on my shoulder. Someone else butted up against my crotch. Half of someone else on my legs."

And they began a wait that would last three full days, long enough for death to visit.

"Scoot over."

"My arm is cramped."

"My legs hurt."

"Let me out."

The cave was about 4 feet high and 6 feet long. To get inside, the climbers had to lie down and slide through a tunnel made tight to keep out the wind. They had no insulation beyond the clothes they wore, and much of that was inadequate.

Body heat caused the snow ceiling to soften and fall in on them, the floor to melt and leave them in a shallow lake of slush. Ice formed around the entrance, tightening the hole, which had started out horizontal, but turned upward because of the snow and ice. Climbers took turns crawling out to make space, to get air. Those inside used an ice ax to keep the entrance chipped open.

"But it wasn't working," Thompson says. "Our shovel was lost, buried outside in the snow. And the hole got smaller and smaller."

It was only the first night. But already, Goman was severely hypothermic.

"One time he was outside the cave, shivering so loudly that it scared us. He was just screaming," he says. "I remember that sound."

Thompson struggled out to search for the group's packs.

"The tarp was under a foot of snow," he says. "I couldn't lift it. It was insane -- the wind, the snow, the cold. I couldn't get back in the cave. I panicked and just wrenched myself in."

By morning, most of the 13 were in bad shape. The students were listless. The teacher was no longer talking. Summers asked Goman to count to 10. He couldn't. His mind was gone.

Summers tapped Schula as his partner in the attempt to march out. He told those left behind that he and Schula would "keep walking until we found help or until we died."

Thompson pauses before speaking again.

"We were scared," he says. "That sound of people shivering."

Only the kids were awake. At first, they nursed their hopes. Summers would bring help. The weather would blow over. Rescue would come.

But the hours passed, and kept passing. Someone asked whether they were going to die. There was no answer. They lost track of time. At one point -- most likely Tuesday night -- three students went outside.

"Maybe to pee, maybe they were claustrophobic, I don't know," Thompson says. "But they couldn't get back in. We tried. All that could fit through that tunnel was a leg. I saw this boot. That's all. I chipped away with the ice ax, trying to make the hole bigger. But the boot disappeared.

"I looked through that hole," he says. "It was like looking through a telescope, just an image of gray. I wasn't at peace or terrified. They were out there and we were in here."

Thompson had no way of knowing that searchers were on the slopes, desperately probing the snow. He didn't know that they had come within 15 feet of the buried snow cave the day before. All he knows is that only he, Brinton and Richie Haeder were awake at the end. Their friends and teachers, cradled with them in that icy hollow, were dead, or near death.

"We hadn't eaten," he says. "We had no water. The weather wasn't getting better. We were cold. So cold. I never thought I would die, but I was pretty scared. It was so bizarre. This howling wind outside, the silence inside. And then a lot of hallucinations, pain."

The doctors never lied to him.

"They told me that I lost my legs and that six others in the cave died," he says. "I just cried. I cried. And I cried some more."

He returned to OES the next school year in a wheelchair and his physical recovery progressed rapidly. It wasn't until he went to Colorado College that the depression seeped in.

"I had to let my old self go," he says. "I just wanted to be like everyone else, and I wasn't."

He went to a counselor. He dropped out of school and began skiing in competitions for disabled people.

"I needed some success," he says. "I found it."

He returned to school, where he earned a degree in drama and met his wife. Their son Lewis, 2 1/2, looks like his father.

"I'm not rooted in the past," he says. "Nothing is going to change. I am rooted in reality. Every morning I put on my legs."

He stands up and walks down the hallway of his home. He returns with a piece of graph paper. He has drawn a pencil rendering of the cave. He does not want it to be reproduced, but he needs me to see it, to understand.

It is a simple sketch and small. But the terror cries out.

The cave is shaped like an old-fashioned water bottle, the kind tucked at the end of a bed to warm your feet. A side view shows there was no room to sit up. Thirteen bodies are jammed together. There is no free space. They are curled and draped, in balls and angles, clinging to one another.

The drawings have few features, but neither are they stick figures. Here is a boy, there a girl. There are shadowy eyes, almost personalities. One girl holds a head in her lap. Another, her head buried in someone's shoulder, seems so sad.

Thompson points to a figure shoved against one wall, hugging the girl next in line.

"This was me," Thompson says.

He doesn't know why he lived.

"I was slightly bigger, I had skied more and was wearing some ski gear," he says. "I don't know. I gave up second-guessing long ago."

There was a time he felt guilty, like giving up.

"But eventually I realized I could not give up or waste an opportunity that none of them would have."

He sighs.

"Erin and Susan and Eric and Patrick and Richard and Tasha . . "

His wife rubs his arm.

"They all had such special qualities," he says. "They all paid such a terrible price. In my heart, they are all with me. Not daily, I don't live for them. But they are there. The reality is that they are with me, and I with them."

Thompson's son toddles over to him.

"When I held my child for the first time, I realized that I am part of the cycle of life," he says. "And for the first time, I understood what those parents went through. Those hours, those days of waiting."

He bends down. He kisses his boy.

CHRISTMAS ADOPTION

With one little word -- "yes" -- a journey began.

The Christmas gift arrived unexpectedly in the heat of summer when a woman in rural Washington County picked up the phone and confronted a choice that she knew would ultimately alter the course of a life.

What if she hadn't been home? Or had declined, saying the timing wasn't right? Both haunting questions that get to the core of love, sacrifice and family -- concepts people focus on so intently this time of year.

With one little word --"yes" -- a journey began.

Though it may have started out of desperation, it ended in joy Friday afternoon, just two days before Christmas, when a family gathered in a courtroom for a simple ceremony that couldn't begin to do justice to all that had transpired during the past five months.

The call came July 13 when Sandi Brannock's husband was at work and the couple's six kids were busy playing in another part of the house. At her desk, she glanced at the caller identification and read Cincinnati. Brannock knew only one person there. And, sure enough, when she picked up it was Robin Steele, coordinator for the National Down Syndrome Adoption Network.

Five days earlier, a mother had given birth in Washington state to twin girls. One was healthy. The other had a heart defect and Down syndrome, both a complete surprise. The parents had decided they were going to take the healthy twin home and leave the other behind. Called boarder

267

babies, these children become wards of the state, which places them in foster care. Steele, who 35 years ago adopted such a child, searched her organization's database to find someone who might take this child.

The parents were checking out of the hospital in two days.

She needed to find a family who not only had an interest in adopting a special-needs child, but who had also completed a detailed home study, the first step in the adoption process. The computer came up with Sandi and Kirk Brannock. Eighteen months earlier, the couple, both 46 and married for 17 years, had adopted Amira, a 2-week-old Washington baby girl with Down syndrome. Steele had an important question for Sandi: Were they interested in adopting again?

Brannock asked whether any other families had expressed interest.

No.

———◆———

The circumstances touched a nerve with Brannock, a registered nurse who had worked in a hospital's postpartum and neonatal unit before quitting to raise her children. She knew of a single mother who planned to put her unborn child up for adoption, but the adoptive family backed out when the child was born with cerebral palsy. The birth mother also walked away, and the child was institutionalized. The story hit close to home because one of the Brannocks' sons, Cole, 12, has cerebral palsy.

Brannock told Steele she had to talk with her husband, who works in high-tech. After a quick phone conversation, she got back to Steele and said yes.

That evening, the couple gathered their five sons, ages 6 to 16. Before they adopted Amira --who now walked around the living room during the discussion --they talked with their boys about what it would mean for their lives. Once again, they wanted their boys to weigh in. One day, when their parents were gone, the responsibility of having sisters with special needs would fall to the boys, they told them. The answer was unanimous. They were gaining another sister, one they would love as much as they loved Amira.

—◆—

The next morning, the family climbed into their 10-seat bus and set out to bring another little girl home. On the way, the adoption caseworker called and told the Brannocks to go to the hospital where paperwork giving them legal permission to see the baby would be waiting.

They arrived at the hospital early in the evening. The boys and their sister stayed in the neonatal waiting room. Their parents were each given a wristband that read "Baby A." On the band was the date the unnamed girl was born. Sandi Brannock studied the band, trying to remember what she'd been doing the day the girl she now considered her daughter was born. A nurse led the way to a room with a sliding glass door. She passed a crib where a healthy baby girl slept and stopped in front of a crib near the back of the room. She picked up a bundle and placed it in Sandi Brannock's arms. Brannock scooted over so her husband could sit next to her. She pulled back the blanket to look at the little face.

The baby was small and pale, more fragile than Brannock had expected, and she said a silent prayer asking for strength.

Kirk Brannock took pictures of the baby on his cellphone, then went to show the kids her image. Nurses told Sandi Brannock the baby had heart problems and had undergone blood transfusions, which was why she was so pale. Brannock handed the baby back to a nurse. She said she and her husband would return Friday, and the family checked into a nearby motel.

Sandi Brannock didn't want this newborn girl to leave the hospital without a name. She researched names online, studying the meaning of each one. None felt right.

Then she found Elyana -- God has answers.

—◆—

The next morning, the Brannocks drove to the adoption agency to complete the paperwork and to meet the parents who decided to give up one of their daughters.

At 11:30 a.m., the parents walked into the room with Elyana's sister in a baby carrier. Sandi Brannock expected a drug-addicted mother, or maybe a young girl. Instead, she found an attractive couple who appeared to be at least middle class. The parents were too nervous to sit, and they stood in the middle of the room. At one point, Brannock studied Elyana's sister. She saw the clear resemblance between the two girls, save for the distinctive facial features that indicated Down syndrome. The couple told the Brannocks they had a 3-year-old son who knew his mother had given birth to twins. The parents said they planned to tell him one of his sisters had gone to live with a family who would care for her.

As gently as possible, Kirk Brannock asked why they'd decided to give up one daughter. When the Brannocks had decided to adopt Amira, some people couldn't understand why. Even though it felt right to them, they approached it analytically, listing the pros and cons. The only con was fear. And that was not enough to stop them from going ahead.

Fighting tears, the woman said she and her husband were their parents' only children. They had no family in the area to help them raise a special-needs child. They both had demanding careers. They said they wanted the baby girl to live with a family who could do a better job than they could. The birth mother, clearly hurting, began crying. She said she loved the little girl.

The Brannocks would never judge this woman and her husband, a couple so full of fear and doubt. Better than anyone else, they knew what they were going through and would never want them to feel guilty. A little baby, made the way Sandi believes God intended her, would soon be joining a family eagerly awaiting her arrival. But it was impossible to say it just then. All the Brannocks could do was wrap their arms around this couple and hug them tightly.

The Brannocks returned to the hospital, where they filled out more paperwork and scheduled appointments in Portland with a pediatrician and a heart specialist.

Then they carried Elyana Brannock to meet her brothers and sister.

———◆———

Elyana was so small and fragile that doctors had to wait three months before she gained enough weight to fix the hole in her heart. She was eventually released from the hospital and sent home, but the recovery took more than a month. It wasn't until late November that their little girl was clearly healing.

A date -- what the family called "the day" -- was set to make the adoption official.

Two days before Christmas, they all gathered in the Washington County Courthouse, waiting to be brought into a courtroom where U.S. Circuit Judge Rita Batz Cobb would sign the adoption papers. All the Brannock kids, their parents, grandparents and family friends packed the hallway, waiting for the signal that it was time.

Kirk Brannock reached for his cellphone, tapped the picture icon and up popped a photo of Elyana.

"The rough patch in her life is over," Brannock said. "She smiled for the first time two days ago.

"We got it on film."

THE CAT'S STORY

Slow down and pull up a chair. Get a cup and slip into a small town's history.

Big cities are known for amenities, trendy restaurants, art museums and upscale stores. What's harder to find are the characters, the ones found in tiny communities, those little dots on the Oregon map where everyone knows everyone and their business.

Down in Tangent -- south of Albany and east of Corvallis -- there's never been a character quite like John Bass.

When Bass died in 1983, he left everything -- a five-bedroom house, a big barn and $70,000 -- to his beloved pet Kitty Kat with the stipulation that when the cat died, the estate would pass to Tangent, a town of about 1,185 people.

Bass, married twice, outlived his second wife. The couple had no children, but there were several nephews and nieces. No one is sure if Bass was sending a message to his extended family, or if he wanted to make sure Kitty Kat lived out the rest of its years in the lap of luxury.

The will was drawn up by Albany lawyer Roger Reid, who said he's never met a man quite like Bass. Reid laughed when he told the story about the time a bartender at Tangent's Dixie Creek Saloon refused to serve Bass -- a man who liked his drink -- another round.

Bass solved the problem by buying the place.

"That," Reid said, "is John Bass."

The Bass legacy continues Sunday when people will gather at his estate to watch a massive tractor-trailer haul the red barn, built in the 1920s, over the equivalent of two city blocks to a new home. The barn, by the way, measures 92-by-36 feet, is 40 feet tall and, with metal supports needed to help with the move, weighs 140,000 pounds.

All in all, the production would make John Bass proud.

Yet as interesting as the spectacle will surely be, the real story is how Tangent came to own the barn, who rescued it and why it's moving.

So slow down and pull up a chair. Get a cup and slip into a small town's history.

———◆———

Tangent, known as the grass seed capital of the world, is so small that when visitors need directions to City Hall, they're told to "take a right" at the Dixie Creek Saloon.

Don't go looking for anything fancy. City Hall is headquartered in the Bass house. The City Council meets there on a Monday night once a month. The council chambers are in the living room.

The town has no tax base and limited resources, getting a bit of money from state cigarette and liquor taxes and franchise fees from cable, electric, gas and garbage companies. It has just two employees: town coordinator Georgia Edwards and the budget and finance director, Bev Manfredo, who also answers the City Hall telephone.

The ghosts of John Bass and Kitty Kat are everywhere. Photos of Bass are scattered through the house. A framed photo of Kitty Kat has a place of honor on a table in the council chambers.

"You can't spend anytime in Tangent and not know about John Bass and his cat," Edwards said. "They're part of our history."

No one, however, knows if Kitty Kat, a gray and white mix, was a male or female.

"There were never any babies, if that helps," Edwards said.

Reid, the attorney who drew up the will, said he never bothered to ask Bass, a rye grass and wheat farmer and tavern owner, the cat's gender.

"He was kind of a rough guy," Reid said. "He was a fast talker. He knew my dad, and he came to see me to represent him on some farm problems.

One day he asked me to draw up this will. First time I've ever been asked to find a way to leave everything to a cat. Here was an old guy who wanted his cat to have first crack at the estate."

Bass died of old age, Reid said, but neither he nor City Hall officials can remember his age.

After the funeral, it came time to read the will.

"I was the mayor back then," said Jim Wagner, now a Tangent councilman. "The attorney called me and told me about the will. It came out of the blue."

The will said that a Bass friend, a man who lived on a mobile home on the property, could stay there with Kitty Kat and feed it. The $70,000 that Bass left was to pay for cat food and maintenance to the house and barn.

"The cat had been an outdoor cat," Edwards said. "After Mr. Bass died, people were afraid someone might kidnap Kitty Kat for ransom. So we had to keep the cat indoors."

Kitty Kat, Edwards said, wasn't great at using a litter box, perhaps making a statement about the nature of politics.

"It did try and run outside," Edwards said. "A few council meetings were stopped to go rescue the cat."

As Kitty Kat aged, the cat's hearing failed.

"It wouldn't hear me," Edwards said. "I'd turn around and accidentally step on it."

Kitty Kat -- at age 19 -- died in 1993.

"Naturally, we had a funeral," Reid said. "I was there. We had 20 people and had some music playing on a recorder."

The cat was buried in front of the Bass home under a small stone marker that reads: "Kitty Kat, a true friend."

The barn became an albatross for Tangent, Edwards said. The $70,000 maintenance fund was long gone, and the structure deteriorated and the roof had to be repaired. When shingles began falling off a second time, the council proposed a city levy to see if citizens would pay for the barn's upkeep.

"That was turned down," Edwards said. "We had a barn that was a liability."

The council tried selling the barn but got no takers. Several firms offered to dismantle the barn and take it to a landfill at a cost of more than $15,000, money that Tangent couldn't spare.

In February, a woman walked into City Hall to say she wanted the barn.

"I came to Oregon State University 30 years ago from Seattle and never left," said Beth Timmons. "I was a veterinarian technician, and a year ago I moved to Tangent as a hobby farmer. I raise sheep. When I got here, I heard all about John Bass and his cat."

When she learned the barn was going to be demolished, she said she "couldn't imagine this beautiful barn going to a landfill."

She showed up at a council meeting to announce her plan to buy it.

The council sold the barn to Timmons for $1 and helped get the permits to transport it to her place, the Circle of Life Farms. Her father, Mike Timmons, who lives in Washington, took over the planning needed to move the barn.

"When my daughter moved here, the first thing we heard was the Bass barn was going to be torn down," Timmons said. "Bass was a unique character. His barn needed a benefactor. I guess that's why I am down here."

He hired a company experienced in moving homes and structures. He didn't want to say how much it's going to cost him but said it would be far cheaper to tear down the barn and be done with it.

"The barn has been jacked up and has three dollies under it," he said. "It's going to be hooked up to an eight-wheel truck and towed like a little red wagon."

Beth Timmons said she received permission from two farmers to tow the barn across the fields to her property.

"One of them was a field of mustard seed, and we had to wait until it was harvested," she said. "But we had to do it before the rains came because it would have been impossible to move the barn. They harvested the field last week, and we're ready."

Timmons said she doesn't need the barn.

"I have three already," she said. "But this barn is a piece of this town's history. If it had been torn down, there would be a hole in the ground. I'm going to open it up as a community meeting place and museum where people can enjoy it."

Timmons calls herself a cat person with multiple cats and feels linked to the spirit of Tangent's character who so loved Kitty Kat.

"I think," she said, "this is what John Bass would have wanted."

Taking a Shot

If anyone asked what happened, he'd laugh the whole thing off as a joke.

Part 1

Mike Luckenbaugh sat at the workbench and concentrated on his first-quarter art project. Around him bantering classmates rehashed the weekend. But Mike, as always, was a couple of beats behind. By the time he thought of something to say, the clever, popular kids had moved on. So Mike sat silently, his face as impassive as the green ceramic mask he held in his hands.

He wondered whether his junior year could get any worse.

The school year wasn't 2 months old, but in Mike's world, everything was unraveling. His grades were good, he liked his teachers and they liked him. But high school has always been more than textbooks, grades and projects, a truth parents sometimes forget. The real battle, the one that keeps a kid up at night, is finding his place and himself. And, at 16, Mike Luckenbaugh was struggling.

He turned the mask in his hands, studying it from different angles. He was tall and slender, and he wore his brown hair spiked, with highlighted burgundy tips. That, along with a quiet, contemplative personality, set him apart from the bustle of students that swirled around him. So Mike went his own way, drawing, taking guitar lessons and writing stories about video game characters.

His artistic side had, in a way, created the challenge he was facing. Over the summer, administrators at Southeast Portland's Marshall High School had broken the school into four academic units. Mike enrolled in the arts division, but familiar faces from his first two high school years went elsewhere. Mike, who was naturally shy, suddenly felt like a stranger.

Art class drew to a close. Students tucked their projects away, gathered books and made plans for lunch. Mike moved slowly. He had no one to meet, no one to catch up with. A few weeks earlier, the friend he'd eaten lunch with every day, the buddy he'd had since middle school, quit showing up at his lunch table. Mike kept returning to the same table, and one day the friend showed up with a group of strange boys. They stood around Mike and teased him about the clothes he wore.

Mike, the last kid out of art class, stepped into the hallway. Locker doors slammed. Students yelled to one another and traded good-natured insults. They huddled in small groups and passed along the latest gossip.

Mike looked straight ahead, walking slowly, his brown eyes moving from side to side. He stayed close to the wall, poking along while others rushed up a staircase. When he reached the main floor, he turned a corner and walked past a case that displayed one of his art projects -- a pencil drawing of an open hand.

Mike had accepted that he would never be popular, never receive the magical anointing bestowed on a handful of students who seemed to have it all. He didn't feel sorry for himself, but he still wanted to fit in -- somewhere.

Up ahead he heard noise echoing off the walls. As in most high school cafeterias, students had to shout to hear one another. And this cafeteria was near the gym, where boys ran up and down the basketball courts, dribbling, passing and yelling. In the lunchroom, everyone segregated. The jocks held court at one end. The skaters owned that table. Across the way, the Goths, decked out in black, drifted toward one another.

Mike retreated from the cafeteria and returned to the main hall, where he sat on a bench with his back against a window. After a few seconds, he stood and walked across the hall. An 8-1/2-by-11 sheet of paper was taped to the wall.

Seeing it made his palms sweat. At home, his decision had been easy. At home, though, everything was easy. There, he moved with grace and confidence, sure of himself and his place in the world. But Mike didn't live just at home. He slept there, ate meals with his parents and older sister. But his crucible, the other place where he lived -- and died small deaths each day -- was in this high school.

He touched the paper and read the words: "BOY'S BASKETBALL TRY-OUTS."

He'd quietly signed up with the coach, a mild-mannered math teacher he once had. One of his classmates, though, caught wind of his plan and blurted it out in English class.

He was committed. Sort of. He could back out, just not show up in the gym Tuesday after school. If anyone asked what happened, he'd laugh the whole thing off as a joke. Because who -- in the entire high school -- wouldn't laugh at Mike Luckenbaugh's dream of making the basketball team?

───────◆───────

The school day ended, and Mike threaded his way through the crowded hall, out the main door to where his mother's car waited at the curb. His mother quizzed him on his day, the way she did every afternoon when she picked him up. But this day, he grunted one-word answers. He turned on the radio, bounced around a couple stations until he found a song he liked and stared out the window.

He thought about what he and his father had talked about that morning on the drive to school. Real failure, his father had told him, isn't trying and losing, but in never trying and never knowing. That sounded good, but his father wouldn't be at the next day's tryout.

By the time his mother turned into the driveway, Mike's spirits had lifted. Not only was he going to try out, he also was going to make the cut. He saw himself wearing uniform No. 19, his favorite number, and slipping into a letterman's jacket when the season ended.

His mother led the way into the house and headed to the kitchen. Mike sat on the living room floor and thought about his best basketball moves -- a jump shot and the ability to shoot with his left hand. He stood 6 feet 1 and weighed 145 pounds -- a basketball player's body, and he'd honed his touch out on the driveway, where he'd launched thousands of shots at the hoop hanging above the garage door. Stray balls had broken nearly every garage window. His father had nailed plywood over the vacant frames, even though his mother thought that made their house look trashy.

Each night, when his mother called him in for dinner, he'd always take a final shot while in his mind an announcer called out the play: "The game is tied . . . game on the line. Luckenbaugh has the ball. Three seconds to go. Luckenbaugh takes the shot. It's in!!! Luckenbaugh wins the game."

In the living room, Mike rose from the carpet, crouched and shot an imaginary ball. Swish. As soon as he landed, though, he stared at his tan surf shoes, the slip-on canvas style popular at school. The surf shoes were fine in a high school corridor, but they weren't basketball shoes. Mike didn't own a pair. He could rattle off the models named after famous players -- Vince Carter, Michael Jordan and Kevin Garnett -- but he knew what they cost. He'd heard his parents talking about household bills, and he knew where the money went in this family. He had running shoes. He'd wear those to the tryout. They'd be more practical than surf shoes.

He watched his mother bustling around the kitchen. She drove a 13-year-old car; his father had a pickup. The family didn't have cable television or cell phones. Neither parent had gone to college. His father worked as a property manager, and his mother worked the 6 a.m. shift in a Mervyn's shoe department. She shopped at discount stores for Mike's school clothes, the off-labels that popular kids sometimes ridiculed.

In the living room, Mike launched another imaginary shot, flipping his wrist the way Jordan used to do when he backpedaled down the court after making a three. Jordan's championship years with the Chicago Bulls back in the early 1990s had hooked him on the game. And, as much as he loved art and music, Mike Luckenbaugh was a closet basketball nut. He read newspaper sports pages and sports magazines. And, although he held back from the sports conversations among boys at school, he knew the teams, players and statistics as well as anybody.

Mike heard the truck door slam. His father, who played a year of high school basketball, shot hoops with his son in the driveway. But Mike had never played on an organized team, or even in an open gym with other boys playing a pickup game. Being in front of people made him nervous. During his sophomore year, when he presented his Global Studies report about life in Germany, he blushed, his cheeks turning so red that he ended up holding the paper in front of his face.

Simple conversations sometimes left him tongue-tied. He self-edited while he talked, thinking that what he was saying was stupid. He couldn't figure out how to casually break into a conversation. But he was working on being bolder. This very Monday, he'd said hello to the guy next to his locker.

The front door opened and his father walked in. His parents hugged and Scott Luckenbaugh sat in a living room chair.

Mike studied his father. Over the past year or so, he'd discovered a new side to the man. His father drove him to school each morning, and on the way he told his son about his own life.

As a young man, Scott Luckenbaugh also had been shy and lacked confidence. It was only now, at 45, that he realized he hadn't achieved some of the things he'd hoped for because he'd been afraid to take a risk. That fear of failing -- not the actual failure itself -- is what had held him back.

Over the summer, Mike thought about what his father had taught him. He started working out, running and taking guitar lessons. He decided to study hard his junior year. His father's mantra -- Dream big -- stuck with him. And when he saw the sign announcing basketball tryouts, he heard his father's voice.

As the afternoon gave way to the evening and the living room grew dark, Mike cast a glance at his father. He remembered the look on his father's face when he told him he was going to try out for the team, the way his father smiled at him and threw his arm around his shoulder.

Some of his classmates in the arts academy, though, told him he was stupid. Jocks, they said, were jerks.

———◆———

Mike lay back on the living room carpet, worrying about looking like a fool and daydreaming about jump shots and LeBron James, the kid drafted into the NBA right out of high school.

Mike's mother, Connie Luckenbaugh, came out of the kitchen and sat on the sofa. "Shall we get you some basketball shoes?" she asked.

Mike sat up.

"What?"

"I think we can afford it," his mother said. "We can use my discount and see what's on the clearance rack at Mervyn's."

And for the first time since he'd left school that day, Mike smiled.

After dinner, he and his mother drove to the Clackamas Mervyn's. They made their way to the shoe department where his mother would start work in less than 10 hours. She said hello to the other clerks, pointed to her son and announced he was trying out for the basketball team.

Mike went straight to the shoes. He held them in his hand, ran his fingers over the leather and touched the laces. He looked at one shoe, but spotted the price tag and quickly set it back on the shelf. He picked up another. His mother looked at the box and frowned.

"Geez," she said. "They're $50, and that's a little spendy right now."

Mike wandered over to the clearance rack. Nothing caught his eye. And then he found shoes that were white, with red-and-black highlights, two of his favorite colors. He bent down to look at the boxes, pulled a shoe out and searched for the price -- $39.99.

Mike shoved the box back onto the shelf, stood and moved on. His mother tapped him on the shoulder.

"Honey," his mother said, "I saw you looking at that red-and-black pair. Do you like them? Why don't you try them on. What are you a 12?"

"A 13."

"Wow."

His mother found the size and handed the box to her son. He slipped off his surfers and laced up the basketball shoes.

He grinned.

"Well," his mother asked, "how do they feel?"

"Really good."

"What's the price?"

He looked at the box.

"Almost $40."

She opened her checkbook and flipped through the register.

"With my discount," she said, "I think we can do that."

She thought some more. Her son waited.

"Yes," she said, "we can do that."

Mike followed his mother back to the counter, still wearing the shoes, and a clerk rang up the sale. His mother hugged him, pulling him in close.

"Thanks, Mom."

"I'm glad you got them," she said. "I'm really happy."

"Me, too."

Mike stepped away from his mother. He crouched. He jumped. He shot. Swish.

"I'm ready now," he said.

———◆———

As soon as his Tuesday afternoon art class ended, Mike ducked into a bathroom and changed into a black T-shirt, shorts and his new shoes, which squeaked with each step. When he was sure no other students were around him in the hallway, he thrust his hands over his head, flicked his left wrist and shot an imaginary ball.

"Five seconds to go, game on the line, Luckenbaugh with the ball . . . swish."

His smile vanished when he spotted dozens of students jammed in the narrow corridor by the gym, anxious to see who was trying out. Potential players thrived on the attention. They greeted friends with fancy street-style handshakes, flirted with girls and imitated the confident strut of professional players ready to take the court.

Mike stood with his hands at his side, looking down a short stairway at the corridor scene. He felt cool air on his back and toyed with slipping out the open side door. Tryouts started in 10 minutes. If he was going to escape, this was the moment. Not one student in the corridor would ever realize that Mike Luckenbaugh had, at the last minute, backed out.

But he'd know.

He remembered what his father had told him, walked into the crowd, pulled open the metal gym door and stepped inside.

Part 2

At the far end of the Marshall High School gym, five boys passed a basketball back and forth. Every few seconds, the door banged open behind Mike Luckenbaugh and more boys ran onto the court.

A few gave Mike the once over. Although tall for his age -- about 6 feet 1 -- the 16-year-old junior lacked the upper-body muscle of other boys trying out for the team. His brown hair was cut in a style unlike anyone in the gym -- tight on the sides and gelled into spikes, each dyed a deep burgundy.

Mike was different from the athletes around him in other ways, too. He was drawn to art and music. So when Marshall introduced a new system that divided the high school into smaller academic units, he chose the arts academy. That separated him from most of the school's jocks and also isolated him from old classmates. And Mike was shy, hesitant to call attention to himself. So his decision to try out for the basketball team was a real reach.

But his father had told him that the real failure was giving up without making an effort. That way, he said, you defeated yourself.

Mike looked around the gym and spotted Don Elwell, the 29-year-old math teacher who coached Marshall basketball, talking with an assistant coach. Elwell had taught Mike math the previous year, and Mike remembered him as easygoing and relaxed in the classroom. When Elwell seemed to look his way, Mike raised his hand to wave. But the coach quickly turned away without responding. Mike's face reddened, and his hand dropped to his side.

Other players yelled to one another, trying out fancy moves. Mike, who'd only shot baskets at the hoop hanging over the garage at home, knelt and tied new shoes, the red-and-white model his mother had bought off a discount shelf the night before.

He stood up, glanced around the gym. He retied his shoes. He adjusted his lucky wristbands, imprinted with the names of two favorite rock bands. He wiped the palms of his hands on the soles of his shoes, hoping a little dirt from the floor would improve his grip. He'd learned the move from the pro players he'd seen on television.

He'd never been to a Marshall basketball game and didn't know who'd been on the previous year's team. He recognized Daniel Tinnon-Brooks, also a junior. They had no classes together, but Mike had seen Daniel in the cafeteria with other jocks, the athletes many of his classmates in the school's arts academy thought were stuck up. Even from across the gym, Mike saw Daniel's well-defined arms. He dribbled easily with either hand and banked in jump shots from 25 feet.

A group of players walked onto the gym floor. Mike tagged along, falling farther behind with each squeaky step he took in his new shoes. When the boys started shooting, Mike hovered nearby, ignored, and drifted around the gym, trying to fit in. He retied his shoes.

A whistle blew. Don Elwell marched to the center of the gym.

"Let's go," he bellowed. "In formation, four lines."

Each time a player joined Mike's line, he cut in front of Mike, slowly pushing him to the rear. Coach Elwell waved his hand, then Daniel faced the lines and dropped into pushup position.

"All together," he called out.

"That guy," said a kid in the line next to Mike's, "is going to be a team captain."

The boys did pushups to Daniel's count.

"Do it right, do it right," the coach yelled. "This is no time to play."

Mike struggled to finish.

Another whistle.

Elwell told the players to practice defensive slides. Mike had no idea what the coach wanted. He moved to the side, watching Daniel. The flashy guard spread his arms and crouched. He slid three quick steps to his right, then left and repeated the move, as though he were guarding an offensive player. Mike copied the moves, but when he was ready to make the final step to the right, his line was already moving left.

Mike's arms hurt -- he'd never held them in a raised position for so long. His legs burned and sweat ran down his face.

"Too slow," the coach hollered from the front of the gym. "Everyone drop and give me 10 pushups. And pick up the pace."

By the eighth pushup, Mike's arms trembled. He was one of the last to complete 10.

The coach wandered through the hopeful boys, clipboard in hand. He wasn't anything like the easygoing math teacher Mike remembered.

"How many guys we got in here?" Elwell yelled. "Count off. "

He listened and studied his clipboard.

"We have 56 guys," Elwell said as he wandered up and down the rows of players. "It can be louder in here."

He blew his whistle, and told the boys to make two lines. He surveyed them. He'd be picking the varsity, junior varsity and freshman teams.

"Fellas," he said, "I hate to be the bearer of bad news, but 20 of you will be gone by the end of the week because you're not able to play at this level. Your services will not be needed. If your work ethic is not good, change it now. If your attitude is wrong, fix it now."

Elwell bounced on the balls of his feet.

"NOW," he bellowed, "is your chance to show ME that YOU deserve to play on this TEAM."

———◆———

The boys finished a running drill, and the coach called for the weave, a practice exercise that requires five players to move down the court, passing the ball back and forth until the final player makes a layup. On organized teams, even the youngest players know the weave. But Mike stood with his back against the wall, watching the other players and trying to make sense of the drill. He discreetly stepped aside to let other players move in front as they stepped forward to take their turns.

But he eventually arrived at the front of the line. A group assembled, and Mike joined them, taking off as fast as he could.

"Five man weave," Elwell yelled. "Luckenbaugh, five man. You're the sixth."

He felt the heat rise to his face, and he slid to the back of the line, hiding behind taller players. But then Daniel was there, refusing to move in front, pushing Mike. Someone tossed him the basketball, and it was up to him to start the weave. He took off down the floor, dribbling, uncertain of his next move.

"Ball," a player screamed at him. "Ball."

Mike still didn't pass, and the weave fell apart.

"He doesn't know what he's doing," someone yelled.

Elwell called for layups, breaking the players into two groups. Each boy had to run down the court and make a layup, the two teams competing against each other. Mike watched from the rear, listening to Elwell shout: "Run faster. Concentrate. We're watching you. The guys who can't handle it at this level, we send home."

Mike waited his turn.

"Come on now," the player behind him said. "Hurry up, buddy."

He moved as fast as he could, but missed. The players on his team grumbled, wondering why they were stuck with him.

"It's OK," Daniel said. "It's all right, man. We all miss. We're all human. Go for the square, you'll make it."

Daniel held up his right hand. Tentatively, Mike raised his. Daniel slapped a high five.

Soon, it was his turn again. He followed Daniel's advice, made the layup and made three more. He cheered with his teammates when they beat the other group.

Elwell called for a final drill. Defenders guarded shooters and then blocked a third player to get the rebound. Elwell pointed to Daniel and two other players.

"This is a demonstration," Elwell said. "We're showing you what to do. There will be no excuses."

For Mike, this was nothing like shooting ball with his father. He moved to the side, alone, and wondered whether he was fooling himself. He moved closer to the action to study the drill.

A whistle blew and the first day of tryouts ended with the coach demanding that everyone do 25 pushups. Mike's arms gave out at 18.

———◆———

When Mike walked into the gym the next afternoon, he saw fewer boys. Some, realizing they had no chance of making the team, hadn't bothered to show up. Others had been called to a small room just off the court where Elwell delivered the bad news -- they'd been cut.

The players lined up for the weave. Mike overcame his natural shyness and asked another player to explain the drill. Two boys stepped out of line and pointed to the players running down the court, showing Mike how they passed the ball and shifted positions. Mike got back in line. He rubbed the palms of his hands on his soles of his shoes and waited for the ball, which popped into his hands. He moved quickly onto the court, throwing a perfect pass to a player to his right, and returned to the line to receive a high-five from Daniel and two players standing with him.

Elwell walked to the middle of the gym. It was time to scrimmage.

"I do not want to go 2 and 24 like last year," he shouted, "or 2 and 24 the year before that, or 0 and 26 the year before that."

While Elwell divided the players into teams, Mike asked an assistant coach how to block someone while fighting for a rebound. The coach grabbed another player and showed Mike how to use his arms and legs. Elwell yelled out five names, and Mike walked onto the court. He'd never played organized basketball, never stepped onto a court like this with a group of guys. He wasn't even sure where to stand.

The opening tip somehow bounced straight to him. He grabbed the ball, dribbled down court and stopped. Two defenders rushed him. He looked at the basket, jumped and fired a shot from beyond the three-point line.

Swish.

Daniel, watching from the sideline with four players, cheered. He pointed at Mike and clapped. Mike tried to stifle a smile. A smile flickered across Elwell's face, too, but he quickly put his poker face back on.

Mike's moment was short-lived. He lost the man he was supposed to defend. The strong players pushed him around. He fumbled a pass. He dribbled the ball off his foot, and it bounced out of bounds. When the game ended, his team had lost and Mike was out of breath.

Elwell blew a whistle and told the boys to line up and run circuits around the gym. Mike kept pace for five laps and then faltered. His side ached. He felt like throwing up. When he was positive he couldn't take another step, he felt a hand on his back.

"Keep going, man."

He turned and saw Daniel.

"Keep going. You got it in you."

He ran two more laps and pulled out of line, gasping. He saw Elwell watching him. He put his hands on his knees, breathing in deeply, his face flushed. His hands trembled. Another player dropped out of line and stood next to him.

Elwell came to check on the boys.

"I can't do it," the boy next to Mike told the coach. "I'm done."

"What? You're quitting."

The player nodded.

Elwell shook his hand.

"Maybe we'll see you next year."

When the line of boys came around the gym again, Mike joined in. He ran four laps and dropped out. He lay on the floor, his heart racing. One by one, other boys dropped out. Any boy who dropped out, the coach said, had to do pushups in repetitions of 10 until the running ended.

Mike did his 10 and realized the coach wasn't watching him or the three boys next to him. Two of the boys sagged onto the floor.

Mike took a sip of water and got into pushup position. He took a deep breath.

Down.
Not for the coach.
Up.
Not for his father.
Down.
For himself.

———◆———

Mike nodded to other boys when he arrived for the third day of tryouts. One bounced him a ball, and he joined six other players at the basket. He'd just made his first shot when he heard the coach call him. He followed Elwell into a small room and sat on a bench. Elwell sat on a desk. Rob Reynolds, his assistant, closed the door.

"There's good news and bad news," Reynolds said. "The good news is that we loved having you here. The bad news, well . . . You haven't played basketball before, right? I mean not real ball. Just goofing off?"

Mike nodded.

"Your skill level isn't where it needs to be to make the team," Elwell said. "But we'd like you to stay on and be the manager with an option to practice and work on your game."

Mike remained silent, biting his lip.

"You got heart," Elwell said. "But this isn't going to be a storybook ending."

Mike took it all in.

"You have an athlete's body," Elwell said. "But you just need to work on it. You said you ran in the park. Coming out here, you see it's a different kind of running."

Elwell stood up. He had other players to cut.

"I want you to feel we gave you a fair shot," he said.

"You did."

"Think about the manager's job tonight," Elwell said. "Let us know either way. No hard feelings if you don't think it's for you."

He shook Mike's hand, opened the door, looked at his clipboard and yelled for another player to come into the office.

Mike lingered at the edge of the basketball court and watched the boys shoot and stretch. There'd be no uniform. No letterman's jacket. Only then, as he stood on the sidelines, did he realize just how desperately he'd wanted those things.

He hung his head, looking at his shoes. They were scuffed, broken in. He held up his right hand, then his left. His slender fingers had scratches on them from fighting for the ball.

He walked onto the court, passing through clumps of boys who would make the team. He stopped in front of Daniel.

Mike held out his hand.

"I was cut," he told Daniel. "But thanks for helping me."

Daniel took Mike's hand.

"I respect you," Daniel said. "Respect you for coming out and trying."

They shook hands.

Mike turned away, ready to change his clothes and get a ride home.

"Hey," Daniel called.

Mike turned around.

"I'll see you at lunch one of these days."

———————◆———————

On the way to school the next morning Mike told his father he was going to turn down the manager's job. He'd been thinking about other goals, other dreams. He wanted to start a band. He'd write his own songs, play guitar. His goal was to get up in front of an audience and sing.

He knew, he told his father, what he wanted. College. He was going. Somehow.

Yes, the past couple of months had been a struggle. He was still a shy kid, and Marshall's new system of separate academies would still isolate him from the faces most familiar to him. But life is what you make of it, his dad had told him. Sometimes, you just have to take a shot and see what happens.

He'd always love basketball. He told his father they'd shoot around that night at the hoop hanging from their garage. And he might even drop by Marshall's open gym so that he could work on that box-out technique Daniel had taught him. It could come in handy if friends dropped by for a game on the driveway.

He was eager to get to school. If anybody asked about tryouts, he was going to set some of the art crowd straight. Jocks weren't always the stuck-up jerks they were made out to be. The high school basketball season was approaching, and Mike planned to cheer from the stands.

His father told him to have a good day at school.

"I will," Mike said. "You, too, Dad."

He climbed out of the pickup, slammed the door and joined the crowd of students swarming toward Marshall's front door.

THE COP HELD HOSTAGE

That cop in the uniform had disappeared, and he had to find him.

In the middle of the night, when the nightmare jolts him awake, Larry Strayer slips quietly from his bed and escapes to the solitude of his den.

He stands still for a moment in the dark, listening in case his wife has once again been awakened by his whimpering cries.

But everything is quiet, the house peaceful. His warm bed beckons, but sleep is impossible. The nightmare always seems so real. He is in uniform again and back in Room 14. Al and Mike have his gun. He is their hostage, and he is waiting to die.

Even now, fully awake, his body tenses, and Strayer flips on a light to chase the bogymen. The den's walls are covered with pictures and mementos, but Strayer focuses on one ornamental frame.

Behind the glass, set on a mat of dark fabric, his Portland Police Bureau badge gleams. Once, it gave him strength. Now, it mocks him.

Thirteen years ago he had pinned that shield to his uniform. In time, he discovered that suit of blue had a life and power all its own. In time, it became his second skin. In time, the lines in his life blurred so that he didn't know where the uniform ended and he began.

People saw him as Officer Strayer. Even when he was off duty, they treated him differently. That was fine. He was different. He was a cop.

Then, in the space of nine hours, everything changed. Al and Mike threatened to blow off his head with his own gun. Strayer escaped without a scratch. He thought he'd take just a few days off before returning to the street.

But the days turned into weeks. And then months. He couldn't face the uniform. It was hanging there in his Central Precinct locker. Waiting for him, clean and pressed. It was ready. So where was he?

He told himself he just needed time. He puttered around the house. He read books. He watched television. He visited friends who told him how great he looked. But all he really thought about was that uniform and how scared he was to put it on.

He took a leave of absence, collected disability and tried to sort things out. He'd go back. He knew it.

But nothing worked, and in time Larry Strayer realized he had lost more than a job. He had lost himself. That cop in the uniform had disappeared and he had to find him. Because without him, Larry Strayer had no idea who he was.

———◆———

Cold, steady drizzle made it an uneventful shift for Officer Larry Strayer, patrolling Southwest Portland with a criminal justice student, a young woman interested in police work.

On this night -- May 12, 1988 -- she wanted to know about Strayer, who was more than willing to talk and took her back to the beginning, back to when he decided to become a policeman after getting to know the officer who worked the football games and dances at his high school.

After graduation he moved to California and worked a series of jobs until he turned 21, the required age for police work. But California departments turned him down because he packed only 145 pounds on his 5-foot 11-inch frame.

So he ate more, enrolled in college and hired on as a guard at San Quentin, a maximum-security prison. Two years later he became a sheriff's deputy. After stints at a couple of small California departments, he applied to the Portland Police Bureau, only to be told that at 34 he was too old.

He signed on with the Washington County sheriff's department. Two years later, when the bureau dropped its age requirement, Strayer came back.

At 36, he told his guest with pride and pleasure, he became what he had wanted to be all along, a big-city cop.

Strayer stopped talking. The police radio squawked and the dispatcher reported that a Safeway store on Southwest Barbur Boulevard had been robbed. At the market, Strayer was given a broad, almost useless description of the departed robber: white male, 5-feet-11, slender build.

On a hunch, Strayer headed south on Barbur, toward a string of dreary little motels that get no stars in the travel guides.

He stopped at two places before the manager at the Portland Rose Motel said a man who kind of matched the description had rented Room 14 with another guy. They were Albert Reinhart, 42, and Michael Ager, 37.

By the time Strayer returned to his patrol car to ask for backup, it was almost 7 p.m. His ride-along asked what would happen if the motel guest was the robber and had a gun.

"Well, you can't live forever," Strayer replied with a wry smile. He told her to stay in the car.

The backup arrived, and Strayer and another officer knocked on the door of Room 14. A curtain moved, someone peeked out the window and Reinhart opened the door. Strayer saw that he looked like the suspect, but so did hundreds of other men.

When Strayer explained why he was there, Reinhart smiled and asked Strayer to excuse his friend. Strayer stepped into the room, looked through an open bathroom door and saw Ager sitting nude on the toilet.

With no direct link to the robbery, Strayer could not search the room. But he was suspicious and asked another backup to fetch a store employee, who arrived a few minutes later and identified Reinhart as the gunman. Strayer handcuffed him.

When Strayer told Ager he wanted to question him, Ager asked for time to finish in the bathroom. Strayer told him to get dressed and looked away.

Then he heard Ager's voice: "Don't do anything stupid."

Strayer turned around.

Ager was pointing a gun. Strayer recognized it as a .357-caliber Magnum and saw a bullet in the cylinder. As he raised his hands, his heart thumped and his stomach twisted.

"Take it easy. Don't shoot me."

Strayer's two backups drew their guns and ducked outside while Ager backed into the protection of the bathroom. Ager told the backups to leave.

"Get them out of here or I'll kill you."

One of the backups, looked up at Strayer. Strayer spoke slowly.

"Just go."

Strayer was alone.

Within moments, Ager had slammed the door, told Strayer to radio other officers to leave and ordered him to free his buddy. Reinhart rubbed his wrists, grinned and slid Strayer's .45-caliber semiautomatic from its holster. Strayer was shoved against a wall and searched.

Reinhart told Ager he didn't feel comfortable with semiautomatics and left the room to get a gun out of his car. When he returned to the room he told Ager the cops were gone and it was time to split.

"What are you guys going to do with me?" Strayer asked.

"Nothing," Reinhart said. "We just want to get out of here."

"Hey, the longer you wait, the more police are going to show up."

Ager ignored Strayer. He had decided to stay long enough to get high and demanded that Strayer get on his radio and tell the police to deliver Dilaudid, a powerful narcotic. Let's go, Reinhart said. But Ager was adamant.

Strayer didn't like junkies because they were unpredictable. He knew the police wouldn't send drugs, which meant Ager and Reinhart would soon turn irritable and paranoid because of their cravings.

Somehow, he had to calm them. He remembered defusing tense situations at San Quentin and forced himself to seem less like a cop by appearing to be relaxed, almost friendly. Somehow, he realized, he would have to symbolically shed his uniform.

Strayer was confident that a hostage negotiator and a swarm of officers were on their way. With any luck, Strayer figured, he'd soon be free. But then he watched as Ager locked the door and frantically barricaded all of them inside the room, overturning the bed and moving the box spring up against the window. Ager said he was afraid police were going to storm the room.

"If that happens," he warned Strayer, "you die."

Strayer believed him. Trained to maintain control, Strayer felt it slipping away. He was scared. He wondered if he had left enough life insurance for his wife and kids.

Ager, too, was thinking of family and telephoned his wife in Washington to tell her what was happening. His wife didn't believe him, so Ager put Strayer on the phone.

"Are you really a cop?"

"Yeah."

She apologized for what was happening.

"He's really not a bad guy."

Yeah, right, Strayer thought as he handed Ager the phone.

The room was silent. Strayer was asked what he did at the bureau. He said he used to work with kids in the juvenile unit. He didn't mention his time in the drug squad.

He wanted his captors to forget he was a cop. When they said they were hungry, Strayer offhandedly offered to run across Barbur Boulevard to get some food. They all laughed. But when Ager and Reinhart tried to order out for pizza, they discovered police had taken over the motel switchboard.

A hostage negotiator came on the line and demanded Strayer's release. No way. They wanted drugs. The negotiator said he was working on it.

Within a matter of hours, Ager needed a fix and paced the room. Some junkies pass out, Strayer thought. Others lash out in anger. What do I have on my hands, he asked himself.

Strayer was relieved when Ager said he wanted to lie down. He walked to a ledge used to store suitcases. The ledge was about 3 feet off the ground, and Ager used it to shield himself. He lay down.

With the lights off, the room was illuminated by the television's blue glow. The sound was turned low so they could hear if anyone approached. Strayer sat on a bench next to the TV.

The room had become a prison for all three men. The negotiator had not called back and Reinhart was edgy. It was his turn to pace. Where Ager had been sleepy, Reinhart was angry.

He kept Strayer's gun cocked and held it in his hand. Strayer calmed him by asking about family and background. Soon Ager joined in the conversation. They said they were career criminals and had robbed the Safeway for drug money. Then the conversation fell off.

They all were thinking the same thing. The police weren't going to send drugs. There were only two endings: Ager and Reinhart would surrender or the police would storm the room.

Time dragged on. There was no more pretense, no more laughing about running out for pizza. Strayer was a hostage, something to bargain with.

When he shifted his weight, Ager and Reinhart leveled guns at his head and chest. If he scratched his face, the guns came up. A drink of water, a trip to the bathroom -- always a gun in his face.

By 10 p.m., almost three hours after the door slammed behind him, Strayer was exhausted and scared.

Once, when he was a young cop in California, a robber had shot at him. The incident had been over in less than 45 seconds, and he hadn't had time to think about the danger.

But this was different. Death was in the room with him. He could feel it, almost see it in the dark. That line about being brave in the face of death was nonsense: Earlier, he'd taken the phone to ask the hostage negotiator if his life wasn't worth just a few drugs.

Now, sitting alone on the motel floor, he realized he had groveled. Pleaded. Begged. He was a policeman; he knew what the negotiator could and couldn't do. But now. . . . Now he wasn't a policeman anymore. He was just a tired, terrified 43-year-old man who wanted to go home.

He wondered if he would live to see the sunrise. He thought about his family. He wondered if this was what they meant when they talked about your life flashing before you.

Shortly before 11 p.m., Ager woke up and told Reinhart to handcuff Strayer. Strayer forced himself to appear lighthearted. He told Ager not to worry: Hey, you've been sleeping and Reinhart had dozed off and I didn't bolt the room. Ager turned angrily to the sleepy Reinhart and forgot about the cuffs.

On the late news, Reinhart and Ager learned the motel was surrounded by the Special Emergency Response Team. Reinhart looked directly at Strayer.

"They come through that door and you're dead," he said.

At midnight Reinhart could no longer be calmed. He threatened to kill Strayer. Forget the drugs. He was fed up. He held Strayer's .45 in his hand.

Strayer didn't care.

Countless times he'd been told he would die. He didn't cry, or beg for his life. He didn't think about escaping. He said a prayer and made peace with himself.

Strayer knew he would die quickly. The .45-caliber slug would take care of that. He hoped he wouldn't feel pain. More than anything, he was afraid that Reinhart would torture him, make him pay for being a cop.

He told Reinhart he had one request: "Make it quick." Then he waited for the gun blast. Instead, Reinhart turned away and resumed pacing. For the first time that night, Strayer felt hopeful.

About 2 a.m. Reinhart flopped down on the mattress and ordered Strayer to lie near him on the floor. Ager was asleep and within minutes so was Reinhart.

Huddled under a blanket, Strayer started thinking like a cop again. Both men were asleep. Maybe he could make a break for the door. He was up on hands and knees when the phone rang. It was the negotiator.

No drugs.

Reinhart slammed down the phone. Strayer had seen Reinhart take about five seconds to wake up, and knew he would have another chance to escape. He just had to keep Reinhart calm.

But Reinhart whirled on Strayer and demanded the extra bullets to the .45. He said he was going to kill Strayer. Earlier, Strayer had tucked the spare ammunition under a mattress. He now insisted he had no more. Reinhart searched the room with Strayer's small flashlight but gave up and lay down again.

Were they sleeping? Strayer shined his flashlight around the room. If they saw the light, they'd react. Nothing.

Strayer saw a dark object lying next to Reinhart. He knew Reinhart had two guns, the .45 and the .357. He guessed the dark object was one them.

He called to Reinhart. Nothing.

Strayer moved slightly. His leather shoes creaked. He took them off. He called out to Reinhart. Nothing.

Twice he started toward the dark object and stopped. Too afraid. He sat back against the wall. He had to take the chance. He crept across the carpet and reached out. It was the leather holster -- the .357.

Slowly, he pulled the gun free and flopped back against the wall. He stood, walked carefully to the door and felt for the light switch. He wanted to stun his captors by blinding them momentarily. He rubbed his hand along the wall. Where was the switch?

The sound awakened Ager.

"Al, Al. What's that?"

Reinhart sat up and turned toward Strayer.

Strayer knew Reinhart had the .45 cocked and ready.

Strayer fired four shots. Reinhart groaned and rolled over.

Ager tried to scramble out from behind the mattress against the ledge. Strayer stepped around the mattress. Ager pointed a gun. Strayer fired once, then ran for the door.

He had his hands in the air. He was yelling.

"I'm a police officer! I shot them! I'm a police officer!"

———◆———

Strayer's peers congratulated him as he was hustled away from the motel and taken to the bureau to be interviewed by detectives. When they were done, his wife, Evelyn, and daughter, Kirsten, took him home to Southwest Portland.

Although he had been awake more than 24 hours, Strayer couldn't sleep. A Valium pill had no effect. He listened to the phone ring with the calls of friends and co-workers.

After he dressed and drove back to the Portland Rose. Outside Room 14, a detective told Strayer his gunshots had killed Reinhart and wounded Ager, who fatally shot himself when police lobbed tear gas into the room.

The detective said he had to hold Strayer's .45 for evidence, but Strayer could have it when he came back to work.

Strayer forced himself to look into the room. The bodies were gone. That's why Strayer had needed to come back -- to make sure Al and Mike were dead.

As he left the room, his sergeant threw his arm around Strayer's shoulders. "I'll be back in a few days," Strayer said. "See you then."

But by the end of the week, Strayer knew something was wrong. Physically, he felt fine. But he couldn't put on his uniform.

He didn't even like to hunt and thought maybe he was troubled over killing someone. He took comfort in a letter from Reinhart's sister.

"The terror and trauma you suffered at his hands must have been horrible. Our concern and sympathy is for you and your family. Such moments must be a policeman's nightmare. It would be natural to look back on them and wonder if you could have avoided the violent end. Do not let self-doubt and recrimination undermine your effectiveness as a policeman. Your life was threatened, and you had a clear duty to perform. Sorry as we are for those awful hours, the Reinhart family will always be grateful that Al did no greater harm."

He filed the letter away. No, there was something else.

Maybe he needed a visit to Central Precinct. Officers dropped what they were doing when he walked through the door. His lieutenant told Strayer to go home, take it easy. They'd see him soon enough.

But as he talked with his colleagues, Strayer realized he was glad he didn't have to wear the uniform. He didn't say that, of course. See you soon, he said on his way out the door.

He took a trip back East to see his 20-year-old son, Craig, graduate from the U.S. Coast Guard Academy. When he came home, he found that his friends at Central Precinct had taken up a collection to send him on another trip, one he'd been talking about for years -- visiting Civil War sites in the South.

He came back rejuvenated. He was ready to put on the uniform. But one day, driving downtown, Strayer casually glanced at the car next to his. He could have sworn the two men in the front seat were Al and Mike. Strayer drove straight home. He couldn't sleep that night. He told his wife he needed more time.

A few weeks later his uncle came to town and Strayer took him to dinner. On the drive home, Strayer made up his mind to go to work the next day. When they got home Strayer and his uncle went to the living room to watch television. There on the screen, a man pointed a handgun straight at the camera. And Strayer was right back in Room 14.

Strayer shut his eyes and turned his head away. His pulse raced. He was petrified. What would happen if he saw a real gun?

He called his commanders. Won't be back as soon as expected, he said. His .45 caused too many bad memories so he sold it to a sergeant.

Is this what it's like to go mad he wondered. He wanted only to sit in a dark room. He didn't want to have to talk to friends or family. He thought about killing himself.

He sought help. A counselor said Ager and Reinhart had irrevocably changed his life. The doctors called it acute stress, which meant he qualified for disability payments from the city.

He took a leave of absence from the bureau. Almost a year after being taken hostage, Strayer and his wife decided to move to Colorado Springs, the city where he first thought of becoming a police officer.

But before they left Portland, Strayer had an errand to run. He drove to Central Precinct at a time when he knew the Justice Center station house would be nearly deserted. He nodded to the man at the desk and walked back into the bowels of the precinct.

Then he opened his locker door. Inside was his life.

There hung his uniform and his bulletproof vest. He could see his nightstick and belts, his keys, his legal books, his ticket book. Numbly, he stuffed it all into a bag. Then he took the elevator to the 16th floor and handed everything to a supply clerk.

Now he could move to Colorado.

———◆———

The Strayers were there more than a year before they admitted life wasn't better. Strayer continued counseling, but Evelyn Strayer noticed the little things. He didn't smile much anymore, he'd lost his sense of humor and seemed moody, preoccupied with thoughts he didn't care to share.

Strayer found that he needed to be in control at all times. He was no longer upbeat and optimistic about life. He brooded about his mortality. He had nightmares.

Evelyn had been married to Larry for more than 20 years, but at times was living with a stranger. Who is this man? Strayer felt much the same way: If he wasn't a policeman, what was he?

The kids had moved away, so it was just Larry and Evelyn. He pushed her away and refused to discuss his demons. They argued over minor things until, finally, she said she couldn't take it anymore.

One morning she packed her car for the drive back to Portland. Strayer didn't try to talk her out of it. He stood in the middle of the street and watched her car disappear around the corner.

He enjoyed the solitude. In the next weeks, he busied himself remodeling the basement, building a deck and working in the yard. He continued his counseling. In time he believed he would be a policeman again and bought back his gun from the Portland sergeant.

He had it with him as he drove through Idaho on his way to visit some Portland friends. He was traveling at 6 miles an hour over the speed limit when a trooper pulled him over and asked for identification. It's in the trunk, Strayer said, in a briefcase that contains a gun.

The trooper took the gun and ID and walked back to his patrol car. A few minutes later a second trooper showed up. A backup. Something was wrong. Strayer opened his car door.

"Get back in your car now," came a command over the loudspeaker.

Several minutes passed. The trooper told Strayer the gun was listed as stolen. Strayer said there must be a mistake. He had used the gun when he was a Portland policeman. He asked the trooper to call the bureau.

The trooper made the call. No one in the Portland Police Bureau's record unit had ever heard of a Larry Strayer. Strayer panicked. Check again. More minutes passed.

The trooper came back. A records supervisor had remembered Strayer. And because of a computer error, the gun, first reported stolen when Reinhart took it from Strayer, had never been taken off the list. The trooper handed Strayer his gun.

"You'd better get this straightened out," he said.

Strayer wanted nothing more than to straighten out his life. If he could have anything, it would be to go back to Portland, put on the uniform and hit the street.

He just couldn't do it.

Every time he thought about police work, he got scared. He knew he'd be a disaster. He'd overreact, pull his gun when he shouldn't or shoot too soon to protect his own life, not someone else's.

In the months alone, Strayer thought about a lot of things. What he kept coming back to was the price he had paid for the job he had loved.

As a child, Strayer's son had been an athlete. How many games had Strayer seen? A handful. He had been too busy.

How many family picnics were canceled because Dad was immersed in an investigation? Too many.

How many times had he turned his kids away when they wanted to talk with him? Next weekend, he would say. Tomorrow. But he never had time. He was always too tired or getting ready for court.

Strayer, alone in his home, thought about all that.

And he decided that if he couldn't be a cop, he could be a father.

He reached out to his children, who were in their 20s and lived far away. He didn't mumble or hem and haw. He said he loved them. And they said they loved him. The tears came.

He decided he could be a husband.

He called his wife. They talked. He admitted he was a different man from the one she had once known. It wasn't his choice. Maybe he was a better one. Maybe they could find out together.

She came back.

When he'd go back to Portland to visit old friends he'd occasionally see a policeman and his heart would ache a bit. One day, after he had been gone for more than two years, he went back to Central Precinct.

There had been so many changes that Strayer didn't know most of the crew. He talked to a couple of men he knew and found they didn't have much to say to each other. He was an outsider now. He accepted it. He didn't plan to visit again.

Strayer returned to Colorado convinced he had survived that night in Room 14 for a reason. He didn't know what the future held, but he felt patient enough to wait and see.

His disability payments, good for only a couple of years, were drastically reduced and he began looking for new work. He lectured at the Colorado police academy, volunteered at an agency that helped the retarded. When people asked what he did, he said he was a retired policeman.

Retired? You're awfully young.

I've done my time, he'd say.

One Saturday last fall, Strayer got in his pickup and drove out to see how the leaves on the aspens had turned from light green to bright gold to mark the change of seasons.

He left behind the busy streets and headed up Ute Pass. He passed ghost towns and abandoned railroad grades, until finally he found himself alone in the isolated high country.

From a distance he could see the aspens. The brilliant flame colors of the leaves covered the valley floor.

He pulled his truck to the side of a road, turned off the engine and rolled down the window. A cold wind whistled through the cab. Yes, winter was coming.

He stared out at the trees. The leaves were dead. And so was Officer Larry Strayer.

He was gone. Strayer accepted it. It wasn't easy, but he had buried the cop, that man in the blue uniform. He had let him go. He had been a good man. A brave man.

But he was gone.

In his place was simply Larry Strayer -- a new man it would take some time getting used to.

Strayer looked out the window. The snows were on their way. The aspens faced another vicious Colorado winter. But they would survive. And in the spring, the leaves would blossom and life would begin anew.

Of that, Strayer was sure.

THE PROM

For one night these boys and girls could be teenagers.

The children who will arrive here within the hour exist in life's shadows. At school they're teased. Or, even worse, ignored. They're the kids who ride the short bus, the boys and girls who don't fit in, the ones who struggle down hallways in wheelchairs or on crutches.

They're different.

But only on the surface.

And that's what this night is all about.

The volunteers began transforming the lobby at Portland's Shriners Hospital for Children after Friday's last appointment. They had to get the room ready for a prom thrown for children who've been coming to this hospital most of their lives.

For one night -- for at least a few hours -- these boys and girls could be teenagers. They didn't have to worry about fitting in. Or being understood. Or being accepted. They could reveal what lay hidden in their hearts and souls.

Crews quickly got the decorations on the walls. A DJ tested the sound system. Volunteers shoved chairs to one side, hung white sheets from the ceiling to hide a long bank of intake desks and ran a length of black plastic to cover windows, giving the room that necessary dark ambience that lets everyone look good and feel a bit glamorous.

Nurses -- the women these children see before surgery, the ones who offer a gentle touch when a child is scared and lonely -- hustled from the lobby to transform themselves. They ditched the practical cotton pants and oversized blouses with pockets and slipped into dresses and high heels. They fixed their hair just so and applied makeup and lipstick.

And then they waited.

———◆———

An elevator door opened and Megan Johnson, who just turned 17, stepped into the lobby in a long prom dress. She's been coming to the hospital since she was 5. She's had 24 operations on her face. A 25th is scheduled for August. While Megan stopped at the front desk to register for the prom, her mother found a seat and served as a reminder that these children don't travel alone on their journeys.

"I had to home-school my daughter in fourth grade," Jill Johnson says. "She was teased all the time. Girls teased her about her face. They told her to kill herself. Other girls told her to turn the other way, they didn't want to see her face. Those were terrible years. She now goes to a small high school. It's better, but she's not included in so many things.

"My daughter will go to college next year," Johnson says. "She's a straight-A student. We came from Seattle for this prom. She's been looking forward to this night for months."

Johnson waved to her daughter.

"Tonight, no one will laugh at her," Johnson says. "No one will snicker at her behind her back. Tonight, she can just be Megan."

———◆———

Shriners hospital began holding a Halloween dance nearly 20 years ago after a mother told a nurse that her child had never been invited to a dance.

The hospital, which treats the spirit as well as the body, tries to give its young patients the life skills they need to transition into full lives as adults. An important part of that is learning how to socialize and be comfortable with the opposite sex. The dances were so successful that four years ago the hospital began the spring prom.

Everything -- the food, DJ and decorations -- is donated. Five girls from area high schools -- all of them in elegant prom outfits -- volunteer to run the check-in desk and mingle with the guests.

The night is like any high school prom. Kids get their picture taken. They want to look good, cool. A shy boy doesn't know what to say to a girl who's caught his eye from across the room.

There are differences, of course. A girl on crutches dances, standing in one place, but swaying to the beat. A boy in a wheelchair dances with her, his wheelchair twisted back and forth by one of the high-school volunteers.

And yet, they're just teenagers. The DJ plays a slow song.

A boy and girl -- hardly able to look each other in the eye –f umble for each other's hands in the dark room and lean into each other, knowing and feeling that for three precious minutes nothing else in the world matters or exists.

Christopher Mitchell, 17, stands on the sidelines but then moves to the center of the dance floor and begins to move to the beat, attracting a group of teens who dance with him. Across the room, his father, Lee, smiles.

"I like to see him have a chance to do things with other people," Mitchell says. "When he was young, he had club feet and ear issues, and he's developmentally behind."

Mitchell watches his son spin on the floor.

"He has trouble fitting in with kids his own age," Mitchell says. "He doesn't make friends easily. Kids in his high school know him, but they say 'hi' and move on. He's not the kind of kid that they want to spend time with."

On the dance floor, Christopher held a girl's hand and spun her.

"He's a good boy," his father says quietly. "A good son."

The children continue to arrive. Parents make sure a long, burgundy gown doesn't get tangled up in a wheelchair. A boy needs his father's help to straighten a tie.

After Eleanor Crawford gets her daughter, Ashley, registered, she takes a seat and watches her 17-year-old daughter, who has spina bifida, slowly move to the dance floor on crutches. Her daughter, who's undergone 20 major operations at Shriners, begins to dance.

And Crawford finds herself starting to cry.

"My daughter never had any friends," she says. "Everyone's nice to her at school, but she's never been invited to a birthday party or sleepover. She's never had a friend spend the night at our house."

At last year's dance, Ashley met a girl in a wheelchair. They became friends. Best friends. They now text-message each other so often that Crawford has had to buy more cellphone minutes.

She's not complaining.

"That one dance," she says, "changed my daughter's life. It gave her the confidence to open up to other girls in school. She blossomed."

A few weeks ago, her daughter did something unusual. She asked Abbie Peterson, a 17-year-old girl in her school, if she'd like to come to the prom as a guest. Abbie, who's mildly autistic, said yes and wore a long black dress.

The two girls stopped by to say hello to Crawford and finalize the evening's plan -- Abbie is spending the night.

Just hearing the words makes Crawford choke up. She runs a finger across her eyes. She smiles, telling her daughter that they're happy tears.

"I love you," she calls to her daughter, who's heading back to the dance floor. "Have fun."

GIFT FROM A STRANGER

Their story begins with a brutal murder.

H e was the kind of man she hated.
She was the type of woman he ridiculed.

Velazquez Polk was rough.

Janet White was refined.

He's black.

She's white.

Polk arrived in Northeast Portland when he was 10. His mother, raising him alone, moved from Tennessee in the early 1980s in search of a better life. Instead, her child surrendered to the siren of the streets and joined a gang. In time, he assumed command of a crack cocaine operation that he protected with his wits, his fists and an arsenal of guns.

White, 16 years older than Polk, was raised in Alameda, an upper-class neighborhood in Northeast Portland that's less than 10 miles from Polk's turf. Her mom was a homemaker; her dad a dentist. She made the honor roll and won a spot on the cheerleading squad. For fun, she figure skated and rode horses.

Two worlds.

Two lives.

And then their paths crossed.

———◆———

Their story begins with one of the most brutal murders in Portland's history.

Sixteen years ago, White's sister, Donna Kuzmaak, was beaten, raped, stabbed and then strangled with her pantyhose during an attack inside her home. Authorities never caught the killer.

Kuzmaak was 26.

"I was one year younger than her," White says in a soft, hesitant voice. "She was my big sister and. . . ."

The years have left not a scar, but a scab easily ripped away with a word or two. Emotions and pain ooze to the surface and seep out. Her eyes water, her voice quavers and her hands tremble.

She collects herself and forces a smile.

"Donna always looked out for me," White says. "She wanted to know who I was dating and how school was going. She was always there for me. She was more than a sister, she was a best friend."

Crime had always been abstract, a faraway war that never reached the Kuzmaak family's shore.

Until Donna was murdered.

"I remember the police coming to her funeral," says White.

She stares at the floor.

"They thought the killer might show up to get a thrill," she says. "So they took pictures of everyone there."

That day, as Donna was laid to rest, part of White also died.

Hope.

Innocence.

Soon, shock turned to anger and then to bitterness. Strangers aroused suspicion.

She needed a goal, something to make her stop dwelling on the horror. She pursued her dream of becoming a nurse and ended up in charge of the surgical recovery unit at Providence Medical Center. At the hospital she met the man she would marry, a Portland policeman in for a minor operation.

Their union meant more barriers for White, though, because their friends were other cops. Conversation at parties and dinner turned to crime and the criminals who ruled the streets. As time passed, every criminal represented Donna's murderer.

White became a cop without the badge. She thought and talked like the worst of them, someone hardened from patrolling the street for too many years.

Criminals were animals.

Punks.

Scumbags.

———◆———

The street radiates off Velazquez Polk the way the smell of garlic lingers long after a meal. It's in his voice and the carriage of his body. It's there when he stares, sizing someone up in a heartbeat.

He makes the small room his, sitting in a chair and waiting, deciding what to say and when to say it.

"I was a gang banger," he finally says. "They were my family."

Childhood meant surviving. He had to be strong enough to take what he wanted. And tough enough to keep it.

"Man, I was in fights all the time."

The memory brings the first smile. He chuckles and clenches his right hand, creating a fist, which causes his bicep to ripple.

Then the smile fades.

"I been shot. Hit my leg. Man, it burned."

He juts out his chin.

"And I shot back."

He's animated now.

"I had guns. Let's see. . . ."

He uses his fingers as he counts -- 9mm, .22, .45, .357, .44 Magnum.

He slouches in his seat, then tilts forward.

"Oh yeah, I forgot the Uzi."

His business was selling crack cocaine. That ended with an arrest. As a first-time offender he received three years of probation and a spot in a Job Corps program where he learned cement masonry.

It was a joke.

He spent four months working on a building in Estacada. When he was done he didn't get a job or even a lead on how to find one.

So he drifted back to what he knew best.

He was arrested again. This time he spent two months in jail. When he walked out, police were lurking.

He vowed to be sucker free, avoiding people who did stupid things that attracted cops. His two rules: Deal only to close friends and tell everyone else to get the hell away.

That worked for a while.

Then his best friend, a fellow dealer, was arrested and sentenced to eight years in the penitentiary.

The sentence scared Polk. He had to find something else to do.

But what?

In the midst of his confusion he heard about a meeting of community leaders talking about gangs. He decided to go. But as he listened to their spiel he grew angry.

Who did they think they were? Sitting there in their suits and ties and high-priced dresses. Coming to his neighborhood to tell him about the street. Bull. They weren't here for him. They were here for themselves, here so they could say they did their good deed for the year.

He raised his hand.

Hey, theories and programs are fine. What about reality? They should get people from the street to talk about the street.

How about you? they asked. He was taken aback, but accepted the challenge.

A few weeks later he spoke at a downtown luncheon. He meant only to explain his past, his frustrations and to introduce the mostly white audience to the reality of the street.

But as he began speaking he surprised even himself when the words came from his heart.

"I need help," Polk admitted. "I need someone to believe in me."

In the audience was Providence Medical Center's chief executive officer. He asked if Polk was serious about finding a job.

———◆———

For months White had pestered hospital administrators to let her hire a surgical aide, someone to transport patients from the operating room to the recovery unit.

Now word came that the position was approved. With a caveat. She had to grant a specific applicant an interview. When she learned he was a gang member trying to straighten out his life, White was outraged.

Narcotics were all over the unit, along with blank, signed prescription pads that could be sold on the street. And they wanted her to consider letting a criminal inside?

Fine.

She'd play their game.

Talk to this guy and hustle him out of the hospital. She didn't buy into liberal guilt about rehabilitation. Let them all stay in jail. Forever.

When Polk arrived for his interview, his shaved head and swagger irritated White. A cocky guy looking for an easy landing. He wasn't going to find it here.

But orders were orders.

She made small talk about the weather and sports. She had the power. Whatever happend to Polk was up to her. Be courteous and polite. Jump through the boss's hoops and be done with it.

Polk said he wanted a job.

No, there was nothing particular about the hospital. He filled White in on his background.

An unrealistic street kid, she thought.

But she better be careful. A black kid dealing with a white-run institution was touchy. Someone higher up was pulling strings. She had to make everyone look good. New employees were on probation for a month. Then she'd get rid of him.

Two days later, Polk started.

White kept watch. She was pleasant, but when he wasn't looking, she counted the prescription pads and checked the drugs.

Nothing missing.

Give him time, White thought. He'll mess up.

They always do.

———◆———

"Let's go for a ride."

Two gang buddies had pulled up in front of his mother's house. Polk climbed into the back seat. They cruised Northeast Portland. Talking and laughing. Just like old times.

Except . . . something was wrong. Tension. Then a question.

"How come you don't hang with us anymore?"

"What you mean?"

"You know. You don't come around."

Polk chose his words carefully.

"I have a job."

"A job?"

The two men in front glanced at each other.

"We don't believe you," one said. "You're a snitch. We think you're working for the police."

The car was silent.

"We don't know if we should put a bullet in your head."

One of them turned and glared at Polk.

"Whatta you think?" he asked.

Polk returned the stare.

"If you're going to do it, you better do it now. I'm telling the truth. I have a job."

The two in the front seat said nothing.

Polk looked out the window.

"OK," came the verdict. "But come around."

That night, Polk sat in his bedroom and held his hospital paycheck.

$280.

A week.

When he was dealing, he'd make that in an hour. By dawn he'd have $1,500 tucked in his pockets.

He looked at the check.

$280.

But this . . . this was a life.

————◆————

Polk spotted the cop coming down the hallway toward him. Instinctively he assumed the pose -- hands on the hospital wall, feet spread -- and waited to be questioned.

He felt foolish when White said the cop was her husband and was here to take her to lunch.

There was an embarrassed silence that afternoon. Keeping out of each other's way. Always having busywork to attend to.

During a lull, Polk asked White if he could talk. They walked to her small office. He sat down. He didn't know where to start or how. Then everything spilled out.

The problems with the gang.

How he knew people were waiting for him to fail.

How he wanted to flee his old life.

How he was going to move from his mother's home and get an apartment in another part of town.

And, well, maybe it was foolish, but he liked working here and he saw a future and he had found a program at a community college where he could become a nurse's aide.

There.

He just wanted White to know.

When Polk returned to his duties, White remained behind.

She thought about his past.

Her own.

She felt her sister's presence.

She remembered that Donna had befriended a gas station attendant. The man trusted Donna and confided he was on parole. When Donna told her family, they said she was crazy. He could be dangerous and should be avoided.

Donna said she believed in people. Everyone needs a chance.

After her murder, her family wondered if that had been her fatal mistake. Had she given the wrong person a chance? Detectives investigated and ruled him out.

Now, sitting in her office, White felt Donna enter her heart.

Everyone needs a chance.

And then she was extending her hand, reaching for the telephone.

She had never done this.

Not for the brilliant college kids.

Not for the friend of a friend.

She dialed the number of the hospital's human resources director. She explained. She lobbied. She cajoled. Finally, it was settled. The hospital would pay for Polk's tuition and books.

Now, one final act.

Janet White took Velazquez Polk off probation.

He was hired.

When this good Samaritan euphoria of hers faded, there were doubts. If Polk stole drugs, walked off with a nurse's purse or hurt a patient, White wouldn't be able to blame her boss or some distant administrator. It would be her fault.

Since the other nurses knew nothing of his background, White suggested Polk say nothing until they knew him better. In the meantime, she'd continue to monitor him.

The days turned to weeks and then to months and there seemed to be no problems.

At least nothing obvious.

One day, though, White heard a patient sobbing. She was an older woman and White saw Polk standing beside her bed. White moved to intervene, but hesitated.

She saw Polk lean into the bed, clasp the woman's hand in his and caress the tired flesh. He bent toward her face, whispered to her, nodded and whispered once more.

White checked the woman's chart. Cancer.

White walked toward Polk, trying to listen without being obvious. She never heard what Polk said. But she heard the woman's quiet reply.

"I want you to know you made all the difference in the world just by being here for me."

White felt a surge of pride. Her eyes were damp. She turned away before he saw her.

She realized then that it was time to share her secret, the one few in the hospital knew.

One afternoon she called Polk into her office. She closed the door. There was a false start. Then another. Then everything came out.

"I once had a sister. . . ."

———————●———————

The power-assisted doors to 3F2 swoosh open, and the secrets of the Recovery Unit are revealed.

Inside, Polk and White tend to a patient, communicating with glances and gestures -- the language of best friends, which is what this nurse and the stranger from the street have become.

For the most part they take each other for granted.

And yet. . . .

When Polk hears about an old buddy being hauled off to jail or reads about a gang member being killed, he silently thanks Janet White for taking him to a world he did not know existed. She showed him he belonged, and he plans to become a physical therapist.

Although the pace here is hectic, White occasionally looks up from her paperwork and sees Polk. She really looks at him and realizes that once she hated such a man.

The pain of the past remains, but Velazquez Polk's gift was to help her find the person she once was and sweep away the bitterness that poisoned her heart.

Now, they stand over a patient.

Polk says something.

White chuckles.

Soon they are both laughing.

No Excuses

There is no agenda. The power comes from talking and listening.

Seventeen inmates gather at a long table and chat, glad to be out of the general population for a few hours. But they fall silent when Travis Gamble and Nate Roberts appear in the doorway and settle at the head of the table.

Inmate Dana Andrews, following the lead of the older men on either side of him, holds a blank 1,000-yard stare. Gamble and Roberts say nothing.

Finally, Gamble speaks. "I want you to listen," he says with quiet intensity. "When a man's talking to you and trying to get your life in order, listen."

Andrews, in prison-issued jeans and a sweat shirt, stops feigning boredom. So do the others.

Gamble and Roberts, Multnomah County parole and probation officers, have come to Northeast Portland's Columbia River Correctional Institution to offer the men a chance to join their group, a chance to avoid returning to prison. A chance at redemption.

Men allowed into Multnomah County's groundbreaking African American Program attend weekly sessions where they get a mix of high-five peer support and in-your-face reality checks.

Part of what makes the group work --and it does work, drawing national attention --is that Gamble and Roberts know the street. Gamble was the only one among high school buddies who stayed straight. Roberts' brother died after drug dealers shot him and injected him with rat poison.

They don't tolerate excuses.

Yes, Gamble tells the inmates, racism is real. Black men face special challenges. Even so, that's not a free pass.

"While you're in here, your kids have no guidance," he says. "Accept your responsibility as a black man. It's your responsibility, not always someone else's. Black men are in peril. It's not the fault of white people, the judge or because your mom didn't hug you enough."

He pauses. "It's you," he says. "Yeah, you."

He and Roberts, both built like linebackers, ask pointed questions aimed at cutting through barriers built by men who think they have to act tough to survive.

"My dad's in the pen," one says. "I'm 32 years old. I grew up in the visiting room. I thought all black fathers were in prison. I'm living my father's life. Other criminals run into me in here and tell me they know my dad from the joint."

He cries.

"My heart breaks every morning," another says. "I'm 55. I get out and always go back to my old ways, the old flash, the devil. My two brothers are in federal prison."

Another says his grandmother told him she's glad he's in prison.

"Got to change," a fourth man says quietly. "My kids is all smarter than me."

"I want you to stay free. But a lot of you are going to be coming back," Gamble says, knowing that drugs, booze and the old crowd appear the moment a man walks out the gate. "Blacks are a small percentage of the population, but we make up a large percentage in prison."

He leans forward. "This isn't about Nate and me," he says. "We're gonna help you all we can. If you want to change, we can help. If you don't, then it's going to be cops and robbers. It's your life. We get paid the same for your destruction or reconstruction."

At the far end of the table, Andrews raises his hand.

"I don't know if I'm going to make it when I get out," he says. "This is my fourth time in here. I'm 26. I've never had a job, never worked a day in my life. All day long, we glorify drugs and crime. It has power. Part of me wants to make one last good run, dealing the dope. It's the world I know. Do I want to flip burgers at $7.25 an hour, or sell dope for a $30,000 score?"

He shakes his head.

"I fear the unknown," he says.

But he wants in.

———————◆———————

The African American Program began in 1997 when a parole/probation officer and supervisor wanted to do something about the disproportionate number of black men in prison, says Erika Preuitt, interim district manager for Northeast and Central Field Services with the Multnomah County Department of Community Justice.

"Even now, it's unique," Preuitt says. "The officers involved in this project have flown around the country to talk about the work they're doing."

In Oregon, African Americans make up less than 2 percent of the population but account for just more than 9 percent of the prison population, says Debbie Hazapis, public affairs assistant for the state Department of Corrections.

And black men are more likely to return after they're released, with a 39 percent recidivism rate compared with 31 percent for white men.

Evaluations of the African American Program show more needs to be done to keep black men from cycling back into prison, Preuitt says.

"The people in our program do get re-arrested," she says. "But in a state-wide comparison with Multnomah County, the African American Program had a lower recidivism rate. But it's a snapshot in time, and the program continues to change to meet the needs of the community."

Once a year, Gamble and Roberts visit Oregon prisons to meet with administrators, counselors and inmates to explain the program. Inmates interested in joining must get approval from their prison counselor to be transferred to Columbia River. Then they must write a letter of interest that's screened by corrections counselor Dorothy Steele; inmates already at Columbia River apply directly to Steele. Sex offenders and the severely mentally ill aren't allowed, and inmates must be within six months of release.

Steele looks for an inmate's sincere commitment to change. Those accepted attend a weekly class, limited to 23, at which Steele encourages them to think about their lives, relationships and crimes. She leads discussions about current events and issues affecting black culture to prompt the men to think about the world beyond the razor wire.

She assigns homework. If an inmate struggles, Steele finds someone in the class to help, teaching the men to trust one another. When they're released from prison, they join Gamble and Roberts' group.

Gamble, 38, and Roberts, 44, get the life.

Gamble, raised in Sacramento, had relatives involved in crime. Kids he ran with went bad; one is doing a life stretch at Folsom State Prison in California.

Roberts grew up in Oakland, Calif. At 16, two friends went on a nationwide crime spree and ended up in prison, one serving life. Drug dealers tortured and killed Roberts' brother, shooting him six times, then injecting him with poison.

Roberts, with the program eight years, has spoken with parole officers in Missouri, Wisconsin, Texas and Tennessee.

"Some are excited by it," he says. "Others have an us-against-them thing going and think we're crazy. Some offenders call me an Uncle Tom. But over time, I think they understand my role. Other than church, there are few places where men -- especially felons -- can talk. We get them talking about good things, bad things, worries. They tell them to find peers experiencing the same things."

Preuitt says the goal is to keep the community safe by breaking a cycle of crime that often stretches back generations.

Sometimes the program works. A man Roberts considered hopeless turned his life around, has a job and is now a group mentor. Sometimes it doesn't. The meetings often feature an announcement that a member is back in jail.

The heart of the program is a Thursday evening group held in a Northeast Portland church. The setting is spare. The men push chairs over to a far corner of a large room, forming a circle so they must look one another in the eye.

They've come from work. Or they've faced yet another disaster -- or temptation -- on the street. There is no agenda. No one takes notes. The power comes from talking and listening. Some stay with the group for years, long after they're "off paper" -- no longer having their post-prison life watched..

Dana Andrews, on the street for less than a week, arrives early, not knowing what to expect.

"The thoughts come," Andrews says while enjoying the sun on the church steps. "I see guys drive by in nice cars. I see the flash. I know my old crowd. I don't have one cent to my name. If someone had told me a week ago that I'd be out on the street, I'd figure I'd be smiling. But I can't find happiness."

Other members arrive, and Andrews follows Richard Brown inside. Brown, a Northeast Portland activist, so believes in the program that he moderates the group.

"I understand a lot of the issues," Brown says. Early on, he says, a young man fed the group excuses. "I let him spout off even though I knew he was fooling himself. He ended up getting shot downtown. I was so angry with myself. I didn't challenge him. I said I'd never make that mistake again."

If a man's at work, he's excused from group. On this night, about 30 men fill out the circle. Andrews takes a seat in the corner and -- living by prison code -- acknowledges no one and keeps his eyes focused on the carpet.

Andrews looks up when Gamble starts the meeting by announcing that a member has been arrested for selling drugs to an undercover cop. Then Gamble sits back and lets Brown take over. Brown asks: How has the week been?

"I have a restraining order on me from my ex-wife," a man offers. "Now she's calling me to come see my daughter."

"Got to watch that," a man warns.

"You back him up on that, Pete," someone says.

"Baby's mama is crazy," the father says. "I think she's bipolar."

"Like Bobby Brown," someone calls out.

The group laughs; Andrews, too.

"We laugh about this, but it's serious," Brown says. "You come see your daughter, and the cops going to put you in jail. You keep your distance."

One man, off parole, says he'd been to Disneyland and had his photo taken with Mickey Mouse. The others laugh. The man glowers, then settles back in his chair and smiles. "Ain't nothing wrong with that," he says. "It was nice being on vacation with my family."

A man to his right says he'd just started taking a parenting class. "Already I'm seeing the things I'm not doing," he says.

The group claps. "You're opening up, man," one member says in support. "Hang in there."

A man says quietly that he'd been in touch with his wife.

"She been clean a couple days, and I went to see her," he says. "I wanted to boost her self-esteem. She borrowed $100 from me and went on the run. She got her money, and I haven't seen her since. It was a trip for me. In that relationship, I've never been clean and sober. I see what's going on now. I realize it's not my fault. I'm an addict. She's an addict. Don't mean I got to accept it."

The group applauds. One man walks across the circle to slap hands. "You on the ball, man."

The ex-addict shakes his head. "I'm 47," he says. "At a certain age, an addict's got to get it together or it ain't never getting done."

Drugs have been Andrews' downfall. Even though he's more than 20 years younger than the man speaking, he knows how much of his life has been wasted.

Byron Maddox speaks up. "I'm not well," he says. "I know I could get dope. I got to work on success. All I got is one day, one second. I know I got a criminal record. All I want is a shot. I'm tired of hurting people. I've done that all my life."

He cries. "I need this group," he says. "I got no one else in my life but the men in this room."

"Brother," member Larry Turner tells Maddox, "I like the emotion you showed out there. That's a hell of a feeling, man."

He looks at his watch. "You know what they're doing now?" Turner asks the group. "They're in the yard. We can go anywhere we want."

Browns turns to Andrews. "You see the format," Brown says. "How you doing?"

Andrews glances around the room. "All this is new to me," he says. "I'm trying to deal with stuff instead of running. I'm happy to be free, but I got some immediate needs. I need glasses. I went to Lloyd Center and walked out heavy. The glasses were $300."

A man in the circle snorts.

"What you lookin' at? Gucci?"

"It was the prescription," Andrews stammers. "I got the frames on the inside. They're old."

The circle doesn't buy it.

"I think you're hooked on the name on the side," Maddox says. "You lookin' for the top of the line, and you ain't going to get it."

"Listen," Turner says, "go to Outside In. They'll give you a voucher for glasses. Transition services will pay for the prescription."

He gives him the address.

"The men in this circle will be your resource," Brown tells Andrews. "You'll hear your stories here. You won't go through anything that no one else didn't go through. When you are tired, talk to these brothers."

He reaches over to shake Andrews' hand.

"I'm glad you are here, Dana."

———◆———

Nate Roberts swivels in his chair and types a name -- Dana Andrews -- into the computer to see whether he's been picked him up on the arrest warrant Roberts requested. Weeks after leaving prison, Andrews started using drugs again and quit the group.

"Typical addict," Roberts says. "He tried to handle it on his own. A cop caught him using in a park. I gave him 15 days in jail and got him to commit to drug treatment. He did what most guys do with addiction -- he failed to show up.

"I'll try and help," Roberts says. "But this isn't about a friendship. Don't play the race card on me, either. I had a guy call from jail and ask why I -- a black man -- put him back in. I hung up. He called me back 14 times. On the 15th, I took his call. He apologized. . . .

"It's not my fault he's in jail. It's not my fault any of them are in jail. Some of these guys are full-fledged criminals who think they can pull it off. I got one guy looking at a 15-year term for drug-dealing. He's 30. All he knows is drugs."

During the year, men in the African American Program die.

"There was one guy that the whole group pleaded with to stay off the street," Roberts recalls. "He wouldn't. He got shot in the chest for dealing at the wrong corner. He died in a police officer's arms."

Roberts refuses to attend the funeral of any member who dies because of drugs or crime.

"Natural causes, I'm there," he says. "I have a difficult time at other funerals. The last one I went to, this guy was shot because he continued the lifestyle. At the funeral, everyone was moaning and groaning about what a good man he was. It was all so dishonest. Come on. I have a difficult time with that, so I won't go. It's a waste of my time."

A board on his office wall lists members on the run -- three names this day -- and the lockdown crew, 12 men who've been returned to Columbia River.

Weeks after Andrews skips, he's arrested. Roberts adds him to the lockdown list.

"If I can change one life out of 50, it's a big deal," Roberts says. "I can't write these people off. They're human beings. They need a chance. A couple days ago, I talked with Dana. He says he did it his way. Maybe now he'll try my way."

Two fans cool off the church room. Even so, the men are hot. A man in the circle says being off-paper changed his view. "I've had no contact with the police since I've been out," he says. "It's a trip. What I worry about now is being a father to my daughter."

Brown smiles. "There's good stuff happening here tonight," he says. "We got to keep brothers from going in and out of jail."

Brown moves around the circle, letting each man speak. Ken Shephard, a newcomer, spent 12 years in prison.

"I went to three interviews, and those robberies don't look good," he says. "Some of the choices I made, I got to live with. I'm staying humble, but it's a struggle. Strength in prison is different than the kind of strength I need out of prison,"

"It's a process," Gamble tells him. "You can't expect the skies to open up."

"For those of you struggling," one man says, "keep on. I just got promoted on my job to supervisor. I get benefits now."

Halfway through the session, Andrews arrives from work: In March, he had gone straight from prison into a drug treatment center. Nate Roberts had picked him up at Columbia River and delivered him to its door. He got clean and found a job as a telemarketer in Old Town.

"I'm starting to adapt," Andrews tells the group. "I'm going to my program and have a sponsor. He's been clean 22 years, and I've learned to listen."

From his window at work, Andrews says he can see a corner where drugs are sold.

"I see it all day, the twisting, just like I used to be," he says. "So much pain in that. At lunch, I go to this little store. One day a dealer came up to me and wanted to sell. I'm an addict. I didn't get mad. I just told him I was working and not to ask me again."

The group applauds.

Andrews tells the group that he's learned to appreciate what it means to be free.

"A couple weeks ago, we had that big thunderstorm in Portland," he says. "When I was locked up, I never got to see something like that. The thunder and lightning were amazing. I walked out of my house and stood on the sidewalk just watching. I didn't care if it was raining on me. It was beautiful. It was powerful."

He closes his eyes, remembering.

"This woman came by and asked me why I was just standing there getting wet," he tells the group. "I said she wouldn't understand."

Double Life

For those who knew the man, it was unthinkable that he would meet his end this way.

H e had them all fooled.

Even up to the end, when he forced the police to gun him down in the middle of a Northwest Portland street, he remained true to form. He was a character come to life from a cheap mystery novel.

Lover. Con man. Bank robber.

That was Charles Glenn Ferguson.

His friends -- good people throughout Oregon, Washington and Northern California -- knew him as high-living Jim Malone, a wealthy entrepreneur who owned an Alaskan gold mine.

His competitors -- men who battled him on a West Coast drag-racing circuit -- also knew him as Malone, a fearless 57-year-old who spent $100,000 for a dragster that would turn 180 mph.

The women in his life -- who knew him as Malone or Ferguson -- described him as loving, caring and kind.

That was one life.

But there was another, one he kept hidden from the world, one stocked with a fully automatic Uzi machine gun and a cache of rifles, shotguns, pistols and revolvers worth more than $10,000.

On June 23, light began filtering into the dark corners of his life when Ferguson, armed with two pistols and a police scanner, took over an Aloha bank hours before it opened for business. He handcuffed six employees and made off with more than $71,000 from the vault.

The getaway, like all his others, would have been clean. This time, though, a Beaverton policeman spotted his car. Ferguson took off, leading law enforcement authorities on a high-speed chase that ended when Portland police surrounded his car on Northwest 23rd Avenue and Thurman Street.

Ferguson got out of the car. He held a 9 mm pistol to his head.

"Shoot me or I'll shoot you."

Police told Ferguson to put the gun down.

But Ferguson pointed the gun at the officers. They opened fire.

Who was this man?

After Thursday's funeral, many of the questions followed him to his grave. So far, detectives have linked Ferguson to at least seven bank robberies in the Portland area in the past eight years. In each instance he made off with between $15,000 and $75,000.

And as Portland Police Bureau Detectives Kerry Taylor and Joe Goodale dig into his past, they believe there's a good chance that Ferguson has robbed banks throughout the Pacific Northwest.

Next week they will put the finishing touches on a Ferguson dossier, which Portland FBI agents will distribute to West Coast FBI offices to see if agents in other cities have unsolved bank robberies committed by a man using Ferguson's M.O.

Each day, Taylor and Goodale peel back another layer of Ferguson's life.

"He was a bank robber, but he was also a mild-mannered good friend to a lot of people," said Taylor. "He lived an upper-middle-class lifestyle.

"The average bank robber doesn't drive a 1993 Suburban, wear a gold Rolex watch, have a private pilot's license and consider drag racing a hobby," Taylor said. "But then this guy was not your average person."

———————————◆———————————

For those who knew the man named Jim Malone, it was unthinkable that he would meet his end this way. Not in a black, 1976 Chevy Malibu Classic, an 80,000-mile beater he bought in January for $800.

It just wasn't Malone's style.

But it was Ferguson's.

The Chevy was his getaway car, a throwaway, one he could dump when the job was over, leaving behind a paper trail that would lead law enforcement authorities into a maze of aliases and phony addresses and dead ends.

There was just one problem.

This time, a cop spotted the car.

A Beaverton policeman on routine patrol along Southwest Murray Boulevard heard his dispatcher broadcast a description of the Chevy. A short while later, he couldn't believe his luck when he saw it headed his way. When he turned to follow, Ferguson took off.

A 1976 Chevy should be no match for a police car.

Usually.

But Charles Glenn Ferguson was behind the wheel.

In addition to running dragsters, Ferguson spent a week last year at a road race class at the Roy Hill Race School in North Carolina. Now, he pulled out every trick.

At one point he passed several cars by manuevering his car so two wheels hung on the sidewalk and two were on the street. He sped through Beaverton at 50 mph, eluding a growing number of police, and turned onto Northwest Cornell Road where his car reached nearly 90 mph.

He was headed to Portland.

Waiting for him, where Cornell meets Lovejoy Street in Northwest Portland, was Portland Officer Ken Zahler. He was in a 1994 police car outfitted with a Corvette engine. Ferguson blew by Zahler.

"The guy could really drive," Zahler said. "Right away I realized he was an expert because he was never out of control. But it was insane. It was scary. Damn scary. Scary as hell."

Zahler said Ferguson hit 65 mph as he headed down Lovejoy. Other police cars joined Zahler, not only to stop Ferguson, but to warn pedestrians and other motorists to get out of the way.

"He never touched his brakes, never slowed down for lights, people, stop signs or other cars," Zahler said. "He went through one intersection and just missed a car. I mean by inches. Some of the things he was doing were suicidal."

Eventually, Ferguson led police into the heart of Northwest Portland. There he began making a series of evasive moves, the type that are usually seen in Clint Eastwood movies. Residents and pedestrians stood on the sidewalk directing police on where to go.

"He'd go left, left, left and then go a few more blocks and make a right and then a left," Zahler said. "And he's doing all this at high speed and never once losing control of the car. If police hadn't flooded the area, he would have gotten away because of his ability to handle that car."

Finally, at 23rd Avenue and Thurman Street, Ferguson was caught in heavy traffic.

It was there that he was shot and killed.

"I've been in high speed chases," Zahler said. "This guy was good. Very, very good. He was as good as anyone I've ever chased."

———————◆———————

The police cars skidded to a stop, and the officers, guns drawn, took cover and watched Ferguson play his deadly game with the gun pressed to his skull.

He was his own hostage. He wasn't going anywhere. He must have known, as he pointed his gun at the police, that he was sentencing himself to death. There would be no more running.

The officers' gunshots knocked him to the pavement. He moved. He was alive. On the way to the hospital he spoke only once, to tell a paramedic his name was "Chuck.'

Within minutes of the shooting, Taylor and Goodale arrived on the crime scene in Northwest Portland. Taylor is in the homicide unit; Goodale in robbery, where he specializes in bank heists.

While other detectives interviewed witnesses and talked with the officers, Taylor and Goodale looked in Ferguson's car. Right away they knew this was no nickel-and-dime case. Inside the car they found a police scanner, a book listing radio frequencies for police agenices around the country, another 9 mm pistol and a white box stuffed with money. Goodale had never seen so much cash. There were wads of bills in denominations from $1 to $100.

When they couldn't find any identification in the car, Taylor hustled to the hospital. He arrived only to learn that Ferguson had died without speaking again. He carried no wallet or identification. A doctor handed Taylor the only thing the dead man carried -- a $10,000 Rolex watch.

The body was hauled to the medical examiner's office, where fingerprints were lifted. The prints were then taken to a sophisticated Police Bureau computer that scanned them and searched through hundreds of thousands on file to come up with a match.

Soon, the computer spit out a name.

Charles Glenn Ferguson.

Taylor checked police records and found that Ferguson had his fingerprints taken in the mid-1980s by the community corrections office in Washington County when his parole status was transferred to Oregon from the state of Washington. Taylor drove to the office and found that Ferguson was no longer on parole and his file was locked in the archives.

So Taylor ran Ferguson's name through the Oregon Division of Motor Vehicles and learned that Ferguson lived in Beaverton and owned a 1993 white Chevy Suburban. Taylor drove to the address, but it turned out to be a business that rents post office boxes.

The place was closed, but Taylor peered inside a window and saw someone walking around. He banged on the door. A woman let him in. He showed her his badge.

"Who has Box 233?" he asked.

He waited while the woman searched her files.

There were two names.

Charles Ferguson and Jim Malone.

———◆———

Goodale, meanwhile, was tracking Ferguson's two handguns. His contacts at the U.S. Bureau of Alcohol, Tobacco and Firearms traced the guns and found that one had been sold in 1991 to a Seattle policeman. Goodale called the officer. He said he had sold the gun to a friend who in turn sold it at a gun show in the Seattle area.

Who did his friend sell to? Goodale asked.

The officer didn't know.

Did he remember anything about the guy?

Just that he said he was in the merchant marines.

Goodale and Taylor huddled.

Taylor said he had been researching tax records to see if Ferguson or Malone owned homes in the Portland metropolitan area. He found nothing for Ferguson, but Malone owned a home near the Hoyt Arboretum in Washington Park.

Taylor drove up to take a look.

It was a nice place, appearing to be worth at least $250,000. He wanted to talk to this Malone and ask him why his name was on a post office box along with a guy who was a bank robber.

He had just two questions for Malone.

Who's Charles Ferguson?

And who are you?

Taylor rang the bell.

No answer.

He knocked on the door.

No answer.

He wandered around the neighborhood ringing doorbells.

One man said he knew Malone.

Tell me about him, Taylor said.

A nice man. A great neighbor.

Ever see a white Chevy Suburban around here? Taylor asked.

Sure. It was here last week.

Tell me more about Malone, Taylor asked.

Not much more to tell.

What do you know? Taylor asked.

He was a merchant marine. And he died at sea.

———◆———

Taylor and Goodale were confused. They searched police files, located a copy of Malone's fingerprints, but found they didn't match the prints taken from the bank robber.

Goodale began tracking Ferguson's criminal history. In 1958 Ferguson had been convicted of fraud in Nevada. For the next six years, there were a string of arrests for fraud, auto theft, grand theft auto in cities throughout Arizona, Nevada, Utah and California.

And then Ferguson disappeared.

He resurfaced in 1984 in Spokane, where he was selling heavy construction equipment. He tried passing a bad check, which caused his company to investigate his accounts. They discovered that he was selling some equipment and pocketing the money. For his crimes, he ended up at a local work camp.

While in Spokane he met a woman. Her name: Carol Malone.

In 1986, Ferguson moved from Spokane to Roseburg, where he got married and began working once again as an equipment salesman. But he traveled frequently to Portland and kept in touch with Malone.

He also robbed a West Slope bank.

Ferguson soon divorced his wife, quit his job, moved to Portland and began an affair with Malone, whose husband, Jim, was a merchant marine who spent months at a time at sea.

"When he was gone, Ferguson started using his credit cards and assumed his identity," Goodale said. "Everyone in Portland knew him as Jim Malone. Everyone thought they were a couple. The real Jim Malone did actually die at sea."

———◆———

And so began this double life.

Ferguson robbed banks.

Malone was the man about town.

He traveled throughout Oregon, Washington and California.

Money was never a problem. When he became interested in drag racing, he started buying cars and racing on the circuit. He paid $50,000 for a Corvette, and at the time of his death he owned a $100,000 Willys Roadster.

"He was a great fellow," said Robert Whitcomb, a Portland businessman. "He was a quiet, personable guy. He dressed real nice, not flashy, just nice. He worked out in the gym and was in good shape.

"He was an intelligent man who could pick stuff up quickly," Whitcomb said. "If I made a list of all the things he might have been into, robbing banks never would have been on it."

Another Portland businessman said he "trusted Jim with anything."

He does not want to be identified because "as a friend I can go along with Jim, but as a businessman I can't afford to be associated with a bank robber. The whole thing is bizarre."

"He told everyone he didn't have to work because he had a trust fund set up through investments," the businessman said. "He also said he owned a gold mine in Alaska. None of us ever met anyone from his past, and now we know why. He was a little strange that way. Secretive."

Goodale has interviewed Carol Malone. She told him that she had no knowledge of Ferguson's criminal activity, that she believed his cover story. Goodale said that Carol Malone is not under investigation.

Malone said Ferguson's death -- as well as finding out about his bank robberies -- has left her shocked.

"He was a wonderful man," she said. "That's all I want to say. I just can't believe it all."

In January 1993, Ferguson and Malone split up, although Ferguson continued to live in Portland.

While at a drag race in Bakersfield, Calif., he met his new love -- Evelyn Carlson. They became engaged and decided to move in together, although Ferguson didn't want to live in Bakersfield. Carlson didn't want to move to Portland. So they settled on Redding, Calif., and in August 1993 Ferguson and Carlson moved into a rental home in a quiet suburb.

Ferguson bought an airplane and made frequent trips to Oregon, telling Carlson that he had business in the state. His hangar was at the Hillsboro Airport, just a few doors down from the FBI hangar.

One day, Carlson stumbled upon receipts made out to Charles Ferguson. She confronted her fiance. He said it was his old name. He said he had been adopted by the Malone family in Montana when he was a child, and that his real name was Ferguson.

"This has been a total shock," said Carlson. "I'm grieving. All this other stuff has been very difficult to hear. This was not the man I knew and loved. I knew him as a very kind, caring and generous man."

Two weeks ago, Ferguson told Carlson he had to go to Portland for business.

———•———

He had told Carlson he would be staying at a Beaverton motel. When she hadn't heard from him for several days, Carlson called the motel. An employee said he was a registered guest. Carlson asked the employee to check his room while she waited on the telephone.

A few minutes later the employee returned to say that Ferguson was not in his room. His belongings were there.

Oh, and there is a lot of money in the room.

Carlson hung up and called the Beaverton Police Department.

Taylor was notified and went to examine the motel room. Inside, he found two expensive two-way radios and stacks of money taken during an April robbery of a Beaverton bank.

And the mystery was over.

Or was it?

———•———

The old man had a story to tell.

It has been bothering him for years. And now, Jim Wiggs wanted to tell it before it's too late.

After all, he is 71, tired and, well. . . .

"His name was Charles Wiggs. He was my brother."

His story -- their story -- unfolds.

"He was born on Feb. 6, 1937, into the Wiggs family," he said. "Our mother died of pneumonia right after he was born. She never came home from the hospital. She was 39.

"We lived in Grandview, Texas, and my dad was a sharecropper," he said. "We were poor. There was no money, and when my mother died, my father was left with five kids and this new baby, Charles, who was sickly."

An aunt in San Antonio offered to take Charles and temporarily take care of him.

"My aunt's husband was in the Air Force, and there was another Air Force couple, the Fergusons, who were moving to Hawaii," Wiggs said. "They offered to take Charles there because the climate would make him better. He had real problems. My aunt convinced my father that this is what should be done, and that's what happened.

"We'd get a letter every month, then it tapered off to every few months and then no letters," he said. "At one time, I remember my father coming home from the courthouse after he signed some papers to give Charles away to the Fergusons.

"And then we lost contact with him."

Over the years, Wiggs tried asking his father about Charles.

"Dad said it was better to leave it alone," he said. "So I did."

Wiggs has no memory of his brother. But for decades he has carried in his wallet a picture of Charles when he was 2 years old.

"A few years back, this really started bothering me," Wiggs said. "Dad died, and so I started searching for Charles."

He used public records -- Social Security numbers, anything -- and traced his brother through the Western United States. But he was always a year or two late.

Ferguson had moved on.

"I finally traced him to Roseburg, and when I checked I heard the authorities were also looking for him," Wiggs said. "I wondered if I really wanted to find this guy.

"Something inside told me I still had to look."

Two weeks ago, Wiggs, who lives in Harrison, Ark., learned that Ferguson had an address in Beaverton.

That night, he sat down and wrote to him.

"I really don't know how to start this letter. I don't know what you were told when you grew up, but you do have an extended blood family. I would be your only blood brother that you have. You have four sisters living.

"We have tried to get in touch with you. If you would like to get in touch with us, here are three phone numbers.

"Charles, this will be your call.

"We would love to talk with you."

He mailed the letter.

He waited for a reply.

There was none.

When police searched Ferguson's post office box they found the letter.

It was unopened.

The Twins

Hard work and talent shaped her life. As did fate.

The hallways were the worst place. The boys -- the athletes, the ones who seemed so sure of themselves -- would plot the ambush, waiting until they caught him alone. Then they'd pounce, surrounding him, taunting him, calling him "retard."

They'd keep it up until they spotted tears. Then they'd laugh, congratulate themselves and run away. Sometimes, just for fun, they'd shove him into a locker and watch him bounce around, a scared and confused look on his face.

Teachers tried to keep an eye out for him. But a school playground is a big place, and a middle school hallway can be as treacherous as a battlefield.

He turned to one person. His sister, his twin.

But she turned away.

Even after 17 years, Alisa Sinnott can still remember the internist telling her an ultrasound showed twins. And later, in the recovery room, learning the boy had Down syndrome. She knew her son's future because of her past. In high school, she'd volunteered at Fairview, the state institution where severely retarded adults and children were housed. Later, she'd worked in a Portland high school's special education program.

Patrick's distorted features and empty gaze would always set him apart. He would be slow to develop, would struggle with physical handicaps and might not outlive his parents. His father had been a college football player, but Patrick lacked the coordination he'd need to play varsity sports.

When the twins were 2 months old, the Sinnotts enrolled Patrick in a program where the parents learned how to help him develop. Because the twins were nursing, his sister, Colleen, joined the group. And she, too, did the exercises needed to strengthen Patrick's body. Later the twins joined an early intervention program for Down children. Colleen was the only child who didn't need to be there.

Patrick's demands soaked up his parents' attention. When another baby arrived, Colleen lost her place in the side-by-side stroller she had shared with Patrick. She could walk. He couldn't.

When it was time to enroll in first grade, school officials in Northeast Portland said Patrick had to go to a developmental class across town. Colleen's Catholic school, where she was in second grade, refused to admit him. The Sinnotts had friends with a mentally disabled daughter, and they spoke highly of the Tigard school district's efforts to mainstream her. The Sinnotts called the elementary school, spoke with the principal and decided to move.

Colleen didn't want to leave her friends or her school. She wanted to try out for the Junior Rose Festival a few years down the road, but if she left Portland, she'd be ineligible. Nonetheless, for Patrick's sake, the family moved.

Patrick was assigned to the first grade. Colleen was in third. They saw each other in the halls and at lunch. At home, Colleen helped Patrick with his simple assignments. They played games, and she taught him to dance. Colleen knew Patrick was different from other kids. But in those days it didn't matter.

Then, as she grew older, she became self-conscious. She wanted to fit in, to be popular. And having Patrick as a brother didn't help.

———◆———

Patrick sat quietly in the front seat while his father drove him to his first day of high school. Colleen had already begun her day at Central Catholic High School, where she was a junior. Their Roman Catholic faith was important to the Sinnotts, and they'd wanted both the twins to attend Central. They offered to pay a tutor who'd help Patrick at school, but school administrators turned them down. That irritated Nick Sinnott, who'd been a teacher and head football coach at Central in the 1970s before becoming a textbook salesman. So Patrick enrolled at Tigard High School.

He didn't know what to expect. Colleen liked high school. He had heard her talking about it, but they didn't do as much together as they once had. Her bedroom was in another part of the house. She had a boyfriend, a job and friends who kept her busy. Even so, he looked up to Colleen. He wanted to be like her. When she took her driver's test, he told his parents that he wanted his license. But he couldn't read the driver's manual. They made him a deal: When he could read the manual, he could learn how to drive and eventually get his license. On the day Colleen took her exam, he went, too. He got his Oregon Identification Card, and both twins came home with something they could put in their wallets.

His father swung the car into the Tigard parking lot and found a spot. They both walked toward the door. When they entered the building, they found the school's seniors lining the hallway. The school's tradition was that the graduating class welcomed the freshman with cheers and applause. The commotion was intimidating, and Patrick kept his eyes on the floor.

Patrick filled out some paperwork, said goodbye to his father and followed an aide to his first class. He met his case manager, who had enrolled him in a mix of classes: physical science, English 9, typing and then special classes that would give him skills to live an independent life. He would learn what he could in class, but much of the true learning, the caseworker hoped, would come in other ways.

He had limitations. He couldn't use a locker because he couldn't remember the combination. He couldn't tie his shoes. But he was a boy of routine, and he learned his way around school.

Patrick was in the hall that first week when Tigard's head football coach, Frank Geske, stopped him and said he wanted him to come down to the weight room the next day. Patrick's father had coached Geske at Central, and Geske was surprised to learn his old coach's son was at Tigard.

The next morning, Patrick walked into the weight room and found it filled with big guys, members of the football team, the kind of kids who used to tease him in middle school. He hesitated. Then Geske waved him into the room. He called the team to attention.

"This is Patrick Sinnott," Geske remembers saying.

Patrick looked up from the floor and into the eyes of all the boys. No one said anything. He was about to look back at the floor when Geske put his hand on his shoulder.

"Patrick," he asked, "do you want to be a part of the football team?"

Patrick didn't say a word, and no one was sure if he'd heard Geske. And then, as the coach remembers it, Patrick nodded, almost imperceptibly. Geske reached into a paper bag and pulled out a jersey. He handed it to Patrick. The boy held it in his hands. He felt the fabric.

No. 31.

"Put it on," Geske said.

Patrick slipped the jersey over his head.

He was No. 31.

The football players surrounded him, slapped him on the back and welcomed him to the team. Geske told Patrick he was the official tee-runner. His job was to run out onto the field after the kickoff and pick up the tee used by the kicker. He went home and told his parents he'd be busy that Friday night. Just like Colleen, he had plans.

The season sped by, and the night of the last game, Geske called Patrick to the center of the locker room. He handed him a package. With awkward fingers, Patrick ripped open the paper. Inside was a black letterman's jacket with green sleeves. A football patch was sewn onto the front.

"It's yours," Geske said as Patrick slipped the jacket over his shoulders. He wore it to school every day, and his caseworker remembers him showing it off to her and talking about what his family thought about it. She asked him to slow down and repeat what he'd said because it didn't make sense.

"A twin," he said again. "I have a twin."

———◆———

As she walked down the hallway, Colleen saw the notice for the upcoming three-day student retreat for juniors. Central Catholic wanted seniors to lead the sessions, which focused on religious values. She applied and was selected to be one of five leaders to guide a February 2002 retreat.

She was near the end of a wonderful high school career. She'd made the honor roll and was involved in theater, school politics and sports. But she hadn't thought much about religious values. She sat in her room and worked on the speech she would give the juniors. She didn't like writing speeches, and this one seemed particularly hard.

She had Christian faith, certainly, but what, exactly, were values? Did they come from the Bible? Or sermons? Or going to Mass?

She scribbled some thoughts, re-read them, crumpled up the paper and left her room. She had four more days to finish the speech, and then she'd have to give it in front of the other team leaders and teachers. Each day brought more frustration.

At home, listening to her brother talk about being manager of Tigard's basketball team was a welcome diversion. She knew some of players.

She'd always been haunted by the knowledge that while hard work and talent shaped her life, so, too, did fate. Had something different, something random, occurred in her mother's womb, she'd be the one who struggled to spell simple words, to button her shirt, to add 8 and 3.

One morning, she watched her brother sit on the edge of his bed and tie his shoes. He had taken 16 years using one red lace and one blue lace to master that simple task.

She returned to her room, grabbed a yellow legal pad and began to write:

I never really believed that Christian values were important. . . . I guess you can say I was looking in all of the wrong places, because my signal of where to find my values ended up being right in front of me the whole time. This sign in my life was my very own twin brother.

She thought about his life, her life and their lives together. She remembered the way she had treated her brother:

I was being just as blind and ignorant as the bullies. . . . I was shocked and disgusted with myself.

Patrick, she realized, had taught her something. Suddenly, the words, the feelings, came easily:

From never judging others, loving enemies who mistreated him to being able to strive for a goal with inspiration, he possessed the Christian values I wanted to achieve. . . . I wanted to be able to walk down a street or school hall and only see people. I wanted to set my mind toward a difficult task and do it. All I really wanted was to be like Patrick.

When the time finally came to give her speech, Colleen read the first line and began to cry. She told herself to keep going. With shaking hands and a quivering voice she made her way through the speech. When she finished, she went to the bathroom and broke down.

———◆———

On March 9, the Sinnotts' doorbell rang. Colleen's boyfriend, a Jesuit High senior, was there to take her to the state high school basketball championship -- Jesuit versus Tigard. Colleen sat with the Jesuit supporters and watched from across the floor as her brother, the Tigard manager, led the players onto the court and then slowly jogged over to the Tigard student section. Students reached out to slap his hands in greeting, and Colleen realized how well-liked Patrick was.

She watched the teams warm up, but kept an eye on her brother, who arranged the towels on the bench. She saw him look into the stands and find their parents to make sure they were watching him. He concentrated, trying hard to articulate the words, and finally yelled "Go Tigers."

After a close back-and-forth contest, Tigard's Eric Doak sent the game into overtime with a spectacular shot. Colleen hadn't seen Eric since middle school. He'd never teased her brother, but he was the type of kid -- popular and athletic -- who had made Patrick's life miserable.

During overtime, Eric led Tigard to the championship, and someone hauled out a ladder to cut down the net. One of the players motioned to

Patrick, who'd been off to the side, watching. Someone handed him the scissors and told him to go up the ladder and get a bit of history.

He climbed two rungs and stopped, unsure of himself. His arms weren't long enough to reach the net unless he climbed to the top. He held on tightly and peered over the sides, a frightened look on his face.

And then from behind he felt someone. He carefully turned and saw Eric. The player whispered in his ear. Patrick took a hesitant step. He looked down at the court and grabbed the ladder with both hands. Another whisper. A step. He looked up, close enough to see the net. But he couldn't take another step, and he didn't know what to do. Eric took the scissors from his hand. With long arms he reached around and snipped a piece of the net. He handed it to Patrick and backed down two steps.

Patrick held the piece of net in his left hand. He was alone in the spotlight. He raised it over his head. Below him the players and Tigard fans applauded.

And tears rolled down Colleen Sinnott's cheeks.

———◆———

Four days later, Colleen arrived at Central Catholic High School in a gown. After listening to her and the other candidates speak, her fellow students would vote for the school's ambassador to the 2002 Rose Festival Court. Her brother stood by her side in a tuxedo. She'd chosen him to be her escort as she played this very public part in the city's biggest civic celebration.

Patrick offered his arm and led Colleen to the stage. A spotlight dazzled him, and his smile vanished. But he kept walking; his sister was counting on him.

She'd confessed that she had no real expectation of winning. One of her best friends was also a contestant, and Colleen usually came in second to her. Even her parents would later admit that they expected the other girl to win.

But Colleen still walked to the stage with special pride. For the first time, she was introducing her twin brother to all her Central High classmates.

And, for the first time, she had a full understanding of just how much he'd accomplished and how much he meant to her.

The contestants lined up for a photographer, and Patrick's short figure disappeared between Colleen and the tall girl behind him. Colleen reached around and pulled his arm forward. She wanted him in the picture.

And then it was time for her speech, built around the official Rose Festival theme: "Imagine the Possibilities."

We all imagine doing something with our lives, she told the crowd, following our dreams. She had dreams. And so, too, did her brother: "Being able to read a new word like 'cat,' 'tiger,' or 'basketball' every day," she said, "allows him to imagine the possibilities of one day being able to read a whole book."

And Patrick's dreams, she said, were just as important within the context of his own life as hers were within her life.

She looked into the audience. Tears welled in her mother's eyes. She turned to her right, where Patrick sat with the other escorts. He smiled at her.

After the speeches, each contestant selected a rose from a vase. Attached to the stem were two pieces of paper, each containing a question. The contestants were to pick one and answer it briefly.

Colleen looked at the first question, thought a moment, then opened the second. She smiled and handed the paper to the master of ceremonies. "Who," he read, is your role model and why?"

"My brother Patrick," Colleen said. "He has shown me how to strive toward a goal." She turned and looked directly at her twin, smiling broadly.

When everyone had finished answering the questions, the eight contestants walked backstage and waited. The students cast their votes. The girls filed back on stage.

The master of ceremonies stepped to the microphone and made the announcement. Colleen looked stunned. She buried her face in her hands. The other girls swarmed around her and the previous year's winner placed the crown on her head.

On the crowded stage, she looked around for the person most important to her. Patrick appeared at her side. She slipped her arm through his, and the twins stepped off the stage and into the crowd.

DADDY'S CAR

You couldn't mention his name without someone mentioning the DeSoto.

When Ernie Rigotti died in 1978, he left behind the loves of his life: a wife, four daughters and a green 1951 DeSoto.

Bought new off the lot, the car reminded Rigotti that he'd made something of himself. Other men, he could say with pride, called him a good provider.

He was a self-made man. In 1947, he managed to scrape together enough money to buy a garbage truck to service routes in what was then called Portland's Italian section.

Rigotti worked alone, rising at 3 a.m. Day after day for nearly 30 years, Rigotti hoisted heavy metal cans onto his back, pulled himself up the truck's small ladder and dumped the load. His body took a beating. But Rigotti never complained. The truck put his girls through private Catholic schools and gave the family a house, clothes and food.

But the truck was a tool, no different than a carpenter's hammer or a plumber's wrench. His DeSoto was something special. In the Rigotti home, it was called "Daddy's car." He babied the car, driving it gently and washing it once a week, sometimes twice if the family had a special outing.

Over the decades, the car and the man became one. You couldn't say the name Rigotti without someone mentioning the DeSoto, with its distinctive hood ornament and blaring horn.

In 1973, Rigotti's back gave out. The doctor told Rigotti to quit the garbage business or risk being disabled. So he sold the truck. Five years later, he and his wife traveled to Italy for his first trip to the old country. He had been there less than 48 hours when he settled into a chair to enjoy a meal and glass of red wine.

He looked at his wife and said two words, "Tutto passa" -- everything passes. Then he was gone, dead of a heart attack at age 65. It was Aug. 31, 1978, the exact day the DeSoto's Oregon vehicle registration expired.

His wife renewed the tags, and the family continued using Daddy's car. It kept Rigotti's memory alive. By 1989, though, his wife, Flora Rigotti, was considering selling the car. The kids were gone, and she had bought a newer car.

When grandson Christopher Cettina, then 13, heard she might sell the DeSoto, he told his parents they should buy it. Cettina had only vague memories of his grandfather, who died when Cettina was not yet 3. Yet when the boy rode in the DeSoto surrounded by his aunts and grandmother, the talk inevitably turned to the family patriarch. Through the stories, Cettina felt his grandfather's presence.

But his parents didn't want to buy the car. Besides, they told him, his grandmother was only thinking about selling it. Then, unbeknownst to anyone, Rigotti's widow placed a classified ad in the newspaper asking $2,000 for the DeSoto. The next day, a man came by and offered $1,800. She accepted and handed over her husband's keys and black leather fob.

The DeSoto rolled out the garage and down the driveway. Flora Rigotti shed a tear for the man she'd loved and the car he'd treasured. She went inside and called her daughters to tell them the car was gone. And in that moment, they felt as if their childhood was gone, too.

Everyone has something from the past they wish they could retrieve. In a turbulent world, objects from the past can serve as personal anchors, reminders of a simpler time.

That's how it was for the Rigotti clan, which grew to 24 people as the daughters married and had kids and grandkids. What they thought about -- what they missed -- was the DeSoto.

When they got together and talked about the past, they talked about the car: how the four sisters, driving and singing, got a ticket for driving without headlights. The time they got a flat tire and sat quietly while Daddy jacked up the car. The trips to the beach, the dog sleeping on the floor and the youngest daughter up front between her parents.

And they talked about Ernie Rigotti. How he insisted on taking water on long trips in case the car overheated, though it never did. How he covered the car, though it was in the garage, with a blanket in winter because he wanted it to stay warm. How he insisted there was a certain way to wash and dry the car.

A year ago last May, Christopher Cettina, then 32, was going through a divorce. One Monday night, feeling low, he thought about his grandfather. He turned on his computer and typed into Google: 1951 DeSoto.

A list of links popped up, the first from eBay. The seller had photos of the car, inside and out. The car looked like his grandfather's -- same color, same interior. He clicked on a photo taken from the passenger seat toward the steering wheel. He enlarged it and spotted the key in the ignition.

It was on a black leather fob.

In a heartbeat, Cettina was a little kid. He scanned the rest of the ad and found that the seller had posted a phone number. He called.

A Salem man told him he bought and sold cars and had owned the DeSoto for about six months. He knew the car's history. He told Cettina that previous owners -- there had been several -- had each agreed to keep the car out of the rain and in a garage. The original owner, the seller said, was "a little old lady" in Southeast Portland.

Cettina waited while the man went to check a tag in the car's door jamb; it was a service sticker from a Shell gas station off Southeast Hawthorne Boulevard, the shop Cettina's grandmother used.

Guess what, Cettina told him: I'm the grandson of the car's original owner.

—◆—

The seller had posted the car the day before and believed that fate had intervened. Cettina had to have this car. The man knocked $1,000 off the $8,500 price.

I'll call you right back, Cettina said. He called his parents to tell them he'd found the DeSoto. They didn't believe him. Neither did his grandmother or his aunts.

He wired the man money to hold the car and drove to Salem with his parents later in the week. The car was in the back of a long garage. His mother examined the car and found where her father had tried to touch up a scratch with paint and the spot where battery acid had caused the paint to bubble.

Cettina bought the car. He brought it home and washed and waxed it until it gleamed the way his grandfather would have liked. He asked relatives to meet at his grandmother's house that Sunday after church.

That day, the house was packed. Miles away, Cettina slid behind the DeSoto's wheel. He wore Ernie Rigotti's old fedora, the hat his grandmother had given him after his grandfather died.

———◆———

A few blocks from his grandmother's home, Cettina began honking the horn. The aunts and grandmother remembered the sound. Could it be? From a window, they spotted a flash of green. They piled outside, just in time to watch the DeSoto lumber up the driveway.

They erupted into tears and laughter.

How? Where? When?

Cettina explained the best he could, but everyone was talking and reminiscing and hugging.

In the middle of all this, Flora Rigotti made her way to the car. At 95, she walks with a cane. The family parted so she could stand in front of the car. She looked at it for a moment, then leaned down and kissed the hood.

In that moment, everyone agrees, it was as if Ernie Rigotti himself had come home.

THE MURDER VICTIM

He returned to the scene of the crime.

He had just finished dinner and settled into the living room with his acoustic guitar, working out a version of "Making Whoopee" and toying with some 1940s swing tunes. The telephone rang, and he tried to ignore it.

By nature, Gus Lamm is a private man, a reserved 42-year-old who lives in Southeast Portland near Clackamas Town Center. His one-bedroom apartment is hidden away in one of those anonymous complexes where neighbors remain strangers. Only his closest friends know that he has led two lives.

The only clues to Lamm's past surface during his group sessions at Providence St. Vincent Medical Center, where he's a mental-health therapist. He tells his clients, troubled souls trying to rise above their own crises, that the difference between him and them is only a matter of degree.

The telephone's incessant ringing finally forced Lamm to set down the guitar, walk across the room and pick up the receiver. The woman on the line introduced herself once, then twice, but he could not speak.

He hadn't heard her voice in 18 years, and the sound of it brought the memories flooding back.

"Hello, Nancy," he finally said.

They made small talk. Nancy Mesner wanted to know how his daughter was doing. Lamm, a lean 6-footer with salt-and-pepper hair and horn-rimmed glasses, said Audrey was 21, in college and studying to be a special-education teacher. She lived, he said, in her own Southeast Portland apartment.

Mesner paused.

"Gus," she finally said, "I'm not calling just to make conversation. Something is happening in Nebraska. You need to know that they've set an execution date for Randy."

A woman named Paula Hutchinson had more details, she said. Lamm thanked Mesner, hung up then punched in the 402 area code for Lincoln, Neb., and the number Mesner had given him.

"Paula," he said when she answered, "my name is Gus Lamm. Vickie was my wife."

And then he started to cry.

———◆———

Her name was Victoria Zessin. She was born and raised in Lincoln, Neb., and strayed from the homeland in 1971 when she climbed into a Volkswagen bus with two friends and visited Oregon. She met Lamm in Portland. When they married, they moved to Tillamook, where Lamm ran a group home for mentally retarded adults. Zessin worked as a nurse practitioner specializing in social services. Before long, they had a baby girl.

In March 1980, Zessin was three months pregnant with her second child when she took her daughter, then 3, to visit her family. On her last day in Lincoln, she and her daughter spent the night with her oldest friend, Janet Mesner, a caretaker at a Quaker Friends Meeting House.

That same day, rain washed out a construction job about 100 miles from Lincoln. Randy Reeves and the rest of the crew found their way to a bar and began drinking. Then Reeves and a buddy decided to drive to Lincoln, where they continued to drink. Some time during the night of March 29, Reeves asked a friend to drive him to Mesner's home. As a boy, he had been adopted by a Quaker family, and Mesner's mother had taught him in Sunday school.

His friend couldn't find the place, so Reeves, who had a blood-alcohol reading of .23 nearly three times Oregon's legal limit got out of the car and walked away, wandering the neighborhoods until he recognized the Meeting House. He climbed through a rear window.

Police theorized that Reeves then attempted to rape Janet Mesner, who fought back. Vickie Zessin, sleeping in another room, ran to help. Reeves stabbed Zessin once with a kitchen knife, killing her on the spot. He then stabbed and slashed Mesner several times before running. Mesner lived long enough to call 9-1-1. Police found Zessin's daughter unharmed in another room, asking for her mother. A cop shut the bedroom door so the child wouldn't see her mother's body.

About 30 minutes later, police found Reeves walking down the street, covered in blood, and arrested him. A Lancaster County District Court sentenced Reeves to death. But his attorneys filed appeal after appeal.

During the telephone conversation, Hutchinson, Reeves' attorney, told Lamm that in November 1998, the state of Nebraska had set a date for Reeves' execution: Jan 14, 1999.

He was stunned.

After the murders, Lamm flew to Lincoln to retrieve his daughter. He came home to Tillamook, quit his job and moved with his daughter to Central Oregon. He did not follow the trial, and he never went back to Nebraska. He had minimal contact with the Zessins, who had had a strained relationship with their daughter, a hippie as they put it who married barefoot, with flowers in her hair.

Lamm told Hutchinson he had always believed Reeves would die in prison. The attorney told him that since 1990 three inmates had been executed in Nebraska, and that Reeves could very well die in two months. Lamm thanked her and hung up the phone.

That night he thought about his wife and Janet Mesner and Randy Reeves. He mulled over Vickie's values. He believed his wife, as he did, would have opposed the death penalty, even for the man who had murdered her.

In late November, he told his boss he needed to talk with her. "I guess the only way I can tell you this," he remembers saying, "is that 18 years ago my wife was the victim of a homicide in Nebraska. The man who killed her is going to die, and I have to have time off to go back and ask for clemency."

"Take all the time you need," she said.

He called Hutchinson that day.

"I can't let this happen," he said. "I'm coming back to Lincoln."

———◆———

His daughter, Audrey Lamm, had been close to her grandparents and spent part of several summer vacations with them. But she hadn't been back in nearly 10 years. When she heard what her father planned, she wanted to join him. The two gave up buying Christmas gifts for each other so that they could afford two airline tickets.

The week before they left, Lamm invited his daughter to dinner. He had always spoken honestly, without graphic details, about what had happened on his wife's last trip home. And he never shied away from Audrey's questions.

His daughter had no memory of that night in Lincoln, no memory of her mother. After dinner, Lamm pulled out mementos: old pictures of his wife, her Oregon Driver's License, their wedding invitation and pictures of the ceremony. He spread them out. He showed Audrey letters her mother had written. He played songs she had loved.

Audrey had questions.

Yes, he had been angry. Angry at God. This had happened in His house. Where was He that night? And Lamm could never forgive Reeves for what he had done.

But for the evil to end there, Lamm had cast off his bitterness. He had to raise a daughter, to shape a life. She was ready to bloom and needed to be surrounded by love and kindness, and a belief that the future, her future, was full of hope and promise.

Always, Lamm explained, he tried to raise Audrey by asking one core question: "What would Vickie have done?"

Whatever the particulars, the overarching answer was always the same: to reaffirm that life was precious.

And that is why he had to go to Lincoln.

Not for Randy Reeves.

But for Victoria Zessin.

———◆———

They arrived in Lincoln on Jan. 7. Hutchinson put them up in her apartment and updated them on the case and the attention it was getting in Nebraska. She said she had told Randy Reeves what Lamm was doing and Reeves was humbled and overwhelmed.

Reeves was a Native American, a member of Nebraska's Omaha Tribe. Activists from the Omaha Reservation were helping to fight Reeves' death sentence. So, too, was the American Friends Service Committee, the country's largest Quaker organization. A contingent had flown in from Philadelphia to join organized protests by Quakers across the state. Reeves' father, a prominent Quaker who sits on the national board of directors, was the first conscientious objector in Nebraska history and did alternative service to avoid the Korean War. Even after the murders, the Reeves and Mesner families remained close friends.

Lamm listened carefully and then told Hutchinson that she had his support.

Her goal, she said, was to have Lamm and his daughter, as well as the Mesner family, testify before the Nebraska Board of Pardons the day before the execution. The board, made up of the governor, the secretary of state and the attorney general, could vote to give Reeves clemency.

Lamm told Hutchinson to use him in any way she wanted. She began contacting television stations and newspaper reporters to set up interviews with the Oregon man who had traveled to Nebraska to save the life of the man who had killed his wife.

His daughter, meanwhile, set out to meet with the Zessins. She traveled to a small town in central Nebraska to meet with her grandfather to explain why she and her father opposed the execution.

Her grandfather told her they were on opposite sides. He hated Randy Reeves and what the killer had done. The murders, he told his granddaughter, had killed his own wife. The light went out of her when Vickie died. She withered. Then a stroke took her life. He, too, had suffered a stroke.

Goodbye, he told his granddaughter. Don't bring any more misery into his life. And then he ended the conversation.

She drove back to Lincoln.

That night Lamm told Audrey that her grandfather was a good man with a broken heart. He was a product of the life he had lived. He was a hard worker and, without being demeaning in any sense of the word, unsophisticated. He was a blue-collar man who had worked in the Goodyear plant his entire adult life.

His daughter, Audrey's mother, was different from anyone in the family. She embraced the larger world. During the Vietnam War, she joined protests and was quoted in the newspaper. She took on unpopular causes, provoking running debates with her father. Debates that often ended in arguments.

When Victoria Zessin was murdered, Lamm tried to explain, she and her father were torn apart without a chance to make peace with each other. That lack of a resolution, regrets over things said and not said, had consumed him from March 29, 1980. It had hardened and embittered him. One day, Lamm told his daughter, she would understand.

Victoria Zessin's brother, Greg, and his wife invited Lamm and his daughter over for breakfast at their home, just outside Lincoln. Greg Zessin told Lamm he didn't want to talk about the death penalty or Reeves. He just wanted to see his former brother-in-law and his niece.

Over breakfast, they talked about good memories: fishing at the family's trailer in Republican City. Going to the zoo with grandpa. Being towed on a tube behind the boat. Shopping with grandma.

After breakfast, Lamm walked outside for a smoke.

"I'm just coming here to express my opinion," he told Zessin.

"I can understand," Zessin said. "I don't have a problem with Reeves rotting in jail, but no one can guarantee me that he won't get out."

Lamm smoked in silence.

"I can understand you, Gus, but does that make us the bad people," Zessin said. "I just want this behind us. I don't want to hear about Randy Reeves anymore. He started this. He climbed into that window."

Lamm finished his cigarette. They walked inside, said their goodbyes, shook hands and exchanged awkward hugs.

Then it was just the two of them, a father and a daughter driving along a lonely, quiet stretch of road the locals call Purple Heart Highway.

———————

The Meeting Hall is a two-story building in a middle-class neighborhood. Audrey and Gus Lamm got out of the car and walked toward the place.

"I don't remember anything at all," Audrey said. She took her father's hand in hers as they walked to the back of the house.

"This is where he must have climbed in," her father said.

"It's strange," Audrey said. "It's just a building."

Her father pulled his daughter close to him.

"We don't get a choice of how we pass away," he said. "When a person goes, I think they want friends around. Those two women loved each other."

He stared at the window.

"I'm sure Vickie was fighting back real hard."

He began to cry. His daughter hugged him.

"Let's go," she said.

On Jan. 11, the Lamms joined Hutchinson and a group of supporters at the state capitol for the Board of Pardons meeting. More than 60 spectators crowded into the room. Another 40 watched from another room on a closed-circuit TV.

Audrey and Hutchinson sat in the front row next to Greg Zessin and the Mesner family. The secretary of state opened the meeting by making a motion to allow the Lamms to speak. The motion was defeated 2-1. The board then voted 3-0 to deny Reeves' clemency. He would die in three days.

The crowd, realizing what had happened, began to boo. The governor called a 15-minute recess. Hutchinson held up a large poster-sized photograph of Victoria Zessin and her sisters. Hutchinson gave Audrey Lamm three roses representing the lives of Zessin, Mesner and Reeves to present to the governor. He refused them. Gus Lamm approached the governor and asked why he had not been allowed to speak. The governor refused to answer.

Audrey turned to her uncle.

"You know your sister would not approve of that," she said.

"But she's not here, is she?" he replied.

"Are you happy now?" she asked.

He had no answer.

Audrey hugged him.

"I love you," she said. "I will always love you."

Then she joined Hutchinson, who was telling reporters she planned to file an immediate appeal.

That afternoon, less than 30 hours before Reeves was to die, the Nebraska Supreme Court granted a reprieve, ruling that it would not have time to consider the appeal before the execution. It will be months before the court hears arguments in the case. If another execution date is set, the process the protests and media events and appeals will begin again.

The Lamms have vowed to return.

———————————

Gus Lamm is back in Portland and has returned to work. Other than his boss, he's told no one of his trip to Nebraska. When he looks at his wife's picture and listens to the music she loved, he knows he made the right choice.

His two lives are both special in their own ways. He has been blessed with a wife he loved, and who loved him. And with the daughter they created. When he looks at Audrey, he sees his wife in her eyes. In her laugh, he hears the echoes of a sweet voice long ago silenced.

Last week, his daughter told him she had decided to move in the coming months. She will enroll at the University of Nebraska and finish her education. Part of the blood that surges through her lies in those broad flatlands and fertile soil.

She has written letters to her grandfather and uncle to tell them she is coming. They are family.

Her father will miss her. He will send her away with tears in his eyes and an ache in his heart. But it will be the right thing. He knows it is what Vickie would have wanted.

FINDING FREMONT

The psychics and white witch couldn't tell him where the dog was.

Doug Baker settled into a chair at the head of the dining room table and added up the figures. He could hardly believe the search had set him back $15,000.

"Fifteen grand?" he muttered.

He checked his figures again.

"Fifteen grand," he sighed. By the end of the week, he'd have to make another withdrawal from his retirement account. He pushed the grim numbers to the far end of the oval table, his back to the kitchen and the forlorn sight of a blue bowl sitting by itself on the floor. Just a glance at it triggered tears, and Baker had been crying daily since the night of Sept. 27 when Fremont vanished.

A gust of wind rattled a window and reminded Baker that a cold front was moving in. He worried out loud about his 8-year-old buddy, out there alone, tired and hungry. Baker said he had to stay strong and calm, to think for both of them. Even so, an air of desperation hung like a cloud over the 45-year-old bachelor. Baker's eyes were red and watery. His clothes were wrinkled and his hair uncombed.

In his right hand, he held a journal that detailed every aspect of the search. The book was a testament to his love.

Or his obsession.

Baker slowly turned the pages, reviewing the case. The white witch hadn't been much help. But the three psychics did connect with Fremont.

Or at least they claimed they'd spoken with him and that he was still alive. And that opened up possibilities for the $200-an-hour animal tracker.

He put the journal on the table, pushed back the chair and dared to look into the kitchen at Fremont's bowl and the blue leash hanging on the wall.

"He's not just a dog," Baker said. "He's my soul mate."

The relationship began nearly four years ago. A traffic jam stalled Baker on the lower ramp of the Fremont Bridge. He saw cars slowing to avoid hitting a long-haired German Shepherd mix limping along next to the railing. For some reason, Baker decided to stop. He now believes that God himself planned for him to be on the bridge at 9:17 p.m. on June 17, 1999.

"The dog was scared out of its mind," he recalled, smiling for the first time in hours. "I stopped and he ran right under my truck and started whimpering. Cars were whizzing around me, but I pulled him out and put him in the back of my truck. Our eyes met, and we connected.

"My life's never been the same."

He called his girlfriend, Lisa Klein, and said he'd found a stray that was in a bad way. He drove to Klein's Southeast Portland home, picked her up and took the dog to an emergency clinic. The vet discovered the dog's leg was broken in five places. Surgery would be difficult and expensive, and the best choice would be to put the animal down.

Baker said he'd pay for the operation. The bill came to $4,000, no small change to a guy who ran a small auto-repair shop in downtown Portland.

"People thought I was crazy," Baker admitted. "But I'm telling you, God wanted me to save him."

The clinic searched for the dog's owner, found none and Baker agreed to adopt the animal he wanted to call Four Grand. His girlfriend suggested Fremont.

The dog weighed 79 pounds, but quickly grew to 125. He couldn't live on Baker's houseboat; so Klein kept him at her house, where Baker stayed on weekends. During the week, he'd pick Fremont up each morning and take him to his repair shop where the dog spent the day lying on a blanket in the office. He barked and growled at any stranger who dared to enter.

"He was with one of us nearly 24 hours a day, and he really only trusted us," Baker said. "He was scared of people, and if someone got too close to him, he'd snap and lunge at them. When we had to leave him, and that was not very often, we had a professional dog sitter take care of him. This was not your regular dog. He was something special."

On Sept. 27, Baker took Klein to dinner for her birthday and left the dog with a sitter who charged $30 to watch him at her mother's house in Gresham. But Baker and his girlfriend came home to a chilling telephone message: Fremont was gone.

A truck had backfired. That apparently spooked the dog, and he took off, escaping through a gate that, Baker said, had accidentally been left open.

Baker searched Gresham for three straight days, but found nothing. He ran a small display ad in The Oregonian with a photograph of Fremont, an offer of a $1,000 reward and a plea to return the dog who was "the love of our life." He spent thousands of dollars to run the ad for 10 consecutive days, and he placed ads in several other area newspapers. He paid to distribute hundreds of fliers and to create a Web site devoted to his search.

He had lost his lease on the auto-repair shop and he needed to relocate. He was just getting ready to move when Fremont took off. So he concentrated on finding his dog and simply let the shop go out of business.

He took a leave from the Scappoose volunteer fire department. And he put off asking his girlfriend to marry him. His plan had been to tie the engagement ring around Fremont's collar so the dog could deliver it. But Fremont disappeared the night before the planned proposal.

Lisa Klein's dining room became what Baker calls Command Central, the place where he sorts through tips and possible sightings. Papers related to the search cover an antique hutch. And the wall behind the table. And the walls in the living room and kitchen.

Baker spends every night in Command Central, going over the paperwork and planning his next moves. On an evening three weeks into the search, he rose from the dining room table and led the way to the den.

"Two weeks after we got Fremont he came in here," Baker said. "Lisa and I were sitting on the double love seat, and he came up and gave each of us a lick. He was telling us thank you for saving him."

Now, though, the den is a place that haunts Baker. Taped to the walls are cards from sympathetic animal lovers and more clues related to the case.

"Excuse me," Baker said as he turned back toward the dining room. "It's just too much for me in here."

Days after Fremont ran off, Baker heard about Harry Oakes, a professional animal tracker who looks for lost pets. Oakes has his critics, but he says business is booming. One client spent $1,500 to fly him and his search dog to New Jersey to look for a lost cat, Oakes says. They found it hiding in the owner's attic.

Valorie, Oakes' border-collie mix, tracked Fremont's scent to an isolated road on the way to Dodge State Park. The scent stopped right at the road. Oakes and Baker searched the woods, looking for Fremont's body, and checked with the few homeowners in the area to see whether a stray had turned up. Oakes concluded that Fremont had been abducted, and he put Baker in touch with animal psychics.

Baker hired all of them, paying between $55 and $100 a session. Each psychic claimed to have spoken with Fremont. One said someone had dragged Fremont into a car after putting something around his neck. Another said Fremont spoke to her, telling her that he saw a fence and the dogs were kept out of doors, sometimes in a kennel with a cover. Fremont told her, the psychic said, that the people holding him called him "Pal" and "Chief." He added that he missed his home.

But the psychics couldn't tell Baker where Fremont was.

Baker then turned to a white witch, a woman brought in to cast spells with candles, herbs and dream cards. She had given Baker two cards to put above his bed so he could tap into the spiritual world, where he'd connect with Fremont. Although Baker had a vision of an orange license plate, he'd never had a solid dream because, he said, his girlfriend kept waking him when she got up to go to the bathroom.

Oakes, who had worked on only one other case as long as Fremont's, suggested that Baker slow down and wait for a break. Baker pressed on. "I'll do whatever it takes to find him," he said. "This has become a full-time job."

Baker hired a fourth psychic and continued to rely on Oakes, asking the tracker to meet him at the spot where the scent ended along the road. He planned to drop off a placard and look for more clues.

While Baker waited for Oakes to arrive, he dug through files in his pickup. During the past few weeks, he's driven more than 2,000 miles looking for Fremont. In his files were copies of a letter he's sent to 400 veterinarians and plans to get space on billboards around the region.

"If he was dead, his body would turn up," Baker said. "If he was at a shelter, he'd be home by now. Harry's experience says that Fremont is alive."

Baker pulled out a file labeled "Urine Drops," read through it to see whether he needed to update anything.

"I went out and put my own urine in the area where Fremont was last seen," he explained. "He might smell my scent and then stay put."

Oakes pulled up and let Valorie out to stretch her legs. Baker hurried off to discuss the day's plan and catch up with Oakes, who had just arrived back in Portland. Days earlier, he'd been flown to Los Angeles where a Playboy Magazine Playmate -- January 1997 -- had paid him to look for her lost dog.

"A miniature pinscher," Oakes told Baker. "We went on the Malibu Canyon road and found the dog's footprints and the poop."

Baker looked puzzled.

"Miniature pinscher poop is discernable," Oakes explained. "It's tiny. Now, coyote poop is larger."

Baker held a piece of paper in his hand, anxious to get started on the search for Fremont. The new psychic said his dog had told her that the property where he was being held had junk on it. Baker wanted Oakes to drive around with him, looking for junk-filled yards. They climbed in their trucks and disappeared around a bend, Baker using his left hand to point out possible places to search.

Last Tuesday -- the 60th day since Fremont's disappearance -- Baker sat at the dining room table and added up the figures. The total tab had climbed to $20,000, and it was still growing. Oakes was still on the case, and Baker planned to hire yet another psychic.

"Frustrated, angry and scared," he said. "That's what I am. Just before Lisa got home, I was out on the porch crying. It just came over me."

Earlier in the day, Baker and Klein had talked with Geordie Duckler, a Portland attorney who specializes in the new and evolving area of animal law, as they finalized a suit to be filed against the dog sitter. The couple plans on asking for economic damages of $63,000 -- which they say covers the search costs and the loss of Baker's business because of the search -- and $100,000 for pain and suffering. Duckler says he is the only lawyer in Oregon who specializes in representing pet owners who've suffered a loss. He has 50 active cases of that sort, he says, and he has represented owners of exotic birds, a lynx and an alligator.

What Baker wants most is his pal.

"I want Fremont," he said. "As each day goes by, I think I'll never see him again. I try and brush that off and keep going. I don't want another dog."

Then he broke down in tears.

"I saved him once," he said, "and here I am trying to save him again."

Epilogue:

A 68-day search that included advice from a white witch, four psychics and a professional animal tracker ended Wednesday when Doug Baker, who spent nearly $21,000 looking for his dog Fremont, happened to see the long-haired German shepherd trotting across a road about two miles from where he was last seen.

Baker and his girlfriend, Lisa Klein, had spent more than two hours searching throughout East Multnomah County, focusing on an area where the dog was last seen, when Baker decided to follow up on a tip he received earlier this week from someone who'd read about his plight in The Sunday Oregonian. The caller told Baker he'd seen a large dog matching Fremont's description running in an East County field.

Baker drove there, but found nothing. As he was pulling away, though, he spotted a crumpled, unreadable flier nailed to a telephone pole. It looked like one of the thousands of fliers he'd distributed since Fremont ran away. He climbed out of his truck and walked across the road to fix the flier, which turned out to be from someone else also looking for a lost dog.

"I was walking back to my truck when out of the corner of my eye I saw this German shepherd crossing the road about 200 yards away," Baker said. "I jumped in my truck and roared down the road. I just had a feeling it could be him. We got out of the truck and saw the dog disappear into the brush. We called to him real softly and he came out. He was whimpering and in shock, but it was Fremont."

The couple helped the dog into their pickup, and sped to the Woodstock Veterinary Hospital to have Fremont examined by Dr. Kirk Miller.

"He's alive," Baker shouted as he pulled into the hospital's parking lot. "He's alive. He looks like hell, but he's home."

Baker helped the dog out of the truck and put a collar around Fremont's neck. He got down on one knee, buried his face in the dog's body and began crying, overcome with relief.

The saga began Sept. 27 when Baker took Klein to dinner for her birthday and left the dog with a dog sitter who charged $30 to watch him at her mother's house in Gresham. The couple came home and learned that Fremont was gone. A truck had backfired. That apparently spooked the dog, and he took off, escaping through a gate that, Baker said, had accidentally been left open.

Baker searched Gresham for three straight days, but found nothing. He ran a small display ad in The Oregonian with a photograph of Fremont, an offer of a $1,000 reward and a plea to return the dog who was "the love of our life."

He spent thousands of dollars to run the ad for 10 consecutive days, and he placed ads in several other area newspapers. He paid to distribute hundreds of fliers and to create a Web site devoted to his search. He then brought in an animal tracker who charges $200 an hour and used four psychics and a white witch.

The tab for the search grew daily, but Baker refused to quit, even though he'd lost his small auto-repair business because the search consumed all his time.

The psychics -- all said they communicated with Fremont -- told Baker the dog was being held with other dogs. The tracker, who said Fremont's scent stopped right at the edge of a road, surmised the dog had been lured into a car and secreted away.

But Miller, who gave Fremont a cursory exam in the waiting room, said it appeared the dog had simply been living in the wild for 68 days. He wasn't far from where he disappeared. His coat was matted and he weighed in at 90 pounds, down from 125 pounds.

Fremont's discovery followed a bad scare. On Tuesday night Baker went out to search for Fremont, as he did every day the dog was gone, and stumbled on animal remains not far from where Fremont was last seen. He was afraid the remains were Fremont's.

He took parts of the carcass to Miller for identification. Miller had just determined the remains had come from a deer when Baker called him to report that he'd found his dog.

Fremont, who had a reputation for snapping and lunging at strangers, sat quietly in the hospital waiting room, not even paying attention to Louise, a black-and-white cat curled up on a sofa not 10 feet away.

Baker said he wouldn't have found Fremont if it had not been for the hundreds of telephone calls from people who responded to the story.

"You made it, buddy," he told Fremont.

Baker said Wednesday that he plans to talk with his attorney next week to decide whether he'll go ahead with a lawsuit against Fremont's dog sitter.

"All I want to do now is rebuild my life," said Baker, who hasn't shaved since his dog disappeared. "I know that Fremont is never going to leave my side.

Sister D

She was the heart and soul of the school.

Life's most powerful forces are invisible. How do you begin to explain faith, perseverance and love? The best you can do, at least in this case, is to stand outside a Southwest Portland home in an early morning rain and wait for a 79-year-old woman to start her day.

She limps out -- cane in hand, right shoe an inch taller than the left -- and is helped into a van that will carry her to a school at the foot of the hill. Although she's in constant pain, she settles into the seat with a smile. Her name is Sister Dolores Doohan. But everyone calls her "Sister D."

Just down the street is St. Clare School. Sister D has taught there for 38 years. She's the heart and soul of the place. Now she's leaving and moving across the country. Yet she refuses to say goodbye. Uttering the word would make it so final.

When it comes up, she changes the subject, explaining that Iowa isn't that far away and that people travel all over these days and that no one can be sure when two paths might cross. The truth is that saying goodbye makes Sister D cry.

Leaving St. Clare and its 234 students -- kindergarten to eighth grade -- has been one of the most difficult decisions in her life. No one has been at the school longer than Sister D. To many people, she is the school.

So she's prayed over this, relying on God's guidance the way she did long ago when she left home against her father's wishes and took the train from Oakland, Calif., to Dubuque, Iowa, to join the Sisters of Charity of the Blessed Virgin Mary.

In a matter of days, she'll fly from Portland back to where she began her spiritual journey at her order's Motherhouse. She left there in 1949 to teach at Catholic schools across the country, eventually landing at St. Clare. Now, in the autumn of her life, she returns to the place where she learned a valuable lesson.

At the time she was a white-veil nun -- what they called newcomers. She'd gone to the infirmary and felt compelled to stop at a bed where an elderly nun lay. The woman summoned all her strength to say just one thing to this 19-year-old girl: Pray, she whispered, for the grace to persevere.

The message made no sense. Didn't for years.

And then, suddenly . . . persevere.

A child believes a teacher has no life beyond the classroom. A teacher is the face in the front of the room, the person who hands out assignments and issues grades. Where she came from, or how she got there, doesn't register.

But decades later that child is wiser to the ways of the world. From the past, the adult hears the echoes of a special teacher's voice. Something sticks, something that has nothing to do with math or science or social studies or all those things that once seemed so important. The gift that was given is that teacher's very essence.

From an old woman dying in a bed to a girl who thought she knew it all to a child who one day will certainly remember the sister with a limp.

Mention Sister D to kids who've graduated from St. Clare School and in their eyes you'll see her soul. One word from her past -- persevere -- lives on in them.

And when you learn where she came from, it makes sense.

———————

An intensely private woman, she avoids questions by waving her hand as if swatting a fly. A weary "Oh, my goodness" shows her irritation. Talking about herself, she believes, is nonsense. And so no one knows Sister D's story.

Life was a struggle for Dolores Doohan. Her parents, Irish immigrants who met in San Francisco, told her that at birth she weighed just over 4 pounds. The doctor asked her father whether he wanted to see his daughter before she died. But the baby fought for life. They put her in an incubator and hoped for the best.

When she began walking, her father noticed she frequently fell. Finally, at 7, her parents took her to a doctor who discovered the girl's hip had been dislocated since birth. Surgery corrected the problem, but the damage was done.

Her father supported two kids and a wife on a longshoreman's pay. Dolores needed a scholarship to attend the neighborhood Catholic high school run by Sisters of Charity of the Blessed Virgin Mary. As graduation neared, she felt a call to be a nun in the same order.

The sisters at school told her mother that they weren't sure it was a wise choice. Her bad leg would make a lifetime of service to others difficult, if not impossible. Dolores was adamant.

If she was sure, the sisters said, she had better include anything in her application that showed she'd have the ability to rise to the task. The girl looked back over her relatively short life and wrote that since fourth grade she'd never missed a day of school.

Her father, though, was disappointed. His sister had been a nun. When their mother died, the church had refused to let her travel from England to Ireland for the funeral. Dolores and her father shared a bond. He wanted her to attend college near the city. But she felt sure that it was time to start the journey that would carry her far from her home and family.

As she reveals that nugget from her past, there's something in her eyes that reveals the girl who remembers breaking away.

"It was very hard on my father," she says quietly. "He was so sad. The sisters sent me a trunk to pack my clothes. When he saw it in the living room he realized I really was going."

In that era, every nun was given the name Sister Mary. Dolores requested that she also be given her parents' names, Sarah and James. Two years after leaving home, Sister Mary Sarah James was ready to take her final vows. Two weeks before that ceremony, she learned her father had died.

"My parents never came to see me," she says. "It was too expensive."

Her father had managed to scrape enough money together to buy her a watch. On it he had this engraved: Sister Mary Sarah James. "Giving me the watch was one of the last things he did in life," she says. "He'd accepted my choice."

When it was time to leave the Motherhouse, Sister D began a nomadic journey, dispatched to teach in schools in Montana, California, Illinois and Hawaii. While in Hawaii, the church decreed that nuns could shed their church-given names and use their baptismal names. Sister Mary Sarah James grappled with the idea. Both her parents were dead, and she felt that giving up their names would seem ungrateful. A fellow sister reminded her that her parents had named her Dolores.

Sister Dolores remembered the old nun's message: Pray for the grace to persevere.

A voice from her past spoke. But what did that mean and how did it apply to her life?

For as long as she could remember, she'd been a fighter. Even simple things that others took for granted -- walking -- were a struggle. There'd been moments when she'd been discouraged.

But that's life. No one has it easy. Everyone has a limp. With some people, it's just more obvious.

The message, she decided, was to realize that in life there will always be moments of loneliness and doubt. In the end, it's just you and what you're made of. Children grow up and leave the safety of their parents' home and venture into a world that is both beautiful and harsh. In the midst of every struggle, there remain only two choices: Quit or persevere.

And in the clarity of that moment, she knew that the old nun -- a teacher of sorts -- had given her a wonderful gift that she must now share.

A short time later, she received a flier showing available jobs in the nation's Catholic schools. She believed she was being called to continue her journey. She applied to three schools on the West Coast and was asked to teach fifth grade at St. Clare. She had no idea how long she'd be at the school. But she liked the building. There weren't too many steps.

———◆———

With a wince, Sister D climbs from the van. Doctors fused her hip when she was 23, but it's now cracked and held in place with pins, screws and plates. Over the years, she's tried shots, pills and patches, even a morphine pump to try to stop the pain. A month ago, while recuperating in a convalescent center, she felt it was time to return to the Motherhouse, where she may undergo more surgery.

Her work at St. Clare was done. "As a baby, I was supposed to die," she explains as she hobbles to the school door. "God gave life to me for a reason."

She pushes the elevator button with her cane tip. Upstairs she steps into an empty hallway and slowly makes her way toward a classroom. She lingers, stopping along the way to admire student projects taped to the wall.

Poor health forced her to give up classroom teaching a few years ago, but she felt such a bond to students that she set up a desk in a hallway where she spends the day tutoring kids.

She stops at the desk to get her papers, then makes her way to an empty classroom where she gathers the school staff and leads the morning prayer before school starts. Ever the teacher, she makes a firm request that "everyone quiet down. Let us remember we are in the presence of God."

Her prayer sums up her life and their lives. The core of teaching, she says, is learning about yourself and finding ways to give that to the children.

Back in the hallway, she makes her way to her desk. Two children hug her. They start to say that dreaded word.

"Remember," Sister D interrupts, "no goodbyes."

———◆———

And so, just a few weeks before the students leave school for Christmas vacation, the curtain draws to a close.

Sister D stands in a corner of the school gymnasium watching young faces file through the door. "Oh, my goodness," she whispers. "This is marvelous."

She turns away.

Something in her eye? Adjusting the glasses?

Possibly.

At first, she wanted nothing special to mark this moment. She relented, but insisted that only the children, teachers and school staff be invited to this afternoon assembly. As much as the parents wanted to wish her well, she believed the children to be her flock.

There are songs and prayers, high squeaky voices and shy kids who can't believe they're up there in front of the school. But they catch Sister D's eye and smile and everything is just fine.

Then it's Sister D's turn to take the microphone. She remains seated. The room falls silent. She contemplates, trying to sum up 38 years and a lifetime of lessons, trying to offer a last gift.

"I really want to say thank you," she says. "Being with all of you every day has been wonderful. I'm going to miss you."

She has one parting message.

"Persevere."

———◆———

The final steps of her journey begin very early on a bitterly cold morning. She stands in the kitchen of her home one last time. Then with a smile she limps down the steps and into the garage.

Everything she owns is in three small suitcases packed in the trunk. She arrived at the Motherhouse with only a trunk. She returns with not much more. She eases into the front seat.

"Ready to go?" asks the driver who took her to the airport last week.

The passenger nods.

"Thank you, God," she whispers. "Thank you for all these years here."

The car backs onto the street and heads toward the freeway.

In a matter of moments, the taillights vanish.

ONE NUMBER AWAY

All he had to do was pick up the phone.

When he was sure he was alone, Shaun Wright dug deep into his pants pocket and pulled out a scrap of paper on which he had written a single telephone number.

For more than three weeks, he had been doing this, waiting each morning for his mother and brother to leave the house before sitting in the living room to stare at the paper.

A couple of times, he had picked up the handset. But that triggered the memories. He'd remember the girls who said they loved him, the boys who put tacks on his chair and that day in the eighth grade when it all became so clear.

And as the past swirled round him, sometimes bringing tears to his eyes, Shaun Wright would hang up the telephone, fold up that scrap of paper, stuff it back into his pocket and tell himself that tomorrow, yes, tomorrow, he would make the call.

Then, to cheer himself, he'd listen to his country-western tapes. But sometimes, even that led to regrets: He had always wanted to play the guitar. In junior high, he had envied the kids in the band because they seemed popular. So did the athletes. With music impossible, he went out for track.

One afternoon after practice, he heard a girl call his name. He didn't know her, but she was pretty and popular. Track was a great move, he thought.

He was always looking for new friends and walked over to where she stood with a group of students. She smiled.

"Shaun, I really want to be your girlfriend," she said. "Can I hold your hand?"

All right! He couldn't believe his luck. Nothing like this had ever happened. He didn't know what to say. So he just reached out and put his hand in hers.

She pulled away.

"Oh, yuck. He touched me."

He heard people laughing. What, what's going on?

"Hey, retardo," one boy yelled. "You think she was serious? Get back to your retardo class, you dummy."

He ran inside, just one step ahead of the hooting. Down through a maze of hallways he ran until, finally, he collapsed on the floor and cried. His teacher found him there and led him back to his empty classroom.

"Don't let them get to you."

He thought about what they had said. His mother had told him that he was slow. He knew he needed extra help to learn things. He knew he was in a special class.

Even so, he had believed he was like them -- the kids he saw every day in the hallway, on the school bus, in the lunchroom. As he sat there in short pants and tank top he realized, really for the first time, that he wasn't like them.

He was different. He was retarded.

Years later, he sat listening to his country music and trying to forget that day and all the others like them. He looked around his mother's house. He was 20 years old and he hated living here.

He wanted to live in his own apartment, but he'd never shared the dream with anyone. He was afraid they'd say it was out of the question.

A retarded guy living by himself? Even he wondered if he could do it.

At times, he felt as if his mind taunted and played tricks on him. Sometimes it let him think he was normal. Then it would do something to remind him he wasn't.

And on days like today -- when all he wanted to do was find the courage to make the phone call -- he felt only fear.

It was as though he were being held just below the surface of a swimming pool, close enough to the top to see the sunlight, but drowning just the same.

There was always something he couldn't do.

As an infant, he had a short esophagus and couldn't keep his food down. When other kids walked, he crawled. When other kids chattered, he mouthed his first word.

By the time he entered school, he still couldn't handle scissors; when handed a crayon, he drew only circles. At a teacher's request, his parents had him tested and learned that he was mildly retarded. He would be able to master some skills, they were told, but he would never advance beyond the intelligence of a fifth-grader.

He met his first best friend on the playground of his West Linn school. Her name was Megan. She, too, was in a special education class. She was two years older. A car accident at 4 months of age had left her brain-damaged. Each day, Shaun and Megan ate lunch together and then played tag.

When he was 10, his parents divorced. Shaun, his mother and brother moved to Hillsboro. It was there, after that track practice in the eighth grade, that he first comprehended that he was retarded.

After that, he looked around his special education classroom. He saw with new eyes the girls and boys who were just like him and felt embarrassed. When he walked the halls, he heard other kids' comments and felt ashamed.

If he had been teased before, he hadn't heard it. Now, it was all he heard.

The catcalls -- "Dummy," "Goofy," "Freak" -- followed him into high school. At times, he felt he was the butt of everyone's practical jokes.

The boys put tacks on his chair in the lunchroom. Usually, he spotted them and brushed them off. One morning, he didn't see the tack, sat down and cried while the boys laughed.

The girls were worse. He wanted them to like him and he believed it when they said they loved him. Time after time, they said they wanted to hold his hand. When he offered it eagerly, they would laugh at their joke and run back to their smirking friends.

Had Shaun been severely retarded, the isolation of his own private world might have protected him from the jeers. But he knew why they laughed. He understood what they said.

Beyond these daily ordeals, Shaun faced constant doubt deep within. His mind, and its limitations, terrified him. Things disappeared into its black hole. A person could explain a task to him and he'd understand it fine. But when he tried to do the job himself, he was lost. He couldn't remember what to do.

And then there were the thoughts and feelings that bounced around in his head like balls in a pinball machine. They just wouldn't come out. He knew what he wanted to say but couldn't find the right word. Or he had thoughts and feelings that he couldn't explain or even understand.

His life seemed like the bingo games he played. He was always just one number away from winning. But the number, his number, never came up. Someone else always won.

It wasn't all bad. He had nice teachers and some friends. But there was always something he couldn't do. His friends took up skateboarding; Shaun's poor sense of balance kept him on the sidelines. When other kids played baseball, Shaun watched from the bleachers; his reflexes were too slow to swing a bat or field a ball.

On Sundays, he went to church and listened to lessons and sermons about a great, kind God. He didn't understand. If God was great and kind, why was Shaun retarded? Had he done something wrong? Was he being punished? There were times when he hated being alive.

Normal kids avoided him. No one begged him to eat lunch with them. No one talked to him about upcoming dances. The kids in his special ed class selected him to be their senator for the student council, but it wasn't the same as being popular. It wasn't like being selected by the kids down the hallway in the other classrooms.

When his mom asked how school was going, he'd only tell her he was having some problems. Then he'd look in the mirror. He wasn't tall and didn't consider himself good-looking; he wondered what he could do to make the other kids like him.

Still seeking the popularity accorded athletes, Shaun decided to go for a high school letter. He asked the varsity football coach if he could be team manager. The coach agreed.

The football players affectionately called him "Radar" because he reminded them of the company clerk on the television show "M*A*S*H."

Before games and practices, Shaun bustled around the locker room getting the pads ready or tracking down tape for someone's ankles. When the game was over and the players scattered to meet girlfriends or go to parties, he stayed behind to help clean up.

But it was worth it. At the end of the season, Shaun was invited to the lettermen's banquet in the school cafeteria. He wore his best shirt and tie and made sure his family had good seats.

When dessert was over, the coach called each player onto a small stage to hand him his letter and shake his hand. When it was Shaun's turn, the players shouted, "Good job, Radar!" He grinned and gave them a thumbs-up sign.

About a month later, the team's letter jackets arrived. Shaun tried his on at home that evening. It felt so good. He looked closely at himself in the mirror. He looked like . . . a jock. That's right. A jock.

He couldn't wait to see everyone's reaction at school. He was a jock. And jocks were popular. He got to school early. He wore his jacket to every class. He waited for the comments.

No one said a word.

At graduation, Shaun received what was called a modified diploma, which meant he had taken different classes. But life changed very little. The other kids went to college or started jobs. He lived at home with his mother.

One afternoon as he boarded a city bus, he spotted a familiar face near the back. Could it be? Yes. He never forgot her face. He walked down the aisle and stood beside her. It had been eight years.

"Is your name Megan?"

"Yes."

"Is your last name Mahoney?"

"Yes."

"I thought so. I'm Shaun Wright. Do you remember me?"

"No." The young woman's eyes were bad. She didn't recognize him.

"We went to school. You used to chase me on the playground every day. You could never catch me."

"I remember."

She moved over and made room for Shaun. As the bus bounced along, they talked about the old days and what they had been doing. When Megan's stop was nearing, Shaun stood up and asked for her telephone number.

Two days later, they had their first date.

Since neither drove, Megan's father chauffeured them to a Gladstone restaurant. He dropped them off and said he'd be back in a couple of hours.

Over dinner and soft drinks, they got to know each other. Shaun liked watching World Wrestling Federation bouts. Megan took guitar lessons as part of her therapy.

Before long, Megan's father was back. Shaun and Megan climbed into the van and sat far apart. The radio was on and the windows were down. Warm summer air washed over Shaun's face. He didn't want the night to end.

He looked at Megan. She was so nice. And funny. The wind tousled her hair. And so pretty.

Shaun looked up and caught Mr. Mahoney's eyes in the rearview mirror. Shaun looked away. His hands were sweaty. He wiped them on his pants.

Slowly, he reached across the dark seat and found Megan's small, warm hand. Gently, he wrapped his fingers around hers. He squeezed softly.

He looked out the window. He didn't want to see Mr. Mahoney staring at him. He didn't dare look at Megan. What if she was mad? What if she thought he was pushy? Why did he do it?

And then softly, ever so softly, her hand squeezed his.

What he had with Megan was like nothing he had experienced.

She unlocked love for life he didn't know existed. He groped for words to explain how he felt. He tried "happy" and "on fire" but they seemed inadequate. When he thought about Megan, he felt something in the pit of his stomach that he couldn't explain.

Talking with her on the phone at night, he confided he was worried about being fired. He had lost jobs before.

In high school, he'd worked at a McDonald's restaurant frying chicken. His boss had spent hours training him. Even so, he made plenty of mistakes. His boss would slow everything down and start over.

But when it got busy, Shaun couldn't slow down. The counter help yelled orders so fast he couldn't keep up. He could do only one thing at a time or he'd forget everything. He'd cook too many breasts or too few. Or he'd forget an order.

After three months, his boss called him into the office. Sorry, you're not McDonald's material.

Shaun found a job in a nursing home. He helped cook, mashed food for people who couldn't chew and mopped floors. He struggled with all his boss' instructions and lasted three months before she told Shaun he wasn't what they were looking for.

By the time he finished high school, he was a restaurant busboy. He didn't mind the work, but a cook and some waiters teased him. He came to dread going to work.

One day, he wandered over to an Albertson's grocery store where a sign said they were hiring bag boys. He started two weeks later. He did well enough that Albertson's transferred their new employee to another store soon after that.

As Shaun told Megan on the phone, he liked his job, but was worried about losing it. He was making mistakes again.

If, on his way to return bottles, he walked by an empty display case, he wouldn't think to fill it -- he was concentrating on the bottles. If a customer asked him to run back and get a brand of bread while he was bagging groceries, he'd get back among the aisles and forget what he was looking for.

Shaun was sure he was going to be fired and went to see his boss, Lonnie Walter. Walter told him not to worry; the world won't end because of a few mistakes.

Some frustrated employees then asked Walter to fire Shaun.

Walter listened to their complaints but said the subject was closed. As long as he was the boss, he said, Shaun had a job.

Finding the right job was the challenge. Walter discovered that Shaun was one of his hardest workers. If he gave him a simple job and showed him how to do it, Shaun worked like a machine.

He gave Shaun different jobs to see what he could do. Stocking shelves and setting up food displays were impossible because Shaun forgot what he was doing midtask.

He refined Shaun's work until it was clear what he did well -- return empty bottles, fill up the checkout counters with grocery bags, and bag and carry groceries to customers' cars.

Walter also experimented with Shaun's hours and found that after working about six or more hours a day, he had problems. Walker changed the schedule so Shaun worked about five hours a day.

Shaun's fellow employees noticed the changes. They enjoyed working with him, and he enjoyed the camaraderie. Customers called him by name.

One afternoon, after he'd been at the store for several months, Shaun picked up his paycheck. He stared at it. Something was wrong. He checked the pay stub.

He had earned a raise.

Within the year, he was making $5 an hour, more than enough to occasionally take Megan to a movie or buy another country-western tape to add to his collection.

Because he had problems with math, he'd cash his check and let his mother handle his finances. He knew she worried about him, but he was tired of living under her protective wing.

He felt like a kid, and it seemed they disagreed about everything. He wanted to stay up late; she wanted him in bed early. He wanted to play his music loud; she wanted it softer. She wanted to know where he was going; he didn't want explain his every move.

When he was younger, home had been a place where he could escape from the rest of the world. But now it seemed like prison.

Some of the kids he knew from school had moved away. They were going to college, starting careers and getting their own apartments. He didn't plan on college and he had a job, not a career. But an apartment . . . boy, he'd like an apartment.

He didn't dare tell his mother. She'd worry about him living all by himself. She'd say an apartment was out of the question.

In late 1990, when he thought he couldn't stand it anymore, he remembered the woman he had met on a fishing trip the previous summer. The trip had been sponsored by the Association for Retarded Citizens of Clackamas County and she had been a case worker with the group. He remembered her name, Jo Ann Staino. He remembered she'd told him to call if he ever needed anything.

He looked through the phone book, found the association's telephone number. He was too scared to call, so he wrote the number down on a scrap of paper.

He tried the next day. He couldn't do it.

What if she said no? He didn't think his life could stand another no. What if she didn't think a man like him could live alone?

Each morning, when he was sure he was alone, he would pull the scrap of paper from his pocket and stare at it.

For three weeks this went on. Be brave, he told himself. Make the call. He couldn't do it.

Some days just thinking about making the call almost had him believing he'd done it. He'd leave for work in a great mood. But later on, when he'd be carrying out groceries or counting empty bottles, he'd start thinking about what it would be like to have his own apartment.

One morning, he studied the telephone number. Then he got up and searched the house until he found a pen and another scrap of paper. He looked at the clock and wrote down "11."

At 11 a.m., he would decide. He would call Jo Ann Staino then or forget about it forever.

If he made the call, he risked embarrassment and humiliation. If he didn't make the call, he risked nothing -- except his happiness.

He took his pieces of paper -- the one with Staino's number, the other with the time -- and set them on the kitchen table near the telephone. Then he went to his bedroom. He put on a country-western tape. And then he waited for the time to pass.

A while later, he glanced at the clock.

11 a.m.

He walked into the kitchen. He looked at the telephone number. He picked up the handset. The memories came back. He pushed away his demons. He dialed the number.

He asked for Staino.

He was put on hold. He thought about hanging up.

Staino came on the line.

"My name is Shaun Wright. I want to live in my own apartment. Can you help me?"

That night, he told his mother he was going to leave home. He explained he would soon be on a waiting list for a subsidized apartment from the Clackamas County Housing Authority.

His mother said she was happy, but she worried about him. He knew right from wrong, but what if someone took advantage of him? A part of her wanted him to get the apartment. And a part of her did not.

Activity around her home picked up over the next several months. She taught him a few recipes and advised him to dry his dishes right after washing them to avoid spots.

He met with Staino to learn what he needed to live alone. She helped him fill out forms to verify his income and apply for Social Security benefits and food stamps.

About 30 percent of his income would go for rent. He practiced making a budget by setting aside portions of each paycheck. He learned how to buy money orders so he could pay his bills, how to read labels at the grocery store to figure out which product was the best buy.

Staino quizzed him: What do you do if a stranger knocks on your door? What is the 9-1-1 system? What do you do if you see flames in another apartment? What do you do if the lights go out?

Sometimes he didn't think he could remember everything. Then Staino would start again.

One day a letter arrived at his mother's home. He was No. 1 on the waiting list. The next apartment was his.

Four months later, a housing authority official called. An apartment was available at the Hillside Manor in Milwaukie. His mother drove him over to look at it.

When he stepped inside it seemed so empty and big. He walked into one of the rooms and looked out the window. He could see Portland. It would look nice at night.

"I'll take it," he said.

The next few weeks were a blur.

He and his mother bought some secondhand furniture. In his mother's closet, he found some of his grandmother's old lamps. He began packing up his bedroom.

One Friday, in December 1990, it was time to move.

His mother's next-door neighbor had a pickup and offered to help. By Sunday, they had only one load to go. They hauled the couch and chair out of his mother's house and put them in the truck.

Shaun went back inside to say goodbye to his mother.

She waited in the living room. Her baby was leaving home. A part of her was leaving home. She knew it was for the best, but the tears fell anyway. She hugged her son. He hugged his mother.

"Good luck," she said.

Then he was gone.

He and the neighbor drove to Hillside Manor and moved the couch and chair into Shaun's apartment. Shaun walked his neighbor back to his truck.

"Thanks," he said.

"You have a good life," said the neighbor.

Shaun stood outside the building and watched until the truck disappeared around the corner.

He went back into his apartment building. The hallways were empty. He didn't know anyone. He walked down the hallway to his unit, opened the door and started crying.

He walked from room to room, listening to his footsteps echo off the walls. He turned on his television, glad for the comfort of its noise. He opened his refrigerator, got something to eat and felt better.

He figured his mother would be worried and decided he'd better call her. His telephone wasn't hooked up, but he remembered seeing a pay phone up the road. He walked there and punched in his mother's telephone number.

They talked for a while.

"Mom, I'm fine," he said. "I'm fine. Everything is fine. I'm going home."

He hung up the phone. He walked back up the street.

Night was falling.

He couldn't wait to see the city lights from his living room.

Born of Tough Country

The boy picked up his arm and went two miles for help.

Michael Adams fumbles a bit with his left hand before opening the car door and sliding into the front seat. He frowns slightly when he realizes he can't shake hands with a right arm that, for now, is useless.

He was raised, though, to be polite. So the 13-year-old nods, touches the brim of a white baseball cap smashed down over red hair and flashes a smile to reveal a mouth full of braces.

"Want to see where it happened?" he asks. "I haven't been back there since that day, but I'm ready to see it. Really, I am."

He points to a field about a mile away from his school, the biggest building in Crane, a town nearly 130 miles southeast of Bend, then settles into the seat while the car bounces out of town.

In a farming community where accidents are commonplace, what happened to Michael on July 17 still makes grown men twinge. He was moving an irrigation line when a set of moving gears snagged his sleeve. The machinery cut off his right arm at the shoulder.

What happened next stunned everyone who heard about it: The boy picked up his arm and went two miles for help. That afternoon, the arm was surgically reattached in a Portland hospital.

The extraordinary incident attracted attention from across the country, and interview requests besieged the family. But the Adamses are a private bunch, and they shunned the attention. They went back to Crane so their son could heal in private.

Months passed before they felt Michael was ready to reveal exactly what happened on that terrible day in July.

———◆———

Crane is just a speck on a road map, a detour off U.S. 20 in a section of Harney County, a 10,300-square-mile chunk of Eastern Oregon larger than most New England states.

Only 100 people call Crane home. The Adams family, which works a 550-acre alfalfa and cattle ranch outside of town, settled in here 22 years ago. They've battled bitter weather, ornery equipment and stifling isolation, existing in a land where survival depends on doing whatever it takes to get the job done. The Adams family believes those lessons, ingrained in Michael Adams from birth, saved his life.

"Stop here," Michael says. "See that black cow? That one, right there. That's exactly where it happened."

There was, he says, no pain.

"You know what I remember more than anything?' he asks. "It felt hot. My shoulder was so hot. Then I looked down, and there was my arm. My arm was just lying there on the ground."

He rode his all-terrain vehicle out to this field about 7 a.m. on a Saturday to move irrigation lines. His job was to engage the gears on a motorized wheel attached to the line, move that section, walk to the next wheel and repeat the process. Each line had seven wheels, and he took home about $14 for three hours of work, good pay for a kid in Crane where nearly every child has family chores.

Michael had moved one wheel and started on the second. He reached over the wheel's motor, pushed a lever and felt a tug on his right arm. He saw the sleeve on his jacket slowly disappearing into the gears.

"I tried pulling my sleeve out, but it was stuck," he says. "I tried pulling my jacket off, but the zipper was broken, and I couldn't get it over my head. I tried shutting off the motor, but I couldn't reach the lever.

"The gears were moving kind of slow," he says. "It seemed like it took about 20 seconds. I knew what was going to happen. All I could do was watch."

The gears slowly pulled his arm into the mechanism, and then the gear teeth severed it at the shoulder.

"I wasn't in shock," Michael says. "That was weird. You know, I'd heard stories about people who had their fingers attached again; so I figured I better take my arm with me when I went for help."

"Hey, stop the car here." He points toward the field.

"I ran to that power pole, where I had my ATV parked," he says, moving his arm across the windshield to cover a distance that appears to be the length of a football field. "I got on the ATV, stuck my arm between my legs and took off towards Crane."

The throttle was on the right handle, so Michael had to reach across his body and drive left-handed. He had the ATV running as fast as it would go and, in his words, "wiped out," rolling when he couldn't negotiate a corner leading to the road.

"I picked my arm up and ran to that shed over there," he says. "I knew there was another ATV. I got that one started and took off."

"OK," he says. "You can go into town now. I'll show you where I went."

The car eases down the road toward Crane. As the minutes pass, it's almost possible to see a ghost of a 13-year-old, racing ahead.

"No, I never thought I wouldn't make it," Michael says. "Where did I get my strength? Faith in God. And football, I guess. See, Crane is a small school. So I play back and defensive end. OK, that first house over there, I knew no one was at home. Why? Well, the gate was closed. When people around here aren't home they close their gates."

As he approached the Miller place -- now about two miles from the field -- he rolled the ATV again. He picked up his arm and ran about 300 yards to the Miller house. First, though, he made sure he closed their gate.

"Well, they have dogs," he says. "That's why. I knew they wouldn't want their dogs to get outside.

"When I got here, I started banging on their door, yelling for help. They were in bed. When they opened the door they didn't recognize me because I was covered with dust and dirt. The gears had twisted all the veins closed so there wasn't a lot of blood. When they saw it was me, they let me in their house. I gave them my arm and then I lay down on the floor.

"I asked for a glass of water," he says. "Boy, was I thirsty."

———◆———

Kathy Ann Miller called 9-1-1 to have an ambulance sent out from Burns, about 45 miles away from Crane. Her next call was to Jean Goff, who the previous year had retired as the school's secretary. Goff is a first-responder, a volunteer who has taken advanced first-aid classes. Because they live so far from medical help, townsfolk frequently turn to volunteers such as Goff until the ambulance arrives.

Goff, who lives a quarter-mile from the Millers, hustled over and got to work. She wrapped the boy's arm in a towel, sealed it in a plastic bag and then put it in a chest and filled the chest with ice.

By then his parents, Richard and Nancy Adams, had arrived. The first thing their son did was to apologize to them for what had happened.

The ambulance raced up the driveway, and the family was told that a fixed-wing plane was waiting for them at the Burns airport. From Burns, the pilot flew Michael to Hillsboro. A LifeFlight helicopter then carried him to Oregon Health Sciences University, where nurses whisked him into the operating room.

"The first thing we did was hook up a temporary artery and vein to get blood flowing in that arm," says Dr. Reid Mueller, assistant professor of plastic surgery. "We have a six-hour limit before the limb is dead, and by the time we got him, 21/2 hours had passed since the amputation. We had to move fast." A team of surgeons reattached bones and muscles. From his leg, they harvested a vein and fashioned it into an artery to allow blood to flow into the arm. They used muscles from his back to replace damaged muscle in his forearm.

Michael spent three weeks in the hospital, and family members took turns by his bedside. Then the family took him home to Crane. A week later he was doing chores. His family needs every hand to make the ranch work.

In early November, Michael returned to the hospital, where surgeons took nerves from his leg and grafted them to his shoulder.

"The nerve fibers in his arm had died," Mueller says. "Think of it like a cable without a wire inside. The cable is still there. The nerve fibers will grow down that cable about an inch a month. His forearm muscles will start to work in about a year. In about two years the nerves will reach his fingertips. He has a good chance for movement of the hand. To predict more is difficult. But he's young, and that's good."

———

O n this day, a weekday in late November when it feels as if snow will fall, Michael waves goodbye to his mother and says he'll see her in Burns, where he's headed for a session with the physical therapist.

"You know," he says, after Crane has faded in the rearview mirror, "I don't think I want to be a farmer when I grow up. It doesn't pay enough, and that's kind of sad. I want to go to college. That's what I was saving my money from moving the lines for. I had a little college fund."

His right arm, wrapped up in a navy blue sling, rests in his lap. The skin is pink, and it looks healthy. His left hand is busy -- the radio dial, the window, his baseball cap -- but the right hand, it just lies there.

"Want to hear something?" Michael asks. He starts making bird noises. He smiles proudly.

"I just figured out how to do that," he says. "I was doing them in music class today, and the teacher couldn't figure out where they were coming from. I play the bass drum in the band. You know that song 'Wipeout'? I can do that good. I mean, I could, until this happened."

Night is falling over Harney County, and there are just two cars on this stretch of U.S. 20.

"No, I don't ever get nightmares," says Michael. "No, I don't wonder, 'Why me?' I can't worry about that. Worrying about it won't change a thing. The only thing I feel sorry about is math. I have a hard time with math. Now math, that's tough.

"My chores were cut back a bit," he says. "But nobody was waiting on me hand and foot. Now I just feed the dogs and chickens and gather the eggs and work the gate when my dad gathers the cattle.

"That's not too bad. You know, I had this pig I was raising for 4-H. His name was Sprocket. When I got hurt, my sister -- she's 16 -- she had to take care of him. I was supposed to pay her $50, but I haven't yet, and she's kind of mad at me."

In early September, Michael showed Sprocket at the Harney County Fair, where the 4-H animal projects are sold.

"You know what was the worst part?" he asked. "People felt sorry for me. I know they did. I got $6 a pound for Sprocket, and everyone else got about $3 a pound. My pig wasn't that much better. Come on. I ended up making $1,400, but I felt bad about it."

When school started, Michael was a celebrity. Even the girls were sympathetic. At least for a while.

"Then I started teasing them, and now they hit me," he says. "You know how girls are always talking about how heavy they are? Well, my friends and I tell them to not jump or they'll crack the floor. That's when they hit me. On the left arm only, though."

The sports report comes on again and Michael falls silent, and an unspoken truth fills the car.

"Well, yeah, there are some things I miss," he says. "Sports. Eighth grade was supposed to be my year. I can't play football or basketball. I go watch the practices, but that's hard, you know. I had to learn how to write with my left hand and use a fork again. That was weird.

"Sometimes I get discouraged, and I feel down," he says. "But I sleep it off. It helps to be around people because I have to act happy and before I know it I am happy. That's kind of strange how that works. I can't give up. I'm young. I have a life to live, you know. Say, listen to this."

He reaches up with his left finger and starts to pluck a rubber band in his braces.

"Recognize that?"

He plays it again.

"Wipeout," he says.

THE BARISTA

Move before you think you are ready.

Until the blonde walked into the place, it had been a day like all the days that had come before and all the days he thought would follow.

"Americano."

"Tall nonfat, no-whip mocha."

"Vanilla latte."

His name was Richard Miller. He was 25 and had blown into Portland more than a year before from Eugene. He brought with him $1,000 and a dream of finding wealth as a guitar player in a big-time rock band. His groups never amounted to much. The sure deals and lucrative contracts were wisps of smoke. Before he knew it, the grand was gone and he was looking for work.

He signed on as a barista, serving coffee at a Starbucks Coffee shop on Southeast Hawthorne Boulevard near 20th Avenue. Although he had sworn the job would be temporary, he had been at it for a year, long enough to receive a raise to $6.40 an hour. He counted on tips.

He shared a house with two guys and couldn't afford a car. He hung out on Hawthorne with others of his generation -- pizza makers, waiters, bike messengers and clerks. Many, like Miller, were dreamers. They scribbled in journals, creating poetry, songs, scripts or stories. They waited to be discovered. When they were not, they grumbled about injustice, corporate greed and the foolish ways of the Establishment.

Within this world, Miller was well-liked. A clerk in a gift store had a crush on him. And he couldn't walk more than a block without a friend waving or calling.

He stood 6-foot-1 and weighed just over 200 pounds. He wore a goatee and granny glasses. His black hair, uncut in eight years, hung in a ponytail. His dress rarely varied: black jeans, black combat boots and a long, black coat. At a distance he looked ominous. Up close, though, he had twinkling blue eyes and the unmarked face of a boy.

He was, though, a troubled man. All his life he had been convinced that if he could have nice things -- a decent car, a substantial house and a big paycheck -- this ache inside him would disappear.

Some of the Hawthorne regulars played poor. They wore secondhand clothes but attended college and could afford to shop at Nordstrom. Or they had graduated and were taking it easy for a while. If they ran into trouble, their parents were there with checks to bail them out. They lived in dingy apartments and considered themselves bohemians.

All dumps did for Miller was remind him of what he thought he had finally escaped. As he arrived for this Saturday shift, he was sure of only three things in life.

He made a great latte.

He was no rock star.

He was going to end up like his father.

Then the blonde walked in.

———◆———

To this day, Starbucks regulars swear they've never seen anything like the vision that crossed the threshold that sunny autumn day in October 1997. Conversations stopped. Customers quit reading newspapers. A man at the counter fumbled his change. When she said she was looking for Richard Miller, the cashier looked as if she'd pulled a pistol.

Rich?

Yes.

The Richard Miller?

Yes.

Stunned, the cashier walked to the back room, where Miller was fiddling with supplies. When Miller appeared in the doorway, the blonde waved him over. Miller walked to her. They talked quietly. He nodded. Then he followed her outside to meet a sharp-dressed man leaning against a car. He talked on a cellular phone. He wore a Rolex watch that cost more than Miller earned in seven months.

His name was Eben Pagan. He was a ghost from Miller's past.

And the past was something Miller avoided.

The truth was that Miller was still running from Grover City, a small western Pennsylvania town where he had been considered poor white trash. He and his family lived in trailers. They wore clothes from the Salvation Army and drove $600 beaters. In the fall of 1981, when he was 9, the school nurse pulled him out of class and took him shopping to buy him new shoes with the school's poor fund. When he got home that day, his mother looked at the nurse and the shoes and cried.

After his parents divorced, he and his sister moved with his mother into a place above a beer distributor. Most nights it was so cold that Miller couldn't sleep in his bed. The only warm spot was on the floor, next to a space heater.

When his mother remarried, they moved into his stepfather's apartment, which had been converted from a one-man barbershop. The place was so small that Miller and his sister slept on the closet floor.

When he was in the sixth grade, his stepfather moved the family west for a job in Alaska. It fell through. They landed in Roseburg and stayed with a relative before moving to Eugene. Miller lingered a couple of years before returning to Pennsylvania to live with his father.

He came back after graduating from high school. Other kids were off to college or planning their futures. He had no money for college and no one to give him advice. In his family, success meant a steady paycheck. When his father got out of the service, he married and took a job driving truck. He never did anything else with his life.

Miller played piano, drums and guitar and decided music was his way out. In Eugene, he worked in the Sacred Heart Hospital cafeteria, joined

and formed bands, wrote songs and took guitar lessons. His teacher introduced him to a student named Eben Pagan.

Music brought them together, but their friendship grew out of their
common backgrounds. Pagan, a year older than Miller, had also grown up
poor, and Miller never felt inadequate around him. They were each other's
cheerleaders, both convinced they'd be rock stars.

On the side, Pagan built up a thriving business buying and selling
used guitars. He discovered he was a natural salesman. He took some business classes at Lane Community College, earned his real-estate license and
hooked on with an agency.

Miller felt betrayed. He accused Pagan of selling out his talent, his
dream and their friendship.

Pagan rose through the ranks and was recruited by a Southern
California-based company that trains real-estate types in marketing techniques. Pagan became a consultant, speaker and one of the company's
most valuable employees. Miller, meanwhile, quit the hospital. He took his
$1,000 retirement payout and headed to Portland, determined to start over
in the music scene, to become a star and to find the wealth that would make
him happy.

While in Portland on business, Pagan decided to find Miller. He pulled
up to the Hawthorne Starbucks. Then his cellphone rang -- an important
call from a client. He stayed outside, did a little business and sent his girlfriend in to see if this was the place where Miller worked.

Pagan and Miller shook hands on the sidewalk. Miller took in the
expensive watch, the tailored clothes and the blonde. He wondered how he
looked in his green apron. He felt like a chump.

Their conversation was mercifully short. Before parting they agreed to
have a few drinks that night.

Miller walked back inside a somber man.

"So," a customer asked, "who were those two?"

"An old friend," Miller said. "Just call him an old friend."

He took his place behind the espresso machine.

"Grande mocha."

"Childs hot chocolate."
"Latte."

———————

P agan and Miller went out that night, listened to music and had a few drinks. They talked about old days and old dreams. As the night wound down, Miller admitted how he was feeling to the one person who could understand.

As he talked, though, Miller realized Pagan was different. He listened but offered no encouraging words. Finally he interrupted. He told Miller to stop whining. Pagan said Miller had to be responsible for his life. If he wanted to move to the next level, he had to let go of the past.

Moving on, he said, was scary. He knew that. He reminded Miller of where he had come from. There was no reason for what Pagan did next. Maybe it was out of friendship or a shared history. Maybe it was just late and the drinks were working their magic. Whatever it was, Pagan proposed that Miller come visit him in Southern California. He would see if he could get Miller a job at the company.

Miller mulled it over. He knew that Pagan pulled down a tremendous salary and lived in a great apartment on the beach. Earlier Pagan had told him how he had looked out his living-room window and watched a photo shoot with actress Pamela Anderson.

That's what Miller wanted.

But Starbucks, along with the Hawthorne culture that surrounded it, was the only world he knew. He understood the rules and mores. He felt safe.

And yet . . .

Miller enjoyed reading biographies of achievers who had accomplished great things in politics, music and business. If there was a common thread in their lives, he believed it was this: Move before you think you are ready.

He certainly wasn't ready.

So he had to move.

He used his vacation time. Pagan paid for the airline ticket and warned Miller that life as he knew it was over.

In November, Pagan took Miller to a hair salon and told the stylist to go to work. The goatee was gone. When she attacked his hair, Miller told Pagan that he was freaking out. Pagan told the stylist to keep cutting. When she was done, Millers hair lay above his ears. She rubbed gel into his hair. When he left the salon he carried his ponytail in a plastic bag.

At a clothing store, Pagan paid for pants, shoes and a sports coat. At his apartment Pagan told Miller he looked like a poodle shaking after a trip to the groomer.

Now it was time for the final touches. A splash of cologne. A decent watch. Pagan took the cheap plastic thing Miller wore. He rummaged around a drawer and found a fake Rolex that looked like his real Submariner. If a person knew watches, he could tell it wasn't real. But it was heavy and shiny, and from a distance it made Miller look as if he were a man of substance.

Richard Miller's debut would be at dinner with Joe Stumps, the owner of the company, and the man who ultimately would decide if Miller could be hired. So much was at stake that Pagan decided Miller, who had been eating in fast-food restaurants all his life, needed a practice meal.

Pagan took him to an Italian place. While they ate, Pagan critiqued. Keep the fork in the left hand and the knife in the right, European style. Once they were used, they shouldn't touch the table again. If there was something he needed across the table, ask to have it passed.

The meal was intense. Miller hardly enjoyed the food. He never realized there was a place for the bread plate. And Pagan chided him when he used his fingers with the appetizer, some bread thing with diced eggplant, tomatoes and cheese. Miller laughed. This is the shovel method, he told Pagan. Pagan didn't think it was funny. He told Miller to cut the appetizer on his plate and to use his fork.

As they approached the restaurant the night they were to meet Stumps, Pagan told Miller to maintain eye contact and act comfortable. Introductions were made and the meal began.

Left: Fork.

Right: Knife.

Don't reach.

Look him in the eye.

Napkin on the lap.

When the table was cleared, Pagan told Stumps he planned to find a spot in the company for Miller.

Stumps said nothing -- he just stared at him. Miller wondered if Stumps saw through him. Finally, Stumps reached across the table and grasped Miller's hand.

"Welcome aboard."

———◆———

The rumors swept up Hawthorne Boulevard block by block. At first no one dared believe them. Then he appeared with a navy blue sports coat, dress shirt and slacks. His hair glistened with gel. He wore tan leather slip-on shoes without socks.

Friends didn't know what to say, the girl who had a crush on him got over it, and no one waved.

One guy took a look at his hair and clothes and asked if he still played the guitar. A fellow musician called him a cold businessman. He was criticized for selling his soul to the corporate devil. Old street buddies told him he was making a mistake. They said he'd fail.

He continued working at Starbucks to save money for the move. He had to sell some of his guitars and musical gear to raise money to buy his first suit and tie.

He finally quit Starbucks because he wanted to use his remaining time in Portland to prepare for the consulting world. With Pagan clearing the way, he remembers thinking, there was no doubt he'd be in demand.

Each day he sat down with a stack of books he bought at the used-book store: Advertising Magic, The Complete Guide to Creating Hot Ads and Sales Letters That Work. He read, took notes and devised campaigns. He imagined himself giving advice.

"Mister Miller.

He liked the sound of it.

Although his exact duties were still being worked out, he learned his monthly salary would be about $2,500. The $30,000 he'd make in the first year was about triple what he earned at Starbucks. This sudden wealth convinced him that finally he would get the things he had lived without for so long.

What was the point of living in California without a bachelor pad on the beach? And a nice car? Never again would he walk or take the bus. When Pagan mentioned he was selling his $40,000 Lexus to buy a new luxury car, Miller said he'd take over the payments. Pagan warned him about the expense. Miller scoffed.

When Miller arrived in California, he settled in Oceanside, a town near the company's headquarters and about an hour north of San Diego. He found his place on the beach. Well, not on beach. The complex, which butted up against the freeway, was two blocks from a street that separated him from the ocean.

The car, though, made him feel as if he was living the California dream. No one in his family had ever owned such a car. To celebrate his good fortune, he put on his sunglasses, rolled down the windows and cranked up a funk tape.

He cruised the beach, enjoying the view and trying to get women to notice him. But after about 30 minutes, he realized that a Lexus was no big deal in Southern California. He was getting passed by Mercedes and Ferraris and Porsches.

But he didn't care.

He was Richard Miller.

Mister Miller.

In early January 1998, he showed up for work. He wondered about his office. He required a window. And, of course, a secretary. But she could wait until he determined how much paperwork and correspondence he generated.

A receptionist led him to Reese Harris, the company's assistant general manager. Miller sat down in Harris office. The previous night he had been reading his marketing books and studying his notes. He was ready for the first question. He hoped it dealt with advertising because he felt particularly strong when it came to campaigns. In fact . . .

"Do you have a resume? Harris asked.

"Uh, no.

"Have you sold real estate?

"No.

"Know how to use a computer?

"No.

"Can you write a marketing report.

"No.

"Can you type?

"No.

Harris led Miller out of his office and down the hall to a small window-less room. He saw two boxes. One contained monthly marketing letters to real-estate agents. Envelopes filled the other. Miller's instructions were simple: Take a letter, fold it and insert it into an envelope. A postage meter and an automatic licking machine should make the job easier.

Welcome aboard.

He stuffed envelopes all day and went home that night to his place near the beach and seethed. All this knowledge. All this learning. All this talent. And he's sitting on his butt stuffing envelopes. Any moron could do that.

He called Eben at home to complain. His old friend was no help. He told Miller to learn the company from the ground up.

The envelope stuffing went on for a couple of weeks until the company discovered Miller understood public-address systems, amplifiers and recording gear. Harris put him in charge of the company's sophisticated audio equipment and said he was going on the road to work the seminars. Suits were required. When Miller explained he had but one, the company shelled out $900, outfitted him and put him on a plane to Phoenix, Ariz.

He felt like a big shot on the plane. New suit, attaché case, a drink.

Not a bad life at all.

When the plane landed, he followed other business travelers to the baggage claim. The carousel spun round and round. He took his luggage. He waited for another box. Round and round. Then the carousel stopped, and he was alone. He told an airline employee that an important case containing cables he needed was missing.

When he got to the hotel, he told his boss the airlines had messed up. Stupid box is probably in Chicago. His boss shrugged. He had just two words: Fix it.

Miller wasn't sure his boss understood. He didn't lose the box. The airline lost the luggage. It was their problem.

Your problem, the boss said. You're the audio guy.

But he had just arrived in town. He was tired. He was hungry. He wanted to check into his room and relax.

Fix it. Make it happen, his boss said. He didn't care how Miller did it. Do it.

Now.

The rest of the day, Miller called electronics stores and drove around town buying cords and cables to patch together a system that was ready at 7 the next morning when more than 600 real-estate agents arrived in the hotel ballroom to hear Stumps, Pagan and other consultants.

The second day of the seminar, just when he was going to lunch, the microphone quit. Miller worked on it, grumbling and pouting. Pagan pulled him aside and told him he was the stupidest guy he had ever met. Miller didn't understand why Pagan was so mad. He just wanted to eat. Didn't he get a lunch?

Denver.

Las Vegas.

Orlando.

At one point, Miller was on the road for 13 days.

There always seemed to be a problem. The sound and recording equipment was far more sophisticated than anything he had ever worked with.

Austin.

Minneapolis.

Detroit.

For the first time in his life Miller mingled with people who had careers and long-term goals. During breaks they talked with him. At night they invited him to join them at dinner.

Some told him they made $700,000 a year. And they were nice, something he never would have believed when he was at Starbucks. Then he and his street buddies assumed that all the wealthy had shadows in their lives. They had to be bad or messed up.

When a series of trips ended, he returned to his apartment by the beach and found a stack of past-due bills. He took his clothes to the cleaners and the bill was $30. He needed more pants. Another $100. Rent was $602. The car payment was $450.

He was ready to go on another trip when the company handed him his per-diem check to cover meals on the road. He cashed it and sent most of it to the phone company, which was going to shut his phone off if he didn't pay the bill in full.

A week later he was on the road. He had $20 to last four days. Everyone else was going out to a restaurant. He was in his room eating New Balance bars he brought from home.

He didn't think it could get any worse. Then Pagan quit to start his own consulting business.

Miller was stunned. Pagan had been his sponsor. Miller needed more money, a raise. He was frustrated that no one saw how hard he worked. The shelves in his apartment were lined with consulting books: Psychology of Power, How to Speak, How to Listen, Tested Advertising Methods and Subliminal Seduction.

All he needed was a chance to prove that he could be a consultant. All anyone wanted him to do was make sure the microphone stopped squealing.

One day he was so mad about his situation that he yelled at and nearly got into a fight with a driver who cut him off.

In April, the fake Rolex broke.

———◆———

The lie of it all hit him one spring morning when he looked around his apartment. The sofa was something the company had thrown out. The table had been sitting on the curb outside his apartment waiting for the garbage man when he snagged it. He slept on the floor, just as he had in that dump above the beer distributor.

On his refrigerator was a pawnshop claim for the $50 he got for his expensive tape recorder. Reclaiming it would cost $83. He was hungry, but there was no money. And the only things in the refrigerator were an old frozen burrito, margarine and Bloody Mary mix. He felt as if he was back in Pennsylvania.

Struggling in Portland had been different. He could tell himself then that he chose to be that way. In California it was different. Never in his life had he felt so vulnerable, so scared. His Hawthorne buddies had told him he was making a mistake that he would fail. They had been right. He had fooled the world, fooled even himself for a while. Miller concluded he was as phony as that stupid watch.

He worked, fiddled with the audio gear and made copies of tapes that would be sent to real-estate agents. Day after day he listened to the tapes. He remembers thinking that he should have been the one talking.

One night, he sat in his apartment and took stock of his life. He was in serious debt with no savings or credit cards to tap. Pagan was unavailable, busy with his own business. Millers father, a man who had stayed with the same trucking company for 25 years, had never understood why his son left a good company like Starbucks.

He was on his own.

He could go under, let the water wash over him and drown. Declare bankruptcy or something, get out from under the car payments and go back to Portland. He could get his job at Starbucks. Give it six months and his hair would be longer. He'd fit back in on Hawthorne. Tell some great stories, get some good laughs. Practice guitar a bit, call a few musicians and get a band and a gig and . . .

Or he could be honest.

He was at the bottom.

Ground zero, he called it.

And he didn't want to go back.

He was listening to the tapes one day -- listing agent, appraiser, escrow -- and realized what he heard were just words in some book he had read. He had no idea what they really meant.

He remembered how when he had first picked up the guitar he had learned the most and grown as a musician when he set the books aside and actually played with musicians who were better than he was.

During the next few weeks he called real-estate agents. He introduced himself, explained where he worked and said he wanted to learn about the business. He volunteered to work without pay. Nights, weekends, doing odd jobs, whatever they needed.

Someone took him up on the offer, but he realized he couldn't type. He asked a company secretary if there was a spare laptop computer he could borrow. Someone found one. Instead of going out to dinner or listening to music, he practiced typing. Night after night. He discovered it was like learning scales.

The hardest decision was calling his landlord and giving notice. He found a small place, far from the beach. It was nothing like what he wanted, but he saved $150 a month. He found a second job helping hotels with their audio gear. He quit going to the clubs, restaurants and bars. He learned how to cook. He stocked his refrigerator. He got his tape recorder out of hock.

In May 1998, Harris, the company's assistant general manager, called Miller into his office. He told him to sit down. He had been watching him, he said, talking with employees around the office and checking with consultants who had been with him on the road. Harris said he still had some reservations, but he was willing to take a risk.

He offered Miller a promotion.

He'd be the full-time assistant to a top trainer and consultant. Miller would produce smaller seminars around the country. He would be responsible for the sound, dealing with the hotels, the travel plans, getting seminar participants registered and making sure they were satisfied.

Harris warned it was a high-visibility job. Down the road, there could be a raise, maybe a promotion. But if Miller messed up, just once, the wrath of the company would crash down on him. Hard. The offer, Harris said, was Business Boot Camp 101.

When he was finished, Harris posed a final question: Are you up for the challenge?

Miller had no answer.

Once, he would have shot his mouth off, prattling on about marketing shares and subliminal messages and advertising magic and campaigns and his office with his window.

Now the truth was that he wasn't sure.

And then he remembered what he had told himself a lifetime ago.

Move before you think you're ready.

———————— ◆ ————————

The man walks into a Starbucks coffee shop in Oceanside. He comes in the morning. He is always alone. He sits at a table and reads the newspaper before he goes to the office. Each time, the same drink -- tall, nonfat, decaf coffee with a shot of Hazelnut.

He slips $2 in the tip jar.

If the baristas are lucky, a customer might leave a quarter or two, maybe a buck.

Not this guy.

Always $2.

The employees can't figure him out. He doesn't look wealthy, but always the $2.

One morning, business is slow and the only customer in the store is this guy. The baristas start talking about work and the goofy customers they deal with. They are laughing. Their voices carry.

Then this guy, the $2 tipper, starts laughing, too. He walks up to the counter. He tells them a Starbucks story. It's a good one, and there's more laughter.

How do you know about Starbucks, they ask?

Worked there once, he says.

You?

He reaches into his back pocket and hauls out his wallet. He thumbs through his cards until he finds an old Oregon ID card he carries to remind himself of, well, just to remind him.

That's me, he says.

They peer at this picture of this longhaired hippie.

No way. That doesn't look like you at all.

It's me, he says. Me, at Starbucks.

They look at the picture.

At this man in front of them.

What happened?

Well, one Saturday this blonde . . .

Gossip Columnist

She's just an old woman living alone in the country.

Dinner can wait. So too the books on the nightstand. The television screen remains blank. Time is too valuable to waste. Myrtle Slanger -- "I'm 78, but don't dare call me elderly" -- is on deadline.

She bustles about her rambling old farm house, puttering here and there before stopping in front of a kitchen wood stove fire, which she expertly stokes and prods until it crackles and smokes.

She shuts the door with a satisfying thump and walks to a table piled high with bills, letters and knickknacks. After adjusting her glasses, Myrtle reaches for an indestructable 30-year-old rotary phone and slowly dials a number.

And with that, the last old-time newspaper gossip columnist left on the north Oregon coast finally gets down to business.

"Hi, this is Myrtle. How you feeling?"

She listens. She scribbles something on a piece of notebook paper. She frowns.

"That miserable? Listen, take butter and crackers. Works on my upset stomach every time."

She nods her head.

"That's right, butter and crackers. Now, can I put in the column that you were in for surgery? Oh, good. Thanks. Take care. Goodbye."

A week later, Seaside Signal newspaper readers learn through Myrtle's Nehalem Valley column that Helen Nordstrom of Jewell is home and doing well after surgery.

Once, nearly every weekly paper in Oregon had someone like Myrtle. They were usually women and called themselves correspondents. They wrote about life in their small towns, usually in excruciating detail.

Their columns, typically named something like "Chit Chat" or "Over the Fence Post," were found in the back of the paper next to such items as recipes for tomato suprise.

The Seaside Signal used to have correspondents reporting from Cannon Beach, Tolovana Park, Clatsop Plains, Gearhart, Birkenfeld, Vesper, Elsie and the Necanicum Valley. Those columnists are gone now. Most are dead. Only Myrtle remains.

To outsiders, big-city folks who stumble upon her column during a visit to the coast, Myrtle Slanger is a relic, an anachronism, a leftover from a bygone era.

"I'm not a journalist or a reporter or a writer," she admitted with a smile. "To be truthful, I'm just an old woman sitting alone in the country. But these are my roots. This is where I live. This is where I'll die."

During the past twenty years, Myrtle has written more than 1,000 columns and used nearly 700,000 words documenting valley life. Those columns, many of them now yellowed and frayed with time, are her legacy.

They have been cut from the paper and mailed to relatives who live across the United States. They have been carefully glued into family scrapbooks. They have been passed down through the generations.

They have been saved and treasured by people who took pride in the fact that someone took notice of their lives.

She is not paid for her column and has a hard time explaining why she continues to write.

"I just do it," she says between phone calls. "Habit, I guess. Do something. My Dad was like that. That's the way to stay young. Sit around you get old and depressed.

"Anyway, enough about me," she says as she grabs the phone again. "I've got calls to make."

*B*arbara Hanthorn has been having a bathroom remodeled so has been at the Herbert Twomblys for a few nights and at the Jack Rierson's the last couple. Paul Karhn has been doing the work.

Last Thursday LaVenna Morgan, Ruth Hardwig and Calista Bowles drove to Seaside for shopping. The following day, they drove to Newberg to have work done on LaVenna's car.

Ruby Swipes and Calista Bowles enjoyed a Mother's Day special dinner at Elderberry Inn. Calista also received calls from all her children with special greetings and gifts.

———◆———

Myrtle has but one motto: "News is what people think is important, not what I think is important."

There's no Pulitzer Prize-winning reporting, no investigative muckraking, no knock-your-socks off writing. About the only editorializing you'll find is when Myrtle implores senior citizens to come to the monthly potluck lunch at the grange hall.

"Oh, I do hear some scandal sex wise," she admitted. "But that doesn't get in. No place for that here. Or anything about fights between a couple. And these marijuana busts, I don't touch that kind of thing."

Instead, her columns are filled with news about lunches and dinners, births and deaths, shopping trips, proms, marriages and out-of-town guests. Read enough of them and you begin to believe that a place like Mayberry really does exist.

"I stay away from my impressions," she explained. "People want the news, not my impressions. If someone takes their dog to the vet and they think that's news, well then I'll write it up. Who am I to say that's not news?"

Her contemporaries, men and women who have slowed down, can't figure out what drives Myrtle. You're doing too much, they tell her. They read her faithfully. Many say it's the only thing they look at in the paper.

LaVenna Morgan, 75, appears regularly in the column. People who've never met her might still feel they know her because they read about her so often. Her grandchildren, her illnesses and her recent car trouble have all been grist for the column. Morgan believes that much of what she does is newsworthy.

"When my car heated up, I told Myrtle about it because that's important to people who know me," she said. "Why, after Myrtle wrote me up I went to town and had a lot of people come up to me and ask how the car was doing."

In case anyone's interested, it was a problem with the thermostat.

The people here live isolated lives. There's no reason to drop in at Jewell. In fact, many Oregonians know of it only as that exit off U.S. 26 just past the Elderberry Inn on the way to the coast.

There is no city center. People live miles from each other and often see each other only when they're shopping in Seaside, which is 30 miles away. Many valley residents learn what their neighbors are up to through Myrtle's column.

"We're a small valley," said 73-year-old Ruth Nogle. "Without Myrtle, the people around here would be in the dark. I don't know why she keeps it up, but without her we wouldn't know what our neighbors are doing.

"Remember one thing, people like to read about people," she said. "Never forget that."

———◆———

Mick and Ruth Nogle had a busy day last Thursday when she drove first to Birkenfeld for an appointment, returned in time to get Mick, have a sandwich at Oney's and on to Seaside for business.

Mildred Booth and her son, Brian, were out in the valley shopping on Thursday.

Helen Nordstrom reports a good turnout at the Natal Grange for the annual beef dinner on Sunday. She was one of those working in the kitchen full time.

———◆———

Myrtle began writing the column in 1959. She churns one out each Sunday night.

She writes in longhand on notebook paper and delivers the column to the paper each Monday morning. Her editor has only one complaint: It's hard to read Myrtle's writing.

"Other than that she's great," said Rheta Murry. "She's been around a lot longer than I have. She's just a fixture."

Myrtle comes from pioneer stock. She was born and raised in Birkenfeld, a small town about 12 miles south of the Elderberry Inn. She lived there until she was 13. Her father died that year and her mother moved the family to Tigard.

Myrtle returned to the valley after college. She taught school at a logging camp near Elsie, but had to quit after she got married. The log boss wouldn't let married women work. So Myrtle started a school in her Birkenfeld home. She taught until her first child was born, then quit to raise her children. When they were grown, she started Jewell's first kindergarten. She taught classes out of her home until the program moved to the school.

She now leads a 4-H group that meets each week in her home to study outdoor cooking and child care. Some of the kids are the sons and daughters of students she taught years ago.

In addition, Myrtle has 15 head of cattle on a 27-acre ranch. She also is an avid gardener. She leads a busy life. And that's why people can't figure out why she keeps writing the column.

"I'm pushing 75 now and I'm taking it easier," said Bunny Doar, Myrtle's first editor. "I was with the paper for 25 years, and I did everything from writing editorials to cleaning the floors.

"What Myrtle does is not all that easy," she said. "Would you like to write this stuff week after week? Most people are busy with other things. It doesn't pay.

"Unless you have an abiding love for the written word and this kind of stuff, you're just not going to do it," Doar said. "But she keeps it up."

Mr. and Mrs. CeVern Grit were Sunday evening visitors at the home of Mrs. and Mrs. Herbert Twombly.

Hank and Arneda Taylor were in Astoria on Saturday and drove on to Seaside later where they visited Dan and Dee Hansen.

Jane Reynolds has opened a beauty salon in Birkenfeld a week ago. She already has had a number of customers and last week, one from Jewell.

Although Myrtle prints her home telephone number at the top of each column in hopes of getting people to call with news, most of her information is gathered by calling area residents each Sunday night.

She works out of her kitchen, taking notes as she talks on the telephone. Many of the people know her voice. Instead of saying "Hello," she charges ahead by asking right away, "Got any news?"

"A lot of the older people like to visit," she said. "They haven't had anyone to talk to all week. So sometimes they get to talking and you have to cut them short every once in a while.

"One dear lady, you get a hold of her and she'll talk for nearly an hour," she said. "Another lady is 70, but you'd think she was 100. She's very religious and talks and talks about that."

Some of the people in the valley still use party lines, which means that people can eavesdrop.

"I know when they're listening because you can hear them," Myrtle said. "There was one old fellow who used to go to sleep and we could hear him snoring. But I hated to say anything. His wife had passed away and he was ill and alone."

She gets news mainly from women, but from a few men.

"The Meyers boys are two of the area's chief gossipers," she said. "They're bachelor boys. One's 61. The other is a couple years younger. Two nicer men folk you will not find. If you can't get along with them, you shouldn't come to Jewell.

"And I get a lot of news from Herbert Twombly, who almost always gives the news at his house because his wife is finishing up the dishes or busy doing the mending," she said.

Myrtle begins making calls about 6 p.m. and tries to finish by 9:30. She stays put at the kitchen table until she's done writing, which means she's usually there until after 11 p.m.

Then, and only then, Myrtle finally calls it a day.

———◆———

Mr. and Mrs. Warren Portrey were in Astoria a week ago to help a little grand-daughter celebrate her first birthday. They stayed overnight.

Jewell seniors will hold their regular potluck luncheon on Friday, April 27, starting at noon, to be followed by pinochle, bingo and visiting. It is nice to see so many coming to enjoy.

Myrtle Slanger received word last Tuesday of the passing of Gilbert Raymond, a former logger of Unker and Wicks Camp of Elsie.

———◆———

Myrtle stood in front of her kitchen window. She watched and listened as the dark sky opened up over her valley. Rain pelted her land. A gust of wind shook her old house.

"Getting cold in here," she said as she turned away and stoked up the wood stove fire.

She turned on an overhead light and poured herself a cup of coffee. She walked out of the kitchen and into the living room. A moment later she returned. She dragged behind her a book as long as a newspaper page and nearly a foot thick. She struggled to lift it onto the counter.

"Arm doesn't work as well as it used to," she apologized. "But then what does any more? When you get to be my age though you can't feel sorry for yourself. But enough about me."

Myrtle opened the cover. It was a scrapbook compiled over the years by members of the Nehalem Valley Pioneers Association. Myrtle keeps it in her home.

She turned the pages and showed documents, handwritten letters and photographs revealing the history of the valley -- logging, farming and schools. Lives carved out of the woods. She pointed to a picture of a man and woman sitting close together in a horse-drawn carriage.

"I remember the man who gave us this," she said. "That was his girl. He was courting her. That was a happy time for him. He wanted people to remember him. He's gone now."

She flipped through the pages, stopping when she spotted a picture of her husband. He died three years ago. She said nothing, but gently rubbed her fingers across his face. She pointed to a group picture of five men.

"They were all just full of good history," she said. "And now not a one of them is left."

Myrtle closed the book and walked to the kitchen window. The rain was coming down hard. The wind whipped down the hills.

"Storm's really moving into the valley," she said. "Rain will do us some good."

She poured more coffee. She warmed her hands on the steaming cup and stared out the window.

"You know, the young don't care about history," she said softly.

She sipped her coffee and then set down the cup.

"No, the young don't really care," she said more firmly now. "Until my time comes, I guess that's my job -- keeping the history."

In a moment, she would start making calls. And in a few hours another chapter in the saga of life in the Nehalem Valley would be finished.

Myrtle looked at the clock. Her deadline approached.

People would be settled into their homes by now, trying to stay warm on a cold, rainy night.

Myrtle stoked the fire one more time and then cleared a space at the table. She clicked her pen and straightend her paper. She pulled the telephone close to her.

It was Sunday. She had a job to do. She dialed the first number.

LEVEL 3

Those who stay here are profoundly changed.

Part 1

Relaxed maternity nurses lean against the front counter, chatting. Babies cry in homey birthing rooms. The scent of flowers, recently delivered to new mothers, floats in the air.

But down the long hall, over the blue and pink squares of the maternity ward's buffed linoleum, through two locked doors, past scrub sinks and a security camera, pulses a different world. Life-support monitors, their screens a palette of blues, greens and reds, glow in dim light. Motorized Plexiglas covers glide down tracks and seal artificial wombs that look like compartments for science-fiction space travelers. Respirators hiss, staving off the collapse of tiny lungs.

Death stalks this space. Parents swallow fear every time they step into it, pushing away dread that radiates from the tangle of electronics, pumps and warmers. The patients, premature babies with undeveloped brains, translucent skin and bodies violated by tubes and needles, lie quietly, fighting for life. Barriers shield the most delicate from light that might stress their fragile systems. Most have left the womb so early that even excessive brightness can raise their blood pressure and burst their blood vessels.

Stress is the enemy here, especially for the unit's nurses. Each focuses on a single patient, or maybe two, minute by minute, hour after hour. They never stray far from red panic buttons that can instantly summon emergency-response teams.

The emotional intensity keeps most nurses from ever venturing here, drives away some who do and profoundly changes all who stay.

They call it Level 3.

———◆———

At the maternity-ward counter, a nursing instructor with a student in tow stopped by and joined the conversation. A nurse mentioned Level 3.

Level 3? the student remembers saying. What's that?

Off-limits, she was told. Locked down. Entered only with a special badge. But Tara Graham, a freshly minted 24-year-old nurse on tour to see what the hospital had to offer, was undeterred. She'd been through all of North Portland's Legacy Emanuel Children's Hospital, and she still wasn't sure what her new calling might be. She remembers being intrigued by Level 3 and begging to see it.

The instructor finally gave in, and the two women set off down the hall. Like all Level 3 visitors, they first pushed through swinging wooden doors, leaving the floral scent behind. Then they walked down a long corridor and past a wall covered with memorial panes of glass, each carrying a name: Jake Bartlett Winchester, May 22, 1990. Troy David Fox III, Sept. 11-16, 1995. Baby Boy Hill, Aug. 20, 1964.

The route led them to a locked wooden door with a window that looked into yet another long hallway. A ceiling-mounted security camera monitored them from above. Tara, a lean woman of medium height, has fine, almost delicate features. She nearly always wears her straight hair, the color of copper, pulled back behind her ears in the manner of someone who doesn't like fussing over her looks.

The instructor, following a routine that varies for no one, picked up a telephone and identified herself. Only then did the door buzz open, allowing the women to step into the corridor and wait for someone to greet them.

A unit supervisor appeared and led the pair down the hall to a stainless-steel double sink outside a metal door. Like everyone who entered these restricted areas, they scrubbed from finger tips to elbows for three minutes. Then the supervisor held a card to an electronic pad, a lock clicked, and they entered Level 2, the less intense side of Emanuel's neonatal unit. In this area, bright lights flood the room and nurses routinely dole out parenting advice to mothers in wooden rocking chairs, holding babies who will soon be heading home.

A set of metal doors loomed 25 feet ahead. Tara remembers the supervisor motioning them on and leading the way through them. She and her instructor followed, stepping across an invisible line and into Level 3.

Tara vividly remembers her first sight of the tiny babies who nearly filled the darkened room, slowly squirming or lying motionless in cocoons of machinery, all in critical condition.

The nurses were scattered about the unit, their voices just above whispers. Life-support monitors produced background noise that filled the room like conversation at a cocktail party. As always, the nurses tuned out the general din but noticed individual sounds that signaled a potential crisis -- the unhurried beeps of an alert, the more insistent be-BEEP, be-BEEP of a warning, the unsettling claxon of an alarm. Or, most insistently, the high-pitched sound of an apnea alert, signaling that a baby has quit breathing.

Twenty-one Isolettes, the high-tech bassinets that enclosed the babies, stretched across the room in long rows, each identified by a sign hanging from the ceiling. One showed a ladybug. Another a duck. A third displayed a butterfly. Roughly 100 nurses care for more than 550 babies a year who typically move through Level 3.

Tara's instructor found a former student working in Position 2 of the butterfly aisle. While the two of them talked, Tara peered into the Isolette. A black mask shielded the baby's eyes and most of his face from the therapeutic beam of light that helps fight the jaundice that so often tints preemie skin.

The boy's medical history was taped to the front of the Isolette on a light-blue card that looked like a birth announcement, the facts written in hand. Later, Tara would remember being startled by the realization that this infant wasn't a medical curiosity, but somebody's son.

The boy in Butterfly 2 was nearly 28 weeks old and weighed 2 pounds. From her nursing classes, Tara knew that full-term babies were born between 37 and 42 weeks.

She moved closer, stepping around the lines that ran from his body to banks of machines. She recognized the ventilator line that forced air into his lungs in small bursts. The baby's chest vibrated as if he were having spasms. His transparent skin, still without fat, stretched over bones like a thin coating of jelly. Tara counted each rib and saw blood coursing through veins. The baby looked unnatural, hardly human. Tara had learned about premature babies in nursing school, but she'd never seen one so small, not even in her textbooks. Essentially, he was a fetus that somehow existed outside his mother's womb.

She remembers staring for quite some time. Then she turned her attention to the nurse, her instructor's former student and a woman not much older than she. The nurse moved continuously, checking lines and monitors, moving from one side of the Isolette to the other, referring to a thick notebook, jotting something on a piece of paper. How, Tara remembers wondering, could this woman care for something so fragile?

Then the tour was over. Tara and her instructor followed the supervisor back past the ladybug and butterfly rows to the exit, through Level 2 and out into in the empty hall.

For weeks, images of Level 3 haunted Tara Graham. She left Portland and drove to Medford, where she had been born and raised, to talk with her mother.

After dinner, Tara asked her mother about her brother, a year younger than Tara and still living at home. Her mother left the dining room and returned with a file folder stuffed with medical reports, documents and photographs.

The file brought back painful memories, but Tara's mother was pleased her daughter was taking an interest. Tara had been struggling to find a focus for her life.

After high school, Tara had earned a bachelor's degree in geology, a degree she found impractical. She worked as a clothing-store clerk then joined a program to train buyers for a large Portland department store. She spent two years as an assistant buyer and learned to dread Monday, the day her co-workers studied weekend sales figures and broke down in tears when they missed their targets. She quit, got married and enrolled in a Mt. Hood Community College nursing program.

Tara opened the file her mother handed her. Her brother had been born extremely early, at 26 weeks, and he'd weighed only 28 ounces. The nurses had sent notes when her brother came home after three months: "You were my favorite baby in the unit." "Good job, miracle baby."

What had it been like back then, Tara asked her mother.

Doctors, her mother recalled, had said her son would probably die. There were days when his heart stopped every few hours. But he always rallied.

Tara looked at the photographs of her brother in the hospital. His mother hadn't been allowed to touch him for months, and then only inside an Isolette with built-in plastic gloves. In those days, no one was sure of the best ways to care for such a premature baby. One memory lingered. A nurse asked the doctor about pain medication. He said the baby was a "gork" -- a vegetable -- and couldn't feel pain. The callous comment appalled Tara's mother, and the nurse, too. Together, they complained to the hospital's medical director.

Parts of her brother's brain remained undeveloped. He'd never graduated from high school, and he still read at third-grade level. He kept busy working a series of odd jobs -- gas-station attendant, dishwasher or doing yardwork for family friends.

As her mother packed away the file, Tara asked how she had managed to cope. She never would have made it, her mother said, had it not been for the support of the nurses.

Later, upstairs, Tara lay sleepless in her old bedroom. She remembers thinking about her brother, in his bed just across the hall. Thinking about his life and hers, and about their mother, a young women thrust into a strange and frightening situation.

That night Tara Graham decided what she wanted to do. She wanted to be there for new parents, for a terrified mother who didn't know where to turn, for a baby who needed her skills to live.

Tara returned to Portland, graduated from the nursing program and passed the state boards to earn her nursing license. Although friends and school advisers suggested she apply to several hospitals, Tara sent out only one application -- to Emanuel's neonatal unit. As instructed, she included three letters of recommendation, an essay and a portfolio of schoolwork.

Forty applicants were competing for the four openings in the 12-week orientation program -- the first of several steps needed to become a Level 3 nurse. Seven hospital managers interviewed them, one by one. Three weeks later, the neonatal supervisor gave Tara one of the slots.

She arrived Aug. 21, 2002, and spent three weeks in Emanuel's classroom. The equipment used by Level 3 nurses was among the most expensive and sophisticated. Emanuel was the only Oregon hospital, for example, that routinely used extracorporeal membrane oxygenation or ECMO, a kind of advanced heart-lung technology for preemies, over extended periods of time. So preemies from Alaska, Hawaii and throughout the Northwest who needed that sort of treatment were sent there.

But when it came to keeping extremely early preemies alive, the personal touch could be even more important than technology. Tara's coach, a veteran nurse assigned to work with her during orientation, would guide her into that side of the Level 3 world.

In mid-September, after two weeks on Level 3, she still had trouble sleeping before a scheduled shift. On the first morning of her third week, she joined the 6:45 a.m. stream of nurses walking into Emanuel. After swiping her identification badge against the pad on the wall, she pulled open the doors to the scrub room. She looked to her left and saw the board listing the babies in Level 3 and the nurses on the shift. She pushed through into Level 3 and headed for the break room.

Once they began their 12-hour shifts, Level 3 nurses were on stage, working in front of worried parents, doctors and medical experts. Only in the break room could a nurse truly relax. That's where they went to get off their feet, eat, chat and cry.

Tara walked through Level 3, punched a five-digit code into the break-room door and entered. She settled onto a cushioned bench that formed a semicircle along the outside wall. The day-shift and night-shift nurse supervisors sat at a round table, running down the status of each baby in the unit. Tara listened intently.

When the 15-minute review ended, each nurse chose her shift assignment. Some had cared for a particular baby before and wanted to continue. Some, coming back from four days off, were energized, ready to deal with a baby who would need minute-by-minute care for 12 hours. Others, perhaps those having a rough time at home, or just tired, looked for less-demanding assignments.

Tara waited for her coach to make the day's selection for her. She followed the older nurse through another secure door and into Level 3. The night-shift nurse briefed Tara and the coach on the baby's status.

And then the baby was in Tara's hands: A critically ill boy in Butterfly 4.

Classroom theory was one thing. But suddenly, Tara was dealing with a human being, and she didn't know where to start. She flipped through a notebook at the bedside, a thick record that contained the baby's medical history. He needed an intravenous line placed in a hand smaller than a 50-cent piece. Tara had to get the line in without jostling the baby. If she moved him too suddenly, tiny blood vessels could burst and he could suffer brain damage or even bleed to death.

She walked around the bed, looking at the baby from different angles. She planned her approach and took the IV line in both hands. They shook. She backed away from the Isolette, took a deep breath, stepped into position again and pierced the baby's skin.

The fluid began flowing into her patient's bloodstream.

Over the months, she learned about Level 3's culture and codes, often in the break room or at the scrub sink, where nurses talked about what life in the unit was like. There were joyful moments, and yet every nurse had cases that stayed with her. No one sat and told a story from beginning to end. The stories, and their meanings, spilled out in bits and pieces.

One veteran always started her shift by going to a back room, reaching into a cabinet and pulling out a Magic 8 Ball, asking if she'd have a calm shift, shaking the ball and waiting for her fortune to appear in a little window.

In the break room, nurses complained about husbands and boyfriends who often didn't want to hear about life in Level 3. Tara knew what they meant; talk of blood made her own husband squeamish. She found herself keeping quiet about what she'd seen during her shifts. No one but a Level 3 nurse, she came to learn, could understand what it was like behind those locked doors.

Level 3 nurses worried constantly. They had nightmares about dropping a baby. Nursing in this unit was a high-wire act. If the care wasn't perfect, the baby could end up with vision, lung or hearing problems.

Not every nurse could handle the toll. Some quit after a few months. Others lasted a year and transferred out. Even the nurses who stayed admitted to times when, while driving home, they'd suddenly find themselves crying for no apparent reason.

Some nurses believed in God. They realized that even with the world's most sophisticated technology, much was out of their hands. Babies who had no chance rallied. Babies who were doing fine suddenly died.

Other nurses couldn't see God's touch anywhere. How could a mother who desperately wanted a child lose her baby while in the next Isolette a preemie abandoned by a drug addict thrived?

Tara Graham discovered that no matter what a nurse believed, or didn't believe, all lived by one motto: Every baby who died in Level 3 went to heaven.

———◆———

Leaves drifted down from the maples around the hospital's entrance. Tara took the elevator to the second floor, passed the glass memorial to children who have died and buzzed into the prep area outside Level 3. She scrubbed, walked into the unit and headed for the break room.

The nurses were somber, preparing themselves for a shift bound to end badly. Something had gone terribly wrong with a baby who'd spent months on Level 3. He'd die before daybreak.

Tara walked into Level 3 with her coach and took a position at Duck 5. The baby and his family had been moved away from Butterfly 7 to an isolation room in the back of the unit. As Tara cared for the Duck 5 preemie, she watched family, doctors and nurses stream in and out of the room.

Then the traffic stopped, and the parents left.

Her coach asked Tara to come with her. It was important, she said, for a young nurse to see and feel death up close.

They slid the room's door open and walked to the Isolette. Tara would never forget what she saw there. The child, wearing pajamas and wrapped in a blanket, looked as if he were sleeping.

Do you want to hold him, Tara's coach asked.

It would be good for you to hold him, the coach said. Babies feel different after they've died.

Tara sat in a rocking chair. The nurse lifted the baby out of the crib and placed him in her arms. His skin was cold. She began rocking and studied his face. His hair was reddish blond. He had no bruises, no marks. He looked exhausted. Tara would later remember thinking about how long and hard he'd fought for life.

The baby boy's nurse stepped back into the isolation room. Tara stood up and laid the child in his Isolette and helped the nurse clean him. She walked out of the room, checked in with her coach, finished her paperwork and left Level 3 for home.

She drove in silence, the radio off.

Part 2

The shrill sound of three pagers shattered the evening quiet. Tara Graham glanced up from the preemie under her care and saw three nurses sprint through Level 3. She remembers the resuscitation team members pulling the purple surgical gloves they wore from their hands, tossing them aside and running out swinging double doors.

News worked its way to Level 3 in bits and pieces, floating from aisle to aisle, nurse to nurse, until it reached Tara's isolette. Seconds earlier, someone from the Legacy Emanuel Children's Hospital emergency room, two floors down, had called the unit secretary to activate the R-Team.

At that moment, an ambulance was speeding through Northeast Portland, rushing a 23-year-old pregnant woman to the hospital. An hour earlier, she'd been in perfect health. Then she'd collapsed at home in front of her husband and two young children. The patient's name seemed familiar to the secretary, and she called through her open office door to check with the nearest nurse. The patient, it turned out, was good friends with another Level 3 nurse.

The ER called. The woman had just arrived and died on the table, the victim of a blood clot in her lungs. With her last breath, she gave birth to a 23-week-old boy. The R-Team struggled to keep him alive long enough to reach Level 3.

Tara, a nurse who'd already spent nearly four months on Level 3, knew 23 weeks was in the gray area. Even the most sophisticated technology might not be enough for this child.

The doors next to her burst open, and the R-Team rushed a rolling isolette by her, frantically working on the baby. They wheeled the isolette into an empty room next to Tara's station. She remembers seeing nurses hustling in and out during the next few hours, but tests indicated the baby was fighting a losing battle.

Eventually, the doctor in charge pulled the father out of the room where his son lay. Tara heard him break the news: This is where we're at. The baby's blood-gas levels are incompatible with life.

The baby struggled for another 45 minutes, and then he died.

The personal connection gave the case a dimension the Level 3 nurses tried to avoid. More than 20 babies in the unit needed care, and the nurses couldn't let their emotions revolve around only one. But they'd just been touched by two deaths, and they needed to grieve. Co-workers juggled assignments, and supervisors stepped in so that the nurses could escape to the break room.

Tara remembers standing at her spot on the aisle and watching each nurse pass by with tears in her eyes. She heard the family's sobs. She watched a nurse carry the baby's body to the morgue. And then her shift ended. Just like that. With no one to talk to about what she'd seen.

She pushed through the swinging doors, leaving Level 3 behind. She wound her way through the empty hospital halls, out of the sprawling complex and into the parking garage. She kept seeing the baby and the father's face as his son died.

The Level 3 nurses had done all they could. And it hadn't been enough.

Nothing in nursing school had prepared her for this moment. She knew about intubation and blood, how to handle intravenous lines. The controls that ran the Level 3 machines were as familiar to her as the buttons on the remote control for her television. And yet for the first time since she'd started working in this strange new world, she felt lost.

She later would remember arriving home and crawling into bed, sleepless. She lay there hearing the pagers and crying nurses. She remembers thinking about how the man had been at home with his pregnant wife and two children. Just living a normal life. Then, hours later, his wife and baby were gone.

She cried, quietly so as not to wake her husband.

She remembered what the supervisor told her when she graduated from orientation and became a regular Level 3 nurse. "OK," he'd said. "That's it. Starting Sunday it's your nursing license on the line. And the patient's life."

Could she make it as a Level 3 nurse?

It wasn't just death that bothered her. Hospitals, by their very nature, were places of death. But death was always so close in Level 3. And on each 12-hour shift, she worked with one baby and one family. That was almost unheard of in medicine. Doctors often saw dozens of patients in a day. Other nurses, even those with critically ill patients, might have six or more. And hospital patients typically came and went in a few days, at most.

But in Level 3, a patient might stay for three months, and the same nurse might care for a baby again and again. Professional distance dissolved. Nurses couldn't help it. Level 3 touched their hearts as much as their heads.

Tara remembers thinking about requesting a transfer to short-stay, or to the dialysis unit. Someplace with some distance between her and her patients.

She had a week off. She gave herself a deadline -- seven days -- to decide whether she had what it took to stay with the preemies.

The week passed, and Tara Graham drove back to the hospital, took the elevator to the second floor and reported for duty . . . in Level 3.

———•———

As the months went by and winter passed into spring, Tara Graham had fewer questions about techniques and procedures, but continued to grapple with life on Level 3. Then she discovered she was pregnant.

Her husband was delighted, but Tara worried constantly. All pregnant mothers worried, of course, especially in an age when books and Web sites inundated them with information about everything that could go wrong. But a neonatal nurse had an entirely different perspective.

When it was time for an ultrasound test, Tara grilled the technician: Could he see the heart's chambers? she remembers asking. What about the spine? Any sign of birth defects? It was too early to tell, the technician said. He asked where she worked. Level 3 in the neonatal unit at Emanuel Children's Hospital, she told him. She remembers him shaking his head. He couldn't imagine, he said, a worse place for a pregnant woman.

Weeks later, another baby died on her shift.

The girl had been born severely premature and weighed less than 2 pounds. Three days after her birth, her parents, on the advice of their doctor, turned off the life-support machines.

When Tara left Level 3 that day, she walked by Cathy Pollock-Robinson, a 46-year-old nurse who had cared for the baby the previous day. Tara wanted to know what it had been like for Cathy, but she didn't want to bring up such a sensitive subject.

The two nurses passed each other with nothing more than a hello.

Cathy had worked in the neonatal unit for 24 years. Like the other nurses, she'd tried to explain her job to family and friends but found that the details made them uneasy. So she'd quit talking about her work except in the most general way.

Every Level 3 nurse led two lives -- one in Level 3, the other outside. Getting from one to the other was a challenge. Although she lived only 11 miles from the hospital, Cathy often took a long, winding route home, driving aimlessly to help make the transition.

Sometimes she approached her house overcome with love for her two children, wanting to rush inside and hug them, simply because they were alive and healthy. Then she'd walk in the door to a dirty kitchen and the sound of video games. The kids would glance up and ask about dinner.

Cathy headed into the nurse's break room, preoccupied with the high-risk birth she'd been told to expect that afternoon. As the admit nurse, Cathy was on the resuscitation team and wore a pager. When it went off, she'd be helping direct a tense team effort to stabilize a baby long enough to reach Level 3.

She knew that during a routine ultrasound exam, doctors had discovered a fetus with a congenital diaphragmatic hernia, a severe birth defect. CDH babies were rare -- turning up only once every 4,000 births. But because Emanuel's Level 3 drew the most severe cases from several states, a CDH baby wasn't all that unusual there.

In this case, a hole in the baby's diaphragm had allowed body parts that should have been in the abdomen -- the stomach, liver, spleen and intestines -- to float into the chest. As a result, one lung was just a nub, and the heart had been shoved far to one side, weakening it.

But Cathy had something else to do before her pager beeped, summoning her to help the CDH baby.

She checked in with the charge nurse, told her what she was about to do and headed to the back of Level 3. She pulled two cream-colored folding screens around an empty isolette to shield the scene from the parents in the unit. She flipped the switches to warm the isolette, and then walked to the morgue, where she pulled open the cooler door and found the baby who'd died the day before.

Cathy pulled the little girl's body from the tray and held it against her side, feeling the cold seep through her scrubs. She wrapped the baby in a flannel blanket and discretely carried her back into Level 3. She set the baby in the isolette and loosened the blanket to allow the heat to warm the body.

Years before, nurses had tried to protect parents from death. But that, Cathy was convinced, only prolonged grief. She'd met mothers who had mourned a child for 20 years because they'd never been allowed to say good-bye properly.

As she approached a quarter-century in nursing, she did whatever it took to help a parent come to terms with loss. One mother told her that she'd always dreamed of taking a bath with her baby. Cathy contacted the pediatric ward and found a vacant room with a tub. She brought the woman's dead child to her. The mother slipped into the tub and bathed with her son.

Cathy was four hours into her shift when the unit secretary called. The dead baby's parents were outside, waiting to be buzzed into Level 3. Cathy met them at the front counter and led them to a private room where she'd moved two rocking chairs.

She pulled two blankets out of the blanket warmer, stepped behind the screens concealing the isolette warming the baby's body and wrapped the little girl in the blankets. She cradled the body in her arms -- she never brought a baby's body to a parent on a piece of hospital equipment.

She carried the body to the private room and set it in the mother's arms. The conversations she had in these moments were always intense, one mother to another, and she could always remember them, almost word for word:

She was very cold. I've put a warm blanket on her. You can unwrap her, look at her, touch her. You can do whatever you want. When you're done, tell someone and they'll find me.

Thirty minutes later, she returned. The mother handed her dead daughter to Cathy. The nurse cradled the body in her arms and felt the cold that had returned to the small arms and legs.

I'd like to echo what the doctor told you yesterday. You made a very courageous decision to stop support.

The parents said they were afraid of what their family and friends might say.

I don't want you to ever think that anyone's judged you. You made the right decision for you and your child.

The parents left, and Cathy took the body back to the morgue. She unwrapped the blankets, studying the little face, the hair, the hands. She slipped the child into the cooler and shut the door.

And then her pager beeped.

———◆———

Cathy hustled out of Level 3 and into the resuscitation room near the maternity ward. Other members of the resuscitation team made a final check on the supplies they'd need for the high-risk birth about to take place. Deborah Ross, the Level 3 supervisor in charge of documenting everything that took place in that room, stood behind a table, two notebooks in front of her. Deborah reached into her pocket, pulled out silver rosary beads and whispered a prayer. She checked to make sure she had her lucky blue pen.

If the baby were to cry before the team could shunt air directly into his lung, that might force air into his stomach. putting pressure on his heart. But depriving the baby of oxygen could damage his brain. So, before he cried, the team wanted to get a breathing tube down his windpipe and past his vocal cords to pump oxygen into his one good lung. At the same time, they had to thread a tube down his esophagus to suck out any air that made its way to the stomach and bowel.

Even if they did everything right, this child stood a good chance of dying in the R-Room.

The team members slipped on surgical gloves and masks. Cathy peered through a small window in the door leading to the operating room. Surgeons were poised to perform a Caesarian, to get the baby out of the womb quickly and into the hands of the R-Team.

"They're scrubbed up and ready to cut," she said.

The team members took their positions around the isolette.

Cathy looked at the suction tube running from the pregnant woman's body. When she saw drops of blood, she'd know the operation was under way. She moved to one side and let an R-Team nurse slip into the operating room to be the catcher, the nurse who'd rush the baby from the operating table to the resuscitation room isolette.

"Folks, we're getting close," Cathy said. "They're suctioning away blood."

She moved to one side. The suctioning line was a deep red.

"There's the uterine incision."

"It's out!" she yelled.

The nurse burst through the door, and the team members stepped aside to let her through.

"Boy or a girl?" the charge nurse called out.

"Boy."

He cried.

"Damn it."

"Let's go. Let's go."

The team surrounded the isolette again.

"Can we wipe off his face with alcohol and straighten out the head?"

Cathy swabbed down the baby and studied the boy's face. He was gray from lack of oxygen. She helped position the head while another nurse stood at the foot of the isolette and shoved a metal guide device into the child's throat. A breathing tube quickly followed, along with a tube to the stomach. A nurse attached a bag to the breathing tube and squeezed it repeatedly with her hand, forcing air down the tube. Cathy used a stethoscope to see whether she could hear air moving in the baby's lung. But the sound in the stethoscope reminded Cathy of an old man with asthma, his lung wheezing.

She stepped back to let another team member start an intravenous line.

The newborn didn't have much lung tissue, and his heart was a tiny, undersized motor. The team could breathe for him, but at some point, his body had to take over.

Again, Cathy listened to his lung.

"Hey, it seems louder now," she said. "I think you're in."

"The heart rate! The heart rate! It's going way down."

"What's the rate?"

"About 100 . . . no, now 90, now 80."

"This is bad," a nurse muttered. "We're going to bite this one."

Maybe the breathing tube hadn't reached the carina, the point where the trachea normally branches off to the two lungs. Deborah grasped her blue pen. Her other hand searched for the rosary beads.

"Try the line again."

"We're in."

The heart rate shot up to more than 100 and then began falling: 80, 70, 60, 55.

Cathy climbed on a stool to rise above the crowd and get some leverage. She leaned over the isolette and grabbed the baby with both hands as if holding a mound of clay. She placed her thumbs over the baby's heart and began squeezing.

From her position, Cathy couldn't see the heart monitor. But a nurse had slipped a device for measuring the amount of oxygen in the baby's bloodstream over his right arm. As Cathy pressed down on the heart rhythmically, the device showed oxygen moving through the system. She counted the heart's pulses -- a more normal 120 beats a minute. She looked down at the baby's chest.

It began to rise and fall.

————◆————

A ventilator replaced the bag on the breathing tube. Cathy stepped off the stool, wiped her hands on a towel and helped another nurse slip an IV line into what was left of the baby's umbilical cord. The line, no wider than a strand of angel-hair pasta, carried medications to the baby's heart.

The team sedated the boy to keep him from thrashing, which would use precious oxygen that his tissues required. They administered drugs to buffer the acid in his blood. Then painkillers. But painkillers lower blood pressure; so the R-team watched the monitors closely, keeping the baby's body finely tuned.

Cathy checked a blood sample. It looked like burgundy wine instead of red fruit punch -- oxygen still wasn't flowing properly.

"This isn't good," she told another nurse. "This is serious here."

A team member increased the ventilator settings, forcing more oxygen into the baby's lung. But could the lung and heart handle the increased load?

The operating-room door swung open, and the baby's father walked in, wearing light-green surgical scrubs. He stood at the far end of the room watching the R-Team work on his boy.

"Do you have a name for your son," Cathy asked.

He shook his head, bit his lip and turned away from the isolette.

Cathy touched his shoulder.

"You can look at him," she said. "Here, come with me."

She took him by his forearm and led him to the isolette. She found a place for him next to the resuscitation team, still working frantically.

"You can hold his hand."

She took the father's hand in hers and placed it on top of his son's little fingers. She kept her hand on the father's shoulder.

"Are you OK?" she asked.

He nodded.

"Let's give another dose of morphine," ordered the doctor standing behind the nurses. "Let's take another gas reading in five minutes."

The doctor turned to the father.

"Let's step over here," he said. The father pulled his hand away from his son's and took three steps back from the table.

"The lung on the right side is just a nub," the doctor said. "I have to warn you that this may not go very well in here. This is a significant defect."

The father ran his hand across his face.

"I think I'm going to step outside for a moment," he said. He pulled open a door to a hallway.

The team studied an X-ray.

"The whole side of his chest is bowel."

A machine started beeping.

"He may be coding right now. The circulation is so poor. No blood's going back to the lungs."

Wires snaked out from the baby's head, arms, legs and chest, running to the machines surrounding him.

"Look," the doctor said, "as soon as he's stable enough to move, let's get him to Level 3."

The door to the operating room opened. Attendants wheeled in the mother's gurney. The boy's father stood next to her. Cathy moved to the mother's side, and she crouched down so she could look the mother in the eye.

"It's important for you to see your son," she said.

While Deborah filled out the admission forms, a team member hurried to Level 3 and notified the unit. And she asked the hospital chaplain to talk with the parents about what the night might bring.

Cathy moved the mother's gurney so that it formed a T with the isolette, the mother's head next to her baby.

"Here," she said to the mother, "turn this way a bit so you can see his face."

Cathy took a camera from the father and stood on a stool so she could look down on the isolette.

"OK, hold his hand one more time," she said. The resuscitation team backed out of the frame. Cathy snapped several shots.

"I know you'd like to stay," she said, "but we have to go."

The mother gently rubbed her son's hair. Cathy touched the woman's head.

"It's time." she said. She held open the operating-room door. Maternity nurses led the mother and father back through the operating room. The team unplugged lines from the machines, getting ready for a 50-yard dash into Level 3.

"Disconnect."

Then they were gone.

The baby ended up at the Ladybug 3 workstation. Still no first name, just baby boy Brooks.

At the shift change that night, Tara Graham heard the charge nurse give the rundown on the boy. He was on five intravenous drips, had low blood pressure and high concentrations of carbon dioxide in his system. He was critical and unstable.

At any moment, he could die.

Part 3

Laurie Roberge stepped through the unmarked doors into a room crowded with other day-shift nurses. She quietly waited her turn at a stainless-steel scrub sink, contemplating what lay ahead. She turned to her left and studied a whiteboard listing the Level 3 babies who would require minute-by-minute monitoring during the upcoming 12-hour shift.

Once she entered Level 3, the neonatal intensive-care unit at Legacy Emanuel Children's Hospital, anything could happen, and just showing up for work put her on edge. A newborn, barely clinging to life, might be rushed to the unit. A ventilator tube could pop out, and the resuscitation team would have to scramble. Or everything could go wrong, and one of the names on the whiteboard would disappear.

Laurie never drank coffee until a couple of hours into her shift, once she'd settled down.

When it was her turn to scrub, Laurie stood at the sink and stepped on a pedal to activate the faucet. She wore a pair of $45 shoes, a model favored by marathon runners. She wore out a pair every three months.

At the end of a workweek, the 49-year-old nurse always needed a day to recover. Like every Level 3 veteran, Laurie had problems with her ankles, knees and back. The biggest strain, though, was on her heart. Some nights she just couldn't shake Level 3's spirit-draining sounds and images.

She nodded to other nurses waiting for the sink. They wore the light-green surgical scrubs the North Portland hospital provided. But Laurie paid for her own less-institutional scrub blouses. On this day, she wore white dotted with pink and purple hearts.

Laurie dried her hands, pushed open a swinging door, made her way to the nurses break room and sat on a cushioned bench along the back wall. Moments later, the supervisors sat down at a round table in the middle of the room. The night charge nurse wearily opened a notebook that detailed the medical histories of all the Level 3 babies and read each page aloud.

Laurie listened carefully, trying to figure out what assignment she'd request: A 28-week preemie had just arrived. His 16-year-old mother had claimed she didn't know she was pregnant and went into labor while playing basketball. A set of 26-week-old twins had spent a restless night, and their mother was afraid one would die. Then there was the CDH baby.

Baby boy Brooks lay in the workstation called Ladybug 3 and was one of the sickest babies in the unit. He'd been born six days earlier with a congenital diaphragmatic hernia -- a hole in the diaphragm that allowed body parts to float from the abdomen into his chest cavity. If he remained stable during this shift, surgeons planned to move his stomach, spleen and intestines back into his abdomen.

The supervisor finished her report and looked at the nurses, the signal that it was time for them to request their assignments.

Laurie spoke up: "I'll take baby boy Brooks."

———————

Laurie used her identification badge to unlock the double doors to Level 3, then clipped the badge onto her blouse, next to a gold wedding ring held in place with a safety pin. Two years before, Laurie's husband had a heart attack on the eve of the couple's 25th wedding anniversary. Laurie came home after running an errand and found him dead on their bed.

After the funeral, she took a leave. She returned three months later but no longer had the emotional strength Level 3 demanded. She moved to the pediatric short-stay ward and, later, to Level 2, where she worked with healthier babies who were almost ready to go home. But, eventually, she returned to Level 3.

She walked to the front of the unit and conferred with Abby Archambault, a night-shift nurse caring for baby boy Brooks. She and Laurie talked about whether he would be a good candidate for surgery. Then Abby left, and Laurie looked into the isolette.

The baby looked only slightly pink -- his heart and lungs were still struggling. She touched his torso. Warm. A good sign. A failing system would route blood to vital organs, leaving the skin cool.

Laurie let her hand linger, a way, she explains, of letting the child know she's there.

Tubes ran from baby boy Brooks to a bank of machines: intravenous lines and umbilical arterial lines, a venous catheter, a dopamine drip, morphine and methadone for pain and a drug to keep his body immobilized. Monitors showed adequate levels of oxygen and carbon dioxide in his bloodstream. The high-frequency ventilator buzzed away, causing the baby's one good lung to vibrate at 600 beats a minute, forcing oxygen in without causing the lung to strain from expansion.

She flipped through the medical reports, looking for the baby's first name -- Bryton -- and the names of his parents -- Kyle and Barbara.

The name Kyle sent Laurie back to another time, to another Level 3 baby. That Kyle had been born with seizures and kidney problems. He had lived in Level 3 for three months, and Laurie had often cared for him, growing to know his parents well. On the day he died, his mother had clung to her dead son's body for hours. Laurie had finished her 12-hour shift, but couldn't abandon the mother. She'd spent another eight hours in Level 3 to be with her until, finally, the mother let the body be taken to the morgue.

Laurie jotted "Kyle" and "Barbara" on a piece of paper -- she always greeted parents by name. And she thought about how the other Kyle's mother had asked her to come to her home. For five hours, the two women sat on the floor in what would have been Kyle's nursery, talking about the boy and the random nature of life and death.

On another slip of paper, Laurie wrote "Bryton." She never talked about taking care of a "patient" or a "baby." A name gave the child's life, however short, meaning.

She heard rustling and turned to see a couple standing 10 feet away. They stared at her with red and swollen eyes.

"Hi, Kyle. Hi, Barbara."

She extended her hand.

"I'm Laurie," she said, "and I'm going to take care of Bryton."

Laurie shifted her attention to the isolette to give the Brookses a bubble of privacy in the wide-open expanse of Level 3. Another nurse worked on a baby not six feet away. Level 3 nurses were practiced in the art of discretion, of hearing what went on around them but not giving any indication they'd heard. She glanced up to study the couple, who still had not moved toward the isolette.

"Where do you guys live?" she asked.

"North Bend," said Kyle Brooks, who said he owned a car-stereo business in the small coastal town. He relaxed while talking about work, apparently pleased to be thinking about something familiar. And then, as if realizing where he was, he ran out of things to say. Laurie sensed the couple faltering, and saw that Barbara Brooks continued to hang back.

"Come here," Laurie said softly as she put her arm on Barbara's shoulder. She led her to the edge of the isolette.

Some Level 3 babies couldn't tolerate touch, a fact some parents didn't understand. Laurie remembers a teenage mother who once demanded that the nurse wash her baby's hair even though he was panting, his heart racing. When Laurie explained that a shampoo could be fatal, the mother wouldn't listen. She just yelled that Laurie didn't care.

Laurie had checked Bryton's vital signs and knew what the baby could tolerate.

"It's OK to touch him," she said.

Barbara didn't move.

"Are you sure?"

Laurie took Barbara's hand in hers and gently placed it on Bryton's arm. The sensitive monitors beeped as he responded. She held her hand on top of the young mother's hand.

"That's good," Laurie said. "He likes that."

A tear formed in Barbara's eye.

"Thank you," she said.

"Talk with your son," Laurie said. "He knows your voice."

Barbara leaned into the isolette and whispered into Bryton's ear. She gently stroked his forehead as she watched the monitors. The numbers mirrored the boy's responses to his mother.

"You're doing just great," Laurie told Barbara.

"Before he was born, they told me there was a 60 percent chance he'd die," Barbara said. "Then, when he was born, they told me they were going to lose him."

"We'll get another gas reading about noon," Laurie said. "But for right now, given where he's at, he's cruising."

For the next several hours, the mother, father and nurse huddled around the isolette. Laurie learned about Kyle's achy knee and how the couple had been married for a decade. Bryton was their first child. They'd been trying to get pregnant for nearly four years, had visited a fertility specialist and had been losing hope. Bryton was the only boy on Barbara's side of the family. On Kyle's side, Bryton was the last chance to carry on the Brooks name.

Laurie was working on Bryton when Dr. David Bliss, the surgeon, appeared in light-green scrubs. He conferred with the nurse, studied an X-ray and turned to the parents.

"We're going to have the surgery right here." Bliss said. "It's impossible to safely move the baby. I'll make a cut on his left side, then pull the organs to his belly and unfurl the diaphragm. I figure the operation will take 90 minutes."

He turned away, looked for the wooden top of a cart and knocked twice.

"We don't want problems," he said. "We have to respect the spleen. We lose the spleen, and it's bad news."

He clapped his hands.

"Any questions?"

"When do you do this?" Kyle asked.

"This afternoon," Bliss said. "I have three cases ahead of him. I'm going to go downstairs and do some more work. See you later."

———◆———

A few hours later, the prep team arrived. Surgical nurses pushed tables together around the isolette and unwrapped packages, setting instruments on sterile towels. An anesthesiologist fed new lines into Bryton's body.

A Level 3 nurse grabbed a handful of light-blue surgical masks and walked aisle to aisle, handing them to nurses who put them on and continued working on their babies. A charge nurse walked through the unit telling all parents to leave.

Bryton's parents hovered around his isolette, waiting for the last moment to say goodbye. The operating-room team took control of the baby, monitoring his vital signs and leaving Laurie with nothing to do. She stood with the parents, waiting for the surgeon. He arrived and talked with his team.

"I think it's time for family to leave," Laurie told the couple.

Kyle and Barbara kissed Bryton on the forehead, and Laurie led them to a parents room in back of the unit. She closed the door and walked back to Ladybug 3. On the way, she spotted a nurse standing at another workstation, crying.

"Are you OK?" she asked.

"He's gone," the nurse said.

Hours earlier, a boy she'd often cared for had been taken off life support. The nurse had wanted to say goodbye. After the parents left the hospital, she embraced his cool body.

Laurie barely had time to console the nurse before the surgeon asked her to make a call placing the hospital's blood bank on standby.

"Starting," he said.

Bryton's blood pressure soared, and his heart rate shot up to 202 beats a minute. Bliss used his fingers to probe and search the deformity.

Laurie picked up a teddy bear that had been in Bryton's isolette and carried it back to Kyle and Barbara in the parents room. She knocked on the door and stepped inside.

"They're under way," she said as she handed the bear to Barbara, who began crying. Laurie touched her shoulder. "I'll be back to check on you."

The team pumped medications into Bryton and his heart rate dropped to 150. Each time Bliss probed, however, it shot back to more than 200 beats a minute. The surgery would have strained a normal system. But Bryton had only one lung and a weak heart.

Laurie noticed that the monitor measuring the oxygen saturation rate in Bryton's bloodstream read 60, instead of the normal 100. She stayed near Ladybug 3 and away from the parents room. Unless she could tell Bryton's parents things were going OK, she didn't want to see them.

Bliss opened up a gaping hole in the boy's body and found the space where the bowel should have been located. He muttered -- it was filled with fluid. The heart rate shot up again. Blood pressure climbed, and Bliss moved quickly. He put the body parts back in place and used a fabric patch the size of a silver dollar to close the hole in the diaphragm.

When Ladybug 3 was cleaned, all evidence of surgery gone, Laurie led Kyle and Barbara back to their son. Barbara kissed Bryton on his forehead. She took several steps, then turned and walked back to Laurie.

"Thank you for all you've done," she said.

They hugged.

An hour later, the night-shift nurses arrived. They washed their hands in the scrub room, checked the whiteboard on the wall and went to the break room to hear the updates and select their assignments. Moments later, Laurie Roberge made the handoff and left Level 3.

She arrived home to find that her two grown sons were out, the house empty. She missed her husband. She thought about Bryton and his parents. She thought about other children from Level 3. Those who had lived, those who had died. She remembered the familiar names that often came back to her.

Sadie, Blake, Parker, Colin, Maureen . . .

———◆———

Tara Graham heard about Bryton during evening report, listening to the charge nurse list all the drugs the boy was on. He was so critical that he might not survive the night, and the care he would require was far beyond Tara's expertise. She let a more experienced nurse volunteer for the assignment. During her dinner break, Tara wandered back to look at Bryton and watch the nurse at work. She wondered who this boy's parents were and how they were doing. Families could be tricky in Level 3. One set of parents refused to let any childless nurse care for their son -- they were afraid she might unnaturally bond with the boy. Other families formed bonds with the nurses. And the nurses grew attached to them.

Tara frequently thought about one particular family. The mother gave birth at 26 weeks to a boy, and Tara often cared for him. During the child's stay in Level 3, Tara had learned about the couple's personal lives -- their jobs, the things that were troubling them, how they dealt with stress. She listened to them describe the baby's nursery and shared facts about her own life. During the months the boy spent in Level 3, she became friends with the couple. When they finally took their boy home, Tara was tempted to call the mother and ask how things were going. She missed the baby . . . and his parents. But the hospital administration frowned on nurses initiating contact with families. If a family called, a nurse could respond.

But this couple never called Tara.

———◆———

For weeks, Bryton hovered between life and death. But eventually he stabilized and began improving, day by day. The surgery that moved Bryton's organs back into their proper position and sealed the hole in his diaphragm had pulled him back from the brink. Bryton moved from an isolette into in a crib full of stuffed animals, toys and photographs of his mother and father. Above his head, a mobile revolved, and he followed the movement with his eyes.

A small line still ran into Bryton's nose, supplying oxygen. Beads of sweat formed on his forehead -- he was suffering drug withdrawal from being on methadone and morphine for so long. But his underdeveloped lung was growing, and the prognosis was good. After 10 weeks in Level 3, he was ready to go home.

In a private room just off Level 3, Kyle and Barbara Brooks gathered with the nurses who'd cared for their son. Some of them signed a memory book. The first entry was from Deborah Ross, the supervisor who had been in the resuscitation room, creating the medical log that detailed Bryton's birth and the frantic effort to save his life.

"Hi Bryton. I met you just moments after you were born. We knew right away you were a fighter. When your Daddy came in to see you, we could tell how happy and proud he was. Then we met your Mommy, and we knew we had met a very, very special family. It was a pleasure to watch you grow and get well. I wish you a long and happy life."

Cathy Pollock-Robinson, the nurse who had massaged Bryton's heart in the R-Room, was caring for Jonah Van Arnam. Like Bryton, the boy had been born with a CDH. She took a moment to sign the memory book: "Dear sweet Bryton. You are so lucky to have been born to such a loving family. Take care of each other. Cathy Robinson, Your 'first nurse'."

Bryton's mother had seven medications tucked away in a bag, and Bryton would still be on oxygen once she got him home. But he was leaving the dim, windowless world of Level 3. "In a little while, you're going to go outside and see the sun for the first time," his mother told him.

Level 3 nurses poked their head into the room.

"I'm going to miss you," one said as she hugged Barbara.

"You're leaving us," said another.

"Let me write a note," another nurse said. She scribbled something in the memory book: "What a darling, adorable, sweet and determined little angel you are."

Barbara had heard about Jonah, the new CDH baby. So she sought out Cathy, asked for a piece of paper and wrote a note for Jonah's mother. She included her phone number in case Tracie Van Arnam wanted to talk.

Barbara slipped the note to Cathy and then returned to her son's room for a prayer.

The chaplain moved to the bed and asked Bryton's parents and other nurses to gather around. Barbara took Cathy by the hand and led her to the side of the bed.

"We held him in our prayers when he came in," the chaplain said, "and it's fitting that we bless him on his way out of here. Have a safe trip home. There've been so many ups and downs, and he goes home a healthy baby."

Tears ran down Cathy's cheeks. At the chaplain's request, she joined the others as they placed their hands just above Bryton.

"Bye-bye," she whispered.

She wiped her eyes and cleared her throat.

"I have to get back to work," she said.

Part 4

Tara Graham felt stirrings within her as she moved around her patient, the little movements reminding her that she was carrying a son. The pregnancy was a blessing, of course, but she couldn't push her nagging worries aside. The rows of severely premature babies that surrounded her on Level 3, the neonatal intensive-care unit at Legacy Emanuel Children's Hospital, constantly reminded her of all the things that could happen to a developing baby.

Most of the mothers of these babies had, like Tara, done everything right -- good prenatal care, checkups with the doctor and daily doses of vitamins. Then something had gone wrong. Tara glanced at the mother standing next to her in front of the isolette containing the woman's baby. She remembers wondering if the woman saw her round stomach and resented her.

The new mother -- her eyes red and wet -- looked as if she was in her early 30s. Tara knew her pregnancy had been uneventful until she went into spontaneous labor at home. She was rushed to Emanuel, but doctors heard no fetal tones and performed an emergency Caesarean. The full-term baby looked perfectly healthy. But the medical history revealed she had serious neurological problems.

The baby's mother just stared at her daughter, in shock, and Tara doubted the woman even realized the nurse caring for the girl was pregnant. And yet every time Tara's son kicked and moved, she again felt guilt.

When the mother left Level 3 for the night, Tara studied the child's medical history. The day-shift nurse noted the girl had been unresponsive. Hospital therapists came to the unit to examine the girl, and they left instructions on ways the Level 3 nurses could stimulate the baby's body and brain. But the specialists weren't hopeful. The girl had been deprived of oxygen and had suffered severe brain damage. She was unable to suck, a baby's most basic and natural response.

But Tara wanted a miracle. She got to work, following the therapist's guidelines.

She pushed the bottle's nipple against the roof of the baby's mouth, letting it sit there for five minutes at a time. When nothing happened, she pulled it out and started over. She hoped to trigger something deep within the girl's brain. She put the nipple on the back of the baby's tongue, but nothing happened.

Again and again, hour after hour.

Therapists had noted that it was fine to move the baby into different positions. Tara lifted her into a sitting position, but the girl was limp.

And then -- near the end of her 12-hour shift -- Tara felt the bottle move. Bubbles floated in the milk, a sign that sucking had forced air through the nipple.

Tara cried out, telling other Level 3 nurses that the girl had responded.

The baby drained the bottle.

Tara remembers telling her day replacement to let the parents know what had happened as soon as they arrived. Tara couldn't sleep that afternoon. She fought the temptation to call Level 3 to talk with the girl's mother. She arrived for work at 7 p.m., tired, but in good spirits.

The news she received during the report was devastating. The girl continued to suck, but specialists had conducted extensive tests and determined that the long-term prognosis was grim. The little girl had severe mental and physical deficits. Even if she survived, she'd probably end up in a care center for the rest of her life.

When the supervisor asked nurses to choose assignments, Tara let another nurse care for the girl.

———◆———

During the next two months more children died, on average about one every 10 days. During the evening report, Tara learned that a child with a congenital diaphragmatic hernia was failing. Like other CDH babies, Jonah Van Arnam had been born with a hole in his diaphragm, and the body parts that should have been in his abdomen had floated into his chest.

He'd been placed on the heart-lung bypass machine to let his organs rest, but even that hadn't helped. Medications and a ventilator kept him alive.

But for how long?

Tara was well aware of the little girl who'd been born with multiple defects a month before. Machines and medications kept her heart beating, but she had no real chance at life, a fact her parents had a hard time accepting. They asked that the doctor direct the nurses to do whatever it took to keep their child breathing.

And so shift after shift, hour after hour, the nurses poked the girl with multiple intravenous lines. Tara never volunteered for duty with the girl -- many nurses shied away from the assignment -- but she heard nurses talking in the break room. Some of them thought the extraordinary effort was merely prolonging pain.

Finally, the nurses rose up and confronted the doctor.

He shared their concern and took the case to the hospital's ethics board. Specialists examined the baby and agreed that hope was gone. The doctor sat down with the parents, who agreed to continue pain medication but stop all other drugs.

A day later, infections took the girl's life.

Tara thought about that little girl during her shift. As she worked her assignment -- checking intravenous lines, administering medication and updating medical histories -- Tara considered what the Van Arnams faced when they arrived in Level 3 the next morning.

During breaks, nurses passed along discouraging information about Jonah's condition. His parents, a deeply religious couple, had read from the Bible, sung hymns and prayed at Jonah's bedside.

When her shift ended, Tara headed toward the Level 3 exit, looked to her right and saw that Heather Wells was caring for Jonah.

Heather checked the monitor that showed how much oxygen was getting into Jonah's bloodstream. Despite the nurse's best efforts, the levels were falling. Heather walked across Level 3 to a small office where Dr. Mindy Hendrickson sat at a desk. Hendrickson was a neonatologist, a medical subspecialty that requires six years of training after medical school.

Heather filled Hendrickson in on Jonah's situation, and the two women returned to his isolette. Hendrickson had been in Level 3 the night Jonah was born. She'd tried several courses of care, going as far as to place him on a heart-lung-bypass machine to let his organs rest. But the falling oxygen saturation levels indicated Jonah was dying.

In addition to CDH, he suffered from severe cardiopulmonary hypertension. The high pressure was restricting the flow of blood to his lungs. The ventilator settings were on high, but the machine did no good. His body just wasn't getting enough oxygen.

Hendrickson returned to her office, called a cardiologist and radiologist and asked them to come to Level 3 to conduct tests and examine X-rays and ultrasounds. The specialists confirmed Hendrickson's worst fears. She asked Heather to notify her when Jonah's parents -- Kevin and Tracie -- arrived. Then she went to the coffee bar on the hospital's second floor to prepare for a conversation she didn't want to have.

Minutes after her return, Kevin and Tracie showed up. Hendrickson took a large gulp of coffee, set the cup on her desk and walked over to their son's isolette. She pulled chairs from a counter and set them in a circle. She got right to the point.

"He's going through another crisis," Hendrickson said. "I was hoping things would look better for Jonah at this point."

"What are we supposed to do?" Tracie asked.

Hendrickson looked directly at both parents, shifting her gaze from one to the other.

"What I see isn't good," she said.

Kevin reached out and took his wife's hand.

"Remember when he was born how we talked about pulmonary hypertension being reversible or irreversible?" Hendrickson asked. "I'm now thinking this is irreversible."

"What's the deal?" Kevin asked.

"I know you guys have been thinking since the day this was diagnosed, 'What's it going to be like if Jonah can't be with us physically'?"

The parents looked at each other. They nodded.

"I need to know," Hendrickson said, "what you want for Jonah."

"I want him to come home," Kevin said.

Tracie caught Hendrickson's eye and held the glance. Her face fell. She seemed to realize where the conversation was going.

"We want quality of life for him," Tracie said. "That's what we've always wanted for him."

She let go of her husband's hand and pointed to the isolette.

"Jonah has a closer connection to God at this moment than I do," she said. "Jonah's looking at both sides and figuring out which is better. Heaven or Mom and Dad."

She put her hand to her mouth and bowed her head.

"I told him if his soul is hanging on because of me, because I want him, to let go, go be with God," Tracie continued.

She looked at Hendrickson.

"Do you have kids?"

"No," the doctor said, "I don't. I can't really begin to appreciate the heartache you guys are going through."

"How many more days should we sit like this?" Tracie asked. "How many more hours? How many more minutes?"

She lifted her hands toward Hendrickson.

"Please," she pleaded, "you have to direct us in some way."

"I know," Hendrickson said, "I know."

She sat forward and put her hand on Kevin's knee.

"To make Jonah comfortable, I have to give him a lot of medicine, to knock him out," she said. "To give a medicine to paralyze him isn't treating Jonah. I think it's treating us. So we feel better, so we don't see him gasping . . . . It really hurts me to see a baby fighting like that."

She looked at the floor.

"But I've learned that sometimes that's not my job," she said quietly. "I can't make the babies better."

She raised her head, her voice strong again.

"At that point," she said, "I decide to try to take care of you guys."

She edged in even closer.

"I have little hope that regardless of what we do today, tonight or tomorrow Jonah will survive."

She slid back. Kevin and Tracie fell into each other's arms, and a deep wail echoed through Level 3.

"I'm so sorry," Hendrickson said. "I don't want to take away your hope. We're not stopping care. But since Jonah was born, we've had an honest relationship. I'd rather give you bad news that's true, than good news that's a lie."

Tracie shook her head.

"How am I supposed to explain this to my 3-year-old?" Tracie asked. "She thinks she gets to play with him the second he comes home. What do I tell her?"

"You guys are great parents," Hendrickson said. "Whatever you decide to do, or not do, will be right for you. The hardest thing is forcing yourself to think about something you never want to think about as a parent. And that's having a child die before you do."

Kevin Van Arnam cleared his throat.

"Do we just shut off a machine?"

———◆———

During the report the next evening, the supervisor told the night-shift nurses that Jonah Van Arnam's parents had made their decision. The grim news cast a pall over the unit.

An hour after the night shift began, the couple walked into Level 3 and made their way to their son's isolette, which Heather Wells had screened off for privacy. She greeted them with a hug.

Heather had been on duty for 12 hours and was supposed to go home. But she didn't feel right about leaving the Van Arnams with a new nurse. She called home and told her husband she was staying late.

The nurse and the parents faced one another, silent.

"You've been fantastic," Kevin Van Arnam said finally. "Thank you for everything, Heather. I mean for everything."

"It's been an honor," she said.

Kevin sighed.

"We have some friends, relatives, out there in the hall," he said. "We're going to bring them in to say goodbye."

He shook his head.

"It's kind of strange," he said. "One of our friends had a child die here. The name's on that glass out there in the hallway."

He took his wife's hand in his. They left, disappearing behind the screen.

Heather sat on a stool. There was nothing for her to do. The monitors no longer needed to be checked minute by minute. The only medicine flowing into Jonah's body was morphine to make his last moments painless.

She'd done this at least eight times before, sitting outside a screened-off isolette, waiting for parents to say they were ready to unplug the machines. But she was still terribly moved.

She heard Tracie's voice from behind the screen.

"Heather?"

The nurse peered around the barrier, listened and then walked to the unit secretary's office.

"Mom said to send the visitors in," she said.

One by one, friends and family said farewell to the child. Then the parents were alone.

Five minutes.

Ten minutes.

"Heather?"

The nurse disappeared behind the screen. Minutes later, she emerged and walked to a telephone on the counter. She punched in a number.

"This is Heather," she said. "They're ready."

The unit's night-shift neonatologist had been waiting for the call. He arrived in Level 3 and explained to the Van Arnams how the lines would be removed from Jonah. When they were ready to let their son go, they'd tell Heather, who would disconnect the ventilator.

When the doctor left, Heather and Abby Archambault put on surgical gloves and begin taking away nonessential lines. The two nurses cleaned Jonah and wrapped him in a blanket. Heather placed the boy in his mother's arms.

Tracie Van Arnam had never held her son.

"I'm so sorry," Tracie told Jonah. "I'm so sorry."

"Can you take my glasses off?" she asked Abby. "I want to see him better."

Abby set the glasses on a table, and Heather moved medical equipment out of the way. The life-support monitor had gone black and silent. The only remaining sound was the thump-thump-thump of the ventilator.

Heather used Kevin's camera and took a family picture. Then she and Abby left the parents alone with their child.

Thirty minutes later, Tracie called.

"We're ready."

Heather walked behind the screen, hugged Tracie and took the tube holder from Jonah's face. She pulled the ventilator tube from his mouth, flipped off the ventilator, and the thumping stopped.

Nurses all over the unit looked up as a mother's low moan floated out from behind the fabric screens shielding the Van Arnams. It rose in pitch and volume, becoming a wail that overwhelmed the background noise that filled Level 3.

Tara Graham, working only 25 feet from the screened area, looked up from her workstation. She had spent the past hour watching Heather Wells deal with the drama unfolding at Jonah's isolette. She'd seen the Van Arnams arrive on Level 3, and she'd watched the friends and relatives show up to say their goodbyes. After the ventilator stopped and the mother's sobs died away, she'd watched the neonatologist arrive with his stethoscope to certify the death. She'd seen Heather, cradling Jonah's body in one arm while hugging Tracie. The two women supported each other, their heads together.

Tara had been a Level 3 nurse for nearly 10 months. During that time, one nurse had burned out and requested a transfer to another hospital unit. Another had quit and moved out of state. Soon, a new group of nurses would start their 12-week orientation in Level 3, and Tara would no longer be the rookie.

She picked up a telephone, punched in a number and connected with the nurses station in the maternity ward, to the spot where she'd been standing when she first heard about Level 3.

"I'm going to be doing the 8 o'clock hands on," she told a nurse on the other end of the line. "Does Mom want to see her?"

"OK," Tara said, nodding. "I'll be ready for her."

In the isolette in front of her was a girl born at 32 weeks the day before. She weighed just under 4 pounds and was on medications and oxygen. She was doing just fine, but her mother, still in the maternity ward, had yet to hold her.

During the hands on, Tara changed the baby girl's diaper, did a physical assessment and entered her observations in the log.

The door next to Tara opened, and the new mother stepped into Level 3.

Tara introduced herself, and the mother took a seat next to the isolette. Tara stepped into the line of sight between her and Jonah's isolette. In the background, the Van Arnams were gathering their things and getting ready to leave while Heather prepared Jonah for his trip to the morgue.

Tara leaned over the new mother and spoke to her gently.

"Do you want to hold your daughter?"

"Can I?"

"Yes, and she's going to be a little wriggler."

Tara moved to the isolette. As she pressed up against the Plexiglas, she felt her own son kicking within her. He was most active when Tara was at work, and she'd begun joking to her husband that her son kicked to remind her that he was the most important baby in her life.

She lifted the baby girl from the isolette and set the child in her mother's lap.

Alarms began beeping. The mother panicked and started to hand the child back to Tara.

"It's OK," Tara said. "She's tolerating it. The alarms are going off because she's in a different position."

Tara moved to the monitor.

"See," she said, "the saturation levels are perfect."

The mother looked into her daughter's eyes while tears welled in her own. Tara stood by her side, her hand resting lightly on the mother's shoulder.

"You're doing fine, Mom," Tara said. "That's your baby."

Changing Channels

He's a guy who lost his way and then found it again.

Whitey and Beaver lived in a black and white world. But beyond Mayfield, life plays out in every shade of gray.

Street people called him "Whitey," after the character he supposedly played on "Leave it to Beaver." No one knew where he lived, and no one in the theater scene had heard of him. So the rumors were written off as typical of the ramblings that routinely circulated among Old Town's prostitutes, drug addicts and con men.

He was a shell of a man, they said. A heroin addict, a cocaine dealer on the run from the law. Rummies said they'd seen Whitey drunk, begging along the bus mall. No, it was over at St. Francis Park in Southeast Portland where homeless men waited for a free meal. No, he'd died. No, just a couple of overdoses. He'd almost died.

Street lore had it that Whitey's real name was Stanley. And an Internet search revealed that the kid who played Whitey in the Beav's idyllic 1950s town of Mayfield was named Stanley Fafara. A little digging turned up a telephone number with a Portland prefix. The phone rang three times.

"Yes, this is Stanley Fafara," said the voice. Then there was a long pause, as if he was debating whether to hang up. "Yeah," he finally said, "I'm Whitey."

———◆———

The squat single-room-occupancy building sat on West Burnside Street, in the heart of Portland's Skid Road. To move in, the tenants must prove they've been straight for at least a month. Dealers peddle heroin just a block away, but door buzzers and locks keep the addicts out. Visitors must sign in and meet their hosts in the lobby.

"I'll be down," said the voice on the intercom, and the door leading to the lobby buzzed open. Inside, two men sat on battered sofas and shared a day-old paper scattered on an end table. Outside the window a bum pushed a shopping cart loaded with bottles down the sidewalk, and a woman nursing a black eye wobbled out of the Park Blocks.

The elevator door clanked open. A lone passenger wearing a rumpled black sweatshirt, jeans and tennis shoes ambled into the lobby. Short and stocky, he rocked with the swagger of the street. He wore his gray hair slicked back, carried hard knocks in his weathered face and had a scar that traced a small line along the outside of his left eye.

He extended his right hand. "Stanley," he said.

His bright blue eyes flitted between the street and the lobby. "My room?" he asked, repeating the question. "It's a mess." He nodded toward the sofa. "We can talk here." He looked at the two residents on the sofa. "Lobby lizards," he muttered. "Come on."

With a gentle bounce, the elevator stopped at the fourth floor. He walked down a narrow hallway, past a community kitchen and one of four shared bathrooms. A faint odor of cigarettes hung in the air. Next to his door, inside a metal frame, was a piece of paper with a short phrase: "Last Chance."

"I put that there" he explained. "I want to see it every time I leave here and lock the door. I've been to all kinds of clean-and-sober houses. Twenty years and they just never took. This is my last chance. If I fail, I'll have to set up shop in the street."

The room was about 12 by 12, and at one time the walls might have been called white. He snapped on two lamps that hardly dented the dark. It felt like a place where a man sits alone with dreams that have died hard.

The lone window looked out onto a parking garage. A small color television sat on a metal dresser painted to look as if it were made of wood. The single bed was standard issue. Two hand-me-down chairs and a worn carpet filled out the space.

The Beav's old pal pulled a chair from a desk, shoved a book titled "God's Promise" aside and found a partially filled ashtray. He fumbled with the pack and pulled out a cigarette. He lit it, took a long drag and swiveled in his chair.

"What have you heard?" he asked.

He listened, turning away from time to time to stare at a poster on which he'd written "pray for peace and your enemies." Before long, the cigarette had burned to his fingertips. He crushed it in the ashtray.

"Well," he said. "Sounds about right."

He sighed, lit another smoke, started to say something, but thought better of it. He took a drag, tilted his head toward the ceiling and let loose a plume that collected on the yellowed paint. "You're looking at the loss of a myth," he said. "My life was a blessing and a curse. At one time I had money. Hell, there were times when I'd walk around with $16,000 in my pocket."

He leaned forward, nearly whispering, using his cigarette as a pointer, jabbing empty air.

"You want to know a secret?" he asked. "What's more attractive and powerful than money is fame. Fame never runs out. I had fame. But that's the myth. I wondered if my friends liked me because of who I was, or what I was."

What he is now is a recovering addict with hepatitis C and a Social Security disability payment of $475 a month. The room rent, based on a sliding scale, is $153 a month. He stood up, stretched his arms out and slowly turned around, taking it all in.

"This is where I am," he said. "A guy who lost his way and then found it again. I never really lost faith, but I lost all my hope. Hope is just the beginning of faith."

He flopped in the chair, weary, ready to talk.

"This," he said, "is where Whitey landed."

———◆———

The television was turned to TV Land, a cable channel that recycles nostalgia to baby boomers -- and the screen flickered. The theme, a tune nearly every adult of a certain age can hum, stirred memories of a time when a child's world stretched only as far as a mother's voice carried.

Back then, life revolved around recess, kickball and a handful of friends. Kids got around on their bikes, always Schwinns. They used clothespins on a fender bracket to position playing cards between the spokes. When the wheel turned, the cards thrummed and the bike became a motorcycle.

This night's TV Land episode revolved around an intelligence test given to Beaver's class. He's mistakenly labeled a genius, and his friends shun him because he's too smart. Whitey tells him why he's getting the cold shoulder. By the end of the show the mistake is revealed, and Beaver's friends accept him back into the fold. As the credits roll, the name Stanley Fafara makes its way up the screen.

The show, which aired from 1957 to 1963, has become a metaphor for a sheltered, comfortable and simple American existence that never really was. Beaver, his older brother Wally, slimy neighbor Eddie Haskell and Whitey lived in the world their parents wanted to create for them. For the Beav's parents, Ward and June Cleaver, World War II was a fresh scab. The Korean War had just drawn to a close, the economy boomed and the suburbs exploded with families seeking not just a better life, but the good life they'd longed for through all the sacrifice. White, middle-class Americans lived in a bubble, floating along, optimistic and sure of their places in the world and their ability to control their destiny.

But "Leave It to Beaver" was the world as war-weary Americans wanted it to be, not as it was.

It was exclusively white, even though the battle for civil rights had already been joined and would soon tear the nation apart. Beaver's mother puttered around the kitchen in high heels and pearls, but Betty Friedan's "The Feminine Mystique" was about to unleash a tidal wave of feminism. Within a year of the show's last episode, the Cleavers' world dissolved: Assassinations, uprisings and riots in the cities. The Vietnam War. Political scandals. Divorce and the fragmentation of the American family.

Stanley Fafara grew up in Studio City, Calif., in a "Leave It to Beaver" neighborhood: A sprawling suburban home, two loving parents, four kids and church every Sunday.

He never wanted to be an actor. That was his mother's dream, and she pushed her children into the industry. He appeared in his first commercial when he was 4 years old and later had parts on a string of TV Westerns. His life changed when his mother hauled him and his brother to an open casting call for what would become "Leave It to Beaver." Stanley won the role of Whitey, his brother that of Tooey, one of Wally Cleaver's friends.

The show ran for more than 200 episodes. Hugh Beaumont, who played Ward Cleaver, had appeared as a tough guy in dozens of character parts for B films and television. An ordained minister with a degree in theology, Beaumont found a spiritual element in "Leave It to Beaver." He turned the screen into a pulpit, a place where the actors created weekly parables about life and the way it should be lived.

In his clean-and-sober apartment, Stanley Fafara pointed to some videos on a shelf. "Someone made me some tapes of the show," he said. "I never watch them. But it was a good show with values. It was the way people wanted to live and bring up their children." He chuckled. "What they forget was that it was on a soundstage."

He shook his head. "Maybe we all forgot that."

When the show ended, Fafara's parents sent him to North Hollywood High School, where he had his first taste of fame and its perks. He had his choice of girls, and everyone wanted to be his friend.

Life only became crazier after high school. Being Whitey gave him a backstage pass to a hedonistic banquet that few 18-year-old boys could ignore. For a time he lived in a house with Paul Revere and the Raiders, the Top 40 rock band. He started drinking every day.

"Let's say it was not all a veil of tears," he said. "I had access to all the things that were happening. I knew everyone in Hollywood. All the players. Fame goes to your head. Fame never ran out. Drugs, money, women. I got all of them because I was Whitey."

He stood up and left his apartment, locking the door behind him and rattling the knob. Outside the building, he turned up the collar on his jacket and walked onto Southwest Broadway, past a couple of upscale hotels, the kind of places he stayed in the old days. But on this stroll he looked like a panhandler. The doormen watched him until he made his way up the street and became someone else's problem.

"My parents wanted me out of Los Angeles," he said. "They sent me to live with my sister in Jamaica. She was an artist, and I started painting, too. I drank and used pharmaceuticals. I came back to L.A. when I was 22. I started dealing drugs and met the woman who became my wife when I sold drugs at her apartment complex.

"Man, she was beautiful," he said. "She liked to take chances. Like me. The excitement was as euphoric as the drugs."

In the early 80s he started breaking into pharmacies, seeing if he could beat the clock and get out before the police came. His luck ran out on the seventh robbery.

He pulled open the door to a coffeehouse, ordered a large, found a seat at the counter and stared out the window.

After his arrest, his parents bailed him out of the Orange County jail. A month later the cops nabbed him during another burglary. He was convicted and sentenced to a year. When he got out, he worked as a roofer, waiter and janitor. His real talent was dealing drugs, and the profits supported his own habit.

He failed a drug test given as part of his probation, and he ran rather than deal with the fallout. He cut ties to his old life, divorced his wife and bounced around the country. He repeatedly tried to clean up and stay straight, but failed. He washed up in Astoria, where he found work at the golf course. "I cleaned out the ninth hole," he said. "There was a slough, and I got to keep all the balls I found."

When he learned his mother was dying, he returned to California, cleared up the legal problems and served 300 hours of community service in a charity thrift store. But he was arrested again, and spent 65 days in jail. He entered a drug-treatment program, but left after a month.

"I told my girlfriend we had to get out of L.A. I sold my car, and we jumped on the bus and headed to Portland," he said. "Guys in the jail told me it was an easy place to live because the cops didn't arrest you for being drunk. They just took you to detox and let you out in the morning."

Within an hour after the bus pulled into the Portland depot, Fafara and his girlfriend rented a motel room, shot up and crashed. The plan was to get high one last time and then go make something of life.

Instead the addiction took hold, and the two of them lived in the motel for two years.

He lost nearly everything. His parents, the last people who really cared about him, were dead. He'd alienated his siblings, who washed their hands of him. About the only thing he had left was "Whitey." His screen name was always good for a drink or drugs.

He'd tell people that he'd been on "Leave It to Beaver," but he'd lost most of his teeth and weighed less than 130 pounds. So hardly anyone would believe him. To prove his background, he'd tell them stories about the show and the actors, what it was like behind the scenes.

Someone told him they'd seen the movie "Fast Times at Ridgemont High," released in 1982. He told Fafara that in one part of the movie an old film clip of "Leave It to Beaver" was played. It was Whitey's most famous episode, the one where he talks Beaver into climbing a billboard and into a bowl by telling him there's real soup in the bowl.

Fafara called the Screen Actors Guild in Los Angeles and learned he had some royalty checks waiting for him. He rented a post office box and waited. The check was for $1,000. He cashed it and blew it on drugs.

He rummaged around the desk in his apartment and fished out three checks. "Let's see," he said. "Here's one for $1.90. Here's one for $1. I keep them to prove that I was on the show." He found a third check under a book. "Hey, this one's for $20. I'm cashing that. Twenty bucks is 20 bucks."

He shook his head.

"When people learned I was on the show, they looked at me like I was a dumb-ass for not being rich," he said. "I had no control over royalties. None of us did. We were day players. My parents gave me an allowance of like $5 a week, but I was making about $2,000 a week. All the money went to my schooling and things for me. I went through so many cars, muscle cars, tricked-out cars. But when the show ended, so did the money. The only time I get something is when it's used in a movie or something."

He pushed the royalty check under the mouse pad for his computer and stood up. On the wall next to the door, tucked into the plastic cover for the overhead light switch, was a small black-and-white photograph of Jerry Mathers and Stanley Fafara -- Beaver and Whitey. He paused to look at the photograph. "It's a long way from Studio City," he said.

He rested his hand on the doorknob, and his eyes scanned the room. He paused.

"I know it's a dump," he said. "But it's my dump."

———————

On the way to Portland's East Side, he glanced out the car window at some of the old hangouts and spoke softly, almost to himself: "I was living on the street, anywhere I could flop."

The car turned down one street, then another and passed a group of bums hanging out in St. Francis Park. He leaned forward and peered out the window, looking for familiar faces, for the girl who broke his heart.

"No one I know," he said. He leaned back in his seat and said nothing until he was blocks from St. Francis.

"I had this can of beer in front of me," he explained. "I just wanted it to be over. The pain was killing me. Staying loaded 24 hours a day was a job. I'd do anything to keep the drugs coming. So I said this prayer."

He turned in the seat and smiled.

"I know," he said. "I know. Hell, I thought I was fooling myself, too. I'd said prayers before, ask God to help me. But it was usually when I was being hauled away in handcuffs. But I said that prayer."

No director yelling cut.

No swelling soundtrack.

No "Leave It to Beaver" moment where all is set right in the world after a talk with Dad in the den.

Just a bum pushing away a can of beer and wandering over to the detox center and waiting for the door to open. He checked in and stayed nearly two weeks, eventually graduating to a clean-and-sober house for drunks and addicts. He lived there two years.

"Most people stayed a year, but I figured I needed a double dose," he said with a laugh. "I haven't had a drink since Aug. 22, 1995. I don't know why it took. I should be dead. I had three overdoses in two months and was hanging on for dear life. My associates, most of them are gone. I know they didn't want to go, but they did."

He looked out the car window.

"Lucky?" he repeated. He shook his head.

"I don't believe in luck," he said. "Things happen for a reason."

The years since that August day have been lived in obscurity. He hasn't been able to find his siblings, but he reunited with a daughter and learned he's a grandfather. He took a series of temporary jobs and saved to buy his computer. Recently he took a one-day acting seminar, and at times he thinks about getting in the business again. "I think I've got the gangster look down," he said. "It comes from the L.A. County jail and the street. Nothing fake."

He spends his days in his apartment, smoking cigarettes. Thinking and drawing. Taped to the wall next to his bed is a sketch, in pencil, of a woman. It's his vision of his former girlfriend.

"She's still out there," he said. "I had to leave her, and I lost track of her. A month ago I ran into someone on the street who knew where she was living. I took her to dinner, but it was too sad for me to handle. When I met her, she was gorgeous. Now she's scrawny, lost all her teeth. At dinner, I told her that I loved her and that I wanted her to have a real life. She laughed it off."

He lit a cigarette.

"I used to think about her every day," he said. "Not as much anymore. But I still love her. I told her that at dinner, and she just laughed it off. Hell, we both loved drugs more than anything."

———————◆———————

A cold rain greeted Stanley Fafara when he walked out of the lobby of his building and onto West Burnside Street. Gusts stirred up by the autumn's first storm stripped the last leaves out of the trees in the Park Blocks and sent them swirling down the streets. In the old days, Whitey might have been scouring the neighborhood for a fix or panhandling pedestrians so that he could buy one more beer.

Today, though, he just wanted breakfast. He crossed Burnside and headed north, looking for a plate of bacon and eggs. He pointed up the block. "I saw a woman killed there," he said. "But compared to L.A., the streets here are like a college campus."

He made his way through the Park Blocks headed for a cheap cafe where the few dollars in his pocket would buy a full meal. Cars swooshed through puddles, their drivers ignoring the worn, hatless figure strolling easily along the street. Weather doesn't bother Whitey. He walks like a man who enjoys feeling the rain on his face.

He turned toward Broadway, walked to the corner and opened the cafe's smudged glass door. The cook looked up from the grill when the door squeaked and then went back to work.

Whitey settled into a booth, and the window framed him like the screen of an old TV set. He ordered and sipped a coffee. In a few minutes, the waitress dropped off his food, and Whitey ate slowly, staring out the window at the rain and an empty street.

"I know it hasn't been a pretty picture," he said with a sigh, "but it has a beautiful ending."

The Writers Within

She receives $12 an hour to do something everyone saw as impossible.

Barb Kragrud sees the writing teacher enter the church basement and turns from her project, painting colors on a picture of Belle, the Disney heroine in "Beauty and the Beast."

She skips across the floor, pigtails flopping, to hug Cheryl Adelman.

"Can I be first?" Kragrud pleads. "Can I be first?"

Adelman answers with a smile. She promises other students that they, too, will get a turn. Then she leads the 41-year-old woman to an upstairs room where, each Tuesday, she helps developmentally disabled adults discover their stories.

The results are a blessing -- to the writers and those around them.

Kragrud, 41, and the others are students at PHAME -- Pacific Handicapped Artists, Musicians and Entertainers -- a Northeast Portland fine arts academy.

A Portland woman, Carol Stady, founded the academy in 1992 for adults with no interest in Special Olympics. The nonprofit offers classes in drama, piano, voice, dance and choir to about 65 adults from across the metro area.

"I don't know of any organization west of the Mississippi doing what they do," says Bob Shook, executive director of the Arc of Multnomah-Clackamas, an advocacy group. "It's the best-kept secret around.

"It's so important that creativity is nurtured," he says of developmentally disabled people who drop off the radar after high school. "It allows people to express themselves. We had one man who is 30, and everyone thought he was nonverbal. He comes alive when PHAME puts him on the stage."

When the man from the funeral home put my mom in the black body bag and started to zip it up, I said, "Don't cover her face. I don't want her in the dark." He left the bag unzipped and waited for me to kiss her one last time and stroke her hair before he rolled the gurney out the front door. The door on the hearse closed almost without a sound. Bye, Mom.

Cynthia O'Neal

Stady asked Adelman, best known as the "story lady" who reads to students at Glencoe Middle School, to teach writing at PHAME seven years ago. Adelman agreed. She volunteered for years but now receives $12 an hour to do something everyone saw as daunting, if not impossible.

Her goal is to teach these men and women -- all of whom have various degrees of mental retardation, autism or brain damage -- to write.

It's more than copying words on a page, though that would be an accomplishment. Adelman has learned to pick her way through scrawled sentences filled with misspellings and punctuation errors to help students unlock stories from their lives. Their readers travel to intimate places that even some of their parents didn't know existed.

In spring, the students put on a show featuring music and theater. For the finale, Adelman reads stories -- typed at home on her computer -- to a packed house.

"Some students can't read," she says. "Others have problems speaking. I decided that I should read the stories to honor their work. They deserve a reading on par with their writing."

The audience feels the power, she says. The room falls silent. Parents weep at discovering another side of their child.

The students can't explain where the words come from. They offer a shy smile and a shrug. Others gently touch their hearts.

She was a good woman. She was a good baker. She made bread with yeast. And pumpkin bread with raisins and nuts. And banana bread without nuts. She was a good mom to all six of us. I'm the second to the oldest. She's been gone five years now. I miss her at different times, but especially when I smell bread baking.
    Jeff Deeks

As winter term begins, it's time for new stories that will be read this spring.

Adelman opens a thick binder and selects a story Kragrud wrote in October, a short piece, just four paragraphs, titled "I Didn't Get It."

"Let's talk about it again," Adelman says.

When PHAME mounted a musical, "Beauty and the Beast," Kragrud, who loves Belle and has always wanted to be an actress, tried out for the starring role, sure she'd get it.

Adelman reads the story:

"On Saturday, September 22nd, we had the casting party to find out which parts we got. When my name was not called for the part of Belle, I was so disappointed.

"I will be playing one of the funny girls, and I will work really hard to do the best I can.

"I believe two things: First, there is no such thing as a small part. And second, there's always next year, when we might do 'Phantom of the Opera,' in which case I'll be ready to go after the role of Christine."

"You," Adelman says, "are a true writer."

"I didn't know I could write like that," Kragrud says quietly. "I never told anyone what I was feeling."

She hugs Adelman.

"That's why you're here," the teacher says.

———◆———

It was about 8:30 that night when we finally had my toaster on one counter; my microwave on the other; my kitty potholders in the drawer with my oven mitt; my first cookbook in the cupboard above the stove; and my love seat, recliner and entertainment center in the living room.

Then we celebrated with hamburgers at Dairy Queen. We were so hungry.

The keys to my new apartment are on a Navy key chain in my pocket, and tomorrow night will be my first night sleeping in my new apartment. I know it will be another big day for me, and also for my mom."

Barb Kragrud

———◆———

When Kragrud's mother retired last year, her daughter began writing about it. Adelman helped her refine her thoughts before sending her home with instructions to explore her feelings and write about them. The story was unveiled at the recital.

"I didn't think Barb had given my retirement a second thought," says Shari Kragrud. "I cried all the way through the story. She was seeing life from someone else's point of view. When you do that, you have true compassion. Cheryl pulled all these feelings out of her. The writing program has been so affirming for Barb. It's allowed her to feel good about herself and have the courage to pursue who she really is."

When Barb Kragrud's brother-in-law was killed in a car accident last year, she wrote a story.

"She was moved by his death," her mother says. "It wasn't just about the facts. It went deeper than that. She hasn't always been able to verbalize her feelings. They're trapped inside her. With Cheryl, she's been able to put it down in black and white. For those reasons, I know more about my daughter."

My grandmother died last week. When I saw her for the last time, I held her hand and begged her not to die on me. She had held me in her arms when I was a baby because I was a sweet baby. Now all she could do was tell me that she loved me. It made me feel happy and sad at the same time."
Tracy Franz

Adelman stumbled into PHAME while working on a master's degree in writing from Vermont College. She wrote her thesis about a woman with Down syndrome who attended PHAME; she visited an art class at the encouragement of the woman's mother. The next day, Adelman returned to hear the choir.

"About this time, my husband asked me for a divorce," she says. "I was a mess. Even after my reporting ended, I found myself going back to listen to this choir. There was a feeling of family there, even as mine was being ripped apart."

Then PHAME's founder asked her to teach.

"I was barely holding myself together," she says. "I think I was looking for meaning in my life, which had been shaken. My therapist thought that teaching would be healing for me. I thought I'd go in and talk about first, second and third person in writing. I'd done that with grade-school kids. But this was another world. I discovered the biggest problem was getting my students to feel it was OK for them to tell the truth about their lives.

"They're so pressured to be happy," she says. "Everyone is supposed to have a cheerful face. This is the old special-ed kind of mentality. I wanted to get into the hearts of the kids. If I wasn't dealing with the truth, why be there? It would be a waste of my time and theirs."

She works one on one with each student, talking about feelings and a story's meaning, never imposing her own thoughts, always taking direction from the student. She treats students as real writers, lending structure through homework assignments. She reminds them of writing techniques -- that it's more powerful to show than tell, so they must look for details that make the story come alive.

"There's an element of trust when they lay themselves out," she says. "They've all been laughed at. One woman wrote about a high school teacher who humiliated her and called her stupid. It hurt her so badly. Years later, even after he's died, she still can't forgive him."

"I don't give these students the language," she says. "I give them the right to tell their stories."

———◆———

My parents have always told me to follow my heart. Both my head and heart agree about three things: There's nothing wrong with me; I'm still in love with him; but for now at least, we'll only be together in my dreams.
Katie Dunn

———◆———

Katie Dunn's creative life ended when her church's choir director asked her to leave, telling her mother she wasn't good enough.

"That was so upsetting that our family left the church," says Anne Madden, a member of PHAME's board of directors. "I was so desperate for her to have a social life. I found PHAME. It respects and values these people."

After last year's recital, the board was so moved that it gave Adelman $1,000 to publish the students' work. The result was 200 copies of a 36-page book, "Writing Shotgun." The title, Adelman says refers to the armed man who rode next to the stagecoach driver -- an act of courage. Writers, too, need courage. Especially these writers.

"When the book was published, they were so excited," says Madden. "When you read these stories, you get a window into their hearts. My daughter's stories have been a gift to me. "

In one story, Dunn, 33, wrote about a man she liked who also has Down syndrome.

"My daughter will be an eternal 12-year-old," Madden says. "I thought this was just another adolescent crush. But her heart really was taken by this boy. When I read this story, I kept thinking: 'I never knew. I never knew'."

For about three years I've had a volunteer job at Friendly House. . . . There are some nice people at Friendly House who always say Hi to me and tell me I'm working hard and doing a good job keeping the place clean. Not everybody notices or appreciates what I do, but I know that my job is important because lots of people count on me in lots of ways.
Rachel Borkan

The students have written about death and what it's like when a brother goes off to college. They write about childhood memories, who they are – "I am from a red bike with training wheels I rode on the sidewalk as birds cheered me on" -- and about loneliness and love.

The students remain a mystery to Adelman. That, she's come to believe, is part of the beauty of what she does.

"I don't have any answers," she says. "But in their writing, they reveal themselves. In that, I see there's meaning and purpose in the universe."

THE APOLOGY

In my case, it was something that has haunted me for decades.

When he was 12 years old, the boy did something he only later realized probably hurt his seventh-grade teacher. It was minor -- he was, after all, a kid -- but in time, when he was older and wiser, he wanted to find this teacher and apologize.

But the teacher seemed to have vanished. Over the decades the man occasionally turned to the Internet, typing the teacher's name into the search box. He never found anything. He never quit looking. A few months ago -- by now nearly 39 years after this happened -- he got a hit.

Stunned, he started reading a story that two years earlier had appeared in The Oregonian. He studied an accompanying photograph and recognized his teacher. He cleared his screen and wrote an e-mail that ended up in the newspaper's mailbox. A clerk forwarded it to me. I found it buried in my in-box where it was surrounded by notifications about crimes, road conditions and interoffice messages.

Only by chance was I curious enough about the subject line – "Customer Feedback" -- to open the email from a man named Larry Israelson.

You published an item involving retired teacher James Atteberry and the CASA program. Mr. Atteberry was a teacher of mine in the early 70s, and I wish to apologize to him for a regrettable incident that occurred when I was his student. Can you provide any contact information for him, or would you be willing to serve as an intermediary and deliver a message on my behalf? Thank you for your time, and I await your reply.

In the paper's electronic files, I found a story I had written in 2009. My assignment had been to write a short piece about Clatsop CASA, a program

472

that helps kids. To put a face on the organization I found Atteberry, 75, a retired Southern California teacher. He'd moved to Astoria and joined CASA by chance after a server at his favorite restaurant encouraged him to volunteer.

I called CASA, left a message for Atteberry and then emailed Israelson to ask why he wanted to contact Atteberry. He would only say he wanted to apologize. Weeks later, Atteberry returned my call. I said I had something a bit bizarre. Intrigued when I told him what little I knew, he told me to contact this former student and see what happened.

Soon, I received an overnight package containing a sealed envelope. I addressed it to Atteberry and dropped it the mailbox.

———◆———

As the days passed, I thought about this strange tale. There was no news. If no one ever heard a word about James Atteberry and Larry Israelson, it wouldn't matter.

Or would it?

A good feature story is about something universal. When it comes to apologies, no one gets a pass in this life. Everyone deserves one, and everyone needs to give one. When I mentioned this letter to people, I found a story more universal than any that I'd written in years. They all told me they had someone they wished they could apologize to. And they told me that by the time they realized that truth, it was too late.

In my case, it was something that has haunted me for decades.

My third-grade teacher organized a secret Christmas gift exchange. On the big day, we sat in a circle to open our gifts in front of our classmates. The teacher instructed us to announce the name of the gift giver, who would stand and be roundly applauded.

Every kid ripped open a fancy package containing a new toy. Then it was my turn. The teacher handed me something that had been wrapped in paper that was clearly reused. It was so wrinkled and retaped that the colors had faded. With everyone watching, I peeled back the paper and pulled out a cheap paperback book with torn and dirty pages.

Tucked inside was a handwritten note identifying the girl who gave it to me. When I announced her name, my classmates started laughing. Her gift was yet another indication of just how different this girl was from the rest of us. She'd arrive late to class, her hair wet and unkempt. She had no friends, and the popular students made fun of her because she wore old clothes and shoes.

Only later in life did I understand that she obviously came from a terribly poor family.

Even though this incident happened nearly 50 years ago, I remember that afternoon as if it were yesterday. As the class laughed, this 8-year-old girl turned in her chair to hide her tears while the teacher unsuccessfully tried to restore order in a class that had turned on the weakest among us.

At that moment I was worried that the popular kids would think that this girl and I were friends. So I didn't thank her, or even acknowledge the gift. Only decades later -- like Larry Israelson -- did I realize that what I did next was unforgivable: I tossed the book in the garbage.

Months later, the girl left school. I never saw her again. The school I attended has been torn down. I have forgotten the names of many of my old classmates. But not hers. For years I wanted to apologize. While waiting to see what became of Israelson and Atteberry, I typed her name into an Internet search field. I found nothing. I realized then that my story -- the one with no news -- was about something more powerful than news.

It was about getting a second chance.

———◆———

As James Atteberry read the letter he was brought back to 1973 when he was a middle-school history and composition teacher in Huntington Beach, a wealthy Southern California beach community. He was 37, got great reviews and was well liked. He was also gay, and politicians were working to root out gay teachers.

"If a teacher was found to be gay, his contract would not be renewed," Atteberry said. "Gay teachers kept their mouths shut. People of this era might not understand it. But it was a tense time. An art teacher in the school made a stupid mistake, and that was the end of his career. I never talked about my life."

And yes, he told me, he remembered Larry Israelson.

———————◆———————

I am truly sorry for asking to be transferred out of your seventh-grade social studies class at Sowers Middle School during the 1972-73 school year.

I don't have many specific memories from my two years at Sowers, but at the top of one of my assignments you wrote 'You will go far in life. Your command of the English language is exceptional.' Looking back on my younger self, I am certain that I reveled in being one of the 'teacher's pets.' As comfortable as I was in a classroom, however, the boys locker room was something else entirely.

———————◆———————

On the phone, Israelson's voice is low, strong and confident. He stands, he says, 6 feet 5, and played water polo in high school and in college.

"But when I was 12," he said, "I was a scrawny little kid who wore glasses and was into books. I lived in a beach town, yet I couldn't tan. I was very pale. A lot of the athletic guys loved to tease those of us who were weak. You know what it is to feel powerless?"

Some students suspected Atteberry was gay. A boy in class asked Atteberry what he thought about a proposed law banning gay teachers. When Atteberry asked the boy why he posed the question, the student said his father had specifically told his son to ask Atteberry. The teacher chose his words carefully.

Israelson was one of the best students. Bright and articulate, he submitted essays that Atteberry thought were remarkably good.

"I would praise Larry in class," Atteberry said. "That was his downfall."

In the locker room, boys began picking on Israelson.

"They started saying 'Larry' and then 'fairy' and rhyming it with 'Atteberry,' " Israelson recalled.

When he pleaded with them to stop, he was challenged to an after-school fight. Though scared, he hoped that by agreeing, they'd quit thinking he was gay. Even though he admired Atteberry and enjoyed learning from him, the boys were linking the teacher's life and his in a way that made him someone to be ridiculed.

"I took a couple of hard punches," he said. "I gave up."

The teasing intensified with the taunts becoming more sexually explicit and graphic. Israelson told no one. One day, when he could no longer stand it, he showed up at the principal's office and said he needed to leave Atteberry's class. The principal couldn't understand why. His grades were good.

"He kept pressing me," Israelson said. "I wouldn't say."

Realizing he wasn't getting anywhere, the principal signed a transfer slip and handed it to Israelson. The student walked into Atteberry's classroom, interrupted the lesson and handed Atteberry the slip. Without a word, Israelson gathered his books and walked out the door.

"There was no goodbye, no explanation," Israelson said. "I just disappeared. I never talked to Mr. Atteberry again."

———◆———

When Israelson married, he was the first Anglo to marry into a Mexican American family. More than a decade into the marriage -- by this time he and his wife had two daughters -- his brother-in-law called one night and asked whether he could take Israelson out for a beer. After some small talk, his brother-in-law took a deep breath and got to the point.

"He apologized," he said. "He said that he hadn't wanted an Anglo in the family. He'd lobbied behind the scenes to try and get his sister to break up with me. He said he'd felt bad about it for all these years. He decided it was finally time to make it right."

That phrase, of course, made Israelson think once more about Atteberry. The man had inspired and encouraged Israelson at a time when a compliment or praise scrawled across the top of an essay so mattered in a boy's young life. He thought about what it must have been like for Atteberry to hide who he was.

Israelson intensified his search.

A decade or so later, he found my story.

———

The beauty of an apology is that everyone wins because it reveals not only who we are, but who we hope we are.

Israelson had been writing an imaginary letter to Atteberry for more than 30 years. But now the man became a bit of a boy again, writing an essay to a man who had once mattered. He struggled to find the right words. The issue had been "gently nagging at the back of my brain for more than 30 years." He said he was "truly sorry" for asking to be transferred.

"I know my age was a mitigating factor, but when I replayed this incident in my adult head, it shamed me," he wrote. "Since that realization, I have felt like I owed you an apology."

He sealed the envelope and sent it to me to be forwarded to Atteberry.

He expected nothing more. He had done what he had set out to do, and now it was over.

When Atteberry read the letter, he, too, remembered what it had been like to be a boy. Like Israelson, he had been bullied. For more than 60 years, he had kept it a secret. Two athletes had grabbed him when he was walking home, made him pull down his pants and whipped him with a belt. Shamed, he told no one, the matter made worse when the athletes tormented him by demanding each day that he turn over his lunch money to them.

In a strange way, this letter from the past allowed Atteberry to come to terms with his own past. He was not alone.

Atteberry had always wondered why Israelson had left his class. Had he been the problem? Was it something he did or said to this student?

Now he knew.

He set the letter aside, went to his computer and typed Israelson's name into the search box. He found the address and a telephone number.

Should he?

Of course.

More than 1,000 miles away, a phone rang.

A man answered.

Larry, a voice on the other end said, this is your teacher.

ACKNOWLEDGMENTS

B ill Hilliard hired me at The Oregonian as a summer copyboy when he was the paper's city editor. He brought me back the next year as a summer intern. As an assistant managing editor, he twisted arms to get me on staff as a reporter. Without Bill, none of the stories in this collection would have been written.

Jon Franklin was kind enough to guide and influence me when I was an inexperienced writer. Franklin, the first writer to ever receive two first-in-category Pulitzer Prizes, served a stint as a teacher at Oregon State University. Bold in the way that only a young person can be, I wrote to ask if we could meet. He agreed. I took what I thought was best story for Jon to critique. As I sat next to him, he tore it apart, finding flaw after flaw in each paragraph. I had two choices. I could pretend it never happened. Or I could devote myself to studying the craft of storytelling. From Jon, I plunged deep into the mystery of story. Without Jon's influence, I would have missed seeing the stories that appear in this collection.

Jack Hart was my editor for many years, a relationship that ended when he retired. A writer needs a brilliant editor. And that was Jack. We were a magical team. We loved structure, story thinking and story craft. Jack and I brought out the best in each other. There was nothing like walking into his office and saying "Jack, I have an idea." He was always supportive about pursuing the story.

Therese Bottomly, now the paper's managing editor, and I go way back. Several of the stories in this collection started with Therese calling me into her office to say she had an idea for what she thought "would be a Hallman story." For many years she encouraged me to gather my stories into a collection. And then she made it possible for this book to be published.